Charles E Clegg

Clegg's Elocutionist

A Text-Book on the Art of Elocution

Charles E Clegg

Clegg's Elocutionist
A Text-Book on the Art of Elocution

ISBN/EAN: 9783337179212

Printed in Europe, USA, Canada, Australia, Japan

Cover: Foto ©Paul-Georg Meister /pixelio.de

More available books at **www.hansebooks.com**

CLEGG'S
Elocutionist

A

TEXT-BOOK ON THE ART OF ELOCUTION

(WITH A FULL SCHEME OF VOCAL EXERCISES

FOR PUBLIC SPEAKERS, AND FOR THE USE OF SCHOOLS
AND ELOCUTION CLASSES.

INCLUDING A WIDE AND CHOICE SELECTION OF

*POETRY AND PROSE FOR READING AND
RECITATION.*

BY

CHARLES E. CLEGG,

*Lecturer on Elocution at Yorkshire United College, Bradford, and
Lancashire College, Manchester, and Lecturer on English
Literature and Elocution at the Liverpool Young
Men's Christian Association.*

LONDON:
GEORGE PHILIP & SON, 32 FLEET STREET, E.C.
45 TO 51 SOUTH CASTLE STREET, LIVERPOOL.
1896.
[*All Rights Reserved.*]

PREFACE.

The present volume is divided into two parts : the first deals with the principles of delivery ; and the second consists in a number of literary selections, which are intended to serve as exercises of those principles.

Proceeding to some extent on lines elsewhere laid down, I have enforced that side of the subject which it seemed to me could be most usefully enlarged upon, namely, the *literary*. This appears to be an aspect too much neglected, in favour of mere rules of speech, by many treatises on Elocution.

Aspirants to *public speaking* have been considered in a special chapter, which should in all instances be supplemented by the one on Voice Training, and the one on Gesture.

Elocution *classes*, such as meet in various Public Institutions, will no doubt find the specimens of Prose and Verse well adapted to their requirements, and to students of these classes a study of the introductory argument will hardly be superfluous.

The needs of High Schools and Colleges—especially of pupils from the age of about twelve forward—have been carefully kept in view, the several departments of literature represented providing ample scope for class-reading, and again for public recitation at annual Prize-givings, Speech-days, &c.

Although most phases of Elocution are considered in the pages devoted to the Theory of the art, and the treatment more or less organized and proportioned, yet this work is advanced simply as suggestive of the limits and complexity of the subject, and in no way as exhaustive.

For the exercise on Sub and A-tonics I am indebted to an old master and friend.

Ungrudging thanks are accorded to authors and to publishers who have kindly given permission for certain copyright pieces to be inserted in this collection. E. Nesbit ("The Singing of the Magnificat"), E. F. Turner ("My Dentist"), and R. Blatchford ("A Lifeboat Episode"); and Messrs. MacMillan and Co. (selection from Sir Francis Doyle's "Poems"), Messrs. Trübner and Co. (extract from Sir Edwin Arnold's "Light of Asia"), Messrs. Blackwood and Sons (passage from George Eliot's "Silas Marner"), and J. W. Arrowsmith (selection from J. K. Jerome's "Three Men in a Boat"), are entitled to the heartiest thanks for their courtesy.

It remains for me to say that, should any pieces appear for which due sanction has not been obtained, I offer sincere apology to those concerned, and assure them that no wilful liberty has been taken. If any poem has been inserted without proper permission, it has only been after vain efforts to discover the address of the Author or the Publisher.

C. E. C.

56 MOUNT PLEASANT,
    LIVERPOOL,
        January 1*st*, 1896.

	PAGE
PREFACE	3
HISTORIC OUTLINE	9
THE ART OF ELOCUTION (Introductory)	13
PART 1. THE INSTRUMENT: ITS STRUCTURE, USE, DEVELOPMENT, PRESERVATION. VOCAL EXERCISES	14
,, 2. ELOCUTION IN RELATION TO LITERATURE: MODERN AND BIBLICAL	22
,, 3. ,, APPLIED TO PUBLIC SPEAKING	38
,, 4. GESTURE AND ITS ASSOCIATED MODE OF EXPRESSION	42
,, 5. NATURALNESS	44
,, 6. BRIEF STUDIES	48

SELECTIONS—POETRY.
(A) DRAMATIC.

As You Like It, Act 2, scene 5	*Shakspere*	119
,, ,, Act 3, scene 2	,,	92
Hamlet, Act 2, scene 2	,,	96
,, Act 3, scene 1	,,	95
,, Act 5, scene 2	,,	135
Henry the Fourth, Part I., Act 2, scene 4	,,	82
,, ,, ,, ,, ,,	,,	106
Henry the Fifth, Act 2, scene 2	,,	112
Henry the Eighth, Act 3, scene 2	,,	85
Julius Cæsar, Act 2, scene 2	,,	64
,, Act 3, scene 2	,,	67
,, Act 4, scene 3	,,	74
King John, Act 3, scene 3	,,	110
King Lear, Act 1, scene 1	,,	127
Macbeth, Act 3, scene 1	,,	78
Much Ado about Nothing, Act 3, scene 3	,,	117
Othello, Act 1, scene 3	,,	51
Richard the Third, Act 4, scene 2	,,	99
Richard the Second, Act 5, scene 2	,,	109
The Merchant of Venice, Act 1, scene 3	,,	102
,, ,, Act 4, scene 1	,,	55
The Tempest, Act 4, scene 1	,,	123

SPEECHES, &c.

Gloster's Soliloquy	,,	141
Henry the Fifth before the Battle of Agincourt	,,	143
Queen Mab	,,	140

CONTENTS.

PROSE DIALOGUES.
Bubbles of the Day, Scene from, *Jerrold* 158
She Stoops to Conquer, Scene from, *Goldsmith* 155
The Hunchback, Scene from, *Knowles* 144
The Rivals, Scene from . *Sheridan* 151

(B) NARRATIVE—POETRY.
Bishop Hatto . . *Southey* 165
Baby in Church . *M. M. Gow* 183
Barbara Frietchie . *Whittier* 197
Feast of Belshazzar, The, *Sir Edwin Arnold* 180
Ginevra . . . *S. Rogers* 200
Grace Darling . . *Wordsworth* 163
Grenville's Last Fight, *Gerald Massey* 167
Last Shot, The . *J. R. Reid* 188
Legend of Bregenz, A, *A. A. Proctor* 162
Little Golden-Hair . *W. Carleton* 160
Mary Queen of Scots . *H. G. Bell* 184
Maud Müller . . *Whittier* 198
Paradise and The Peri, *Thomas Moore* 201
Ride of Paul Revere, The, *Longfellow* 178
Singing Leaves, The . *Lowell* 194

Singing of the Magnificat, The, *E. Nesbit* 170
Story of the Faithful Soul, The, *A. A. Proctor* 175

(C) LYRICS, IDYLLS, BALLADS, &C.
Above and Below . . *Lowell* 229
At Last . . . *Whittier* 219
Bivouac Fire, The . *S. K. Cowan* 223
Captain of the "Northfleet," The, *Gerald Massey* 205
David Livingstone . *Punch* 232
Forlorn, The . . *Lowell* 214
First Snowfall, The . *Lowell* 216
In Schooldays . . *Whittier* 219
Lost Found, The . *Longfellow* 209
Maids of Attitash, The . *Whittier* 206
Minister's Daughter, The, *Whittier* 221
Passions, The . *W. Collins* 33
Red Thread of Honour, The, *Sir F. Doyle* 226
Rock of Ages . . *Anon.* 217
Sandalphon . . *Longfellow* 208
Song of the Camp, The, *Bayard Taylor* 213
Song for Stout Workers, A, *J. S. Blackie* 231
Singers, The . . *Longfellow* 229
Three Preachers, The . *C. Mackay* 224

UNCLASSIFIED POETRY.

(A) VARIOUS.

A Character . *M. B. Smedley* 240
Charming Woman, The, *Lady Dufferin* 246
Creeds of the Bells . *I. Bungay* 237
Fool's Prayer, The, *Atlantic Monthly* 242
Great Renunciation, The, *Sir Edwin Arnold* 233

Marit and I. . . . *Anon.* 243
Old Schoolmaster, The, *Lee O. Harris* 238
Only a Wee Bit Bairn . *Anon.* 241
Robert of Lincoln . *W. C. Bryant* 236
Scandal . . . *Anon.* 245

(B) SATIRE AND HUMOUR.
Amen Corner, The . *W. Carleton* 248
Altruism . *J. T. Trowbridge* 267

CONTENTS.

	PAGE
Aunt Tabitha . *O. W. Holmes*	248
Catching the Cat . *M. Vandergrift*	271
Dora's Soliloquy . . *Anon.*	266
In Nevada . . *C. Leland*	264
John Day . . . *Hood*	254
Little Quaker Sinner, The . *Anon.*	250
Lay of Real Life, A *Hood*	256
Little Boy Blue . *M. Carey*	259
Nine Suitors, The . . *Anon.*	253
On the Doorstep . *E. C. Stedman*	252
Our Village . . . *Hood*	261
Owl Critic, The . *F. T. Fields*	263
Philosopher and Her Father, The, *Shirley Brooks*	258

SELECTIONS—PROSE.

(A) SERIOUS.

Blank Bible, The . *H. Rogers*	272
Chariot Race, The . *W. Wallace*	288
Death of Colonel Newcome, The, *Thackeray*	275
Lifeboat Episode, A, *R. Blatchford*	277
Long Path, The . *O. W. Holmes*	283
Noble Revenge . *De Quincey*	282
Poetry of the Bible . *G. Gilfillan*	38
Tale of Terror, A . . *Hood*	296

(B) HUMOROUS.

Art of Proposing, The . *Dickens*	322
Artless Prattle of Childhood, The .	303
Briary Villas . . *Anon.*	307
Discussion at the "Rainbow," A, *George Eliot*	309
Getting into Society . *Thackeray*	327
Gregsbury and the Deputation, *Dickens*	316
Ill-bred Hospitality . *Dean Swift*	325
Membranous Croup . *Mark Twain*	339
Mr. Flutter and the Tea Party, *Anon.*	331
My Dentist . *E. F. Turner*	346
Sam Weller's Examination, *Dickens*	319
Stage Coach, The . *W. Irving*	299
Towing Incidents, *Jerome K. Jerome*	335

(C) ELOQUENCE.

The Wonders of Creation, *Dr. T. Chalmers*	349
The Devastation of Oude, *R. B. Sheridan*	351

LIST OF AUTHORS.

	PAGE
Arnold, Sir Edwin	180, 233
Atlantic Monthly	. 242
Anonymous,	217, 241, 243, 245, 250, 253, 266, 307, 331
Bell, H. G.	. 184
Blackie, J. S.	231
Bryant, W. C.	. 236
Bungay, I.	237
Blatchford, R.	. 277
Brooks, Shirley	258
Carey, M.	. 259
Carleton, W.	160, 248
Cowan, S. K.	. 223
Collins, W.	33
Chalmers, Dr. T.	. 349
Doyle, Sir F.	226
Dufferin, Lady	. 246
Dickens, C.	316, 319, 322
Eliot, George	. 309
Fields, F. T.	263
Goldsmith, O.	. 155
Gow, M. M.	183
Gilfillan, G.	. 38
Harris, Lee O.	238
Holmes, O. W.	248, 283
Hood, T.	254, 256, 261, 296
Irving, W.	. 299
Jerrold, D.	158
Jerome, J. K.	. 335
Knowles, S.	144

	PAGE
Longfellow, H. W.,	178, 203, 209, 229
Lowell, J. R.	194, 214, 216, 229
Leland, C.	. 264
Moore, T.	201
Massey, Gerald	167, 205
Mackay, C.	224
Nesbit, E.	. 170
Punch	232
Proctor, A. A.	162, 175
Quincey, De	. 282
Reid, J. R.	. 188
Rogers, Samuel	200
Rogers, Henry	. 272
Shakspere, W.	51 to 143
Sheridan, R. B.	151, 351
Swift, Dean	. 325
Stedman, E. C.	. 252
Southey, R.	165
Smedley, M. B.	. 240
Taylor, Bayard	213
Thackeray, W. M.	275, 327
Turner, E. F.	. 346
Twain, Mark	. 339
Trowbridge, J. T.	267
Vandergrift, M.	. 271
Wordsworth, W.	163
Whittier, J. G.,	197, 198, 206, 219, 221
Wallace, W.	. 283

INTRODUCTION.

HISTORIC OUTLINE.

THE practice of making formal speeches and of declaiming poetry is not a new custom, nor is it peculiar to any one nation. Among the earliest deliverances of a commanding kind are the orations of Moses; while the rhapsodists of Ancient Greece are, perhaps, the forerunners of the ideal reciters of modern days. With the Hebrews, religion was the sphere that most exercised the powers of speech, in other than the commonplaces of every-day conference. The Greeks had a secular literature, Epic, Lyric, and Dramatic, that called into service the best powers of voice, and at the same time demanded the nicest intellectual appreciation.

This, too, was the land of famous orators :—
"Those ancient, whose resistless eloquence
Wielded at will that fierce democratie,
Shook the arsenal, and fulmined over Greece."

What is true of the Greeks is scarcely less true of the Romans; the name of Quintillian is enough, to witness how carefully Elocution was fostered among the youth of Rome. The forum, theatre, and law courts all speak to the imperial sway of the voice in the Roman Empire ere the brilliance of that empire faded.

From the decline of the Roman Drama to the rise of the Elizabethan Drama popular curiosity was met by Art Story. Stories of every conceivable order, culled from many nations, were sung or recited in all parts of Europe, by that band of vagrant artists, who went under such names as bards, minstrels, troubadours. Thus, during the "Dark Ages" and those immediately following, the public taste in the recitation of thrilling or romantic narrative and half-acted story, was kept alive.

When we reach the days of Shakspere we are in a more or less modern state of things. The principles then laid down by Shakspere respecting delivery (in Hamlet's lesson to the Player) have now been accepted as canons of the speaking-art. No doubt the main means of cultivating Elocution, in the age of Elizabeth, was provided by the stage. Pulpits and platforms as we know them to-day were not then in vogue. Legal advocates may have pursued a course of training in the management of the voice. It is possible also that the widespread interest in national song, by necessitating attention to expression, may have required anything but a mean standard of excellence to be attained in the use of the voice. Having dealt the drama its death-blow, Puritanism takes over the voice and all its resources of strength and modulation, and makes it the organ of paramount power in a cause that was mortified by the "Restoration," towards the close of the 17th century. Then for some little time the drama, especially comedy, employs the vocal art in the interest of a society that was essentially critical, and intolerant of carelessness or incompetency in its purveyors of entertainment.

Judged, however, in the most generous spirit, we cannot but describe the career of the art we name Elocution, as an extremely chequered one, in England, until we arrive at the middle of the 18th century ; then it is that we first find Religion, Politics, and Literature fully investing the voice and the associated art of exposition with rightful devotion and dignity. So that from that time to the present the achievements which have made many of England's noblest sons most famous and influential, have not infrequently been won by that matchless vehicle (and all its significations) the human voice.

PRESENT CONDITIONS.

Considering our own day we find, with the amazing expansion and increasing complexity of the social fabric, a corresponding extension of the sphere of educated speech. In the pulpit, in parliament, at the bar, in various departments of educational work, from university down to the elementary school, the organ of speech is indispensable to a degree never before dreamed of. In these directions it is used towards the end of persuasion, or of instruction. Along with the growth of society is seen improvement in the general taste and ideal: literature, both prose and poetry, and of past centuries as well as of the most recent times, commands an ever multiplying community of lovers. With a vast proportion of the people, the joy in imaginative writings, particularly poetry, is magnified when such works are READ ALOUD by the trained expositor. Thus we see that the two main aims of the vocal art are Utility and Pleasure.

There is a further interesting phase of this well-nigh universal application of Elocution, and that is, that many women, towards practical no less than artistic ends, are pursuing occupations that require special fitness in the matter of Elocution. This is noticeably so in the case of teachers in schools, lecturers on domestic economy and other sciences, and again with those who take to public platforms in the interest of morals or of literature. No wonder, then, that of the several bodies of speakers (many with little training, and more with none) there should be a proportion who fail, from ignorance or abuse of the art upon which they rely. With a due understanding and exercise of the doctrines of delivery, everyone should benefit in health and in general physical power just so far as they give themselves ample exertion, rather than repeated spells of rest.

As a matter of fact, no exercise is more beneficial to body and brain than speaking, provided always that it conforms to physiological laws and the dictates of art. Why then, the virtues of training in the art of delivery admitted, should there be difficulty in securing for Elocution a place in the curriculum of all Educational Institutions? The rudiments of delivery could be taught to even very young pupils, and a practical demonstration of the physical basis of speech would always prove intelligible and attractive. A teacher well informed on the subject would notice defects in production and articulation among his pupils, and, knowing the cause in each case, could point to the cure. So that diseased throats, ruined voices, and stammering would often be averted.

But, startling as it may seem, teachers themselves, except in rare instances, have no preparation in Elocution, practical or theoretical. And if the physical side of Elocution is neglected, the æsthetic side is more grudgingly promoted. Instead of the boys and girls of England being led to love the splendid ballad, narrative, and dramatic literature of our country by its being read and commended to them, and by their own reading and reciting of it in the class-room, they are made to positively dislike imaginative literature; partly because it has been rendered a mere medium for philological inquiry, but mainly because there has been no specific treatment of those beauties and sentiments which reveal themselves only to the magic of the voice.

Schools are the very places where gracious and patriotic feelings should be engendered and nursed in the youth of our nation; and they are, largely, the places where not only is there an absence of stimulus, but where all ardour in the romantic and passionate features of poetry is pitilessly petrified by the chilling processes of examinations in arithmetic, grammar, and the like.

THE OUTLOOK.

This is all truly disappointing to those who long to hear the English language spoken accurately, sweetly, and robustly by the great mass of men and women in society. Still there is hope that trustworthy teachers and sufficing elocutionary literature—aided by an acute sense of need on the part of aspirants—will steadily lead to something like national recognition of the necessity of Elocution. Such a recognition, indeed, as shall make it a compulsory subject in the course of study designed for teachers in public schools, and that shall directly encourage good speech and recitation among children. Certain special prizes might be offered for exceptional excellence in the declamation of prose or the appropriate treatment of poetry. Thus the ambition of many would be healthily excited, and the level of the attainment of all would be greatly raised. Wholesome spurs of this kind are given to students in other departments of scholastic work, and there can be no valid reason why oratory and poetical recitation should not equally enjoy such helpful bribes.

But, already, more has been said than space affords for discursive remarks, and some notion must now be given of the plan and extent of our discussion of the Art of Delivery.

SCOPE AND AIM OF THE PRESENT TREATISE.

Elocution has two main applications, which we shall distinguish as—(A) The *Practical*, all that relates to the speaking of our own compositions, whether extempore or prepared; those addressed to the understanding, and those directed to the emotions. (B) The *Artistic*, affecting the expression of literary works, whether prose or poetry; chiefly those that minister to the imagination and the sentiments.

The present work consists in a brief treatment of four topics of our subject, which are taken in the following order :—

    I. *The Instrument:* its Structure, Use, Development, Preservation.

   II. *Elocution applied to Literature:* (A) Modern Prose and Poetry, (B) Biblical Prose and Poetry: important principles of Literary structure to be observed in Reading and Recitation.

  III. *Elocution applied to Public Speaking:* general, practical considerations.

  IV. *Gesture*, and its associated mode of expression.

The topic "*Naturalness*" will receive separate consideration, and will be followed by a series of "*Elocutionary Studies.*"

In such a scheme, all those who work the voice with any serious aim should be catered for; preachers, advocates, parliamentary speakers, lecturers, teachers, readers and reciters of literature, and various other classes of speakers.

The section that deals with the physiology and the training of the vocal organs, and which includes the system of *exercises* for the voice, has reference of course to everyone alike. Much also of what is said in the several other divisions may be useful to students for whom it was not primarily intended. And in every case it would be well, perhaps, that the whole be read, so that a due impression of the unity of the subject may be gained. Lastly, though by no means least in importance, let it be ever borne in mind that intelligent and sympathetic insight is all-important in an art of this character; it is needed to prevent pedantry and pride, excess of expression, as well as spiritlessness. All the after advice assumes the presence of this faculty in the reader. The standpoint taken is that Elocution is the art of interpreting literature and language, and not the reverse, the standpoint taken by some men and women, reciters and speakers.

THE ART OF ELOCUTION.

All arts agree in being a combination of two elements—the abstract and the concrete, or, more colloquially, theory and practice. Accordingly, Elocution, being an art, consists in certain (abstract) principles or laws, and their (concrete) investment in vocal and bodily expression. Elocution, the art of delivering language, embraces the entire compass of speech, from the simplest articulation to the most passionate expression of which human voice is capable. Its purpose is to express the *meaning* of language, and to reveal the accordant *feeling*, or, as we say, to give full value to the *sense* and *sentiment* of words. The abstract bonds—clearness, accuracy, truth, moderation—are precepts drawn from the "concrete" performances of the best artistes in delivery: not so many rules devised only by unpractical theorists and pedants.

In every art, men, consciously or unconsciously, follow models in one form or other. If not by studying theories, then by observing or hearing the actual doings of men, whether in painting, architecture, sculpture, music, poetry, oratory, or recitation of literature.

Great artists have always their own uncopyable charm, but every effective effort in any department of art will be so because it complies with certain *general conditions*.

These *general conditions*, then, are the canons of art that may be noted and set down in strict terms, and grasped and applied by students.

The successful practice of Elocution (as with all other arts) is dependent to a large degree upon native gifts; but all may attain not a little excellence by (1) "constant and well-regulated exercise, (2) by using the mental faculties to a quick power of analysis of thought, and (3) by the cultivation of the ear and vocal organs for a ready appreciation and execution of tone."

Having agreed that Elocution may be acquired by intelligent people as other arts may be acquired, let us first take up

I.—THE INSTRUMENT,
ITS STRUCTURE, USE, DEVELOPMENT, PRESERVATION.

1. STRUCTURE.—There are three main divisions in the mechanism of the vocal organ: (*a.*) The vocal chords that vibrate and sound in response to the breath; (*b.*) the lungs, that receive the breath and regulate its outgo; (*c.*) the throat, nasal channels and mouth, that unite to modify the quality and volume of tone produced by the vocal chords.

2. The vocal chords vary in size and capacity in different persons, but almost all voices are capable of singing at least two octaves. The female voice begins, usually, an octave higher than the male voice. There is no difference in the structure of the male and the female vocal organ, further than in size—the larynx of woman being somewhat the smaller. This is equally true, also, of the rest of the mechanism—the lungs, throat, and mouth. But the matter of size does not necessarily determine the power of vocal endurance and variability. A small organ, well disciplined, will last longer and do more work than a large one indifferently used. Yet, undeniably, a large instrument (consisting in large larynx, lungs, and well proportioned mouth), skilfully exercised, will in the long run prove the most serviceable and effective.

3. Considering the inimitable beauty, variety, and power of the human voice, it must be admitted that its mechanism is extremely simple. Not so simple as those who are ignorant of physiology suppose, and yet not so complex as the wonderful effects would lead us to expect. Just three or four features can here be described. During silent respiration the two vocal chords lie free and open, and not as when adjusted for tone-production. The adjustment of the voice apparatus for tone consists, roughly speaking, in the closing and stretching of the chords against the moving current of air from the lungs. Each of these actions is brought about by a separate set of muscles. A further scheme of muscles regulates the angles of the chords, so that the pitch may easily be changed, and yet another muscular arrangement raises or lowers the whole larynx through a length of something less than an inch, according to pitch required. Knowledge, however, of the

whole function of muscles that control the vocal chords can best be acquired by a study of the physiology of the voice, along with practical demonstrations under the guidance of surgeon and laryngoscope.

4. The lungs, as we have seen, provide the current or blast of air that, resisted by the vocal chords, becomes converted into sound. Now it is important to notice that the lowest sections of the lungs are less restricted than the upper parts. The lowest extremity, therefore—being the point of least resistance—must be considered the true seat of our command over the use of the whole quantity of air taken into the bellows. It is not sufficient to urge that, as fluids press evenly, there is no need to do more than fill the lungs—leaving the emptying of them to nature. Besides, there is a good in this habit of deep-breathing—over and above that of securing superior control and steadier speech—in the fact that the various parts of the lungs are thus almost uniformly refreshed. In natural, untrained breathing, the low parts of the lungs are often impoverished. Especially is this the case with women : but it is also conspicuously so with men who take little physical exercise.

5. The throat, nose, and mouth are designed to act together as resonators of the sounds created in the larynx, and further, as articulators of these sounds. So influential are these upper cavities in the formation of the voice, that we say they alone make each voice "characteristic." Next to health, the symmetry of these cavities is the best gift in this department. The main office of the throat is to swell and beautify the vowel effects. The channels of the nose are indispensable to healthy breathing, and their share in articulation is not small. Without them the *n*, *m*, and *ng* would be most unpleasant, and, in fact, speech would lose its charm of melody and sweetness.

To the mouth is given the chief business of articulation. It is provided with very simple machinery, which, nevertheless, is ample for the work of moulding sound into intelligible symbols. It is by the conjunctive action of the lips or tongue, or sometimes these parts operating together, that all speech elements, the vowels excepted, are shaped. Even to the vowels the mouth gives the final finishing effect.

6. USE.—We now come to the more practical topic : the *life*, not the form, of the instrument. To a musician it must

be of interest and value to have a clear idea of the architecture of the organ he wishes to play; but full acquaintance with bellows, pipes, and stops would not suffice in itself to draw from the instrument even the most ill-composed melody. It is legitimate in analysis to discover the different constituents, and to assign their functions; but in practice these various powers are merged, and the contrivance is thought of as a working whole and as an unit. To the musician, how distracting, too, would be the task of tracing the inside working of his instrument at the moment that he was striving for supreme effects in the harmony of sensuous sounds. So in speaking. In the actual use of the voice as a vehicle of thought, there should be no need to think about the separate, related processes. We have to play upon our organ—the voice—a particular tune, and nothing should be allowed to interfere with the execution of that tune or message. At such times the voice is one thing, the communicant of our mind to the mind of another person. Full exercise and development of the various parts, separately and in conjunction, as a course of training, is obviously pre-supposed; for increase in the power of each part means increase in the sum of effectiveness.

7. In voice-economics, a learner should decide what range of tone is most natural to him. In some cases this range will be restricted to the very deep tones, in others the high tones; but in most the best scope for speech will be neither high nor low—about the middle of the scale, from lower C to middle C. Never should we strive to copy voices utterly unlike our own, simply because of some superiority in power or intensity. In all cases the voice should be extended and generally enlarged, but it is impossible to change the radical cause of distinctions in voices.

Persistent attempts in this direction have, in numbers of instances, led to a complete break-up of the voice.

Having fixed upon the best series of say five tones, we should strengthen that special part of the voice along with regular cultivation of the whole of the voice; using exercises devised to make the most of its resources. (See the section on *Development*). Note, at the same time, that there will often be a call on the parts of the voice above or below that portion most constantly used. You may desire to relieve the range most exerted, by dropping or by lifting the pitch: good speakers know how to do this with effect to themselves and their hearers alike. The subject-matter, too, will occasionally require the *full compass* of the voice. Clearly, then, the whole voice should be at your command.

8. Secondly, keep the voice well out of the throat, so that all the resounding parts above the larynx may be utilized as aids to the voice. Further, when the voice is properly accumulated in the mouth, the throat is less liable to share improperly in articulation. The habit of arresting the voice in the throat, and so involving the throat to an undue extent in articulation, is ruinous to the voice, and provocative of thick, indistinct, articulation. When the voice is thus badly conducted, there is more difficulty in poising it, and giving it that rhythmic movement which is at once more economical, penetrating, and agreeable. This balance and rhythm may often be superfluous in ordinary conversation, but wherever speaking becomes more formal and impersonal, as in addressing public audiences, the instinctive resort to a slightly musical movement of voice must be encouraged. There is a qualification to be added. The smoothly modulated delivery ought not to be used to the exclusion of those short, sharp, percussions that give such natural emphasis to certain constructions. We know things by their opposites, and so the abrupt, staccato mode, in addition to an interest of its own, makes the even undulations of the voice more tolerable and significant.

9. We have next to inspect what may be called the word-manufactory, the mouth.

All pure tones (oo, oh, ah, ai, ee) come from the vocal chords, and are usually named vowels. The rest of the elements, "consonants," are moulded in the mouth or conjunctive parts, and are best styled either sub-tones or non-tones, according as they do or do not contain a trace of tone. For example, there is a degree of tone in the value of initial *B*, but no tone in the value of *P*. It will be seen from this, perhaps, that speakers will profit by giving attention to the mouth as an organ of speech. Constant exercise of all the muscles implicated in tone-production is no more essential than it is of all muscles that co-operate in word-making. The muscles of the tongue, lips, and other parts of the mouth, may be much increased in strength and sensibility by suitable gymnastics. Foremost among the muscles that must not be neglected in exercise are those upon which the jaw rides; and the exercise suited to them is secured in the adequate action of the jaw in speaking, whereby two advantages accrue to articulation, greater clearness, and firmer grip.

10. A word, in passing, on Stammering. Far better prevent stammering than leave it to be cured. Stammering is a defect of articulation that arises usually from a faulty co-ordination of the muscles of speech. It is often a deep-seated mischief, and hard to cure. But in most cases of mal-articulation (where no structural deformity exists) considerable benefit is derived from exercises designed to train the speech-muscles. Defects of this kind in certain stages may by this means be quite cured. The development exercises that follow will meet the needs of most cases. (See section on *Development*).

11. Finally, we must aim to develop all the voice-resources of power, beauty, and compass. The trifling demands of daily talk form no preparation for an organ that will have to work at high power in large and often trying buildings, and have to minister to the whole scale of the emotions, from the lowliest to the most exalted; to the slightest fancy no less than to the widest sweep of imagination. Everything we can do to fit the voice for its severe performances must be done. Rest is seldom the proper cordial. The judicious course is to put the whole mechanism of speech through such a variety and extent of exertion, daily, as will anticipate pretty fully the after-strain of preaching, speech-making, lecturing, or reciting. This must, of course, stop short of abuse, or its end will be defeated. The equivalent of the public-use of the voice is found in a species of ordered exercises that healthfully tax the lungs, the voice, and articulating mechanism in turn.

These exercises are now provided in their proper place under the head of

12. **Development.**—And along with the articulation exercises are given certain exercises in *pronunciation*. These are meant to correct the numerous blunders in vowel-quality which are commonly called *provincialisms*. The exercises, however, embrace more than the vowels, and will be found to attack most of the errors that make our speech unlovely.

Let the order of the development exercises be observed in practice, as each will improve the effectiveness of the succeeding group:—(1) breathing, (2) vocal, and (3) articulation exercises.

At least ten minutes daily should be given to the following exercises :—

1.—**To develop and to gain control over the lungs :**
   Count to 40, in one breath, or take Alphabet twice in one breath. Gradually increase the exercise till 80 can be easily reached, in one breath.

2.—**Voice Development :**
   A.—Sing up Scale from A to E, below middle C, on oh : and from F to C on ah. Repeat each tone four times.
   B.—Sing as before, using movements of the arms downward from the shoulders, in front, for tones to E ; and backward from chest for tones above E and up to C, to accentuate each tone. Fill the lungs well to start with, then take short breath for each tone.
   C.—Take the same range, holding out each tone with equable power : duration, about half a minute.

All these tones should be produced on the inhalation.

3.—**Articulation :**   *Tonics.*
   A.—Speak [in most useful octave] the Vowels oo, oh, ah, ai, ee. Increase force, steadily, until great power is gained.

   Sub-Tonics and Atonics.
   B.—Speak in one breath, firmly and clearly, each of the following exercises :—

Black babbling brooks break brawling o'er their bounds.
The painted pomp of pleasure's proud parade.
Decide the dispute during dinner-time by dividing the difference.
Tourists thronged from time to time to traverse the Thames tunnel.
Gregory going gaily galloped gallantly to the gate.
Crazed with corroding cares and killed with consuming complaints.
Vanity of Vanities and all is Vanity.
Frank Feron flattered his friends and found fault with his foes.
His zeal was blazoned from zone to zone.
Serpents and snakes were scattered on the sea.
Judge and jury adjourned the judgment.
Chosen champion of the church he cherished her children.
The azure sea is shining with ships that shape their course for home.
This thread is thinner than that thistle there.
Year after year the o'er-ripe ear is lost.
Ye heard him yelling o'er your head.
Up a high hill he heaved a huge hard stone.
We wildly wish while wiser workmen win whate'er will worth reward.

And rugged rocks re-echo with his roar.
Lamely the lion limped along the lawn.
Many men of many minds mixing in multifarious matters of much moment.
None know nor need to know his name.
England's king lay waking and thinking while his subjects were sleeping.

4. **Pronunciation.**—Vowel values.

A, e, i, o, u.

A.	1. All, war, tall, fall. 2. Arm, father, card, dark (long). 3. At, cat, apple, tap (short). 4. Ale, pace, sane, ate (long). 5. Rare, lair, dare, pare (short).
E.	1. Ere, where, there (long). 2. Wet, let, mess (short). 3. Even, me, fee, leave. 4. Fern, mercy, err, learn.
I.	1. Field, shield, wield (long). 2. In, it, twist, rim (short). 3. Fir, first, thirst. 4. Lie, thine, sigh.
O.	1. Sold, no, go, tone (long). 2. On, lot, cough, or (short). 3. Who, soot, whom, do (long). 4. Come, other, son, won (short).
U.	1. Turn, nurse, curd, urn (long). 2. Blush, pun, us, rut (short). 3. True, rude (long). 4. Pull, push (short). 5. Tune, duke, unison.

Syllabification.

1. This, then, rough, fall, fix, dull, moon, broom, last.
2. Conflict, relief, instinct, condemn, reason, morose, prudent.
3. Extensive, completed, reformer, servitude, discursive, protector.
4. Invalidate, penetrative, restoration, conservative, partizanism.
5. Transcendentalism, preservativeness, repository, monumentalise.

6. Congratulatory, supererogation, interpretatively, inhospitality.
7. Plenipotentiary, anti-pestilential, instrumentality, derationalisation.
8. Intercommunicability, latitudinarianism, periodecahedral, unintelligibility.

PRONOUNCE:—

Initial G = Glory, not Dlory.
C = Clearly ,, Tlearly.
D = During ,, Juring.
Final ts = Acts, not Acks.
ing = Walking, not walkin'.
a = Ma ,, mar.
ity = Charity ,, charaty.
ible = Possible ,, possable.

AVOID:—

Melting the last letter of one word into the first of the next word.
Example—An don't = And don't.
Awfulie = Awful lie.
Lodeyes = Law dies.
Yardoor = Yard door.

13. Preservation.—This topic has in some sense been anticipated by remarks in the section on Use; but in point of fact, a large volume could well be devoted to it. Many medical throat-specialists state that by far the majority of their clients —speakers and singers—cripple their voices through ignorance of the structure and use of the vocal organs; the few are those who fail directly from lung and throat weakness.

Writing from an extensive and varied experience with public speakers, it is possible to add, that every case of breakdown, temporary or permanent, I have met with, has been primarily due to wrong production or other form of voice-abuse, and not to a singular physical condition.

The one point of moment for all would-be speakers, readers, and singers to care for is, that they *begin* in the *right way*. All after-work, then, should simply perfect the vocal powers. But start in the wrong way, and they are likely to continue in that way, perverting the whole voice machine. The evil day of collapse may be long deferred, but there cannot, at any point, be in false production the ease and zest which accompany true speaking.

It will be convenient to offer a few definite points of advice on voice-preservation, in the form of maxims :—

1. Exercise the voice vigorously, at least once a day, with a view to keeping it in full health.

2. Do not speak in a cold or damp air directly after sustained use of the voice.

3. Avoid competition with loud noises, whether inside or outside the building in which you speak.

4. Lessen the strain on the voice when the throat is at all relaxed.

5. Vary the pitch of voice frequently, keeping easily within the natural range.

6. Shun nostrums.

II.—ELOCUTION IN RELATION TO LITERATURE.

(A), MODERN POETRY AND PROSE; *(B)*, BIBLICAL POETRY AND PROSE.

(A.) Before we dwell upon the principles of Elocution, applied to modern poetry and prose, it will be expedient for us to fasten on some working definitions.

The word literature, rigorously used, denotes experiences of the human mind recorded in artistic language. Works of literary art have this further test applied to them, that they shall, in virtue of their spirit or their form, or both united, give general and enduring delight. Examine any dozen poems or prose writings, of the first order, that occur to the mind at the moment, and they will be seen to possess this double quality. It is the flower *plus* perfume. A definition of Poetry is not easy to press into the measure of a single sentence. In fact, an adequate definition of poetry in any number of words has been the despair of poets and critics of all ages. Nevertheless, it will be pardonable to compound a definition, out of many, that will answer the present purpose. We need not build a larger house than will meet our requirements. With this apology, we may describe poetry as such an elevated expression in *words* of the imagination and feelings of the poet, as will excite like images and feelings in the minds of others. Poetic language is therefore peculiar in several respects. Poetry dwells upon and elaborates images, and so favours picturesque words. Again, the world of poetry is above that of everyday life, and, accordingly, poetry prefers words that retain their pristine vigour or beauty: words degraded by association with vulgar and mechanical things are inimical to poetry. *Sounds* are inseparable from words, hence sounds are brought under the laws of art, and are disposed according to accent, quantity, and rhyme.

The three great kinds of poetry are :—Narrative, Lyric, Dramatic ; and all, doubtless, have emanated from the one source—the ballad-dance of the early days of each nation's history. The Narrative (notably the Heroic) depicts doings and sufferings of men, and refers incidents to a bygone day : thus appealing forcibly to the imagination.

The Lyric reveals the inner self of the writer, and calls upon the joys or sorrows of the reader. The Dramatic presents the poet's intention by means of an organised group of characters ; and we are required, jointly with the poet, to forget ourselves, and act or suffer with the personages of the play. Next, let us give a passing glance at Prose.

Prose is the second, not the first, great landmark in literary history.

It is traceable rather to the loosening of the bonds that braced Poetry than to a separate creative fiat. Its development is coincident with the growth of civilization. Clearness, simplicity, conciseness, are three of its intrinsic traits, according to the gospel of *modern* taste.

In subject it may often overlap or even transcend the subjects of Poetry. It begins with transcriptions of the homeliest life, and ends in the loftiest sublimities. But in form, Prose ends where Poetry begins. Poetry is intense, prose extense. Poetry isolates a fraction of life and concentrates itself upon it—drawing out the ideal feature, and giving to it a monumental form. Prose admits many more and trifling details, and aims at fullness rather than fineness of treatment.

The two modes will come out clearly by a comparison. The prose writer would not consider that he had overspent himself in composing an essay of 5,000 words on the substance of Shelley's verse—

"We look before and after, and pine for what is not,
Our sincerest laughter with some pain is fraught,
Our sweetest songs are those that tell of saddest thought."

The 20 lines or so of Hamlet's soliloquy, "To be or not to be," &c., could not fitly be rendered in fewer than ten times that number of lines in prose. And so it comes about that poetry, on account of the excessive compression of thought it loves, invites a much more subtle vocalization than is necessary for the fully expanded forms of prose. Further than this in the line of definition we cannot go now.

What has been said will help the beginner to approach the subject of literary structure with more readiness, and, perhaps, make him more willing to accept the reasoning, that the true basis of the art of reading or recitation is the basis of literary design or structure.

The entire scale of inflections and intonations is furnished and fashioned by the composition, and not the reverse, as might sometimes be supposed from the manner of not a few interpreters. These, then, are the two large divisions of our subject now to be examined. (1) Literary Structure (chiefly concerning Poetry), and (2) The Technique of Vocal Interpretation.

1. **Literary Structure.**—No better way is open to us than taking types of structure. Look at six poetical compositions (contained in this collection). "Mark Antony's Oration;" "The Bridge of Sighs;" "Ginevra;" "The Norman Baron;" "A Parental Ode;" "Maud Müller."

The subject of the first is the betrayal of Cæsar; of the second, the pitiful end of a poor outcast girl; of the third, the accidental death of a young bride in the midst of her wedding festivities; of the fourth, the conversion and death of a feudal baron under the influences of song, prayer, and storm; of the fifth, a poet's apostrophe to his mischievous child; of the sixth, the unfulfilled desires of a child of nature. The subjects are each different, and the patterns in which they are woven are different. A plain literary definition of each would be—

1. "Antony's Speech:" Dramatic Oration.
2. "The Bridge of Sighs:" Objective Lyric.
3. "Ginevra:" Simple Narrative.
4. "Norman Baron:" Picturesque Narrative.
5. "A Parental Ode:" Apostrophe and Parenthesis.
6. "Maud Müller:" Pastoral Idyll.

Now, look more closely at these pieces, and they will reveal a shapeliness or proportion, which is named Unity. In modern poetry may be observed a great number of literary unities. In some poems the details unified are few; in others, a mass of details, that give an impression of much complexity, and disclose a beautiful design. Straight lines are interesting in their way, but artfully complicated lines will make lovely forms that gratify our finer sense. The unity of a single element is the slightest design, and is generally too bald to awaken uncommon pleasure. Unity of design is one of the chief of art interests; but before the mind conceives the idea of unity, it must be conscious of some degree of complexity. The unadorned development of a single idea has consequently the faintest hold upon the mind; whilst the most involved pattern, cunningly simplified, will most satisfy the mind.

No. 1 is a remarkable oratorical achievement, suiting its own end perfectly. It is an illustration of *climax as design :* the gradual rise from conversational tone, through various adroit deviations, up to the most resistless climax of passion.

No. 2 is an instance of *dramatic unity* in the lyric. That is, a dramatic *centre-piece* uniting two strains of sentiment.

No. 3 illustrates the common and favorite *unity of antithesis.* In this case the first half of the poem presents unbounded joy; passing at its highest point into shade; thence, by rapid steps, into gloom and appalling calamity.

No. 4 is an example of *unity of parallel* interests, working side by side, and enhancing the effect of each other. The "Songs of the Gleemen" form one element; the actions and demeanour of the "Dying Baron" another; "Prayers of the Monk," and the enveloping echoings of the raging tempest outside the castle, the third.

No. 5 stands almost alone as a specimen of *unity of parenthesis.* The sublime and the ridiculous are bound to each other by means of recurrent parenthesis.

No. 6 exemplifies admirably the *unity of parallel.* Two lives in the light of each other are made to share a parallel fate.

Unity defined and preserved by refrain has endless illustrations in both serious and humorous poetry. Tennyson's "May Queen" and Hood's "Bachelor's Dream," are marked types, the former of serious, the latter of comic poetry.

The real use to the Elocutionist of the study of the literary constitution of a poem is two-fold—first he is saved from that lamentable blunder of treating the parts of a work as if each were the whole; discerning that the constituents of a poem have to be justly subordinated to the dominant tone of the whole. Extravagant "reciters," who associate *pantomime* with their art, insist on making the most out of every separate opening for display, regardless of the injury this inflicts upon the total harmonised effect sought by the author. Secondly, and of primary moment, is the safe dictation it gives to the voice. The workmanship of a poem—in respect of architecture—decides the lines and limits and plan of vocal expression. Roughly speaking, the elements of expression are Tone, Power, Inflexion; and if we may distinguish their offices, the first two are the exponents of the *feelings*, and the last one the chief servant of *sense*. This, palpably, is a very arbitrary division, but not without justification for practical use.

Turning again to the six patterns of unity scrutinised a moment ago, observe what obedience of tone, power, and inflexion they impose upon the voice.

Antony's Speech is a series of ascending steps, culminating in an outburst that well-nigh "moves the stones of Rome to rise and mutiny." The momentum of the delivery is increased by being stayed at intervals with a reference to "the honourable men." Think then what the effect would be if the *structure* of this oration were ignored, and the whole work thundered out at full pressure; or, again, if the several parts were seized upon and magnified out of all spirit with the *central purpose* of the speech.

The Bridge of Sighs consists in a line of impassioned contemplation (over the body of one "more sinned against than sinning") broken in the middle by a *dramatic putting of the catastrophe*, which serves at the same time to unite the severed lyrical strain. Manifestly, the voice will express the first part of the lyrical outflow in a register of tones it will have to resume, in modified force, after the dramatic interruption. To deliver the entire poem as if it were a straightforward dirge, would be like converting a piece of chaste gold into solution.

Ginevra requires the voice to depict the first side of the antithesis cheerfully, with nimble movement; the second side changes the joy and rapidity of the voice into deepening sadness, the pace varying from standstill to moderate. The last portion of the poem dissolves, steadily, the mystery and gloom, and, although never rising to the pitch of either side the antithesis, it acts as a key to the whole, and should be delivered in that simple explanatory manner that such a discovery—long after the tragic event—asks.

The Norman Baron consists in three distinct lines that melt into one another, and re-appear separately. Vocally, these three elements must be well distinguished: the schemes of tones describing the Dying Baron will differ from the tones that echo the approach and full outbreak of the thunderstorm, and different from both will be the chain of tones depicting the Songs of the Saxon Gleemen and the devotions of the Monk. The voice and its intonation thus indicating these three threads will, at the same time, so interlace them that they shall minister to our sense of beauty; in this case the unity of parallels. As to which element dominates here, it is not possible to go wrong; the subject of the poem is the dying experiences of a human being. Only wilful misreaders would give the storm or the singing effect the uppermost place.

A Parental Ode supposes the alternation of two opposite intonations: literally, two apostrophes are being carried on in different vocabularies. The one ideal, the other *real*. The antagonism of the two modes of address determines the course of the voice. A somewhat lofty and mellifluous expression best suits the one, while the other prompts an abrupt drop into the region of conversational tone. Observe, however, that the aside-like nature of the parentheses, abrupt as they are, have still to bear relation to the higher strain. It is nothing short of a feat to present a perfect illusion of such a situation. But to treat the poem as the development of one idea, or to so sharply sunder the ties of the two strains so that they utterly part company, is to wreck the ingenuity of Hood.

Maud Müller is an idyll conceived in soft tones throughout. Two contrasted characters are brought under each other's influence for a few moments, and the whole after-life of each is coloured by the sensations of this single interview.

The parallel is rather real than apparent. Both live a disappointed life, in totally different spheres. At the close of the poem the poet sets future Hope over against the Despair pictured in the two histories of the Rustic Beauty and the Judge. As the voice proceeds to trace the details of design in the poem, it will be artistically natural to relate the fortunes of Maud Müller in a higher and more musical tone than is used for the fate of the Judge. The parallel will thus be brought out and maintained, while the organic unity of the details should be definitely struck by a pervading sympathy of tone.

For the first few lines there is an absence of sentiment—the voice moving in the groove of easy description: the last lines of the poem are impressed with the deepest gravity. Thus the opening and the close. The body of the poem requires the voice to move backwards and forwards along the two streams of experience, at the last flowing into the buoyant sea of Hope.

Of the music or metrical element of poetry a word must be added. All poetic language, as we have seen, consents to inherent music, and, without this musical principle, would cease to be poetry in the exact sense. We cannot, therefore, in our adequate interpretations of poetic works of sense, sentiment and *rhythm*, neglect the last and distinctive feature.

This rhythmic quality we produce by *poising* the voice, so that the words, instead of jostling carelessly as in prose, ride along a propped and balanced intonation. The words are shot through, so to speak, with a cord of elastic tone. By this, be it understood, neither sense nor sentiment is improperly enslaved. Both are even freer than they are in colloquial forms.

MODERN PROSE.—With modification, and some exception, the instruction framed for poetry will be applicable to prose. Several cardinal points will be taken up in the after argument on *Naturalness*. Four large classes of prose may be defined, corresponding remotely with the different kinds of poetry.

In one class we should find the prose of Milton, Burke, De Quincey, and Ruskin; in another, the novels of Scott, Dickens, Thackeray, and Eliot; in another, the eloquence of preachers and patriots; in the other class would come literary essays, such as Addison's, Macaulay's, Carlyle's, and many writings (of literary value) on scientific and philosophical subjects.

Generally speaking, prose is met by a less exceptional manner of delivery than will satisfy poetry. Still, there are passages of prose in each of the above classes that would be suited by nothing short of the grandest elocution.

Apart from logical phrasing and the exhibition of the sense of sentences, the reader has to show, by his perfectly sympathetic voice, the rise in dignity or beauty of the language; he has equally to touch with truth that emotional language characteristic of the third class, and again the words of dialogue characteristic of the second class. It will appear to some people a mere triviality for one to remind students that satire, demureness, irony, and other details, have special intonations of their own. But Swift, Addison, Dickens, Thackeray, and Ruskin, who sprinkle their works liberally with one or other of these qualities, are the writers most often misread by readers unversed in the æsthetics of *expression*. And yet these same readers, for themselves, well know the nature of every element in a composition. The one Changeless Rule in Elocution, to be obeyed by everyone, is *propriety;* but the full acquisition of this great principle will be a life-work. Mind, it has full reference to *demonstration* no less than to suppression of feeling, and is anxious only for *truth* of expression.

2. **Vocal Technique.**—We come now to the more mechanical principles that affect logical expression, and form the ground-plan of utterance generally, upon which feeling or any quality, other than sense, is superposed. Hardly any student of elocution can hope to succeed, either as speaker or reader, without knowledge and mastery of these laws. They are rooted not only in logic, but in expediency; they at once give the true meaning of language, and prevent waste of vocal power. To the forces of expression they are what the rails are to a locomotive. And, considering what directness and ease they secure, they are acquired with small difficulty.

Without presuming to draw an entire network of lines—inflexions—along which the voice shall run on different occasions, various intelligible rules, of the nature of fixed principles, may be given. Further than this it seems superfluous to go; only those laws of inflexion that admit of perfectly clear statement and symbolization should be noted in a text-book. For the rest, the learner will do best to consult the living instructor. The two signs ∕ ∖ represent the two elementary actions of the speaking voice, and form the basis from which spring all complex vocal modulations. They have only two essential attributes—(1) Order ; (2) Length.

With respect to the first, the voice may descend and then rise ∖ ∕, or rise and then descend ∕ ∖.

Respecting the second, the length may vary from a ditone to an octave, thus :—

DITONE.   THIRD.   FIFTH.   OCTAVE.

Mark, that inflexion (the characteristic of speech) is a *glide*, not a definite musical step; still there can be no objection to the use of musical terms as signs of measure. It is desirable to exercise the voice in these upward and downward inflexions, and also in the various lengths. These provide the training for ear and voice, without which sense is liable to be maimed, and sound to be robbed of its melody.

Inflexion constitutes a large part of the technique of elocution. Virtually, it holds the position that *drawing* occupies in relation to painting. Tone, pitch, emphasis, are the colouring and life of elocution.

Inflexion, like drawing, is an exact art. The separate shades of meaning contained in different constructions of language can only be expressed by certain *glides* of a particular length. It is this utmost nicety (which alone satisfies the gifted student) that crowns naturalness in the delivery of artistic compositions.

Taking the **V** as the naked plan of voice movement, let it be noticed that, as the two sides are of equal length—varying from length of ditone to octave—the same sense of completeness will, practically, be felt by the ear whether the voice takes the course of **V** proper, or of inverted **Λ**. This is the principle of complimentary inflexions. Once thoroughly grasped, this idea enables a student to abolish a number of cares about the conduct of his voice. So long as the ear has received the satisfaction at the close of an expression that this law of balanced inflexion gives, it matters not whether the last controlling inflexion has been a downward or an upward one. Or, in stricter words, it may often be preferable from all standpoints to end the sense with a rising inflexion. Consider, *first*, in the most general way, the second feature of inflexion—Length. Bear in mind that simple unimpassioned speech is content with a scale of two tones (ditones), whereas interrogation, wonder, animation, require at least three tones. Take a series of three sentences rising in degree of expressiveness—

1. (Ditones.) Now fades the glimmering landscape from the sight
And all the air a solemn stillness holds.
2. (Thirds.) Thousands of their soldiers looked down from their decks and laughed,
Thousands of their seamen made mock at the mad little craft.
3. (Fifths.) But were I Brutus,
And Brutus Antony, there were an Antony
Would ruffle up your spirits and put a tongue
In every wound of Cæsar.

It will readily be felt that each of these verses demands an inflexion-scale of a particular length. What meets the first is too limited for the last. The beginner needs to realize these different powers.

Prose submits to the same laws of inflexion as poetry.

Second, note the Order of inflexion. On this head there is no necessity to delineate exactly what the voice rightly does without our concern; this kind of teaching bewilders and rebuffs those whom it seeks to attract. Only those rules will be given that affect

Words in (1) Apposition, (2) Opposition, (3) Series, (4) Parenthesis.

1. Words in *Apposition* take similar inflexions:

Ex. "Is a candle brought to be put under a búshel or under a béd, or &c."

2. Words in *Opposition* (antithesis) take opposite inflexions:

Ex. "Do all men kill the things they do not lóve?"

"Hàtes any man the thing he would not kill?"

3. A series of three independent qualities has the upward inflexion on the first and last, with the falling inflexion on the middle member, thus:

Ex. According to your áge, wèight, and wórthiness.

Series of words of the Positive class are taken on upward inflexions, with the exception of the last member but one :—

Ex. "I will buy with you, sell with, talk with, walk with you."

Series of words of the Negative class are inflected in the opposite way, thus :

Ex. "But I will not eat with you, drink with you, nor pray with you."

Thus, it will be seen that whatever order the inflexions follow in the body of a sentence, the last two inflected members have complimentary glides of the voice, giving the ear the requisite sense of finish.

4. Parentheses are spoken slightly quicker than the preceding matter, and dropped a tone or two in pitch. But the last inflexion in the parenthesis should be upward, and form a proper basis for the continuance of the voice beyond the parenthetic words :—The inflexions of a sentence containing parenthesis might be represented thus :—

"Upon my power I may dismiss this court

Unless Bellario (a learned doctor

Whom I have sent for to determine this)

Come here to-day."

The elements of Pitch, Emphasis, and Tone can be but sparingly treated : they belong to life, and cannot well be exhibited by printed signs.

Each will receive general comment in the following Analysis of "*The Passions*" :—

TONE.
1. Fear.   High in pitch.   Slight in power.   Tone tremulous.
2. Anger.   „   „   „   Strong in emphasis. Time quick.
3. Despair.   Low   „   Extremes. From slow to rapid.
4. Hope.   Middle   „   Level, flowing. Easy time.
5. Revenge.   Anger intensified. More guttural.
6. Pity.   Low pitch.   Soft emphasis. Slow time.
7. Jealousy. Low, variable. Tender, then harsh. Slow. Rapid.
8. Melancholy. Low. Gentle in power. Slow time.
9. Cheerfulness. High. Light emphasis. Quick time.
10. Joy.   High. Fuller emphasis. More animated.
11. Love. High. }
12. Mirth. High. } Livelier, almost rhapsodial expression.

The poet has in the most charming and finished manner sketched each passion in its different aspects, and it is to the poem itself that we must all go for our one great lesson in the treatment of the "Passions."

Here everything is considered—pitch, tone, emphasis, and modulation. In directing the student to this poem we may safely leave the subject of feeling; he will secure from this all the training that written descriptions are capable of giving.

THE PASSIONS.

William Collins.
(Verse printed as Prose).

When Music, (heavenly maid!) was young, ere yet in earliest Greece she sung, the Passions oft, to hear her shell, thronged around her magic cell: exulting,—trembling;—raging,—fainting;—possessed, beyond the Muse's painting. By turns, they felt the glowing mind disturbed,—delighted,—raised,—refined; till once, 'tis said, when all were fired, filled with fury, rapt, inspired, from the supporting myrtles round they snatched her instruments of sound; and as they oft had heard, apart, sweet lessons of her forceful art, each—for madness ruled the hour—would prove his own expressive power.

1. First, *Fear*—his hand, its skill to try, amid the chords bewildered laid—and back recoiled—he knew not why:—even at the sound himself had made!
2. Next *Anger* rushed, his eyes on fire: in lightnings owned his secret stings; with one rude clash he struck the lyre, and swept, with hurried hands, the strings.
3. With woeful measures, wan *Despair:*—low, sullen sounds his grief beguiled; a solemn, strange, and mingled air; 'twas sad, by fits—by starts, 'twas wild.
4. But thou, O *Hope!* with eyes so fair, what was thy delighted measure? Still it whispered promised pleasure, and bade the lovely scenes at distance "Hail!" Still would her touch the strain prolong; and, from the rocks, the woods, the vale, she called on "Echo," still, through all her song; and, where her sweetest theme she chose, a soft, responsive voice was heard at every close!—and Hope, enchanted, smiled, and waved her golden hair!
5. And longer had she sung—but, with a frown, *Revenge* impatient rose: he threw his blood-stained sword in thunder down; and with a withering look, the war-denouncing trumpet took, and blew a blast—so loud and dread, were ne'er prophetic sounds so full of woe: and ever and anon, he beat the doubling drum, with furious heat. And though
6. sometimes, each dreary pause between, dejected *Pity*, at his side, her soul-subduing voice applied, yet still he kept his wild unaltered mien; while each strained ball of sight—seemed bursting from his head.
7. Thy numbers, *Jealousy*, to nought were fixed; sad proof of thy distressful state! Of differing themes the veering song was mixed; and now, it courted Love—now, raving, called on Hate.

8. With eyes upraised, as one inspired, pale *Melancholy* sat retired; and from her wild, sequestered seat, in notes by distance made more sweet, poured, through the mellow horn, her pensive soul : and, dashing soft, from rocks around, bubbling runnels joined the sound. Through glades and glooms the mingled measure stole ; or, o'er some haunted stream, with fond delay,—round a holy calm diffusing, love of peace and lonely musing,—in hollow murmurs died away.
9. But, oh, how altered was its sprightlier tone, when *Cheerfulness*—a nymph of healthiest hue,—her bow across her shoulder flung, her buskins gemmed with morning dew,—blew an inspiring air, that dale and thicket rung ; the hunter's call, to Faun and Dryad known. The oak-crowned Sisters, and their chaste-eyed Queen, Satyrs, and Sylvan Boys were seen peeping from forth their alleys green : brown "Exercise" rejoiced to hear ; and "Sport" leaped up, and seized his beechen spear.
10. Last, came *Joy's* ecstatic trial; he, with viny crown advancing, first to the lively pipe his hand addressed ; but soon he saw the brisk awakening viol, whose sweet, entrancing voice he loved the best. They would have thought who heard the strain, they saw, in Tempe's vale, her native maids, amid the festal-sounding shades to some unwearied
11. minstrel dancing ; while, as his flying fingers kissed the strings, *Love*
12. framed, with *Mirth*, a gay, fantastic round ;—loose were her tresses seen, her zone unbound ;—and he, amidst his frolic play, as if he would the charming air repay, shook thousand odours from his dewy wings.

(B) BIBLICAL POETRY AND PROSE.—1. It is a time-honoured habit of critics to molest whatever existing forms of art offend them, ere they erect their own structure.

In dealing with the reading aloud of the Bible, there is strong temptation to question some of the prevalent fashions of elocution before proceeding to advocate other methods.

But the balance of good is invariably in favour of *constructive* work ; and, to men of serious intent, in a matter of such solemnity as the reading of Divine revelation, this constructive mode is peculiarly becoming.

The teaching offered in this section cannot be exhaustive, but it will be none the less devoid of the sting of dogmatism.

2. Where the voice is called in once to treat the scriptures purely as the national literature of the Hebrews, it is employed a hundred times in connection with the solely sacred use of the Bible.

That is to say, Elocution serves the reading of the Bible chiefly in its place in Public Worship. And in this domain two requirements are to be satisfied :—(A) Faultless articulation, (B) Full intelligibility.

The former has had attention ; the latter, as it pertains to reading the scriptures, demands somewhat special counsel. First let me say, that for all reasons a dignified rhythmic elocution (which includes that subliming quality musicians name *sostenuto*) seems, for public uses, the best suited to the Bible. It gives ample room for variation of the temper of language, and the sense need in no degree be made to suffer by it.

3. Besides, there are two positive contentions on behalf of this style. Genealogies and bald chronicles excepted, almost all biblical writing is poetical, and fits itself naturally to this higher treatment. "Metrical beauty is the inborn music which beats a natural accompaniment to the creative toil of the imagination, and vindicates the essential unity of the life which runs through it." This inborn music, from the solitary plaint to the swelling anthem, awaits the thrill that the finely attuned and balanced voice alone can give.

The second positive plea for this voice is, that it *carries* much better than does the homelier manner ; and the sustained carrying power of the voice becomes a grave question when large, and sometimes ill-shaped, churches have to be occupied.

4. Full intelligibility is a requisition as difficult to meet as is faultless articulation. By the term is meant such an appropriation (by the reader) of the writer's mind, and manner of expression, as shall enable him (the reader) to make clear the *substance* of a chapter or a book, and the particular *form* to which that substance consents.

Now, the Bible, independent of its spiritual significance, is incomparably rich in more than one literary department, and great in all others but in drama.

Idylls, lyrics, allegories, odes, are kinds of poetry that abound in scripture : prophecy claims a place to itself as the most exalted form conceivable, and, standing aloof from all other literatures, is the special possession of the Hebrews. In prose, the Bible is remarkable for epic, history, philosophy, biography, and written and spoken addresses. The prose we may pass by here. Two or three kinds of the poetry we must take into account.

5. Of all versions of the Bible extant, the Revised is the one from which the most correct literary effects may be gained. In this version, the old obstacles—the arbitrary divisions of

books into chapters, and chapters into verses—have been removed, and the general trend of the writer has been safeguarded. Further, the Revisers have brought out clearly the poetical features of innumerable passages in various parts of the Bible ; and in their manipulation of the Psalms, they have done a work of literary justice and lasting value. It is now possible for readers to see and to show the organic unity of books and passages, and to perceive metrical beauties and formal unities, to which even discerning students were before oblivious.

This is the idea of higher Unity that requires students to read books as *wholes*, and at one effort. The true literary effect, for instance, of Ruth, Job, Malachi, Habakkuk, Joel, cannot be caught unless the whole book be read, and read as a continuous composition. Sometimes two Psalms (such as 42 and 43) are one constitution, and should be read together as one poem ; by this means the Unity, broken by separation into two parts, is restored.

The only forms of Unity that we can single out in these pages are some of those to be met with in the Psalms. (For full treatment of this subject students should read the *Companion to Cambridge Bible*.)

There are notable Unities which are distinguished as :—

1. *Unity shown in the growth of a single idea.* Ex. Psalm 29. Here a thunderstorm is depicted rising from the Mediterranean, passing over the forest of Lebanon to the wilderness of Kadesh, and there subsiding. The Sun shines out once more, and " In His temple everything saith Glory." " The voice of the Lord " is the refrain.

Now the vocal part would be to trace the development of the main idea in one succession of tones, and the refrain in a deeper and grander quality of voice. This would truly interpret the form and spirit of the Psalm, and give all listeners the requisite key to the structure.

2. *Dramatic Unity* consists in sudden change from one condition of mind to another—from despair to hope, from defeat to victory ; or the reverse order : Psalms 57 and 89 are good illustrations of these opposites. Whilst Psalm 27 is a different instance of Dramatic Unity—verses 7 to 12 are really the language of the mood of depression from which the speaker has been rescued, and for which he is now giving praise to God.

In the case of the first two examples mentioned, the voice would change where the change of spirit begins, and thus reveal the pattern of Unity.

With the 27th Psalm the delivery would correspond in joyfulness to the end of the 6th verse, and continue this key from the 13th to the end. But the Dramatic Centre-piece (from verse 7 to 12) would be spoken in sadder intonation, to mark it off as the language of the state from which the Psalmist has been delivered.

3. *Unity of Parallel.*—Of this class there are numberless examples in the Psalms, but the 19th is the one generally selected for illustration. It is the one which inspired Addison's hymn "The Spacious Firmament," &c. The physical and the moral law come in for equal adoration from the Psalmist, who sees a profound witness in each to the existence and goodness of the Creator.

As the parallels do not shade into one another, but join abruptly, the reader must choose two degrees of pitch—say the higher one for the first declaration of the Psalm, " The heavens declare the glory of God," and the lower pitch for the second, beginning "The *law* of the Lord is perfect." Care must be taken to make the Unity felt by the listener,—to read it as though it were two distinct poems would be an unpardonable blunder.

The Unities of Succession, Historic Narrative, and the several more formal Unities, would demand more space for their discussion than the present allows. Of the voice, in relation to these Unities, two general statements may be made.

First, that as the changes are more sudden and considerable in Hebrew poetry than in any other, the voice has a new and special task. Second, *pitch and inflection* trace the *shape* of the poem : *intonation* follows, and reveals the *spirit*.

But, whether in prose or poetry, the reader, by imaginative vision, should see the whole of the composition, he wishes to read, from beginning to end. By this means he is able to give, as he proceeds, the right value and complexion to every detail in its true relation to the whole work.

In this place, on the ground of fitness and high merit, no lines perhaps will be more welcome than those on—

"THE POETRY OF THE BIBLE."
By George Gilfillan.

"That so much of Scripture should be written in the language of poetry has excited some surprise, and created some inquiry; and yet in nothing do we perceive more clearly than in this, the genuineness, power, and divinity of the oracles of our faith. As the language of poetry is that into which all earnest natures are insensibly betrayed, so it is the only speech which has in it the power of permanent impression. The language of the imagination is the native language of man. It is the language of his excited intellect,—of his aroused passions,—of his devotion,—of all the higher moods and temperaments of his mind. It was meet, therefore, that it should be the language of his revelation from God.

"The language of poetry is thus the language of the inspired volume. The Bible is a mass of beautiful figures;—its words and its thoughts are alike poetical;—it has gathered around its central truths all natural beauty and interest;—it is a Temple with one altar and one God, but illuminated by a thousand varied lights, and studded with a thousand ornaments. It has substantially but one declaration to make, but it utters that in the voices of the creation. It has pressed into its service the animals of the forest, the flowers of the field, the stars of heaven, all the elements of nature. The lion spurning the sands of the desert, the wild roe leaping over the mountains, the lamb led in silence to the slaughter, the goat speeding to the wilderness; the rose blossoming in Sharon, the lily drooping in the valley, the apple-tree bowing under its fruit; the great rock shadowing a weary land, the river gladdening the dry place; the moon and the morning star; Carmel by the sea, and Tabor among the mountains; the dew from the womb of the morning, the rain upon the mown grass, the rainbow encompassing the landscape; the light, God's shadow; the thunder, His voice; the wind and the earthquake, His footsteps:—all such varied objects are made—as if naturally so designed from their creation—to represent Him to whom the Book and all its emblems point. Thus the quick spirit of the Book has ransacked creation to lay its treasures on Jehovah's altar; united the innumerable rays of a far-streaming glory on the little hill, Calvary;—and woven a garland for the bleeding brow of Immanuel, the flowers of which have been culled from the gardens of a universe."

III.—ELOCUTION APPLIED TO PUBLIC SPEAKING.
General Practical Considerations.

1. **Public speaking** is a term we associate with the utterance of our own thoughts and feelings, as distinguished from *Reading and Recitation*, which usually imply the expression of more strictly artistic compositions of other minds in verse and prose.

Here the end in view is either persuasion or instruction, and often both together may be intended in the same effort.

Oratorical speeches, designed to rouse, belong to a different category from that occupied by lectures addressed to the understanding; while those speeches or addresses that first appeal to the intelligence, and then seek to carry conviction by an excitement of the sympathies, should be placed in both classes, unless they may be properly reserved for a third class. By providing a third class it will be possible to put all ministrations of whatsoever kind into one or other of the three. We should then say addresses—used in the widest meaning—are either simple or mixed, and speak to (a) the understanding, (b) the feelings, or (c) to understanding and feelings. As examples of the first description, take any series of lectures on mechanical science; of the second, Chatham's (and John Bright's) orations are often good specimens; and innumerable illustrations may be found in pulpit eloquence. Edmund Burke and Lord Macaulay supply numerous examples of the third kind, as indeed have done most of the first-rank political leaders from time to time. In judging of the true difference of tone between the first two classes, let the speeches of *Brutus* and *Antony*, in Shakspere's "Julius Cæsar," be kept in mind as the very best illustrations of the nature and effect of the two modes to be found in either actual or imaginary utterance.

2. It would not be within the province of these pages to discuss the wide subject of rhetoric, even if the ability were at command. All that can be done is to point out what vocal economics must prevail; and then add a few reasonings, conceived for the beginner chiefly, as to the kind of discipline that will be good for him to undergo.

First, as to the needs common to public speech of every species. A good clear voice, well under control, and possessing both variety and power: this must be striven after. Then the pronunciation should be precise, but not pedantic. The language ought to be appropriate to the theme, and the sentences grammatically constructed; whilst the mass of matter should be informed by evident unity or proportion, that the whole may be easily grasped and remembered.

But among the details that speakers have to consider is one of great importance, affecting so much their own comfort and that of their audience, and yet a detail that has received little comment. I refer to the room or building in which speaking may have to be carried on. Many men know, to their cost, what it means to speak week by week in a church, or in a hall, that defies their efforts to be agreeably heard. Only now and then do we find really large structures that lend themselves faultlessly to the speaking voice. (I am now, of course, assuming that the Elocution is all that it should be). But there are two things, in particular, that speakers might look to with advantage. First, the general design of the room in relation to the position of the speaker—whether a long, narrow, or a short, stumpy room ; or, again, an irregularly-shaped room. Is the ceiling unusually high, or unusually low—little or much wood about the room ? The actual size of the place ; the number of occupants. All these and many other details, trifling as they seem in their relation to speaking, are capable of affecting a speaker physically to an extent he alone experiences.

In most cases a long, narrow room will require a slightly higher pitch and more intense tone than a short, broad room needs. Short rooms enable you to turn from left to right, and so spread the voice gently over the occupied area ; long rooms compel the voice to be on a greater stretch for the convenience of auditors at the most distant point.

3. My main argument for all speakers is this : The *cavity* (as it may be called) in which we speak (be the shape what it will) must be regarded simply as carrying on *the work of the mouth*—that is to say, a resonator or larger mouth, magnifying and modifying at once the tones produced by the vocal chords. Puzzling it will be, no doubt, at first, but we must all strive to use the room in which we articulate vocal tone as we use the mouth. That will lead to this difference of method, that, whereas before we had viewed the room or hall as an enemy, an inevitable resistance, for the voice to either overcome by sheer power and endurance, or surrender to, despite all vocal tactics, we now consider the cavity or room as a *friend*, acting as a larger resonator in the service of the mouth, accumulating and distributing the sound created by the voice. But knowledge of the powers and limits of this friend is the one thing that will bring relief and effectiveness to our own mechanism. Let the guiding principle be—seek nothing from the physical sources of the voice that is securable from the resounding arrangement outside ourselves.

Here naturally follows this important question : How can the mouth situate itself to turn the larger reverberator to best account? By attention to two or three simple points, in addition to humouring the voice with nicety to the encompassing walls.

(1.) The mouth should be well opened, and kept in the best line of resonation.

(2.) Bending the head down, or turning it from side to side, so as to narrow the passage of the throat, must always be avoided.

(3.) Leaning against any fixture, or speaking behind a local obstruction—such as book, desk, or stand—is injurious to free, easy speech.

So much for this confined and hasty view of certain economics of Delivery.

4. Now we are to discuss, in a superficial way, four practices that men who aspire to some distinction in public speaking may not do ill to follow. This advice is for the inexperienced. Three features are present in most successful speeches or lectures. There is a suitable and varied vocabulary; a skilful and exact arrangement of this vocabulary into sentences and sections; and there is an orderly and proportioned setting forth of thought, giving the effect of wholeness. *First:* As a foundation training for the speaker, nothing can excel wide reading, whether for language, ideas, or construction. Poetry should not be excluded from this education, but have a prominent share—especially such masters as Shakspere, Tennyson, Browning, and Lowell. *Second:* It is impossible to over-rate the value of experimental exercise in literary composition. The influence of regular, careful composition (on various themes) over the mind that has often to express itself in public speech, is almost decisive. It begets precision and constructive power, and quickens that larger sense of order that enables a man to rapidly resolve his ideas of a subject into natural groups, and this sometimes in the very course of speaking. The use of such preparation for impromptu speaking is not open to question: the operations of analysis and synthesis so cultivated in written compositions, give the mind just that alacrity and method that mark off the ready, intelligent speaker, from the faulty, incoherent speaker. Depend upon it you will speak very largely as you write, or at anyrate you may do—write, therefore, with care and vigour. *Third:* Study Elocution in connection with literature. A

modulated voice, poised so as to move roundly and sweetly; numberless vocal effects the outgrowth of the study of the extent and depth of life reflected in literature;—these are only two of the blessings conferred on the speaker by the habit of *reading aloud* works of literary merit. *Fourth:* Take advantage of all the offers for practice in speaking you can. Theory alone will take you but one step on the way; practice, ceaseless experiment, is indispensable to the gaining of that self-possession which enables you to trust yourself, and to use your full stock of powers without confusion. Few men, with indifferent experience, reach eminence in any line of activity, but in the field of oratory, practice is a peculiarly royal-road to perfection. First-rate works on rhetoric do not deserve to be despised by the really ambitious student: and speakers of reputed eloquence or trenchancy, whether in the Pulpit, Parliament, or at the Bar, will always be of avail if the admirer will not degrade himself into being a mere mimetic slave.

IV.—GESTURE.

1. Most people in ordinary, as well as extraordinary, dialogue, use some gesture, and, whether they are aware or not, change the expression of their face. Among the many families of gesture used by men and women are (1) those that localise objects, or *indicative* gestures; (2) those that describe shape and action, or *imitative* gestures; (3) movements that act as the alphabet of the emotions, or *expressive* gestures. The countenance, too, is a fairly true commentary on the inner condition of mind. Notice, when anyone is telling a thrilling story, how the face and hands evince the changing spirit. The animating principle moves all the means of expression at its command. Dialogue, also, will bring into play a whole set of gesticulations and facial expressions, without which the *spoken* words would often fail to convey the due sense. Gesture anticipates and takes the place of words, from time to time, in most dialogue. Robert Browning, in numbers of his poems that represent Dialogue, and in his dramatic monologues, faithfully depicts this elliptical language, and leaves the reader to supply, by his power of vivid realization, whatever movement or facial change may be natural in the circumstances.

Well, now, how does this discussion help us to give a place to gesture? This question may be answered, in the first place, by our remembering that literature is a *representation*, no less than an interpretation, of life in some form or other, and, in greater or less degree, will carry the assent of countenance and accentuation of gesture with it.

In the *delivery* of literature, and in the speaking of our own minds equally, the impulse and the need for sympathy of gesture and countenance will be present.

2. Fixing the attention on gesture for the moment, let us decide what sort of expression is meant technically by this term. Nine persons of every ten use profuse gestures that commonly lack both point and grace; or the movements are not more than rudimentary jerks of the elbows or fingers. Other people habitually employ violent gesture, out of all keeping with the value of their talk; and not a few people deliver themselves so tamely that there is nothing inconsistent in their motionless attitude. Awkward, angular, and distracting gestures of many other kinds are characteristic expressions of Englishmen in almost all ranks of society. Only those who have been specially educated to come before the public in one or other of the artistic functions, show freedom from the grosser and clumsier *actions* of the arms.

For one person who learns graceful and appropriate action of the arms, a thousand will train their feet for dancing. There is an abstract conception of gesture no less than of dancing as an art.

The abstract idea of gesture confines the movements of the arms and hands within certain bonds of graceful curves; as moving figures restricted to given bonds of rhythm would theoretically explain dancing. It will now be seen how applicable this more artistic manner of gesture is to literature. Literature itself, poetry essentially, is the artistic interpretation of life by means of language. And just as the poet's view of life is exceptional, so is the language he uses, and the arrangement he gives it, conformable to the laws of Art. The gesture, correspondingly, that is suited to accompany the delivery of purified and metrical expression, is not the spasmodic or spontaneous impulse of the instant, but the gesture which has been brought into obedience to the laws of Art—that is to say, Nature at her best.

3. Before mentioning the elementary laws that must be incorporated by all who come before the public to commend their

subject on artistic lines, let it be said that public speakers and lecturers, quite as much as interpreters of literary works, need to turn the arms to their service if they would prevent them being a distraction, not to say a constant embarrassment.

A little care in the early days of practice will habituate speakers to an easy, graceful, and most helpful use of gesture: allowed to slip our attention during the years of self-discipline, nothing can disturb the serenity of a sensitive man, during speaking, like the lawless action of his arms.

The following are four of the elementary laws upon which graceful action rests:—

(1.) The arms should move first from the shoulders, not the elbows.

(2.) The hands contain all expression, and are informed last.

(3.) The fingers should be so combined as to contribute that help that the mind requires.

(4.) On return to a position of repose, the elbows to be turned outward and the wrists turned in.

The principle of *curves* to prevail in all gesticulation (other than that which is intentionally imitative of the vulgar or peculiar in actual life) in opposition to that of *angles*.

4. *Facial expression* should so accord with the sentiment uttered by the voice as to confer the value of emphasis upon speech. Voice, look, and gesture are an union; their united purpose is to manifest the speaker's mind, or the mind that he has for the time being appropriated.

V.—NATURALNESS.

Many authorities have just one injunction for beginners in any department of Art, and that is, "Be Natural!" It is a state very easily enjoined; less easily acquired. But what is meant by this "Naturalness," so much in request, in Elocution? Opinions differ somewhat. By those who take a sternly practical standing, natural reading or recitation is always in the colloquial vein, and is best when it is nearest to the "talking" manner. Their assumption seems to be, that the art of delivery consists in wrestling with lofty ideas and fine phrases, overcoming them, and making them run in the loose, easy fashion of conversation. Such judgments consider all other styles of delivery *affected*.

An opposite class, who approach the subject intensely, but

partially, regard Naturalness of Elocution, especially so far as it affects poetry, as comprising a full vocal ritual ; and to them, *affectation* would only begin with the so-called "Naturalness" of the other class. Here, then, is a wide divergence of view.

Palpably, these are extreme views. It would never do to read *all* types of poetry and prose in either one style or the other. Each style would suit *some* poems, but, doubtless, a far greater number of compositions would require neither manner. The principle of bringing a stereotyped style of treatment to all literature, regardless of the different degrees of spirit and beauty embraced, is vicious in the extreme.

Our manner of exposition—relating to both sense and feeling—must conform to the literary matter ; not the matter be made to fit a cast-iron manner. By this provision—surely an artistic one—every poem or other literary effort would find its proper place in the scale of our emotions, and receive a true articulation in the voice of the emotions.

Satire and humour in verse would deserve a style far removed from that of pathos or of sublimity. "The Well of St. Keyne," and "Our Village," for instance, proceed from a playful mood that has nothing in common with the pathos of Burns' lyrics, or with the sublimities of Milton. Literature may be said to register all states of mind, from low to lofty, and for every state of mind the voice has a peculiarly appropriate intonation. The range of feeling and the vocal range are co-extensive and co-intensive. Is it not, then, wrong to apply any but the truly consistent voice to each state of mind embodied in separate literary works? Fully elaborated, this *artistically-natural* method would entail many and delicate discriminations. For, as it could be shown that no two literary efforts cover exactly the same ground, so, accordingly, no two vocal duties should be quite identical.

For example, there is a certain *solemnity* about Longfellow's "Sandalphon," that is not wholly dissimilar to the tone of Lowell's "Above and Below ;" nevertheless, there is a distinction of *degree*, if not of kind, and this distinction would be realized and sounded by a reader of insight and sensitiveness.

It is in accuracy and subtlety that Art serves a student so well. Light touches and fine strokes are the acquirements of the Artist—not to be had for the mere asking. Grace and inspiration need to go hand in hand : neither can dispense with the other.

But I have two difficulties, says the scrupulous student, which are not yet simplified. *First*, how freely shall the minor elements of a poem be expressed : second, what method of treatment may properly be adopted for writings (poetry or prose), that apparently are framed on other than the autobiographic basis. In both matters, much rests with the individual, educated taste. But with regard to the 1st point: Most elocutionists of educated taste would keep vividly in view the one thing commemorated in each composition, and would emphasize the various details according to their value in relation to the main theme. Take, for example, the poem entitled, "Barbara Frietchie." Here the prime point is the splendid *loyalty* of a ninety-years'-old woman. Not a *man* in Frederick-Town dare declare his loyalty to the Union in the face of the incoming Rebel army, to whose leader this heroine boldly speaks: "Shoot, if you must, this old grey head, but spare your country's flag." The patriotic act occupies the centre of the poem : all that leads up to it, and that follows it, is subordinate. Of the details leading up to the chief topic, no doubt the one for most emphasis is the unmanly action of the townsmen in timidly concealing the National Flag ; of the particulars that follow Barbara Frietchie's act, the most significant is the *sympathy* and honour that the "loyal winds" and "sunset light" show in such noble human conduct.

Short expressions and dialogues by characters introduced into *narrative* poems should not have the same dramatic distinctiveness and vigour that would be proper to speakers in a drama. In serious Epic or Narrative, speeches are only *recorded* by the Narrator. The composition must not be stayed to admit of full play of the dramatic manner. All parts must harmonize with the governing theme and intent of the author. The habit of pouncing upon fine phrases as prey for exaggerated expression, without reference to their place in the whole work, is unpardonable in anyone but the mountebank.

We come now to the *second* topic—the different *persons* to which pieces may be referred. This is a knotty point, and the source of quite irreconcilable differences of opinion. The solution of the problem may be helped by the following view. All matter—prose or poetry—spoken directly in the person of the writer, may be appropriated and delivered as our own, the writer and the reader being for the time identical. Almost all Lyrical matter, and much Narrative (and all forms of Oratory) would occupy this class.

But sometimes an author chooses a plan of representation by which he briefly introduces a character, and then gives the story over to this invented personage, the author himself winding the work up with some moral or comment.

Longfellow's "Tales of the Wayside Inn" illustrate this class.

As a rule, it is necessary to maintain, appreciably, the relation of the second person to the first: that is to say, you cannot, in the character of the deputed speaker, give yourself the freedom of expression you could if the personage were dramatically independent. The utterances of such a character are always modified by its relation to the master character in whose service the subordinate acts.

A *third* class may be formed of all compositions in which the author sinks himself, and instead of speaking about a character, he creates a character that is self-explanatory. Here, then, is a form of the pure dramatic mode. Such poems as Tennyson's "May Queen," "Northern Cobbler," many of Browning's poems, and all prose sketches in the homely vernacular, come into this category. An adoption of the particular shade of character presented is here needful;—the limits and growth of the imitation to be settled by the poem itself. Lastly, in the treatment of dramatic *scenes* (from Shakspere) by one person, the characters must be clearly distinguished, and yet shaded off into one another and organised, just as the speeches themselves are. A highly defined vocalisation of the different speakers gives the ludicrous effect of a ventriloquial entertainment.

[By way of parenthesis, allow me to add that, among the more general but important concerns of the public reader or reciter of literature, is the question of his audience, with particular regard to what may be styled *breadth of effects* to be used. In the case of an illiterate audience, it would be desirable often to indulge a very pronounced manner; humour as well as pathos would have to be demonstrated more or less fully. An educated audience would be offended by just this kind of thing. You would count on a ready response in the matter of sympathy and intelligence in everything provided. Humour, too, would be caught and fully enjoyed without the exaggeration that might be proper with the opposite class of audience.

This point, then, of the particular quality of our hearers, may be no small determining factor.]

From this argument we may see that to be "Natural" is to be ourselves—augmented.

The scale and varied demand of our task considered, the "Natural," undeveloped, inexperienced self, will mostly be "Naturally" *insufficient*. It is only by steady, liberal training that we become adequate for the immense undertaking of appreciating and revealing the wealth of a literature, by means of human tones.

Naturalness in the sense of vulgarity, insipidity, noisiness, or faultiness of articulation, is not a thing to encourage—nor, indeed, is this kind of naturalness in the minds of those who advocate this quality in the true sense. What we all *really* mean by naturalness—though our own terms are often misleading—is *that* naturalness that results from Art : Art which is artistic enough to conceal itself.

VI. ELOCUTIONARY "READINGS."

(ANALYSES.)

A few simple suggestions on the delivery of certain typical pieces will possibly both interest and help the beginner. Three of the items are in verse and two in prose. The brief treatment of each is intended only to indicate in a general way the line of analysis or "reading" that may be followed by the student, and does not even claim to be the only "reading."

Poems : 1, "Portia's Plea for Mercy." 2, "The Singing Leaves." 3, "The Amen Corner."

Prose items: 1, "A Tale of Terror." 2, "Ill-bred Hospitality."

1. "*Portia's Plea for Mercy*" *(page 57).*

The elements of this speech are—
1. The true expression of mercy is spontaneous, not forced.
2. Its becoming character in those who occupy positions of power.
3. As a human virtue, its superiority to power ; more—
4. It is a chief attribute of the *Creator*. Therefore—
5. Man is more Godlike in the exercise of Mercy than in power ; especially when he tempers justice with mercy.

The central important point of the speech is that
6. On the ground of unmixed *justice*, none are entitled to claim *Salvation*.
7. This life stands in relation to an after-life, and as God deals mercifully with His creatures, and not in the manner of their deserts, they should at least act in God's way towards one another.

Justice and mercy are set over against each other :
Shylock the advocate of the one, and Portia of the other.

2. "*The Singing Leaves*" *(page* 194*).*

In Part I. of this narrative we get a clear idea of the spirit of all the characters introduced. The King is severe and proud, but not devoid of tenderness, as we see in his respect for his dead Queen, whose likeness seems to re-appear in the features of his youngest daughter. The look this beautiful girl gives her father at his savage contempt for her choice, acts as a powerful reproach, and he at once relents. Pride, vanity, and humility are the three qualities severally embodied in the three daughters. Each declares her character in her choice. Part II. sees the King—who has easily secured at Vanity Fair the presents for the two eldest daughters—in vain search for the choice of the third daughter, "The Singing Leaves." Neither in Vanity Fair nor in the Greenwood, but in the realm of the human *heart*, is to be found the three-fold message supplied by the King's Page. Part III. makes no reference to the eldest daughters, but tells how she, "in whose blithesome hair dim shone the golden crown," realises to the full her desire—" they speak to my very heart, and it speaks to them evermore." The Page declares that though his love-songs are his only wealth in the world of tangible things, yet in the region of fancy, melody, and imagination, his lute and he are Lords.

The play on the number "three" is a curious interest in this ballad formed on a Mediæval model.

3. "*The Amen Corner*" *(page* 248*).*

This piece is by an American writer, and as it has an American flavour in both spirit and expression, it would be well to give it with a distinct touch of American intonation and inflexion.

It is scarcely needful to say that the first portion of the poem should be treated in a bloodless, matter-of-fact strain.

In the interview there comes the serene simplicity of the aged man, whose feelings should be expressed in a voice sweet and flowing; but there ought not to be an attempt at literal imitation of a cracked and feeble voice. After the full description of the old man in the poem, it is not justifiable to do more than suggest the fashion of his utterance.

4. "*A Tale of Terror*" *(page 296).*

Deliver this piece of conversational prose in as simple and unaffected a way as you can command—up to the point where the aeronaut begins to query the sanity of his companion.

The climax needs to be thrillingly related, and the method of ending the story must suggest the oblivion that overtakes the balloonist at the embrace of the maniac.

5. "*Ill-bred Hospitality*" *(page 325).*

This is a specimen of Swift's finest sarcasm. To adopt a tone free from sarcastic bite would be as great a blunder in the rendering of this piece as an abusive attack would be.

The tone suited is not utterly free from bitterness, but in the main is unforced. Demureness, sarcasm, irony, have their place in this sketch, and the interpreter must not fail to exhibit in tone the finest distinctions. A very ordinary range of voice will be sufficient, as passion plays no part whatever. It is a pure piece of intellect.

Having dealt with the Art of Elocution, the next thing is to provide such literary compositions as will form suitable exercises for mind and voice.

The *poems* which follow will be found representative of almost every style and spirit to be met with in modern poetry. The *prose* selections—serious, humorous, and eloquent—provide good material for practice.

Whilst all the pieces have been chosen for some intrinsic merit, and for their use to the student, there are very few, if any, altogether unfit for the popular purpose of public entertainment.

The classification of poetry and prose illustrates the plan laid down in the section that discusses Literature.

PART II.—CHOICE SELECTIONS OF PROSE AND POETRY.

DRAMATIC LITERATURE.

Othello.

ACT. I., SCENE III.—A COUNCIL CHAMBER.

Duke. Write from us: wish him post-post-haste: despatch.
1st Sen. Here comes Brabantio and the valiant Moor.

Enter BRABANTIO, OTHELLO, IAGO, RODERIGO, *and Officers.*

Duke. Valiant Othello, we must straight employ you
Against the general enemy Ottoman.—
I did not see you; welcome, gentle signior;
[*To Brabantio.*
We lack'd your counsel and your help to-night.
 Bra. So did I yours: Good your grace, pardon me;
Neither my place, nor aught I heard of business,
Hath raised me from my bed; nor doth the general care
Take hold on me; for my particular grief
Is of so flood-gate and o'erbearing nature,
That it engluts and swallows other sorrows,
And it is still itself.
 Duke. Why, what's the matter?
 Bra. My daughter! O, my daughter!
 Sen. Dead?
 Bra. Ay, to me.
She is abus'd, stol'n from me, and corrupted
By spells and medicines bought of mountebanks.
For nature so preposterously to err,

Being not deficient, blind, or lame of sense,
Sans witchcraft, could not——
    Duke. Whoe'er he be, that, in this foul proceeding,
Hath thus beguil'd your daughter of herself,
And you of her, the bloody book of law
You shall yourself read in the bitter letter,
After your own sense; yea, though our proper son
Stood in your action.
    Bra.   Humbly I thank your grace.
Here is the man, this Moor; whom now, it seems,
Your special mandate, for the state affairs
Hath hither brought.
    Duke & Sen.   We are very sorry for it.
    Duke. What in your own part can you say to this?
                                             [*To Othello.*
    Bra. Nothing, but this is so.
    Oth. Most potent, grave, and reverend signiors,
My very noble and approved good masters,—
That I have ta'en away this old man's daughter,
It is most true; true, I have married her;
The very head and front of my offending
Hath this extent,—no more. Rude am I in my speech,
And little bless'd with the set phrase of peace;
For since these arms of mine had seven years' pith,
Till now some nine moons wasted, they have us'd
Their dearest action in the tented field;
And little of this great world can I speak,
More than pertains to feats of broil and battle;
And therefore little shall I grace my cause,
In speaking for myself: Yet, by your gracious patience,
I will a round unvarnished tale deliver
Of my whole course of love; what drugs, what charms,
What conjuration, and what mighty magic,
(For such proceeding I am charg'd withal,)
I won his daughter with.
    Bra.   A maiden never bold;
Of spirits so still and quiet, that her motion
Blush'd at herself. And she,—in spite of nature,
Of years, of country, credit, everything,—
To fall in love with what she feared to look on?

It is a judgment maim'd, and most imperfect,
That will confess—perfection so could err
Against all rules of nature, and must be driven
To find out practices of cunning hell,
Why should this be. I therefore vouch again,
That with some mixtures powerful o'er the blood,
Or with some dram conjur'd to this effect,
He wrought upon her.

Duke.   To vouch this, is no proof;
Without more certain and more overt test,
Than these thin habits, and poor likelihoods
Of modern seeming, do prefer against him.

1st Sen. But, Othello, speak;—
Did you by indirect or forced courses
Subdue and poison this young maid's affections?
Or came it by request, and such fair question
As soul to soul affordeth?

Oth.   I do beseech you,
Send for the lady to the Sagittary,
And let her speak of me before her father:
If you do find me foul on her report,
The trust, the office, I do hold of you,
Not only take away, but let your sentence
Even fall upon my life.

Duke.   Fetch Desdemona hither.

Oth. Ancient, conduct them; you best know the place—
    [*Exeunt Iago, and Attendants.*
And, till she come, as truly as to heaven
I do confess the vices of my blood,
So justly to your grave ears I'll present
How I did thrive in this fair lady's love,
And she in mine.

Duke. Say it, Othello.

Oth. Her father lov'd me; oft invited me;
Still question'd me the story of my life,
From year to year; the battles, sieges, fortunes,
That I have pass'd.
I ran it through, even from my boyish days,
To the very moment that he bade me tell it.
Wherein I spoke of most disastrous chances,

Of moving accidents, by flood and field ;
Of hair-breadth 'scapes in the imminent deadly breach ;
Of being taken by the insolent foe,
And sold to slavery ; of my redemption thence,
And portance in my travel's history ;
Wherein of antres vast, and desarts idle,
Rough quarries, rocks, and hills whose heads touch heaven,
It was my hint to speak, such was the process ;
And of the Cannibals that each other eat,
The Anthropophagi, and men whose heads
Do grow beneath their shoulders. These things to hear,
Would Desdemona seriously incline :
But still the house affairs would draw her thence ;
Which ever as she could with haste despatch,
She'd come again, and with a greedy ear
Devour up my discourse. Which I observing,
Took once a pliant hour ; and found good means
To draw from her a prayer of earnest heart,
That I would all my pilgrimage dilate,
Whereof by parcels she had something heard,
But not intentively. I did consent ;
And often did beguile her of her tears,
When I did speak of some distressful stroke
That my youth suffer'd. My story being done,
She gave me for my pains a world of sighs ;
She swore,—In faith, 'twas strange, 'twas passing strange ;
'Twas pitiful, 'twas wondrous pitiful :
She wish'd she had not heard it ; yet she wish'd
That heaven had made her such a man : she thanked me ;
And bade me, if I had a friend that lov'd her,
I should but teach him how to tell my story,
And that would woo her. Upon this hint I spake :
She lov'd me for the dangers I had passed ;
And I loved her, that she did pity them.
This only is the witchcraft I have us'd ;
Here comes the lady, let her witness it.

The Merchant of Venice.

SCENE—VENICE. A COURT OF JUSTICE.

Duke. What, is Antonio here?
Ant. Ready, so please your grace.
Duke. I am sorry for thee: thou art come to answer
A stony adversary, an inhuman wretch,
Uncapable of pity, void and empty
From any dram of mercy.
  Ant.   I have heard
Your grace hath ta'en great pains to qualify
His rigorous course; but since he stands obdurate,
And that no lawful means can carry me
Out of his envy's reach, I do oppose
My patience to his fury, and am armed
To suffer, with a quietness of spirit,
The very tyranny and rage of his.
 Duke. Go one, and call the Jew into the court.
 Solan. He is ready at the door: he comes, my lord.

Enter SHYLOCK.

 Duke. Make room, and let him stand before our face.—
Shylock, the world thinks, and I think so too,
That thou but lead'st this fashion of thy malice
To the last hour of act; and then, 'tis thought,
Thou'lt show thy mercy and remorse more strange
Than is thy strange apparent cruelty:
We all expect a gentle answer, Jew.
 Shy. I have possessed your grace of what I purpose;
And by our holy sabbath have I sworn
To have the due and forfeit of my bond:
If you deny it, let the danger light
Upon your charter and your city's freedom.
You'll ask me, why I rather choose to have
A weight of carrion flesh, than to receive
Three thousand ducats: I'll not answer that;
But say it is my humour: is it answered?
 Bass. This is no answer, thou unfeeling man,
To excuse the current of thy cruelty.
 Shy. I am not bound to please thee with my answer.

Bass. Do all men kill the things they do not love?
Shy. Hates any man the thing he would not kill?
Bass. Every offence is not a hate at first.
Shy. What! would'st thou have a serpent sting thee twice?
Ant. I pray you, think you question with the Jew:
You may as well go stand upon the beach,
And bid the main flood bate his usual height;
You may as well use question with the wolf,
Why he hath made the ewe bleat for the lamb;
You may as well forbid the mountain pines
To wag their high tops, and to make no noise,
When they are fretted with the gusts of heaven;
You may as well do anything most hard,
As seek to soften that—than which what's harder?—
His Jewish heart: therefore, I do beseech you,
Make no more offers, use no further means,
But with all brief and plain conveniency
Let me have judgment, and the Jew his will.
   Bass. For thy three thousand ducats, here is six.
   Shy. If every ducat in six thousand ducats
Were in six parts, and every part a ducat,
I would not draw them; I would have my bond.
   Duke. How shalt thou hope for mercy, rendering none?
   Shy. What judgment shall I dread, doing no wrong?
The pound of flesh, which I demand of him,
Is dearly bought; 'tis mine, and I will have it.
If you deny me, fie upon your law!
There is no force in the decrees of Venice.
I stand for judgment: answer, shall I have it?
   Duke. Upon my power I may dismiss this court,
Unless Bellario, a learned doctor,
Whom I have sent for to determine this,
Come here to-day.
   Solan.   My lord, here stays without
A messenger with letters from the doctor,
New come from Padua.
   Duke. Bring us the letters; call the messenger.

Enter NERISSA.

   Duke. Came you from Padua, from Bellario?

Ner. From both, my lord. Bellario greets your grace.
[*Presenting a letter.*

Bass. Why dost thou whet thy knife so earnestly?
Shy. To cut the forfeiture from that bankrupt there.
Duke. This letter from Bellario doth commend
A young and learnèd doctor to our court.
Where is he?
Ner. He attendeth here hard by,
To know your answer, whether you'll admit him.
Duke. With all my heart.—Some three or four of you,
Go give him courteous conduct to this place.

Enter PORTIA.

Give me your hand : Came you from old Bellario?
Por. I did, my lord.
Duke. You are welcome : take your place.
Are you acquainted with the difference
That holds this present question in the court?
Por. I am informed throughly of the cause.
Which is the merchant here, and which the Jew?
Duke. Antonio and old Shylock, both stand forth.
Por. Is your name Shylock?
Shy. Shylock is my name.
Por. Of a strange nature is the suit you follow ;
Yet in such rule, that the Venetian law
Cannot impugn you, as you do proceed.—
You stand within his danger, do you not? [*To Antonio.*
Ant. Ay, so he says.
Por. Do you confess the bond?
Ant. I do.
Por. Then must the Jew be merciful.
Shy. On what compulsion must I? tell me that.
Por. The quality of mercy is not strain'd ;
It droppeth, as the gentle rain from heaven,
Upon the place beneath : it is twice bless'd ;
It blesseth him that gives and him that takes :
'Tis mightiest in the mightiest ; it becomes
The thronèd monarch better than his crown ;
His sceptre shows the force of temporal power,

The attribute to awe and majesty,
Wherein doth sit the dread and fear of kings ;
But mercy is above this sceptr'd sway,
It is enthronèd in the hearts of kings,
It is an attribute to God himself ;
And earthly power doth then show likest God's,
When mercy seasons justice. Therefore, Jew,
Though justice be thy plea, consider this—
That in the course of justice, none of us
Should see salvation : we do pray for mercy ;
And that same prayer doth teach us all to render
The deeds of mercy. I have spoken thus much
To mitigate the justice of thy plea ;
Which, if thou follow, this strict court of Venice
Must needs give sentence 'gainst the merchant there.
    Shy. My deeds upon my head ! I crave the law,
The penalty and forfeit of my bond.
    Por. Is he not able to discharge the money ?
    Bass. Yes, here I tender it for him in the court ;
Yea, twice the sum : if that will not suffice,
I will be bound to pay it ten times o'er,
On forfeit of my hands, my head, my heart ;
If this will not suffice, it must appear
That malice bears down truth. And I beseech you,
Wrest once the law to your authority ;
To do a great right do a little wrong ;
And curb this cruel devil of his will.
    Por. It must not be ; there is no power in Venice
Can alter a decree establishèd :
'Twill be recorded for a precedent ;
And many an error, by the same example,
Will rush into the state : it cannot be.
    Shy. A Daniel come to judgment ! yea, a Daniel !
O wise young judge, how do I honour thee !
    Por. I pray you, let me look upon the bond.
    Shy. Here 'tis, most reverend doctor, here it is.
    Por. Shylock, there's thrice thy money offered thee.
    Shy. An oath, an oath, I have an oath in heaven :
Shall I lay perjury upon my soul ?
No, not for Venice.

Por. Why, this bond is forfeit;
And lawfully by this the Jew may claim
A pound of flesh, to be by him cut off
Nearest the merchant's heart.—Be merciful:
Take thrice thy money; bid me tear the bond.
 Shy. When it is paid according to the tenour.—
It doth appear you are a worthy judge;
You know the law, your exposition
Hath been most sound: I charge you by the law,
Whereof you are a well-deserving pillar,
Proceed to judgment:—by my soul, I swear
There is no power in the tongue of man
To alter me: I stay here on my bond.
 Ant. Most heartily I do beseech the court
To give the judgment.
 Por. Why then, thus it is:
You must prepare your bosom for his knife—
 Shy. O noble judge! O excellent young man!
 Por. For the intent and purpose of the law
Hath full relation to the penalty,
Which here appeareth due upon the bond—
 Shy. 'Tis very true: O wise and upright judge!
How much more elder art thou than thy looks!
 Por. Therefore lay bare your bosom.
 Shy. Ay, his breast:
So says the bond;—doth it not, noble judge?—
"Nearest his heart:" those are the very words.
 Por. It is so. Are there balance here to weigh
The flesh?
 Shy. I have them ready.
 Por. Have by some surgeon, Shylock, on your charge,
To stop his wounds, lest he do bleed to death.
 Shy. Is it so nominated in the bond?
 Por. It is not so expressed: but what of that?
'Twere good you do so much for charity.
 Shy. I cannot find it; 'tis not in the bond.
 Por. You, merchant, have you anything to say?
 Ant. But little: I am armed and well prepared.—
Give me your hand, Bassanio: fare you well!
Grieve not that I am fallen to this for you;

For herein Fortune shows herself more kind
Than is her custom : it is still her use,
To let the wretched man outlive his wealth,
To view with hollow eye and wrinkled brow
An age of poverty; from which lingering penance
Of such misery doth she cut me off.
Commend me to your honourable wife :
Tell her the process of Antonio's end ;
Say how I lov'd you, speak me fair in death ;
And, when the tale is told, bid her be judge,
Whether Bassanio had not once a love.
Repent not you that you shall lose your friend,
And he repents not that he pays your debt ;
For, if the Jew do cut but deep enough,
I'll pay it presently with all my heart.

   Bass. Antonio, I am married to a wife
Which is as dear to me as life itself ;
But life itself, my wife, and all the world,
Are not with me esteem'd above thy life :
I would lose all, ay, sacrifice them all
Here to this devil, to deliver you.

   Por. Your wife would give you little thanks for that,
If she were by, to hear you make the offer.

   Gra. I have a wife, whom, I protest, I love :
I would she were in heaven, so she could
Entreat some power to change this currish Jew.

   Ner. 'Tis well you offer it behind her back ;
The wish would make else an unquiet house.

   Shy. [*Aside.*] These be the Christian husbands ! I have a
                            daughter ;
Would any of the stock of Barrabas
Had been her husband, rather than a Christian !
[*Aloud.*] We trifle time : I pray thee, pursue sentence.

   Por. A pound of that same merchant's flesh is thine ;
The court awards it, and the law doth give it.

   Shy. Most rightful judge !

   Por. And you must cut this flesh from off his breast ;
The law allows it, and the court awards it.

   Shy. Most learned judge !—A sentence ; come, prepare.

   Por. Tarry a little ;—there is something else.—

This bond doth give thee here no jot of blood ;
The words expressly are, a pound of flesh :
Take then thy bond, take thou thy pound of flesh,
But, in the cutting it, if thou dost shed
One drop of Christian blood, thy lands and goods
Are, by the laws of Venice, confiscate
Unto the state of Venice.
  Gra. O upright judge !—Mark, Jew ; O learnèd judge !
  Shy. Is that the law ?
  Por.   Thyself shall see the act ;
For, as thou urgest justice, be assur'd
Thou shalt have justice, more than thou desir'st.
  Gra. O learned judge !—Mark, Jew ;—a learnèd judge !
  Shy. I take this offer then,—pay the bond thrice,
And let the Christian go.
  Bass.   Here is the money.
  Por. Soft ;
The Jew shall have all justice ;—soft ;—no haste ;—
He shall have nothing but the penalty.
  Gra. O Jew ! an upright judge, a learnèd judge.
  Por. Therefore, prepare thee to cut off the flesh.
Shed thou no blood ; nor cut thou less, nor more,
But just a pound of flesh : if thou tak'st more
Or less than a just pound,—be it but so much
As makes it light, or heavy, in the substance,
Or the division of the twentieth part
Of one poor scruple : nay, if the scale do turn
But in the estimation of a hair,—
Thou diest, and all thy goods are confiscate.
  Gra. A second Daniel! a Daniel, Jew !
Now, infidel, I have thee on the hip.
  Por. Why doth the Jew pause ? take thy forfeiture.
  Shy. Give me my principal, and let me go.
  Bass. I have it ready for thee ; here it is.
  Por. He hath refus'd it in the open court :
He shall have merely justice, and his bond.
  Gra. A Daniel, still say I ; a second Daniel !—
I thank thee, Jew, for teaching me that word.
  Shy. Shall I not have barely my principal ?
  Por. Thou shalt have nothing but the forfeiture,

To be so taken at thy peril, Jew.

Shy. Why, then the devil give him good of it !
I'll stay no longer question.

Por. Tarry, Jew :
The law hath yet another hold on you.
It is enacted in the laws of Venice,—
If it be prov'd against an alien
That by direct or indirect attempts
He seek the life of any citizen,
The party 'gainst the which he doth contrive
Shall seize one half his goods ; the other half
Comes to the privy coffer of the state ;
And the offender's life lies in the mercy
Of the duke only, 'gainst all other voice.
In which predicament, I say, thou stand'st ;
For it appears, by manifest proceeding,
That indirectly, and directly too,
Thou hast contriv'd against the very life
Of the defendant ; and thou hast incurr'd
The danger formerly by me rehears'd.
Down, therefore, and beg mercy of the duke.

Gra. Beg that thou may'st have leave to hang thyself :
And yet, thy wealth being forfeit to the state,
Thou hast not left the value of a cord ;
Therefore, thou must be hang'd at the state's charge.

Duke. That thou shalt see the difference of our spirit,
I pardon thee thy life before thou ask it :
For half thy wealth, it is Antonio's ;
The other half comes to the general state,
Which humbleness may drive into a fine.

Por. Ay, for the state,—not for Antonio.

Shy. Nay, take my life and all ; pardon not that :
You take my house, when you do take the prop
That doth sustain my house : you take my life,
When you do take the means whereby I live.

Por. What mercy can you render him, Antonio ?

Gra. A halter gratis ; nothing else, for Heaven's sake.

Ant. So please my lord the duke, and all the court,
To quit the fine for one half of his goods ;
I am content, so he will let me have

The other half in use, to render it,
Upon his death, unto the gentleman
That lately stole his daughter :
Two things provided more,—that, for this favour,
He presently become a Christian ;
The other, that he do record a gift,
Here in the court, of all he dies possess'd,
Unto his son Lorenzo and his daughter.
   Duke. He shall do this ; or else I do recant
The pardon that I late pronounced here.
   Por. Art thou contented, Jew ? what dost thou say ?
   Shy. I am content.
   Por.   Clerk, draw a deed of gift.
   Shy. I pray you give me leave to go from hence ;
I am not well : send the deed after me,
And I will sign it.
   Duke.   Get thee gone, but do it.
   Gra. In christening shalt thou have two godfathers :
Had I been judge, thou shouldst have had ten more,
To bring thee to the gallows, not the font.
                               [*Exit Shylock.*

   Duke. Sir, I entreat you home with me to dinner.
   Por. I humbly do desire your grace of pardon :
I must away this night toward Padua,
And it is meet I presently set forth.
   Duke. I am sorry that your leisure serves you not.
Antonio, gratify this gentleman ;
For, in my mind, you are much bound to him.
                    [*Exeunt Duke, Magnificoes, and train.*

   Bass. Most worthy gentleman, I and my friend
Have by your wisdom been this day acquitted
Of grievous penalties, in lieu whereof,
Three thousand ducats, due unto the Jew,
We freely cope your courteous pains withal.
   Ant. And stand indebted, over and above,
In love and service to you evermore.
   Por. He is well paid that is well satisfied ;
And I, delivering you, am satisfied,

And therein do account myself well paid :
My mind was never yet more mercenary.
I pray you, know me when we meet again :
I wish you well, and so I take my leave.

Julius Cæsar.

Act II., Sc. II.—A Room in Cæsar's House.

Cæs. Nor heaven nor earth have been at peace to-night :
Thrice hath Calpurnia in her sleep cried out,
" Help, ho ! they murder Cæsar ! " Who's within ?

Enter a Servant.

Serv. My lord ?
Cæs. Go bid the priests do present sacrifice,
And bring me their opinion of success.
Serv. I will, my lord.

Enter Calpurnia.

Cal. What mean you, Cæsar ? think you to walk forth ?
You shall not stir out of your house to-day.
Cæs. Cæsar shall forth : the things that threatened me
Ne'er looked but on my back : when they shall see
The face of Cæsar, they are vanished.
Cal. Cæsar, I never stood on ceremonies,
Yet now they fright me. There is one within,
Besides the things that we have heard and seen,
Recounts most horrid sights seen by the watch.
A lioness hath whelpèd in the streets ;
And graves hath yawned, and yielded up their dead ;
Fierce fiery warriors fought upon the clouds,
In ranks, and squadrons, and right form of war,
Which drizzled blood upon the Capitol ;
The noise of battle hurtled in the air,
Horses did neigh, and dying men did groan,
And ghosts did shriek and squeal about the streets.
O Cæsar ! these things are beyond all use,
And I do fear them.

Cæs. What can be avoided
Whose end is purposed by the mighty gods?
Yet Cæsar shall go forth; for these predictions
Are to the world in general as to Cæsar.

Cal. When beggars die there are no comets seen;
The heavens themselves blaze forth the death of princes.

Cæs. Cowards die many times before their deaths:
The valiant never taste of death but once.
Of all the wonders that I yet have heard,
It seems to me most strange that men should fear;
Seeing that death, a necessary end,
Will come when it will come.—

Re-enter Servant.

What say the augurers?

Serv. They would not have you to stir forth to-day.
Plucking the entrails of an offering forth,
They could not find a heart within the beast.

Cæs. The gods do this in shame of cowardice:
Cæsar should be a beast without a heart,
If he should stay at home to-day for fear.
No, Cæsar shall not: Danger knows full well
That Cæsar is more dangerous than he.
We are two lions littered in one day,
And I the elder and more terrible;
And Cæsar shall go forth.

Cal. Alas, my lord,
Your wisdom is consumed in confidence.
Do not go forth to-day: call it my fear
That keeps you in the house, and not your own.
We'll send Mark Antony to the senate-house;
And he shall say you are not well to-day:
Let me, upon my knee, prevail in this.

Cæs. Mark Antony shall say I am not well;
And, for thy humour, I will stay at home.

Enter DECIUS.

Here's Decius Brutus, he shall tell them so.

Dec. Cæsar, all hail! good morrow, worthy Cæsar:
I come to fetch you to the senate-house.

Cæs. And you are come in very happy time,

To bear my greeting to the senators,
And tell them that I will not come to-day.
Cannot, is false; and that I dare not, falser;
I will not come to-day: tell them so, Decius.
   Cal. Say he is sick.
   Cæs.   Shall Cæsar send a lie?
Have I in conquest stretched mine arm so far,
To be afeard to tell graybeards the truth?—
Decius, go tell them Cæsar will not come.
   Dec. Most mighty Cæsar, let me know some cause,
Lest I be laughed at when I tell them so.
   Cæs. The cause is in my will: I will not come;
That is enough to satisfy the senate.
But for your private satisfaction,
Because I love you, I will let you know.
Calpurnia, here, my wife, stays me at home:
She dreamt to-night she saw my statua,
Which, like a fountain with an hundred spouts,
Did run pure blood; and many lusty Romans
Came smiling, and did bathe their hands in it:
And these does she apply for warnings, and portents,
And evils imminent; and on her knee
Hath begged that I will stay at home to-day.
   Dec. This dream is all amiss interpreted;
It was a vision fair and fortunate:
Your statue spouting blood in many pipes,
In which so many smiling Romans bathed,
Signifies that from you great Rome shall suck
Reviving blood; and that great men shall press
For tinctures, stains, relics, and cognizance.
This by Calpurnia's dream is signified.
   Cæs. And this way have you well expounded it.
   Dec. I have, when you have heard what I can say;
And know it now: the senate have concluded
To give this day a crown to mighty Cæsar.
If you shall send them word you will not come,
Their minds may change. Besides, it were a mock
Apt to be rendered, for some one to say,
"Break up the senate till another time,
When Cæsar's wife shall meet with better dreams."

If Cæsar hide himself, shall they not whisper
" Lo, Cæsar is afraid " ?
Pardon me, Cæsar ; for my dear, dear love
To your proceeding bids me tell you this ;
And reason to my love is liable.

Cæs. How foolish do your fears seem now, Calpurnia !
I am ashamèd I did yield to them.—
Give me my robe, for I will go.—

Julius Cæsar.

ACT III., Sc. II.—ROME: THE FORUM.

Enter BRUTUS *and* CASSIUS, *and a throng of* Citizens.

Citizens. We will be satisfied ; let us be satisfied.
Bru. Then follow me, and give me audience, friends.—
Cassius, go you into the other street,
And part the numbers.—
Those that will hear me speak, let 'em stay here.
Those that will follow Cassius, go with him ;
And public reasons shall be rendered
Of Cæsar's death.

1st Cit. I will hear Brutus speak.
2nd Cit. I will hear Cassius ; and compare their reasons,
When severally we hear them rendered.

[*Exit Cassius. Brutus goes into the pulpit.*

3rd Cit. The noble Brutus is ascended : silence !
Bru. Be patient till the last.
Romans, countrymen, and lovers ! hear me for my cause, and be silent, that you may hear : believe me for mine honour, and have respect to mine honour, that you may believe : censure me in your wisdom, and awake your senses, that you may the better judge. If there be any in this assembly, any dear friend of Cæsar's, to him I say, that Brutus' love to Cæsar was no less than his. If then that friend demand why Brutus rose against Cæsar, this is my answer : Not that I loved Cæsar less, but that I loved Rome more. Had you rather Cæsar were living, and die all slaves ; than that Cæsar were dead, to

live all free men? As Cæsar loved me, I weep for him; as he was fortunate, I rejoice at it; as he was valiant, I honour him: but as he was ambitious, I slew him. There is tears for his love; joy for his fortune; honour for his valour; and death for his ambition. Who is here so base that would be a bondman? If any, speak; for him have I offended. Who is here so rude that would not be a Roman? If any, speak; for him have I offended. Who is here so vile that will not love his country? If any, speak; for him have I offended. I pause for a reply.

All. None, Brutus, none.

Bru. Then none have I offended. I have done no more to Cæsar than you shall do to Brutus. The question of his death is enrolled in the Capitol: his glory not extenuated, wherein he was worthy; nor his offences enforced, for which he suffered death.

Enter ANTONY *and others, with* CÆSAR's *body.*

Here comes his body, mourned by Mark Antony: who, though he had no hand in his death, shall receive the benefit of his dying, a place in the commonwealth; as which of you shall not? With this I depart,—That, as I slew my best lover for the good of Rome, I have the same dagger for myself, when it shall please my country to need my death.

All. Live, Brutus! live, live!

1st Cit. Bring him with triumph home unto his house.

2nd Cit. Give him a statue with his ancestors.

3rd Cit. Let him be Cæsar.

4th Cit. Cæsar's better parts Shall be crowned in Brutus.

5th Cit. We'll bring him to his house With shouts and clamours.

Bru. My countrymen,—

2nd Cit. Peace! silence! Brutus speaks.

1st Cit. Peace, ho!

Bru. Good countrymen, let me depart alone;
And, for my sake, stay here with Antony:
Do grace to Cæsar's corpse, and grace his speech
Tending to Cæsar's glories; which Mark Antony,
By our permission, is allowed to make.

I do entreat you, not a man depart,
Save I alone, till Antony have spoke. [*Exit.*
   1*st Cit.* Stay, ho! and let us hear Mark Antony.
   3*rd Cit.* Let him go up into the public chair;
We'll hear him.—Noble Antony, go up.
   Ant. For Brutus' sake I am beholding to you.
[*Goes into the pulpit.*
   4*th Cit.* What does he say of Brutus?
   3*rd Cit.*   He says, for Brutus' sake,
He finds himself beholding to us all.
   4*th Cit.* 'Twere best to speak no harm of Brutus here.
   1*st Cit.* This Cæsar was a tyrant.
   3*rd Cit.*   Nay, that's certain:
We are blest that Rome is rid of him.
   2*nd Cit.* Peace! let us hear what Antony can say.
   Ant. You gentle Romans,——
   Citizens.   Peace, ho! let us hear him.
   Ant. Friends, Romans, countrymen, lend me your ears:
I come to bury Cæsar, not to praise him.
The evil that men do lives after them;
The good is oft interrèd with their bones:
So let it be with Cæsar. The noble Brutus
Hath told you, Cæsar was ambitious:
If it were so, it was a grievous fault,
And grievously hath Cæsar answer'd it.
Here, under leave of Brutus and the rest,
(For Brutus is an honourable man;
So are they all, all honourable men,)
Come I to speak in Cæsar's funeral.
He was my friend, faithful and just to me:
But Brutus says, he was ambitious;
And Brutus is an honourable man.
He hath brought many captives home to Rome,
Whose ransoms did the general coffers fill:
Did this in Cæsar seem ambitious?
When that the poor have cried, Cæsar hath wept:
Ambition should be made of sterner stuff:
Yet Brutus says, he was ambitious;
And Brutus is an honourable man.
You all did see, that, on the Lupercal,

I thrice presented him a kingly crown;
Which he did thrice refuse: was this ambition?
Yet Brutus says, he was ambitious;
And, sure, he is an honourable man.
I speak not to disprove what Brutus spoke,
But here I am to speak what I do know.
You all did love him once, not without cause:
What cause withholds you then to mourn for him?
O judgment! thou art fled to brutish beasts,
And men have lost their reason. Bear with me;
My heart is in the coffin there with Cæsar,
And I must pause till it come back to me.

   1st Cit. Methinks there is much reason in his sayings.

   2nd Cit. If thou consider rightly of the matter,
Cæsar has had great wrong.

   3rd Cit.   Has he, masters?
I fear there will a worse come in his place.

   4th Cit. Mark'd ye his words? He would not take the crown;
Therefore, 'tis certain he was not ambitious.

   1st Cit. If it be found so, some will dear abide it.

   2nd Cit. Poor soul! his eyes are red as fire with weeping.

   3rd Cit. There's not a nobler man in Rome than Antony.

   4th Cit. Now mark him, he begins again to speak.

   Ant. But yesterday, the word of Cæsar might
Have stood against the world: now lies he there,
And none so poor to do him reverence.
O masters! if I were dispos'd to stir
Your hearts and minds to mutiny and rage,
I should do Brutus wrong, and Cassius wrong,
Who, you all know, are honourable men:
I will not do them wrong; I rather choose
To wrong the dead, to wrong myself, and you,
Than I will wrong such honourable men.
But here's a parchment with the seal of Cæsar,
I found it in his closet; 'tis his will:
Let but the commons hear this testament,
(Which, pardon me, I do not mean to read,)
And they would go and kiss dead Cæsar's wounds,
And dip their napkins in his sacred blood;

Yea, beg a hair of him for memory,
And, dying, mention it within their wills,
Bequeathing it, as a rich legacy,
Unto their issue.
　4th Cit. We'll hear the will: read it, Mark Antony.
　Citizens. The will, the will! we will hear Cæsar's will.
　Ant. Have patience, gentle friends, I must not read it;
It is not meet you know how Cæsar loved you.
You are not wood, you are not stones, but men;
And, being men, hearing the will of Cæsar,
It will inflame you, it will make you mad:
'Tis good you know not that you are his heirs;
For if you should, O, what would come of it!
　4th Cit. Read the will; we'll hear it, Antony;
You shall read us the will; Cæsar's will.
　Ant. Will you be patient? Will you stay a while?
I have o'ershot myself to tell you of it:
I fear I wrong the honourable men,
Whose daggers have stabb'd Cæsar; I do fear it.
　4th Cit. They were traitors: honourable men!
　Citizens. The will! the testament!
　2nd Cit. They were villians, murderers: the will! read the
　Ant. You will compel me, then, to read the will?　　[will.
Then make a ring about the corse of Cæsar,
And let me show you him that made the will.
Shall I descend? and will you give me leave?
　Citizens. Come down.
　2nd Cit. Descend.
　3rd Cit. You shall have leave.　　*[Antony comes down.*
　4th Cit. A ring; stand round.
　1st Cit. Stand from the hearse, stand from the body.
　2nd Cit. Room for Antony, most noble Antony!
　Ant. Nay, press not so upon me; stand far off.
　Several Cit. Stand back; room: bear back.
　Ant. If you have tears, prepare to shed them now.
You all do know this mantle: I remember
The first time ever Cæsar put it on;
'Twas on a summer's evening, in his tent,
That day he overcame the Nervii:—
Look, in this place, ran Cassius' dagger through:

See what a rent the envious Casca made :
Through this the well-belovèd Brutus stabb'd ;
And, as he pluck'd his cursèd steel away,
Mark how the blood of Cæsar followed it,
As rushing out of doors, to be resolv'd
If Brutus so unkindly knock'd, or no ;
For Brutus, as you know, was Cæsar's angel :
Judge, O you gods, how dearly Cæsar lov'd him !
This was the most unkindest cut of all ;
For when the noble Cæsar saw him stab,
Ingratitude, more strong than traitors' arms,
Quite vanquish'd him : then burst his mighty heart ;
And, in his mantle muffling up his face,
Even at the base of Pompey's statua,
Which all the while ran blood, great Cæsar fell.
O, what a fall was there, my countrymen !
Then I, and you, and all of us fell down,
Whilst bloody treason flourish'd over us.
O, now you weep ; and, I perceive, you feel
The dint of pity : these are gracious drops.
Kind souls, what, weep you when you but behold
Our Cæsar's vesture wounded ? Look you here,
Here is himself, marr'd, as you see, with traitors.

 1st Cit. O piteous spectacle !
 2nd Cit. O noble Cæsar !
 3rd Cit. O woful day !
 4th Cit. O traitors, villains !
 1st Cit. O most bloody sight !
 2nd Cit. We will be revenged.
 All. Revenge ! About ! Seek ! Burn ! Fire ! Kill ! Slay !
Let not a traitor live !
 Ant. Stay, countrymen.
 1st Cit. Peace there ! hear the noble Antony.
 2nd Cit. We'll hear him, we'll follow him, we'll die with him.
 Ant. Good friends, sweet friends, let me not stir you up
To such a sudden flood of mutiny.
They that have done this deed are honourable ;
What private griefs they have, alas, I know not,
That made them do it ; they are wise and honourable,
And will, no doubt, with reasons answer you.

I come not, friends, to steal away your hearts:
I am no orator, as Brutus is;
But, as you know me all, a plain blunt man,
That love my friend; and that they know full well
That gave me public leave to speak of him:
For I have neither wit, nor words, nor worth,
Action, nor utterance, nor the power of speech,
To stir men's blood: I only speak right on;
I tell you that which you yourselves do know;
Show you sweet Cæsar's wounds, poor, poor dumb mouths,
And bid them speak for me: but were I Brutus,
And Brutus Antony, there were an Antony
Would ruffle up your spirits, and put a tongue
In every wound of Cæsar, that should move
The stones of Rome to rise and mutiny.
  Cit. We'll mutiny.
  1*st Cit.* We'll burn the house of Brutus.
  3*rd Cit.* Away then, come, seek the conspirators.
  Ant. Yet hear me, countrymen; yet hear me speak.
  Cit. Peace, ho! Hear Antony, most noble Antony.
  Ant. Why, friends, you go to do you know not what:
Wherein hath Cæsar thus deserved your loves?
Alas! you know not;—I must tell you then:—
You have forgot the will I told you of.
  Cit. Most true; the will:—let's stay and hear the will.
  Ant. Here is the will, and under Cæsar's seal.
To every Roman citizen he gives,
To every several man, seventy-five drachmas,
  2*nd Cit.* Most noble Cæsar!—we'll revenge his death.
  3*rd Cit.* O royal Cæsar!
  Ant. Hear me with patience.
  Cit. Peace, ho!
  Ant. Moreover, he hath left you all his walks,
His private arbours, and new-planted orchards
On this side Tiber; he hath left them you,
And to your heirs for ever; common pleasures,
To walk abroad and recreate yourselves.
Here was a Cæsar: When comes such another?
  1*st Cit.* Never, never:—Come; away, away;
We'll burn his body in the holy place,

And with the brands fire the traitors' houses.
Take up the body.
  2nd Cit. Go, fetch fire.
  3rd Cit. Pluck down benches.
  4th Cit. Pluck down forms, windows, anything.

[*Exeunt Citizens with the body.*

  Ant. Now let it work : Mischief, thou art afoot ;
Take thou what course thou wilt.

Julius Cæsar.

ACT IV., SCENE III.—NEAR SARDIS. BRUTUS'S TENT.

Enter BRUTUS *and* CASSIUS.

  Cas. That you have wronged me doth appear in this :
You have condemned and noted Lucius Pella
For taking bribes here of the Sardians ;
Wherein my letters, praying on his side,
Because I knew the man, were slighted off.
  Bru. You wronged yourself to write in such a case.
  Cas. In such a time as this it is not meet
That every nice offence should bear his comment.
  Bru Let me tell you, Cassius, you yourself
Are much condemned to have an itching palm ;
To sell and mart your offices for gold
To undeservers.
  Cas.   I an itching palm ?
You know that you are Brutus that speak this,
Or, by the gods, this speech were else your last.
  Bru. The name of Cassius honours this corruption,
And chastisement doth therefore hide his head.
  Cas. Chastisement !
  Bru. Remember March, the ides of March remember :
Did not great Julius bleed for justice sake ?
What villain touch'd his body, that did stab,
And not for justice ? What! shall one of us,
That struck the foremost man of all this world
But for supporting robbers, shall we now

Contaminate our fingers with base bribes,
And sell the mighty space of our large honours
For so much trash as may be graspèd thus?
I had rather be a dog, and bay the moon
Than such a Roman.
  Cas.   Brutus, bay not me,
I'll not endure it : you forget yourself,
To hedge me in ; I am a soldier, I,
Older in practice, abler than yourself
To make conditions.
  Bru.   Go to ; you are not, Cassius.
  Cas. I am.
  Bru. I say you are not.
  Cas. Urge me no more, I shall forget myself ;
Have mind upon your health, tempt me no farther.
  Bru. Away, slight man!
  Cas. Is't possible?
  Bru.   Hear me, for I will speak.
Must I give way and room to your rash choler?
Shall I be frighted when a madman stares?
  Cas. O ye gods, ye gods! must I endure all this?
  Bru. All this! aye, more : fret till your proud heart break ;
Go show your slaves how choleric you are,
And make your bondmen tremble. Must I budge?
Must I observe you? must I stand and crouch
Under your testy humour? By the gods,
You shall digest the venom of your spleen,
Though it do split you ; for, from this day forth,
I'll use you for my mirth, yea, for my laughter,
When you are waspish.
  Cas.   Is it come to this?
  Bru. You say, you are a better soldier :
Let it appear so ; make your vaunting true,
And it shall please me well : for mine own part,
I shall be glad to learn of abler men.
  Cas. You wrong me every way ; you wrong me Brutus ;
I said an elder soldier, not a better :
Did I say "better?"
  Bru.   If you did, I care not.
  Cas. When Cæsar liv'd, he durst not thus have mov'd me.

Bru. Peace, peace! you durst not so have tempted him.
Cas. I durst not!
Bru. No.
Cas. What, durst not tempt him?
Bru. For your life you durst not.
Cas. Do not presume too much upon my love;
I may do that I shall be sorry for.
Bru. You have done that you should be sorry for.
There is no terror, Cassius, in your threats;
For I am arm'd so strong in honesty,
That they pass by me as the idle wind,
Which I respect not. I did send to you
For certain sums of gold, which you denied me;—
For I can raise no money by vile means:
By heaven, I had rather coin my heart,
And drop my blood for drachmas, than to wring
From the hard hands of peasants their vile trash
By any indirection; I did send
To you for gold to pay my legions,
Which you denied me: was that done like Cassius?
Should I have answer'd Caius Cassius so?
When Marcus Brutus grows so covetous,
To lock such rascal counters from his friends,
Be ready, gods, with all your thunderbolts!—
Dash him to pieces!
Cas. I denied you not.
Bru. You did.
Cas. I did not: he was but a fool that brought
My answer back.—Brutus hath rived my heart:
A friend should bear his friend's infirmities,
But Brutus makes mine greater than they are.
Bru. I do not, till you practise them on me.
Cas. You love me not.
Bru. I do not like your faults.
Cas. A friendly eye could never see such faults.
Bru. A flatterer's would not, though they do appear
As huge as high Olympus.
Cas. Come, Antony, and young Octavius, come,
Revenge yourselves alone on Cassius,
For Cassius is a-weary of the world;—

Hated by one he loves; braved by his brother;
Checked like a bondman; all his faults observed,
Set in a note-book, learned, and conned by rote,
To cast into my teeth. Oh, I could weep
My spirit from mine eyes!—There is my dagger,
And here my naked breast; within, a heart
Dearer than Plutus' mine, richer than gold:
If that thou be'st a Roman, take it forth;
I, that denied thee gold, will give my heart:
Strike, as thou didst at Cæsar; for, I know,
When thou didst hate him worst, thou lov'dst him better
Than ever thou lov'dst Cassius.
 Bru.   Sheath your dagger:
Be angry when you will, it shall have scope;
Do what you will, dishonour shall be honour.
O Cassius, you are yokèd with a lamb
That carries anger as the flint bears fire;
Who, much enforcèd, shows a hasty spark,
And straight is cold again.
 Cas.   Hath Cassius liv'd
To be but mirth and laughter to his Brutus,
When grief, and blood ill-temper'd, vexeth him?
 Bru. When I spoke that, I was ill-temper'd too.
 Cas. Do you confess so much? Give me your hand.
 Bru. And my heart too.
 Cas.   O Brutus,—
 Bru.   What's the matter?
 Cas. Have not you love enough to bear with me,
When that rash humour which my mother gave me
Makes me forgetful?
 Bru. Yes, Cassius; and, from henceforth,
When you are over-earnest with your Brutus,
He'll think your mother chides, and leave you so.

Macbeth.

ACT III., SCENE I.—FORRES.   A ROOM IN THE PALACE.

Enter BANQUO.

Ban. Thou hast it now, King, Cawdor, Glamis, all,
As the weird women promis'd; and I fear,
Thou play'dst most foully for 't: yet it was said,
It should not stand in thy posterity;
But that myself should be the root and father
Of many kings. If there come truth from them,
(As upon thee, Macbeth, their speeches shine,)
Why, by the verities on thee made good,
May they not be my oracles as well,
And set me up in hope? But, hush, no more.

Sennet sounded. Enter MACBETH, *as King;* LADY MACBETH, *as Queen;* LENOX, ROSSE, Lords, Ladies, *and* Attendants.

Macb. Here's our chief guest.
Lady M.   If he had been forgotten,
It had been as a gap in our great feast,
And all-thing unbecoming.
Macb. To-night we hold a solemn supper, sir,
And I'll request your presence.
Ban.   Let your highness
Command upon me: to the which my duties
Are with a most indissoluble tie
For ever knit.
Macb.   Ride you this afternoon?
Ban. Ay, my good lord.
Macb. We should have else desir'd your good advice
(Which still hath been both grave and prosperous)
In this day's council; but we'll take to-morrow.
Is 't far you ride?
Ban. As far, my lord, as will fill up the time
'Twixt this and supper: go not my horse the better,
I must become a borrower of the night
For a dark hour, or twain.
Macb.   Fail not our feast.
Ban. My lord, I will not.

Macb. We hear, our bloody cousins are bestow'd
In England, and in Ireland; not confessing
Their cruel parricide, filling their hearers
With strange invention: but of that to-morrow;
When, therewithal, we shall have cause of state,
Craving us jointly. Hie you to horse: adieu,
Till you return at night. Goes Fleance with you?
    Ban. Ay, my good lord: our time does call upon us.
    Macb. I wish your horses swift, and sure of foot,
And so I do commend you to their backs.
Farewell.—   [*Exit Banquo.*
Let every man be master of his time
Till seven at night: to make society
The sweeter welcome, we will keep ourself
Till supper-time alone: while then, God be with you!

              [*Exeunt Lady Macbeth, Lords, Ladies, etc.*

Sirrah, a word with you: attend those men
Our pleasure?
    Atten. They are, my lord, without the palace gate.
    Macb. Bring them before us.—   [*Exit Attendant*
                        To be thus is nothing;
But to be safely thus:—our fears in Banquo
Stick deep; and in his royalty of nature
Reigns that which would be fear'd: 'tis much he dares;
And, to that dauntless temper of his mind,
He hath a wisdom that doth guide his valour
To act in safety. There is none but he
Whose being I do fear: and, under him,
My Genius is rebuk'd; as, it is said,
Mark Antony's was by Cæsar. He chid the sisters,
When first they put the name of king upon me,
And bade them speak to him; then, prophet-like,
They hail'd him father to a line of kings:
Upon my head they plac'd a fruitless crown,
And put a barren sceptre in my gripe,
Thence to be wrench'd with an unlineal hand,
No son of mine succeeding. If 't be so,
For Banquo's issue have I fil'd my mind;
For them the gracious Duncan have I murder'd;

Put rancours in the vessel of my peace
Only for them ; and mine eternal jewel
Given to the common enemy of man,
To make them kings, the seed of Banquo kings !
Rather than so, come, fate, into the list,
And champion me to the utterance !—Who's there ?

    Re-enter Attendant, *with two* Murderers.

Now go to the door, and stay there till we call.
            [*Exit Attendant.*
Was it not yesterday we spoke together ?
 1*st Mur.* It was, so please your highness.
 Macb.   Well then, now
Have you consider'd of my speeches ? Know,
That it was he, in the times past, which held you
So under fortune ; which, you thought, had been
Our innocent self : this I made good to you
In our last conference ; pass'd in probation with you,
How you were borne in hand ; how cross'd ; the instruments ;
Who wrought with them ; and all things else, that might,
To half a soul, and to a notion craz'd,
Say, Thus did Banquo.
 1*st Mur.*   You made it known to us.
 Macb. I did so ; and went further, which is now
Our point of second meeting. Do you find
Your patience so predominant in your nature,
That you can let this go ? Are you so gospell'd,
To pray for this good man, and for his issue,
Whose heavy hand hath bow'd you to the grave,
And beggar'd yours for ever ?
 1*st Mur.*   We are men, my liege.
 Macb. Ay, in the catalogue ye go for men ;
As hounds, and greyhounds, mongrels, spaniels, curs,
Shoughs, water-rugs, and demi-wolves, are cleped
All by the name of dogs : the valued file
Distinguishes the swift, the slow, the subtle,
The housekeeper, the hunter, every one
According to the gift which bounteous nature
Hath in him clos'd ; whereby he does receive
Particular addition, from the bill

That writes them all alike : and so of men.
Now, if you have a station in the file,
Not in the worst rank of manhood, say 't ;
And I will put that business in your bosoms
Whose execution takes your enemy off;
Grapples you to the heart and love of us,
Who wears our health but sickly in his life,
Which in his death were perfect.
 2nd Mur.   I am one, my liege,
Whom the vile blows and buffets of the world
Have so incens'd, that I am reckless what
I do, to spite the world.
 1st Mur.   And I another,
So weary with disasters, tugg'd with fortune,
That I would set my life on any chance,
To mend it, or be rid on 't.
 Macb.   Both of you
Know, Banquo was your enemy.
 2nd Mur.   True, my lord.
 Macb. So is he mine ; and in such bloody distance,
That every minute of his being thrusts
Against my near'st of life : And though I could
With bare-fac'd power sweep him from my sight,
And bid my will avouch it, yet I must not,
For certain friends that are both his and mine,
Whose loves I may not drop, but wail his fall
Whom I myself struck down : and thence it is
That I to your assistance do make love ;
Masking the business from the common eye,
For sundry weighty reasons.
 2nd Mur.   We shall, my lord,
Perform what you command us.
 1st Mur.   Though our lives——
 Macb. Your spirits shine through you. Within this hour, at most,
I will advise you where to plant yourselves.
Acquaint you with the perfect spy o' the time,
The moment on 't ; for 't must be done to-night.
And something from the palace ; always thought
That I require a clearness : And with him,

(To leave no rubs, nor botches, in the work,)
Fleance his son that keeps him company,
Whose absence is no less material to me
Than is his father's, must embrace the fate
Of that dark hour. Resolve yourselves apart ;
I 'll come to you anon.
  2nd Mur.   We are resolv'd, my lord.
  Macb. I 'll call upon you straight ; abide within.
It is concluded :—Banquo, thy soul's flight,
If it find heaven, must find it out to-night.   [*Exeunt.*

King Henry the Fourth.
Act II., Scene IV.

Prince H. Welcome, Jack : where hast thou been ?
  Falstaff. A plague of all cowards, I say, and a vengeance too ! Marry, and amen ! Give me a cup of sack, boy. Ere I lead this life long, I'll sew nether stocks, and mend them, and foot them too. A plague of all cowards ! Give me a cup of sack, rogue. Is there no virtue extant ?
  Prince H. Didst thou never see Titan kiss a dish of butter ? pitiful-hearted Titan, that melted at the sweet tale of the sun ! If thou didst, then behold that compound.
  Falstaff. You rogue, here's lime in this sack, too !—there is nothing but roguery to be found in villainous man ; yet a coward is worse than a cup of sack with lime in it : a villainous coward ! Go thy ways, old Jack ; die when thou wilt, if manhood, good manhood, be not forgot upon the face of the earth, then am I a shotten herring. There live not three good men unhanged in England, and one of them is fat and grows old. A bad world I say !—I would I were a weaver ; I could sing psalms, or any thing. A plague of all cowards, I say still.
  Prince H. How now, woolsack ! what mutter you ?
  Falstaff. A king's son ! If I do not beat thee out of thy kingdom with a dagger of lath, and drive all thy subjects before me like a flock of wild geese, I'll never wear hair on my face more. You Prince of Wales !
  Prince H. Why, what's the matter ?
  Falstaff. Are you not a coward ? Answer me to that.

Prince H. Why, ye fat paunch, an' ye call me coward, I'll stab thee.

Falstaff. I call thee coward! I'll see thee hanged ere I call thee coward; but I would give a thousand pounds I could run as fast as thou canst. You are straight enough in the shoulders; you care not who sees your back. Call you that backing of your friends? A plague upon such backing! Give me them that will face me. Give me—a cup of sack;—I'm a rogue if I have drunk to-day.

Prince H. O villain! thy lips are scarce wiped since thou drank'st last.

Falstaff. All's one for that. A plague of all cowards, still say I.

Prince H. What's the matter?

Falstaff. What's the matter! There be four of us have ta'en a thousand pounds this morning.

Prince H. Where is it, Jack? Where is it?

Falstaff. Where is it! Taken from us it is: a hundred upon four of us.

Prince H. What! a hundred, man?

Falstaff. I am a rogue if I were not at half-sword with a dozen of them, two hours together. I have escaped by miracle. I am eight times thrust through the doublet, four through the hose; my buckler cut through and through; my sword hacked like a hand-saw, *ecce signum*. I never dealt better since I was a man! All would not do. A plague of all cowards!

Prince H. Speak, Jack; how was it?

Falstaff. Four of us set upon some dozen, and bound them —every man of them; and as we were sharing, some six or seven fresh men set upon us, and unbound the rest; and then came in the others.

Prince H. What! fought ye with them all?

Falstaff. All! I know not what you call all; but if I fought not with fifty of them, I am a bunch of radish; if there were not two or three-and-fifty upon poor old Jack, then am I no two-legged creature.

Prince H. I pray, you have not murdered some of them?

Falstaff. Nay, that's past praying for! I have peppered two of them;—two, I am sure I have paid—two rogues in buckram suits. I tell thee what, Hal, if I tell thee a lie, spit

in my face—call me horse. Thou know'st my old ward :—here
I lay, and thus I bore my point. Four rogues in buckram let
drive at me——
  Prince H. What! four? Thou said'st but two, even now.
  Falstaff. Four, Hal; I told thee, four. These four came
all afront, and mainly thrust at me. I made no more ado, but
took all their seven points in my target, thus.
  Prince H. Seven? Why, there were but four, even now.
  Falstaff. In buckram?
  Prince H. Ay, four in buckram suits.
  Falstaff. Seven, by these hilts, or I am a villain else. Dost
thou hear me, Hal?
  Prince H. Ay, and mark thee too.
  Falstaff. Do so, for it is worth the listening to. These nine
in buckram that I told thee of——
  Prince H. So, two more already! (*aside.*)
  Falstaff. Their points being broken, they began to give me
ground; but I followed them close; came in, foot and hand;
and, with a thought, seven of the eleven I paid.
  Prince H. O monstrous! eleven buckram men grown out of
two!
  Falstaff. But, as bad luck would have it, three misbegotten
knaves, in Kendal Green, came at my back, and let drive at
me; for, it was so dark, Hal, that thou couldst not see thy
hand.
  Prince H. These lies are like the father that begets them—
gross as a mountain, open, palpable. Why thou clay-brained
and knotty-pated fool, thou obscene, greasy tallow-keech——
  Falstaff. What! art thou mad? art thou mad? Is not the
truth the truth?
  Prince H. Why, how couldst thou know these men in
Kendal-green when "it was so dark, thou couldst not see thy
hand"? Come, tell us your reason. What say'st thou to this?
Come, your reason, Jack, your reason.
  Falstaff. What! upon compulsion? No! were I at the
strappado, or all the racks in the world, I would not tell you
upon compulsion. Give you a reason on compulsion! If
reasons were as plenty as blackberries, I would give no man a
reason on compulsion, I!
  Prince H. I'll be no longer guilty of this sin. Thou san-

guine coward, thou bed-presser, thou horse-back-breaker, thou huge hill of flesh——

Falstaff. Away! you starveling—you eel-skin—you dried neat's tongue—you stock-fish!—O, for breath to utter what is like thee!—you tailor's yard—you sheath—you bow-case—you vile standing tuck——

Prince H. Well, breathe awhile, and then to it again : and when thou hast tired thyself in base comparisons, hear me speak but this : Poins and I saw you four set on four ; you bound them, and were masters of their wealth.—Mark now, how plain a tale shall put you down.—Then did we two set on you four ; and, with a word, out-faced you from your prize, and have it ; yea, and can show it you here in the house :—and, Falstaff, you carried your mountain sides away as nimbly, with as quick dexterity, and roared for mercy, and still ran and roared, as ever I heard bull-calf. What a slave art thou, to hack thy sword as thou hast done, and then say, it was in fight ! What trick, what device, what starting-hole, canst thou find out, to hide thee from this open and apparent shame?

Falstaff. Ha! ha! ha! I knew ye, as well as he that made ye. Why, hear ye, my masters : was it for me to kill the heir-apparent? Should I turn upon the true prince? Why, thou knowest I am as valiant as Hercules : but beware instinct ; the lion will not touch the true prince. Instinct is a great matter ; I was a coward on instinct. I shall think the better of myself and thee, during my life ; myself for a valiant lion, and thee for a true prince. But I am glad you have the money.—Clap to the doors :—watch to-night, pray to-morrow. What, shall we be merry? shall we have a play extempore?

Prince H. Content ;—and the argument shall be, thy running away.

Falstaff. Ah, no more of that, Hal, an' thou lovest me!

Henry VIII.
Act III., Scene II.
Enter to Wolsey, *the* Dukes of Norfolk *and* Suffolk, *the* Earl of Surrey, *and the* Lord Chamberlain.

Nor. Hear the King's pleasure, cardinal ; who commands
To render up the great seal presently   [you

Into our hands ; and to confine yourself
To Asher House, my Lord of Winchester's,
Till you hear further from his highness.
    Wol.   Stay :
Where's your commission, lords ? words cannot carry
Authority so weighty
    Suf.   Who dare cross 'em,
Bearing the king's will from his mouth expressly ?
    Wol. Till I find more than will or words to do it,
(I mean your malice), know, officious lords,
I dare and must deny it. Now I feel
Of what coarse metal ye are moulded,—envy :
How eagerly ye follow my disgraces,
As if it fed ye ! and how sleek and wanton
Ye appear in everything may bring my ruin !
Follow your envious courses, men of malice ;
You have Christian warrant for them, and, no doubt,
In time will find their fit rewards. That seal
You ask with such a violence, the king
(Mine and your master) with his own hand gave me ;
Bade me enjoy it, with the place and honours,
During my life ; and to confirm his goodness,
Tied it by letters-patent :—now, who'll take it ?
    Sur. The king, that gave it,
    Wol.   It must be himself, then.
    Sur. Thou art a proud traitor, priest.
    Wol.   Proud lord, thou liest :
Within these forty hours Surrey durst better
Have burnt that tongue than said so.
    Sur.   Thy ambition,
Thou scarlet sin, robb'd this bewailing land
Of noble Buckingham, my father-in-law :
The heads of all thy brother cardinals
(With thee and all thy best parts bound together)
Weigh'd not a hair of his. Plague of your policy !
You sent me deputy for Ireland ;
Far from his succour, from the king, from all
That might have mercy on the fault thou gav'st him ;
Whilst your great goodness, out of holy pity,
Absolved him with an axe.

Wol.   This, and all else
This talking lord can lay upon my credit,
I answer is most false. The duke by law
Found his deserts : how innocent I was
From any private malice in his end,
His noble jury and foul cause can witness.
If I lov'd many words, lord, I should tell you,
You have as little honesty as honour ;
That, in the way of loyalty and truth
Toward the king, my ever royal master,
Dare mate a sounder man than Surrey can be,
And all that love his follies.
   Sur.   By my soul,
Your long coat, priest, protects you ; thou should'st feel
My sword i' the life-blood of thee else.—My lords,
Can ye endure to hear this arrogance ?
And from this fellow ? If we live thus tamely,
To be thus jaded by a piece of scarlet,
Farewell nobility ; let his grace go forward,
And dare us with his cap, like larks.
   Wol.   All goodness
Is poison to thy stomach.
   Sur.   Yes, that goodness
Of gleaning all the land's wealth into one,
Into your own hands, cardinal, by extortion ;
The goodness of your intercepted packets
You writ to the pope against the king : your goodness,
Since you provoke me, shall be most notorious.—
My lord of Norfolk, as you are truly noble,
As you respect the common good, the state
Of our despis'd nobility, our issues,
Who, if he live, will scarce be gentlemen,—
Produce the grand sum of his sins, the articles
Collected from his life :—
   Wol. How much, methinks, I could despise this man,
But that I am bound in charity against it !
   Nor. Those articles, my lord, are in the king's hands ;
But, thus much, they are foul ones.
   Wol.   So much fairer
And spotless shall mine innocence arise,

When the king knows my truth.
　　Sur.　　　　　　　　This cannot save you :
I thank my memory I yet remember
Some of these articles ; and out they shall.
Now, if you can blush and cry guilty, cardinal,
You'll show a little honesty.
　　Wol.　　　　　　　　Speak on, Sir ;
I dare your worst objections : if I blush,
It is to see a nobleman want manners.
　　Sur. I'd rather want those, than my head.　Have at you.
First, that, without the king's assent or knowledge,
You wrought to be a legate ; by which power
You maimed the jurisdiction of all bishops.
　　Nor. Then, that in all you writ to Rome, or else
To foreign princes, *Ego et Rex meus*
Was still inscrib'd ; in which you brought the king
To be your servant.
　　Suf.　　　　Then, that, without the knowledge
Either of king or council, when you went
Ambassador to the emperor, you made bold
To carry into Flanders the great seal.
　　Sur. Item, you sent a large commission
To Gregory de Cassado to conclude,
Without the king's will, or the state's allowance,
A league between his highness and Ferrara.
　　Suf. That, out of mere ambition, you have caus'd
Your holy hat to be stamp'd on the king's coin.
　　Sur. Then, that you have sent innumerable substance,
(By what means got, I leave to your own conscience,)
To furnish Rome, and to prepare the ways
You have for dignities ; to the mere undoing
Of all the kingdom.　Many more there are ;
Which, since they are of you, and odious,
I will not taint my mouth with.
　　Cham.　　　　　　　O my lord,
Press not a falling man too far ; 'tis virtue :
His faults lie open to the laws ; let them,
Not you, correct him.　My heart weeps to see him
So little of his great self.
　　Sur.　　　　　　　I forgive him.

Suf. Lord cardinal, the king's further pleasure is,
Because all those things you have done of late,
By your power legatine, within this kingdom,
Fall into the compass of a *præmunire,—*
That therefore such a writ be sued against you ;
To forfeit all your goods, lands, tenements,
Chattels, and whatsoever, and to be
Out of the king's protection :—this is my charge.
  Nor. And so we'll leave you to your meditations
How to live better. For your stubborn answer
About the giving back the great seal to us,
The king shall know it, and, no doubt, shall thank you.
So fare-you-well, my little good lord cardinal.
                     [*Exeunt all except Wolsey.*
  Wol. So, farewell to the little good you bear me.
Farewell, a long farewell, to all my greatness !
This is the state of man : to-day he puts forth
The tender leaves of hope ; to-morrow blossoms,
And bears his blushing honours thick upon him :
The third day comes a frost, a killing frost ;
And,—when he thinks, good easy man, full surely
His greatness is a ripening,—nips his root,
And then he falls, as I do. I have ventur'd,
Like little wanton boys that swim on bladders,
This many summers in a sea of glory ;
But far beyond my depth : my high-blown pride
At length broke under me ; and now has left me,
Weary and old with service, to the mercy
Of a rude stream, that must for ever hide me.
Vain pomp and glory of this world, I hate ye :
I feel my heart new open'd. O, how wretched
Is that poor man that hangs on princes' favours :
There is, betwixt that smile we would aspire to,
That sweet aspect of princes, and their ruin,
More pangs and fears than wars or women have ;
And when he falls, he falls like Lucifer,
Never to hope again.—
        Enter CROMWELL, *and stands amazed.*
                Why, how now, Cromwell ?
  Crom. I have no power to speak, sir.

Wol.   What, amaz'd
At my misfortunes ? can thy spirit wonder
A great man should decline ?   Nay, an you weep,
I am fallen indeed.
   Crom.   How does your grace ?
   Wol.   Why, well ;
Never so truly happy, my good Cromwell.
I know myself now ; and I feel within me
A peace above all earthly dignities,
A still and quiet conscience.   The king has cur'd me,
I humbly thank his grace ; and from these shoulders,
These ruin'd pillars, out of pity, taken
A load would sink a navy, too much honour :
O, 'tis a burden, Cromwell, 'tis a burden
Too heavy for a man that hopes for heaven !
   Crom. I am glad your grace has made that right use of it.
   Wol. I hope I have : I am able now methinks,
(Out of a fortitude of soul I feel,)
To endure more miseries, and greater far,
Than my weak-hearted enemies dare offer.
What news abroad ?
   Crom.   The heaviest and the worst,
Is your displeasure with the king.
   Wol.   God bless him !
   Crom. The next is, that Sir Thomas More is chosen
Lord chancellor in your place.
   Wol.   That's somewhat sudden :
But he's a learnèd man.   May he continue
Long in his highness' favour, and do justice
For truth's sake, and his conscience ; that his bones,
When he has run his course and sleeps in blessings,
May have a tomb of orphans' tears wept on them.
What more ?
   Crom. That Cranmer is return'd with welcome,
Install'd lord archbishop of Canterbury.
   Wol. That's news indeed !
   Crom.   Last, that the lady **Anne**,
Whom the king hath in secrecy long married,
This day was view'd in open, as his queen,

Going to chapel; and the voice is now
Only about her coronation.
  Wol. There was the weight that pull'd me down. O Cromwell,
The king has gone beyond me: all my glories
In that one woman I have lost for ever:
No sun shall ever usher forth mine honours,
Or gild again the noble troops that waited
Upon my smiles. Go, get thee from me, Cromwell;
I am a poor fallen man, unworthy now
To be thy lord and master: seek the king;
(That sun, I pray, may never set!) I have told him
What, and how true thou art: he will advance thee;
Some little memory of me will stir him,
(I know his noble nature,) not to let
Thy hopeful service perish too: good Cromwell,
Neglect him not; make use now, and provide
For thine own future safety.
  Crom.   O my lord,
Must I, then, leave you? must I needs forego
So good, so noble and so true a master?—
Bear witness, all that have not hearts of iron,
With what a sorrow Cromwell leaves his lord.—
The king shall have my service; but my prayers
For ever and for ever shall be yours.
  Wol. Cromwell, I did not think to shed a tear
In all my miseries; but thou hast forced me,
Out of thy honest truth, to play the woman.
Let's dry our eyes; and thus far hear me, Cromwell;
And, when I am forgotten, as I shall be,
And sleep in dull cold marble, where no mention
Of me more must be heard of, say, I taught thee,—
Say, Wolsey, that once trod the ways of glory,
And sounded all the depths and shoals of honour,
Found thee a way, out of his wreck, to rise in;
A sure and safe one, though thy master missed it.
Mark but my fall, and that that ruined me.
Cromwell, I charge thee, fling away ambition:
By that sin fell the angels; how can man, then,
The image of his Maker, hope to win by it?
Love thyself last: cherish those hearts that hate thee;

Corruption wins not more than honesty.
Still in thy right hand carry gentle peace,
To silence envious tongues. Be just, and fear not:
Let all the ends thou aim'st at be thy country's,
Thy God's, and truth's; then if thou fall'st, O, Cromwell,
Thou fall'st a blessed martyr! Serve the king;
And,—prithee, lead me in:
There take an inventory of all I have,
To the last penny; 'tis the king's: my robe,
And my integrity to Heaven, is all
I dare now call mine own. O Cromwell, Cromwell!
Had I but served my God with half the zeal
I served my king, he would not in mine age
Have left me naked to mine enemies.
 Crom. Good sir, have patience.
 Wol.   So I have. Farewell
The hopes of court; my hopes in heaven do dwell. [*Exeunt.*

As you like it.
Act III., Scene II.—The Forest.

 Ros. [*Aside to* Celia.] I will speak to him like a saucy lackey, and under that habit play the knave with him. [*To him.*] Do you hear, forester?
 Orl. Very well: what would you?
 Ros. I pray you, what is't o'clock?
 Orl. You should ask me what time o' day: there's no clock in the forest.
 Ros. Then there is no true lover in the forest! else sighing every minute, and groaning every hour, would detect the lazy foot of time as well as a clock.
 Orl. And why not the swift foot of time? had not that been as proper?
 Ros. By no means, sir. Time travels in divers paces with divers persons: I'll tell you who Time ambles withal, who Time trots withal, who Time gallops withal, and who he stands still withal.
 Orl. I pr'ythee, who doth he trot withal?

Ros. Marry, he trots hard with a young maid, between the contract of her marriage and the day it is solemnized: if the interim be but a se'nnight, Time's pace is so hard that it seems the length of seven years.

Orl. Who ambles Time withal?

Ros. With a priest that lacks Latin, and a rich man that hath not the gout; for the one sleeps easily, because he cannot study; and the other lives merrily, because he feels no pain: the one lacking the burden of lean and wasteful learning; the other knowing no burden of heavy tedious penury: these Time ambles withal.

Orl. Who doth he gallop withal?

Ros. With a thief to the gallows; for though he go as softly as foot can fall, he thinks himself too soon there.

Orl. Who stays it still withal?

Ros. With lawyers in the vacation; for they sleep between term and term, and then they perceive not how Time moves.

Orl. Where dwell you, pretty youth?

Ros. With this shepherdess, my sister; here in the skirts of the forest, like a fringe upon a petticoat.

Orl. Are you a native of this place?

Ros. As the coney, that you see dwell where she is kindled.

Orl. Your accent is something finer than you could purchase in so removed a dwelling.

Ros. I have been told so by many: but indeed an old religious uncle of mine taught me to speak, who was in his youth an inland man; one that knew courtship too well, for there he fell in love. I have heard him read many lectures against it; and I thank God, I am not a woman, to be touched with so many giddy offences, as he hath generally taxed their whole sex withal.

Orl. Can you remember any of the principal evils that he laid to the charge of women?

Ros. There were none principal: they were all like one another, as half-pence are; every one fault seeming monstrous, till his fellow-fault came to match it.

Orl. I pr'ythee, recount some of them.

Ros. No, I will not cast away my physic, but on those that are sick. There is a man haunts the forest, that abuses our young plants with carving "Rosalind" on their barks; hangs odes upon hawthorns, and elegies on brambles; all, forsooth, deifying the name of "Rosalind": if I could meet that fancy-monger, I would give him some good counsel, for he seems to have the quotidian of love upon him.

Orl. I am he that is so love-shaked: I pray you, tell me your remedy.

Ros. There is none of my uncle's marks upon you: he taught me how to know a man in love; in which cage of rushes I am sure you are not prisoner.

Orl. What were his marks?

Ros. A lean cheek; which you have not; a blue eye, and sunken; which you have not; an unquestionable spirit; which you have not; a beard neglected; which you have not;—but I pardon you for that; for, simply, your having in beard is a younger brother's revenue:—then, your hose should be un-garter'd, your bonnet unbanded, your sleeve unbuttoned, your shoe untied, and everything about you demonstrating a care-less desolation. But you are no such man; you are rather point-device in your accoutrements, as loving yourself, than seeming the lover of any other.

Orl. Fair youth, I would I could make thee believe I love.

Ros. Me believe it! you may as soon make her that you love believe it; which, I warrant, she is apter to do, than to confess she does: that is one of the points in the which women still give the lie to their consciences. But, in good sooth, are you he that hangs the verses on the trees, wherein Rosalind is so admired?

Orl. I swear to thee, youth, by the white hand of Rosalind, I am that he, that unfortunate he.

Ros. But are you so much in love as your rhymes speak?

Orl. Neither rhyme nor reason can express how much.

Ros. Love is merely a madness; and, I tell you, deserves as well a dark house and a whip, as madmen do: and the reason why they are not so punished and cured, is, that the lunacy is so ordinary, that the whippers are in love too. Yet I profess curing it by counsel.

Orl. Did you ever cure any so?

Ros. Yes, one; and in this manner. He was to imagine me his love, his mistress; and I set him every day to woo me: at which time would I, being but a moonish youth, grieve, be effeminate, changeable, longing, and liking; proud, fantastical, apish, shallow, inconstant, full of tears, full of smiles: for every passion something, and for no passion truly anything, as boys and women are, for the most part, cattle of this colour: would now like him, now loathe him; then entertain him, then forswear him; now weep for him, then spit at him; that I drave my suitor from his mad humour of love, to a living humour of madness; which was, to forswear the full stream of the world, and to live in a nook merely monastic. And thus I cured him; and this way will I take upon me to wash your liver as clean as a sound sheep's heart, that there shall not be one spot of love in't.

Orl. I would not be cured, youth.

Ros. I would cure you, if you would but call me Rosalind, and come every day to my cot, and woo me.

Orl. Now, by the faith of my love, I will: tell me where it is.

Ros. Go with me to it, and I'll show it you: and, by the way, you shall tell me where in the forest you live. Will you go?

Orl. With all my heart, good youth.

Ros. Nay, you must call me Rosalind. [*Exeunt.*

Hamlet.

Act III., Scene I.

Ham. Speak the speech, I pray you, as I pronounced it to you, trippingly on the tongue; but if you mouth it, as many of your players do, I had as lief the town-crier spoke my lines. Nor do not saw the air too much with your hand, thus; but use all gently: for in the very torrent, tempest, (and as I may say), whirlwind of passion, you must acquire and beget a temperance that may give it smoothness. O! it offends me to the soul, to hear a robustious periwig-pated fellow, tear a passion to tatters, to very rags, to split the ears of the groundlings; who, for the most part, are capable of nothing but inexplicable dumb shows and noise: I would have such a fellow whipped for o'er-doing Termagant; it out-herods Herod: pray you avoid it.

1st Play. I warrant, your honour.

Ham. Be not too tame neither, but let your own discretion be your tutor: suit the action to the word, the word to the action, with this special observance, that you o'erstep not the modesty of nature; for anything so overdone is from the purpose of playing, whose end, both at the first, and now, was, and is, to hold, as 'twere, the mirror up to nature; to show virtue her own feature, scorn her own image, and the very age and body of the time his form and pressure. Now, this overdone, or come tardy off, though it make the unskilful laugh, cannot but make the judicious grieve; the censure of which one, must, in your allowance, o'er-weigh a whole theatre of others. O! there be players, that I have seen play, and heard others praise, and that highly—not to speak it profanely, that, neither having the accent of Christians, nor the gait of Christian, pagan, nor man, have so strutted and bellowed, that I have thought some of nature's journeymen had made men, and not made them well, they imitated humanity so abominably.

1st Play. I hope we have reformed that indifferently with us.

Ham. O! reform it altogether. And let those that play your clown, speak no more than is set down for them: for there be of them that will themselves laugh, to set on some quantity of barren spectators to laugh too! though in the mean time, some necessary question of the play be then to be considered; that's villainous, and shows a most pitiable ambition in the fool that uses it. [*Exit.*

Hamlet.

Act II., Scene II.

Enter Hamlet, *reading.*

Pol. How does my good lord Hamlet?
Ham. Well, heav'n-'a-mercy.
Pol. Do you know me, my lord?
Ham. Excellent well; you are a fishmonger.
Pol. Not I, my lord.
Ham. Then, I would you were so honest a man.

Pol. Honest, my lord?

Ham. Ay, sir: to be honest, as this world goes, is to be one man picked out of ten thousand.

Pol. That's very true, my lord.

Ham. For if the sun breed maggots in a dead dog, being a god kissing carrion,—Have you a daughter?

Pol. I have, my lord.

Ham. Let her not walk i' the sun: friend, look to't.

Pol. [*Aside*] How say you by that? Still harping on my daughter:—yet he knew me not at first; he said I was a fishmonger. He is far gone, far gone: and truly in my youth I suffered much extremity for love; very near this. I'll speak to him again. What do you read, my lord?

Ham. Words, words, words.

Pol. What is the matter, my lord?

Ham. Between whom?

Pol. I mean the matter that you read, my lord.

Ham. Slanders, sir: for the satirical rogue says here, that old men have grey beards; that their faces are wrinkled; their eyes purging thick amber, and plum-tree gum; and that they have a plentiful lack of wit, together with most weak hams: all of which, sir, (though I most powerfully and potently believe,) yet I hold it not honesty to have it thus set down; for you yourself, sir, should be old as I am, if like a crab, you could go backward.

Pol. Though this be madness, yet there is method in't. [*Aside.*] Will you walk out of the air, my lord?

Ham. Into my grave.

Pol. Indeed, that is out o' the air. How pregnant sometimes his replies are! a happiness that often madness hits on, which reason and sanity could not so prosperously be delivered of. I will leave him, and suddenly contrive the means of meeting, between him and my daughter. My honourable lord, I will most humbly take my leave of you.

Ham. You cannot, sir, take from me any thing that I will more willingly part withal; except my life, except my life, except my life.

Pol. Fare you well, my lord. [*Exit.*

Ham. These tedious old fools!

Pol. [*Without*] You go to seek the Lord Hamlet; there he is.

Ros. Heav'n save you, sir!

Enter ROSENCRANTZ *and* GUILDENSTERN.

Guil. Mine honor'd lord!

Ros. My most dear lord!

Ham. My excellent good friends! How dost thou, Guildenstern? Ah, Rosencrantz! Good lads, how do ye both? What news?

Ros. None, my lord, but that the world's grown honest.

Ham. Then is dooms-day near; but your news is not true. But, in the beaten way of friendship, what make you at Elsinore?

Ros. To visit you, my lord; no other occasion.

Ham. Beggar that I am, I am even poor in thanks; but I thank you: Were you not sent for? Is it your own inclining? Is it a free visitation? Come, come, deal justly with me: come, come—nay, speak.

Guil. What should we say, my lord?

Ham. Why, any thing, but to the purpose. You were sent for; and there is a kind of confession in your looks, which your modesties have not craft enough to colour: I know the good king and queen have sent for you.

Ros. To what end, my lord?

Ham. That you must teach me. But let me conjure you, by the rights of our fellowship, by the consonancy of our youth, by the obligation of our ever-preserved love, and by what more dear a better proposer could charge you withal, be even and direct with me, whether you were sent or no?

Ros. [*Aside to* Guildenstern] What say you?

Ham. Nay, then I have an eye of you. [*Aside*] If you love me, hold not off.

Guil. My lord, we were sent for.

Ham. I will tell you why; so shall my anticipation prevent your discovery, and your secresy to the king and queen moult no feather. I have of late, (but wherefore I know not) lost all my mirth, forgone all custom of exercises, and indeed, it goes so heavily with my disposition, that this goodly frame, the earth, seems to me a sterile promontory; this most excellent canopy, the air—look you, this brave o'erhanging firmament, this majestical roof, fretted with golden fire, why, it appeareth nothing to me, but a foul and pestilent congregation of vapours. What a piece of work is a man! How noble his reason! how infinite in faculties! in form and moving, how express and admirable! in action, how like an angel! in apprehension, how like a god! The beauty of the world! the paragon of animals! and yet to me, what is this quintessence of dust? Man delights not me; no, nor woman neither.

Richard III.

ACT IV., SCENE II.—A ROOM OF STATE IN THE PALACE.

RICHARD, *as King, upon his throne;* BUCKINGHAM, CATESBY, *a* Page, *and others.*

K. Rich. Stand all apart. Cousin of Buckingham!
Buck. My gracious sovereign?
K. Rich. Give me thy hand. Thus high, by thy advice,
And thy assistance, is King Richard seated:
But shall we wear these glories for a day?
Or shall they last, and we rejoice in them?
Buck. Still live they, and for ever let them last!
K. Rich. Ah, Buckingham, now do I play the touch,
To try if thou be current gold indeed:
Young Edward lives;—think now what I would speak.
Buck. Say on, my loving lord.
K. Rich. Why, Buckingham, I say, I would be king.
Buck. Why, so you are, my thrice-renownèd liege.
K. Rich. Ha! am I king? 'Tis so:—but Edward lives.
Buck. True, noble prince.
K. Rich. O bitter consequence,
That Edward still should live—'true, noble prince!'—
Cousin, thou wast not wont to be so dull:
Shall I be plain? I wish the princes dead;
And I would have it suddenly perform'd.
What say'st thou now? speak suddenly; be brief.
Buck. Your grace may do your pleasure.
K. Rich. Tut, tut, thou art all ice, thy kindness freezes:
Say, have I thy consent that they shall die?

Buck. Give me some little breath, some pause, dear lord,
Before I positively speak in this :
I will resolve you herein presently.   [*Exit* BUCKINGHAM.
  Cates. The king is angry, see, he gnaws his lip.   [*Aside.*
  K. Rich. I will converse with iron-witted fools,
              [*Descends from his throne.*
And unrespective boys : none are for me
That look into me with considerate eyes :
High-reaching Buckingham grows circumspect.
Boy !
  Page. My lord ?
  K. Rich. Know'st thou not any whom corrupting gold
Would tempt into a close exploit of death ?
  Page. I know a discontented gentleman,
Whose humble means match not his haughty spirit :
Gold were as good as twenty orators,
And will, no doubt, tempt him to anything.
  K. Rich. What is his name ?
  Page.   His name, my lord, is Tyrrel.
  K. Rich. I partly know the man : go, call him hither, boy.
              [*Exit* Page.
The deep-revolving witty Buckingham
No more shall be the neighbour to my counsels :
Hath he so long held out with me untir'd,
And stops he now for breath ?—well, be it so.
              Enter STANLEY.
How now, Lord Stanley ! what's the news ?
  Stan. Know, my loving lord,
The Marquis Dorset, as I hear, is fled
To Richmond, in the parts where he abides.
  K. Rich. Come hither, Catesby : rumour it abroad
That Anne, my wife, is very grievous sick ;
I will take order for her keeping close.
Inquire me out some mean, poor gentleman,
Whom I will marry straight to Clarence' daughter ;
The boy is foolish, and I fear not him.
Look, how thou dream'st !—I say again, give out
That Anne my queen is sick, and like to die :
About it ; for it stands me much upon,
To stop all hopes whose growth may damage me.
              [*Exit* CATESBY.

I must be married to my brother's daughter,
Or else my kingdom stands on brittle glass :
Murder her brothers, and then marry her !
Uncertain way of gain ! But I am in
So far in blood, that sin will pluck on sin :
Tear-falling pity dwells not in this eye.

Re-enter Page, *with* TYRREL.

Is thy name Tyrrel ?
  Tyr. James Tyrrel, and your most obedient subject.
  K. Rich. Art thou, indeed ?
  Tyr.   Prove me, my gracious lord.
  K. Rich. Dar'st thou resolve to kill a friend of mine ?
  Tyr. Please you, but I had rather kill two enemies.
  K. Rich. Why, then thou hast it : two deep enemies,
Foes to my rest, and my sweet sleep's disturbers,
Are they that I would have thee deal upon :
Tyrrel, I mean those princes in the Tower.
  Tyr. Let me have open means to come to them,
And soon I'll rid you from the fear of them.
  K. Rich. Thou sing'st sweet music. Hark, come hither,
    Tyrrel :
Go, by this token : rise, and lend thine ear :   [*Whispers.*
There is no more but so : say, it is done,
And I will love thee, and prefer thee for it.
  Tyr. I will despatch it straight.   [*Exit.*

Re-enter BUCKINGHAM.

  Buck. My lord, I have considered in my mind
The late request that you did sound me in.
  K. Rich. Well, let that rest. Dorset is fled to Richmond.
  Buck. I hear the news, my lord.
  K. Rich. Stanley, he is your wife's son :—well, look to it.
  Buck. My lord, I claim the gift, my due by promise,
For which your honour and your faith is pawn'd :
The earldom of Hereford, and the movables,
Which you have promisèd I shall possess.
  K. Rich. Stanley, look to your wife : if she convey
Letters to Richmond, you shall answer it.
  Buck. What says your highness to my just request ?

K. Rich. I do remember me,—Henry the Sixth
Did prophesy that Richmond should be king,
When Richmond was a little peevish boy.
A king!—perhaps——
  Buck. My lord!
  K. Rich. How chance the prophet could not at that time
Have told me, I being by, that I should kill him?
  Buck. My lord, your promise for the earldom—
  K. Rich. Richmond! When last I was at Exeter,
The mayor in courtesy shew'd me the castle,
And call'd it Rouge-mont: at which name I started,
Because a bard of Ireland told me once
I should not live long after I saw Richmond.
  Buck. My lord!
  K. Rich.   Ay, what's o'clock?
  Buck. I am thus bold to put your grace in mind
Of what you promis'd me.
  K. Rich.   Well, but what's o'clock?
  Buck. Upon the stroke of ten.
  K. Rich.   Well, let it strike.
  Buck. Why let it strike?
  K. Rich. Because that, like a Jack, thou keep'st the stroke
Betwixt thy begging and my meditation.
I am not in the giving vein to-day.
  Buck. Why, then resolve me whether you will or no.
  K. Rich. Thou troublest me; I am not in the vein.
            Exeunt KING RICHARD *and train.*
  Buck. And is it thus? repays he my deep service
With such contempt? made I him king for this?
O, let me think on Hastings, and be gone
To Brecknock, while my fearful head is on! [*Exit.*

The Merchant of Venice.

ACT I., SCENE III.—A PUBLIC PLACE IN VENICE.

Shy. Three thousand ducats,—well.
Bass. Ay, sir, for three months.

Shy. For three months,—well.
Bass. For the which, as I told you, Antonio shall be bound.
Shy. Antonio shall become bound,—well.
Bass. May you stead me? Will you pleasure me? Shall I know your answer?
Shy. Three thousand ducats, for three months, and Antonio bound.
Bass. Your answer to that.
Shy. Antonio is a good man?
Bass. Have you heard any imputation to the contrary?
Shy. Ho, no, no, no, no;—my meaning, in saying he is a good man, is to have you understand me, that he is sufficient. Yet his means are in supposition: he hath an argosy bound to Tripolis, another to the Indies; I understand, moreover, upon the Rialto, he hath a third at Mexico, a fourth for England; and other ventures he hath, squander'd abroad. But ships are but boards, sailors but men: there be land-rats, and water-rats, land-thieves, and water-thieves,—I mean, pirates; and then, there is the peril of waters, winds, and rocks. The man is, notwithstanding, sufficient;—three thousand ducats:—I think I may take his bond.
Bass. Be assured you may.
Shy. I will be assured I may; and, that I may be assured, I will bethink me. May I speak with Antonio?
Bass. If it please you to dine with us.
Shy. Yes, to smell pork; I will buy with you, sell with you, talk with you, walk with you, and so following; but I will not eat with you, drink with you, nor pray with you. What news on the Rialto?—Who is he comes here?

Enter ANTONIO.

Bass. This is signior Antonio.
Shy. [*Aside.*] How like a fawning publican he looks!
I hate him for he is a Christian:
But more, for that, in low simplicity,
He lends out money gratis, and brings down
The rate of usance here with us in Venice.
If I can catch him once upon the hip,
I will feed fat the ancient grudge I bear him.
He hates our sacred nation; and he rails,
Even there where merchants most do congregate,

On me, my bargains, and my well-won thrift,
Which he calls interest. Cursèd be my tribe,
If I forgive him!
    Bass.   Shylock, do you hear?
    Shy. I am debating of my present store;
And, by the near guess of my memory,
I cannot instantly raise up the gross
Of full three thousand ducats. What of that?
Tubal, a wealthy Hebrew of my tribe,
Will furnish me. But soft! How many months
Do you desire? Rest you fair, good signior;
                                    [*To* ANTONIO.
Your worship was the last man in our mouths.
    Ant. Shylock, albeit I neither lend nor borrow,
By taking, nor by giving of excess,
Yet, to supply the ripe wants of my friend,
I'll break a custom.—Is he yet possess'd,
How much you would?
    Shy.   Ay, ay, three thousand ducats.
    Ant. And for three months.
    Shy. I had forgot,—three months, you told me so.
Well then, your bond; and, let me see,————but hear you;
Methought, you said, you neither lend nor borrow
Upon advantage.
    Ant.   I do never use it.
    Shy. Three thousand ducats,—'tis a good round sum.
Three months from twelve,—then, let me see, the rate—
    Ant. Well, Shylock, shall we be beholding to you?
    Shy. Signior Antonio, many a time and oft,
In the Rialto, you have rated me
About my moneys, and my usances:
Still have I borne it with a patient shrug;
For sufferance is the badge of all our tribe;
You call me—misbeliever, cut-throat dog,
And spit upon my Jewish gaberdine,
And all for use of that which is mine own.
Well then, it now appears, you need my help;
Go to, then; you come to me, and you say,
Shylock, we would have moneys. You say so;
You, that did void your rheum upon my beard,

And foot me as you spurn a stranger cur
Over your threshold ; moneys is your suit.
What should I say to you ?   Should I not say,
*Hath a dog money ?   Is it possible
A cur can lend three thousand ducats ?*   Or
Shall I bend low, and in a bondman's key,
With bated breath, and whispering humbleness,
Say this,—
*Fair sir, you spit on me on Wednesday last;
You spurned me such a day ; another time
You call'd me—dog ; and for these courtesies
I'll lend you thus much moneys.*
   Ant. I am as like to call thee so again,
To spit on thee again, to spurn thee too.
If thou wilt lend this money, lend it not
As to thy friends ; (for when did friendship take
A breed for barren metal of his friend ?)
But lend it rather to thine enemy ;
Who, if he break, thou may'st with better face
Exact the penalty.
   Shy.   Why, look you, how you storm !
I would be friends with you, and have your love,
Forget the shames that you have stain'd me with,
Supply your present wants, and take no doit
Of usance for my moneys, and you'll not hear me :
This is kind I offer.
   Ant. This were kindness.
   Shy.   This kindness will I show.
Go with me to a notary, seal me there
Your single bond ; and, in a merry sport,
If you repay me not on such a day,
In such a place, such sum, or sums, as are
Express'd in the condition, let the forfeit
Be nominated for an equal pound
Of your fair flesh, to be cut off and taken
In what part of your body pleaseth me.
   Ant. Content, in faith ; I'll seal to such a bond,
And say there is much kindness in the Jew.
   Bass. You shall not seal to such a bond for me :
I'll rather dwell in my necessity.

Ant. Why, fear not, man : I will not forfeit it :
Within these two months, that's a month before
This bond expires, I do expect return
Of thrice three times the value of this bond.
  Shy. O father Abraham, what these Christians are,
Whose own hard dealings teaches them suspect
The thoughts of others !—Pray you tell me this ;
If he should break his day, what should I gain
By the exaction of the forfeiture ?
A pound of man's flesh, taken from a man,
Is not so estimable, profitable neither,
As flesh of muttons, beefs, or goats. I say,
To buy his favour, I extend this friendship :
If he will take it, so ; if not, adieu ;
And, for my love, I pray you, wrong me not.
  Ant. Yes, Shylock, I will seal unto this bond.
  Shy. Then meet me forthwith at the notary's ;
Give him direction for this merry bond ;
And I will go and purse the ducats straight,
See to my house (left in the fearful guard
Of an unthrifty knave), and presently
I will be with you.   [*Exit* SHYLOCK.
  Ant.   Hie thee, gentle Jew.
This Hebrew will turn Christian : he grows kind.
  Bass. I like not fair terms, and a villain's mind.
  Ant. Come on : in this there can be no dismay ;
My ships come home a month before the day.   [*Exeunt.*

King Henry IV. (Part I.)

ACT II., SCENE IV.—TAVERN, EASTCHEAP.

Characters present, PRINCE HENRY, POINS, *and others.*

Enter FALSTAFF.

  Fal. Hal, there's villanous news abroad : here was Sir John Bracy from your father : you must to the court in the morning. That same mad fellow of the north, Percy, and he of Wales— what a plague call you him ?

Poins. O! Glendower.

Fal. Owen, Owen; the same; and his son-in-law Mortimer, and old Northumberland; and that sprightly Scot of Scots, Douglas, that runs o' horseback up a hill perpendicular.

Prince. He that rides at high speed, and with his pistol kills a sparrow flying.

Fal. You have hit it. Well, he is there too, and one Mordake, and a thousand blue-caps more. Worcester is stolen away to-night; thy father's beard is turned white with the news. Hal, art thou not horrible afeard? thou being heir apparent, could the world pick thee out three such enemies again as that fiend Douglas, that spirit Percy, and that devil Glendower? Art thou not horribly afraid? doth not thy blood thrill at it?

Prince. Not a whit, i' faith; I lack some of thy instinct.

Fal. Well, thou wilt be horribly chid to-morrow when thou comest to thy father: if thou love me, practise an answer.

Prince. Do thou stand for my father, and examine me upon the particulars of my life.

Fal. Shall I? content: this chair shall be my state, this dagger my sceptre, and this cushion my crown.

Prince. Thy state is taken for a joint-stool, thy golden sceptre for a leaden dagger, and thy precious rich crown for a pitiful bald crown!

Fal. Well, an the fire of grace be not quite out of thee, now shalt thou be moved. Give me a cup of sack to make mine eyes look red, that it may be thought I have wept.

Prince. Well, here is my knee.

Fal. And here is my speech. Stand aside, nobility. Harry, I do not only marvel where thou spendest thy time, but also how thou art accompanied: for though the camomile, the more it is trodden on the faster it grows, yet youth, the more it is wasted the sooner it wears. Why, being son to me, art thou so pointed at? Shall the son of England prove a thief and take purses? a question to be asked. There is a thing, Harry, which thou hast often heard of, and it is known to many in our land by the name of pitch: this pitch, as ancient writers do report, doth defile; so doth the company thou keepest; for, Harry, now I do not speak to thee in drink but in tears, not in pleasure but in passion, not in words only, but in woes also.

And yet there is a virtuous man whom I have often noted in thy company, but I know not his name.

Prince. What manner of man, an it like your majesty?

Fal. A goodly portly man, i' faith, and a corpulent; of a cheerful look, a pleasing eye, and a most noble carriage; and, as I think, his age some fifty, or, by'r lady, inclining to three-score; and now I remember me, his name is Falstaff: if that man should be falsely given, he deceiveth me; for, Harry, I see virtue in his looks. If then the tree may be known by the fruit, as the fruit by the tree, then, peremptorily I speak it, there is virtue in that Falstaff: him keep with, the rest banish. And tell me now, tell me, where hast thou been this month?

Prince. Dost thou speak like a king? Do thou stand for me, and I'll play my father.

Fal. Depose me? if thou dost it half so gravely, so majestic-ally, both in word and matter, hang me up by the heels for a poulter's hare.

Prince. Well, here I am set.

Fal. And here I stand. Judge, my masters.

Prince. Now, Harry! whence come you?

Fal. My noble lord, from Eastcheap.

Prince. The complaints I hear of thee are grievous.

Fal. 'Sblood, my lord, they are false.

Prince. Swearest thou, ungracious boy? henceforth ne'er look on me. Thou art violently carried away from grace: there is a devil haunts thee in the likeness of an old fat man; a tun of man is thy companion. Why dost thou converse with that grey iniquity, that father ruffian, that vanity in years? Wherein is he good but to taste sack and drink it? wherein neat and cleanly but to carve a capon and eat it? wherein cunning but in craft? wherein crafty but in villany? wherein villanous but in all things? wherein worthy but in nothing?

Fal. I would your grace would take me with you: whom means your grace?

Prince. That villanous abominable misleader of youth, Fal-staff, that old white-bearded Satan.

Fal. My lord, the man I know.

Prince. I know thou dost.

Fal. But to say I know more harm in him than in myself were to say more than I know. That he is old, the more the pity, his white hairs do witness it: but that he is, saving your reverence, iniquitous, that I utterly deny. If sack and sugar be a fault, God help the wicked! If to be old and merry be a sin, then many an old host that I know is damned: if to be fat be to be hated, then Pharaoh's lean kine are to be loved. No, my good lord; banish Peto, banish Bardolph, banish Poins; but for sweet Jack Falstaff, kind Jack Falstaff, true Jack Falstaff, valiant Jack Falstaff, and therefore more valiant, being, as he is, old Jack Falstaff, banish not him thy Harry's company, banish not him thy Harry's company: banish plump Jack, and banish all the world.

Prince. I do, I will.

King Richard II.

ACT V., SCENE II.

Enter YORK *and his* DUCHESS.

Duch. My lord, you told me you would tell the rest,
When weeping made you break the story off
Of our two cousins coming into London.
York. Where did I leave?
Duch. At that sad stop, my lord,
Where rude misgoverned hands, from windows' tops,
Threw dust and rubbish on king Richard's head.
York. Then, as I said, the duke, great Bolingbroke,
Mounted upon a hot and fiery steed,
Which his aspiring rider seemed to know,
With slow but stately pace kept on his course,
While all tongues cried—*God save thee, Bolingbroke!*
You would have thought the very windows spake,
So many greedy looks of young and old
Through casements darted their desiring eyes
Upon his visage; and that all the walls
With painted imagery had said at once,—
Jesu preserve thee! welcome, Bolingbroke!
Whilst he, from one side to the other turning,
Bare-headed, lower than his proud steed's neck,

Bespake them thus,—*I thank you, countrymen:*
And thus still doing, thus he passed along.
    Duch. Alack, poor Richard! where rode he the whilst?
    York. As in a theatre, the eyes of men,
After a well-graced actor leaves the stage,
Are idly bent on him that enters next,
Thinking his prattle to be tedious :—
Even so, or with much more contempt, men's eyes
Did scowl on Richard ; no man cried, God save him ;
No joyful tongue gave him his welcome home :
But dust was thrown upon his sacred head ;
Which with such gentle sorrow he shook off,—
His face still combating with tears and smiles,
The badges of his grief and patience,—
That had not God, for some strong purpose, steeled
The hearts of men, they must perforce have melted,
And barbarism itself have pitied him.
But heaven hath a hand in these events ;
To whose high will we bound our calm contents.
To Bolingbroke are we sworn subjects now,
Whose state and honour I for aye allow.

King John.
Act III., Scene III.

    K. John. Come hither, Hubert. O my gentle Hubert,
We owe thee much ! within this wall of flesh
There is a soul counts thee her creditor,
And with advantage means to pay thy love :
And, my good friend, thy voluntary oath
Lives in this bosom, dearly cherishèd.
Give me thy hand. I had a thing to say ;
But I will fit it with some better time.
By Heaven, Hubert, I'm almost asham'd
To say what good respect I have of thee.
    Hub. I am much bounden to your majesty.
    K. John. Good friend, thou hast no cause to say so yet ;
But thou shalt have : and, creep time ne'er so slow,

Yet it shall come for me to do thee good.
I had a thing to say; but let it go:
The sun is in the heaven; and the proud day,
Attended with the pleasures of the world,
Is all too wanton, and too full of gauds,
To give me audience: if the midnight bell
Did, with his iron tongue and brazen mouth,
Sound one into the drowsy race of night;
If this same were a churchyard where we stand,
And thou possessèd with a thousand wrongs;
Or if that surly spirit, melancholy,
Had bak'd thy blood, and made it heavy-thick,
(Which, else, runs tickling up and down the veins,
Making that idiot, laughter, keep men's eyes,
And strain their cheeks to idle merriment,
A passion hateful to my purposes;)
Or if that thou couldst see me without eyes,
Hear me without thine ears, and make reply
Without a tongue, using conceit alone,
Without eyes, ears, and harmful sound of words:
Then, in despite of brooded-watchful day,
I would into thy bosom pour my thoughts.
But, ah! I will not: yet I love thee well;
And, by my troth, I think thou lov'st me well.

Hub. So well, that what you bid me undertake,
Though that my death were adjunct to my act,
By heaven, I'd do't.

K. John. Do not I know thou would'st?
Good Hubert, Hubert, Hubert, throw thine eye
On yon young boy. I'll tell thee what, my friend,
He is a very serpent in my way;
And, wheresoe'er this foot of mine doth tread,
He lies before me. Dost thou understand me?
Thou art his keeper.

Hub. And I'll keep him so,
That he shall not offend your majesty.

K. John. Death.

Hub. My lord?

K. John. A grave.

Hub. He shall not live.

K. John.   Enough.
I could be merry now. Hubert, I love thee;
Well, I'll not say what I intend for thee:
Remember.

King Henry V.

Act II., Scene II.—*Southampton. A council-chamber.*

Enter Exeter, Bedford, *and* Westmoreland.

Bed. 'Fore God, his grace is bold, to trust these traitors.
Exe. They shall be apprehended by and by.
West. How smooth and even they do bear themselves!
As if allegiance in their bosoms sat,
Crownéd with faith and constant loyalty.
Bed. The king hath note of all that they intend,
By interception which they dream not of.
Exe. Nay, but the man that was his bedfellow,
Whom he hath dulled and cloyed with gracious favours,
That he should, for a foreign purse, so sell
His sovereign's life to death and treachery!

Enter King Henry, Cambridge, Scroop, Grey, *and Attendants.*

K. Hen. Now sits the wind fair, and we will aboard.
My Lord of Cambridge, my kind Lord of Masham,
And you, my gentle knight, give me your thoughts:
Think you not that the powers we bear with us
Will cut their passage through the force of France,
Doing the execution and the act
For which we have in head assembled them?
Scroop. No doubt, my liege, if each man do his best.
K. Hen. I doubt not that; since we are well persuaded
We carry not a heart with us from hence
That grows not in a fair concent with ours,
Nor leave not one behind that doth not wish
Success and conquest to attend on us.
Cam. Never was monarch better feared and loved

Than is your majesty : there's not, I think, a subject
That sits in heart-grief and uneasiness
Under the sweet shade of your government.
    Grey. True: Those that were your father's enemies
Have steeped their galls in honey, and do serve you
With hearts create of duty and of zeal.
    K. Hen. We therefore have great cause of thankfulness ;
And shall forget the office of our hand,
Sooner than quittance of desert and merit
According to their weight and worthiness.
    Scroop. So service shall with steeléd sinews toil,
And labour shall refresh itself with hope,
To do your grace incessant services.
    K. Hen. We judge no less.—Uncle of Exeter,
Enlarge the man committed yesterday,
That railed against our person : we consider
It was excess of wine that set him on ;
And on his more advice we pardon him.
    Scroop. That's mercy, but too much security :
Let him be punished, sovereign, lest example
Breed, by his sufferance, more of such a kind.
    K. Hen. O, let us yet be merciful.
    Cam. So may your highness, and yet punish too.
    Grey. Sir,
You show great mercy, if you give him life
After the taste of much correction.
    K. Hen. Alas, your too much love and care of me
Are heavy orisons 'gainst this poor wretch !
If little faults, proceeding on distemper,
Shall not be winked at, how shall we stretch our eye
When capital crimes, chewed, swallowed, and digested,
Appear before us ? We'll yet enlarge that man,
Though Cambridge, Scroop, and Grey, in their dear care
And tender preservation of our person,
Would have him punished.—And now to our French causes
Who are the late commissioners ?
    Cam. I one, my lord :
Your highness bade me ask for it to-day.
    Scroop. So did you me, my liege.
    Grey. And me, my royal sovereign.

K. Hen. Then, Richard Earl of Cambridge, there is yours ;
There yours, Lord Scroop of Masham ; and, sir knight,
Grey of Northumberland, this same is yours :
Read them ; and know, I know your worthiness.—
My Lord of Westmoreland, and uncle Exeter,
We will aboard to-night.—Why, how now, gentlemen ?
What see you in those papers that you lose
So much complexion ?—Look ye, how they change !
Their cheeks are paper.—Why, what read you there,
That hath so cowarded and chased your blood
Out of appearance ?
    Cam.   I do confess my fault ;
And do submit me to your highness' mercy.
    Grey.
    Scroop.   } To which we all appeal.
    K. Hen. The mercy that was quick in us but late,
By your own counsel is suppressed and killed :
You must not dare, for shame, to talk of mercy ;
For your own reasons turn into your bosoms,
As dogs upon their masters, worrying you.—
See you, my princes and my noble peers,
These English monsters ! My Lord of Cambridge here,—
You know how apt our love was to accord
To furnish him with all appertinents
Belonging to his honour ; and this man
Hath, for a few light crowns, lightly conspired
And sworn unto the practices of France,
To kill us here in Hampton : to the which
This knight, no less for bounty bound to us
Than Cambridge is, hath likewise sworn. But, O,
What shall I say to thee, Lord Scroop ? thou cruel,
Ingrateful, savage and inhuman creature !
Thou that didst bear the key of all my counsels,
That knew'st the very bottom of my soul,
That almost mightst have coined me into gold,
Wouldst thou have practised on me for thy use,—
May it be possible, that foreign hire
Could out of thee extract one spark of evil
That might annoy my finger ? 'tis so strange,
That, though the truth of it stands off as gross

As black from white, my eye will scarcely see it.
Treason and murder ever kept together,
As two yoke-devils, sworn to either's purpose,
Working so grossly in a natural cause
That admiration did not whoop at them :
But thou, 'gainst all proportion, didst bring in
Wonder to wait on treason and on murder :
And whatsoever cunning fiend it was
That wrought upon thee so preposterously,
Hath got the voice in hell for excellence :
All other devils that suggest by treasons
Do botch and bungle up damnation
With patches, colours, and with forms being fetched
From glistering semblances of piety ;
But he that tempered thee, bade thee stand up,
Gave thee no instance why thou shouldst do treason
Unless to dub thee with the name of traitor.
If that same demon that has gulled thee thus
Should with his lion gait walk the whole world,
He might return to vasty Tartar back,
And tell the legions 'I can never win
A soul so easy as that Englishman's.'
O, how hast thou with jealousy infected
The sweetness of affiance ! Show men dutiful ?
Why, so didst thou : seem they grave and learned ?
Why, so didst thou : come they of noble family ?
Why, so didst thou : seem they religious ?
Why, so didst thou : or are they spare in diet,
Free from gross passion or of mirth or anger ;
Constant in spirit, not swerving with the blood ;
Garnished and decked in modest complement ;
Not working with the eye without the ear,
And but in purgéd judgment trusting neither ?
Such and so finely bolted didst thou seem :
And thus thy fall hath left a kind of blot,
To mark the full-fraught man and best indued
With some suspicion. I will weep for thee ;
For this revolt of thine, methinks, is like
Another fall of man.—Their faults are open :
Arrest them to the answer of the law :—

And God acquit them of their practices!

Exe. I arrest thee of high treason, by the name of Richard Earl of Cambridge.

I arrest thee of high treason, by the name of Henry Lord Scroop of Masham.

I arrest thee of high treason, by the name of Thomas Grey, knight, of Northumberland.

Scroop. Our purposes God justly hath discovered;
And I repent my fault more than my death;
Which I beseech your highness to forgive,
Although my body pay the price of it.

Cam. For me,—the gold of France did not seduce:
Although I did admit it as a motive
The sooner to effect what I intended:
But God be thankèd for prevention;
Which I in sufferance heartily will rejoice,
Beseeching God and you to pardon me.

Grey. Never did faithful subject more rejoice
At the discovery of most dangerous treason
Than I do at this hour joy o'er myself,
Prevented from a damnèd enterprise;
My fault, but not my body, pardon, sovereign.

K. Hen. God quit you in his mercy! Hear your sentence.
You have conspired against our royal person,
Joined with an enemy proclaimed, from 's coffers
Received the golden earnest of our death;
Wherein you would have sold your king to slaughter,
His princes and his peers to servitude,
His subjects to oppression and contempt,
And his whole kingdom into desolation.
Touching our person, seek we no revenge;
But we our kingdom's safety must so tender,
Whose ruin you have sought, that to her laws
We do deliver you. Get you, therefore, hence,
Poor miserable wretches, to your death:
To taste whereof, God of his mercy give
You patience to endure, and true repentance
Of all your dear offences! Bear them hence.

Much Ado About Nothing.
ACT III., SCENE III.—*A Street.*
Enter DOGBERRY *and* VERGES, *with the Watch.*

Dogb. Are you good men and true?
Verg. Yea, or else it were pity but they should suffer salvation, body and soul.
Dogb. Nay, that were a punishment too good for them, if they should have any allegiance in them, being chosen for the prince's watch.
Verg. Well, give them their charge, neighbour Dogberry.
Dogb. First, who think you the most desartless man to be constable?
1 *Watch.* Hugh Oatcake, sir, or George Seacoal; for they can write and read.
Dogb. Come hither, neighbour Seacoal. God hath blessed you with a good name: to be a well-favoured man is the gift of fortune, but to write and read comes by nature.
2 *Watch.* Both which, master constable,—
Dogb. You have: I knew it would be your answer. Well, for your favour, sir, why, give God thanks, and make no boast of it; and for your writing and reading, let that appear when there is no need of such vanity. You are thought here to be the most senseless and fit man for the constable of the watch; therefore bear you the lantern. This is your charge:—you shall comprehend all vagrom men; you are to bid any man stand, in the prince's name.
2 *Watch.* How, if a' will not stand?
Dogb. Why, then take no note of him, but let him go; and presently call the rest of the watch together, and thank God you are rid of a knave.
Verg. If he will not stand when he is bidden, he is none of the prince's subjects.
Dogb. True, and they are to meddle with none but the prince's subjects.—You shall also make no noise in the streets; for, for the watch to babble and talk is most tolerable and not to be endured.
2 *Watch.* We will rather sleep than talk; we know what belongs to a watch.

Dogb. Why you speak like an ancient and most quiet watchman; for I cannot see how sleeping should offend: only, have a care that your bills be not stolen. Well, you are to call at all the alehouses, and bid those that are drunk get them to bed.

2 Watch. How, if they will not?

Dogb. Why, then let them alone till they are sober; if they make you not then the better answer, you may say, they are not the men you took them for.

2 Watch. Well, sir.

Dogb. If you meet a thief, you may suspect him, by virtue of your office, to be no true man; and, for such kind of men, the less you meddle or make with them, why, the more is for your honesty.

2 Watch. If we know him to be a thief, shall we not lay hands on him?

Dogb. Truly, by your office you may; but, I think, they that touch pitch will be defiled. The most peaceable way for you, if you do take a thief, is, to let him show himself what he is, and steal out of your company.

Verg. You have been always called a merciful man, partner.

Dogb. Truly, I would not hang a dog by my will, much more a man who hath any honesty in him.

Verg. If you hear a child cry in the night, you must call to the nurse, and bid her still it.

2 Watch. How, if the nurse be asleep, and will not hear us?

Dogb. Why, then depart in peace, and let the child wake her with crying; for the ewe that will not hear her lamb when it baes, will never answer a calf when he bleats.

Verg. 'T is very true.

Dogb. This is the end of the charge. You, constable, are to present the prince's own person; if you meet the prince in the night, you may stay him.

Verg. Nay, by 'r lady, that, I think, a' cannot.

Dogb. Five shillings to one on't, with any man that knows the statues, he may stay him : marry, not without the prince be willing; for, indeed, the watch ought to offend no man, and it is an offence to stay a man against his will.

Verg. By 'r lady, I think it be so.

Dogb. Ha, ah-ha? Well, masters, good night: an there be any matter of weight chances, call up me. Keep your fellows' counsels and your own, and good night. Come, neighbour.

2 *Watch.* Well, masters, we hear our charge : let us go sit here upon the church-bench till two, and then all to bed.

Dogb. One word more, honest neighbours. I pray you, watch about Signior Leonato's door; for the wedding being there to-morrow, there is a great coil to-night. Adieu, be vigitant, I beseech you.

As You Like It.

Act II., Scene V. &c.—*The Forest of Arden.*

Enter Duke *senior*, Amiens, *and* Lords.

Duke. I think he be transformed into a beast,
For I can no where find him like a man.

1st Lord. My lord, he is but even now gone hence :
Here was he merry, hearing of a song.

Duke. If he, compact of jars, grow musical,
We shall have shortly discord in the spheres :—
Go, seek him; tell him I would speak with him.

1st Lord. He saves my labour by his own approach.

Enter Jaques.

Duke. Why, how now, monsieur ! what a life is this,
That your poor friends must woo your company?
What! you look merrily !

Jaques. A fool, a fool !—I met a fool i' the forest,
A motley fool—a miserable world !—
As I do live by food, I met a fool,
Who laid him down, and basked him in the sun,
And railed on lady Fortune in good terms,
In good set terms—and yet a motley fool.
"Good-morrow, fool," quoth I : "No, sir," quoth he,
"Call me not fool, till Heaven hath sent me fortune :"
And then he drew a dial from his poke,
And looking on it with lack-lustre eye,
Says, very wisely, "It is ten o'clock :
Thus may we see," quoth he, "how the world wags :
'Tis but an hour ago since it was nine ;
And after one hour more, 'twill be eleven ;

And so, from hour to hour, we ripe, and ripe,
And then, from hour to hour, we rot, and rot,
And thereby hangs a tale." When I did hear
The motley fool thus moral on the time,
My lungs began to crow like chanticleer,
That fools should be so deep contemplative;
And I did laugh, sans intermission,
An hour by his dial.—Oh, noble fool!
A worthy fool! Motley's the only wear.

(All retire to the table)

Enter ORLANDO *with his sword drawn.*

Orlan. Forbear, and eat no more!
Jaques. Why, I have eat none yet.
Orlan. Nor shalt not, till necessity be served.
Jaques. Of what kind should this cock come of?
Duke. (*coming forward*) Art thou thus boldened, man, by thy distress?
Or else a rude despiser of good manners,
That in civility thou seem'st so empty?
Orlan. You touched my vein at first; the thorny point
Of bare distress hath ta'en from me the show
Of smooth civility; yet am I inland bred,
And know some nurture: but forbear, I say!
He dies that touches any of this fruit,
Till I and my affairs are answered.
Duke. What would you have? Your gentleness shall force,
More than your force move us to gentleness.
Orlan. I almost die for food, and let me have it.
Duke. Sit down and feed, and welcome to our table.
Orlan. Speak you so gently? Pardon me, I pray you;
I thought that all things had been savage here;
And therefore put I on the countenance
Of stern commandment: but whate'er you are,
That in this desert inaccessible,
Under the shade of melancholy boughs,
Lose and neglect the creeping hours of time:
If ever you have looked on better days:
If ever been where bells have knolled to church;
If ever sat at any good man's feast;

If ever from your eye-lids wip'd a tear,
And know what 'tis to pity and be pitied;
Let gentleness my strong enforcement be:
In the which hope, I blush, and hide my sword.
 Duke. True is it, that we have seen better days,
And have with holy bell been knolled to church;
And sat at good men's feasts; and wip'd our eyes
Of drops that sacred pity had engendered:
And therefore sit you down in gentleness,
And take upon command what help we have,
That to your wanting may be minister'd.
 Orlan. Then but forbear your food a little while,
Whiles, like a doe, I go to find my fawn,
And give it food. There is an old poor man,
Who after me hath many a weary step
Limp'd in pure love; till he be first suffic'd—
Oppressed with two weak evils, age and hunger,
I will not touch a bit.
 Duke.   Go find him out,
And we will nothing waste till you return.
 Orlan. I thank ye; and be blessed for your good comfort!

   Exit ORLANDO. *The* LORDS *advance.*

 Duke. Thou see'st, we are not all alone unhappy:
This wide and universal theatre
Presents more woeful pageants than the scene
Wherein we play in.
 Jaques.   All the world's a stage,
And all the men and women merely players:
They have their exits, and their entrances;
And one man in his time plays many parts,
His acts being seven ages. At first, the infant,
Mewling and puking in the nurse's arms:
Then, the whining school-boy, with his satchel,
And shining morning face, creeping like snail
Unwillingly to school: And then, the lover;
Sighing like furnace, with a woeful ballad
Made to his mistress' eye-brow: Then, a soldier;
Full of strange oaths, and bearded like the pard,
Jealous in honour, sudden and quick in quarrel,

Seeking the bubble reputation
Even in the cannon's mouth : And then, the justice ;
In fair round belly, with good capon lin'd,
With eyes severe, and beard of formal cut,
Full of wise saws and modern instances,
And so he plays his part. The sixth age shifts
Into the lean and slipper'd pantaloon ;
With spectacles on nose, and pouch on side ;
His youthful hose, well sav'd, a world too wide
For his shrunk shank ; and his big manly voice,
Turning again towards childish treble, pipes
And whistles in his sound : Last scene of all,
That ends this strange eventful history,
Is second childishness, and mere oblivion ;
Sans teeth, sans eyes, sans taste, sans everything.

Re-enter ORLANDO *with* ADAM.

Duke. Welcome : set down your venerable burden,
And let him feed.
Orlan. I thank you most for him.
Adam. (*sitting*)   So had you need ;
I scarce can speak to thank you for myself.
Duke. Welcome, fall to : I will not trouble you,
As yet, to question you about your fortunes :—
Give us some music ; and, good cousin, sing.

Song.—AMIENS.

Blow, blow, thou winter wind,
Thou art not so unkind
  As man's ingratitude ;
Thy tooth is not so keen,
Because thou art not seen,
  Although thy breath be rude.

Freeze, freeze, thou bitter sky,
That dost not bite so nigh
  As benefits forgot :
Though thou the waters warp,
Thy sting is not so sharp
  As friend remember'd not.

Duke. (*comes forward*) If that you were the good Sir Rowland's son—

As you have whisper'd faithfully, you were ;
And as mine eye doth his effigies witness,
Most truly limn'd, and living in your face—
Be truly welcome hither; I am the Duke,
That loved your father: the residue of your fortune,
Go to my cave and tell me.—Good old man,
Thou art right welcome, as thy master is :—
Support him by the arm.—Give me your hand,
And let me all your fortunes understand.

The Tempest.

ACT IV., SCENE I.

Enter PROSPERO, FERDINAND, *and* MIRANDA.

Pros. If I have too austerely punish'd you,
Your compensation makes amends, for I
Have given you here a thrid of mine own life,
Or that for which I live ; who once again
I tender to thy hand : all thy vexations
Were but my trials of thy love, and thou
Hast strangely stood the test ; here, afore Heaven,
I ratify this my rich gift. O Ferdinand,
Do not smile at me that I boast her off,
For thou shalt find she will outstrip all praise
And make it halt behind her.
    Fer.   I do believe it
Against an oracle.
    Pros. Then, as my gift and thine own acquisition
Worthily purchased, take my daughter. . . . . .
What, Ariel ! my industrious servant, Ariel !
                Enter ARIEL.

    Ari. What would my potent master ? here I am.
    Pros. Thou and thy meaner fellows your last service
Did worthily perform ; and I must use you
In such another trick. Go bring the rabble.
O'er whom I give thee power, here to this place :

Incite them to quick motion ; for I must
Bestow upon the eyes of this young couple
Some vanity of mine art : it is my promise,
And they expect it from me.
  Ari.   Presently ?
  Pros. Ay, with a twink.
  Ari. Before you can say ' come ' and ' go,'
    And breathe twice and cry ' so, so,'
    Each one, tripping on his toe,
    Will be here with mop and mow.
    Do you love me, master ? no ?
  Pros. Dearly, my delicate Ariel. Do not approach
Till thou dost hear me call.
  Ari.   Well, I conceive. [*Exit.*
  Pros. Look thou be true ; do not give dalliance
Too much the rein : the strongest oaths are straw
To the fire i' the blood.
  Fer.   I warrant you, sir.
  Pros.   Well.
Now come, my Ariel ! bring a corollary,
Rather than want a spirit : appear, and pertly !
No tongue ! all eyes ! be silent.   [*Soft music.*

Enter IRIS.

  Iris. Ceres, most bounteous lady, thy rich leas
Of wheat, rye, barley, vetches, oats, and pease ;
Thy turfy mountains, where live nibbling sheep,
And flat meads thatch'd with stover, them to keep ;
Thy banks with pioned and twilled brims,
Which spongy April at thy hest betrims,
To make cold nymphs chaste crowns ; and thy broom-groves,
Whose shadow the dismissèd bachelor loves,
Being lass-lorn ; thy pole-clipt vineyard ;
And thy sea-marge, sterile and rocky hard,
Where thou thyself dost air ;—the queen o' the sky,
Whose watery arch and messenger am I,
Bids thee leave these, and with her sovereign grace,
Here on this grass-plot, in this very place,
To come and sport : her peacocks fly amain :
Approach, rich Ceres, her to entertain.

Enter CERES.

Cer. Hail, many-colour'd messenger, that ne'er
Dost disobey the wife of Jupiter;
Who with thy saffron wings upon my flowers
Diffusest honey-drops, refreshing showers,
And with each end of thy blue bow dost crown
My bosky acres and my unshrubb'd down,
Rich scarf to my proud earth; why hath thy queen
Summoned me hither, to this short-grass'd green?
   Iris. A contract of true love to celebrate;
And some donation freely to estate
On the blest lovers.
   Cer.   Tell me, heavenly bow,
If Venus or her son, as thou dost know,
Do now attend the queen?
Her and her blind boy's scandal'd company
I have forsworn.
   Iris.   Of her society
Be not afraid: I met her deity
Cutting the clouds towards Paphos and her son
Dove-drawn with her.
   Cer.   Highest queen of state,
Great Juno, comes; I know her by her gait.

Enter JUNO.

Juno. How does my bounteous sister? Go with me
To bless this twain, that they may prosperous be
And honour'd in their issue.   [*They sing:*
   Juno. Honour, riches, marriage-blessing,
          Long continuance, and increasing,
          Hourly joys be still upon you!
          Juno sings her blessings on you.
   Cer.   Earth's increase, foison plenty,
          Barns and garners never empty,
          Vines with clustering bunches growing,
          Plants with goodly burthen bowing;
          Spring come to you at the farthest
          In the very end of harvest!
          Scarcity and want shall shun you;
          Ceres' blessing so is on you.

Fer. This is a most majestic vision, and
Harmonious charmingly.   May I be bold
To think these spirits ?
   Pros.   Spirits, which by mine art
I have from their confines call'd to enact
My present fancies.
   Fer.   Let me live here ever ;
So rare a wonder'd father and a wise
Makes this place Paradise.
   [JUNO *and* CERES *whisper, and send* IRIS *on employment.*]
   Pros.   Sweet, now, silence !
Juno and Ceres whisper seriously ;
There's something else to do : hush, and be mute,
Or else our spell is marr'd.
   Iris. You nymphs, called Naiads, of the windring brooks,
With your sedged crowns and ever-harmless looks,
Leave your crisp channels, and on this green land
Answer your summons ; Juno does command :
Come, temperate nymphs, and help to celebrate
A contract of true love ; be not too late.
           Enter certain Nymphs.
You sunburnt sicklemen, of August weary,
Come hither from the furrow and be merry :
Make holiday ; your rye-straw hats put on,
And these fresh nymphs encounter every one
In country footing.
   *Enter certain reapers, properly habited : they join with the
   Nymphs in a graceful dance ; towards the end whereof*
   PROSPERO *starts suddenly, and speaks ; after which, to a
   strange, hollow, and confused noise, they heavily vanish.*
   Pros. [*Aside*] I had forgot that foul conspiracy
Of the beast Caliban and his confederates
Against my life : the minute of their plot
Is almost come. [*To the Spirits.*] Well done ! avoid ; no more !
   Fer. This is strange : your father's in some passion
That works him strongly.
   Mir.   Never till this day
Saw I him touch'd with anger so distemper'd.
   Pros. You do look, my son, in a mov'd sort,

As if you were dismay'd : be cheerful, sir.
Our revels now are ended. These our actors,
As I foretold you, were all spirits, and
Are melted into air, into thin air :
And, like the baseless fabric of this vision,
The cloud-capped towers, the gorgeous palaces,
The solemn temples, the great globe itself,
Yea, all which it inherit, shall dissolve,
And, like this insubstantial pageant faded,
Leave not a rack behind. We are such stuff
As dreams are made on, and our little life
Is rounded with a sleep. Sir, I am vex'd ;
Bear with my weakness ; my old brain is troubled :
Be not disturb'd with my infirmity :
If you be pleas'd, retire into my cell
And there repose : a turn or two I'll walk,
To still my beating mind.
 Fer. Mir.   We wish your peace.

King Lear.

ACT I., SCENE I.—A ROOM OF STATE IN KING LEAR'S PALACE.

Enter KENT *and* GLOSTER.

Kent. I thought, the king had more affected the Duke of Albany, than Cornwall.

Glo. It did always seem so to us : but now, in the division of the kingdom, it appears not which of the dukes he values most ; for equalities are so weighed, that curiosity in neither can make choice of either's moiety.—The king is coming.

Enter one bearing a Coronet, then LEAR, *then the Dukes of* ALBANY *and* CORNWALL, *next* GONERIL, REGAN, CORDELIA, *with followers.*

Lear. Attend the Lords of France and Burgundy, Gloster.
Glo. I shall, my liege.
            [*Exeunt* GLOSTER.

Lear. Meantime we shall express our darker purpose.
Give me the map there. Know, that we have divided
In three our kingdom; and 't is our fast intent
To shake all cares and business from our age,
Conferring them on younger strengths, while we
Unburthened crawl toward death.—Our son of Cornwall,
And you, our no less loving son of Albany,
We have this hour a constant will to publish
Our daughters' several dowers, that future strife
May be prevented now. The princes, France and Burgundy,
Great rivals in our youngest daughter's love,
Long in our court have made their amorous sojourn,
And here are to be answered. Tell me, my daughters,—
Since now we will divest us both of rule,
Interest of territory, cares of state,—
Which of you, shall we say, doth love us most?
That we our largest bounty may extend
Where nature doth with merit challenge it.
Goneril, our eldest-born, speak first.

Gon. Sir,
I love you more than words can wield the matter,
Dearer than eye-sight, space, and liberty,
Beyond what can be valued, rich or rare,
No less than life, with grace, health, beauty, honour;
As much as child e'er loved, or father found:
A love that makes breath poor, and speech unable,
Beyond all manner of so much, I love you.

Cor. [*Aside.*] What shall Cordelia do? Love, and be silent.

Lear. Of all these bounds, even from this line to this,
With shadowy forests and with champains riched,
With plenteous rivers, and wide-skirted meads,
We make thee lady: to thine and Albany's issue
Be this perpetual.—What says our second daughter?
Our dearest Regan, wife to Cornwall? Speak.

Reg. I am made of that self metal as my sister,
And prize me at her worth. In my true heart
I find she names my very deed of love,
Only she comes too short; that I profess
Myself an enemy to all other joys
Which the most precious square of sense possesses,

And find, I am alone felicitate
In your dear highness' love.
   Cor. [*Aside.*]   Then, poor Cordelia !
And yet not so ; since, I am sure, my love 's
More richer than my tongue.
   Lear. To thee and thine, hereditary ever
Remain this ample third of our fair kingdom ;
No less in space, validity, and pleasure,
Than that conferred on Goneril.—Now, our joy,
Although our last, not least ; to whose young love
The vines of France and milk of Burgundy
Strive to be interessed ; what can you say, to draw
A third more opulent than your sisters ? Speak.
   Cor. Nothing, my lord.
   Lear. Nothing ?
   Cor. Nothing.
   Lear. Nothing will come of nothing : speak again.
   Cor. Unhappy that I am, I cannot heave
My heart into my mouth : I love your majesty
According to my bond ; nor more, nor less.
   Lear. How, how, Cordelia ! mend your speech a little,
Lest you may mar your fortunes.
   Cor.   Good my lord
You have begot me, bred me, loved me : I
Return those duties back as are right fit,
Obey you, love you, and most honour you.
Why have my sisters husbands, if they say
They love you all ? Haply, when I shall wed,
That lord whose hand must take my plight shall carry
Half my love with him, half my care, and duty :
Sure, I shall never marry like my sisters,
To love my father all.
   Lear. But goes thy heart with this ?
   Cor.   Ay, my good lord.
   Lear. So young, and so untender ?
   Cor. So young, my lord, and true.
   Lear. Let it be so : thy truth then be thy dower ;
For, by the sacred radiance of the sun,
The mysteries of Hecate and the night,
By all the operation of the orbs

From whom we do exist and cease to be,
Here I disclaim all my paternal care,
Propinquity and property of blood,
And as a stranger to my heart and me
Hold thee, from this, for ever.
    Kent.   Good my liege,—
    Lear. Peace, Kent!
Come not between the dragon and his wrath.
I loved her most, and thought to set my rest
On her kind nursery.—Hence, and avoid my sight!—
So be my grave my peace, as here I give
Her father's heart from her!—Call France. Who stirs?—
Call Burgundy. Cornwall, and Albany,
With my two daughters' dowers digest the third:
Let pride, which she calls plainness, marry her.
I do invest you jointly with my power,
Pre-eminence, and all the large effects
That troop with majesty. Ourself, by monthly course,
With reservation of an hundred knights,
By you to be sustained, shall our abode
Make with you by due turn. Only we shall retain
The name and all the additions to a king;
The sway, revenue, execution of the rest,
Beloved sons, be yours: which to confirm,
This coronet part between you.
    Kent.   Royal Lear,
Whom I have ever honoured as my king,
Loved as my father, as my master followed,
As my great patron thought on in my prayers,—
    Lear. The bow is bent and drawn; make from the shaft.
    Kent. Let it fall rather, though the fork invade
The region of my heart.
Be Kent unmannerly when Lear is mad.
What wouldst thou do, old man?
Think'st thou that duty shall have dread to speak,
When power to flattery bows? To plainness honour's bound,
When majesty stoops to folly. Reverse thy doom;
And, in thy best consideration, check
This hideous rashness. Answer my life my judgment,
Thy youngest daughter does not love thee least;

Nor are those empty-hearted whose low sound
Reverbs no hollowness.
    Lear.   Kent, on thy life, no more.
    Kent. My life I never held but as a pawn
To wage against thine enemies, nor fear to lose it,
Thy safety being the motive.
    Lear.   Out of my sight!
    Kent. See better, Lear; and let me still remain
The true blank of thine eye.
    Lear. Now, by Apollo,—
    Kent.   Now, by Apollo, king,
Thou swear'st thy gods in vain.
    Lear.   O, vassal! recreant!
                        Laying his hand upon his sword.
    Alb., Corn. Dear sir, forbear.
    Kent. Do;
Kill thy physician, and the fee bestow
Upon the foul disease. Revoke thy gift;
Or, whilst I can vent clamour from my throat,
I'll tell thee, thou dost evil.
    Lear.   Hear me, recreant!
On thine allegiance, hear me!
Since thou hast sought to make us break our vow,
Which we durst never yet, and, with strained pride,
To come betwixt our sentence and our power,
Which nor our nature nor our place can bear,
Our potency made good, take thy reward.
Five days we do allot thee for provision
To shield thee from disasters of the world;
And on the sixth to turn thy hated back
Upon our kingdom: if, on the tenth day following,
Thy banished trunk be found in our dominions,
The moment is thy death. Away! By Jupiter,
This shall not be revoked.
    Kent. Fare thee well, king: since thus thou wilt appear,
Freedom lives hence, and banishment is here.—
[*To* Cordelia.] The gods to their dear shelter take thee, maid,
That justly think'st, and hast most rightly said!—
[*To* Regan *and* Goneril.] And your large speeches may your
    deeds approve,

That good effects may spring from words of love.—
Thus Kent, O princes, bids you all adieu ;
He'll shape his old course in a country new.   [*Exit.*

   Re-enter GLOSTER ; *with* FRANCE *and* BURGUNDY,
                    Attendants.

  Glo. Here's France and Burgundy, my noble lord.
  Lear. My Lord of Burgundy,
We first address toward you, who with this king
Hath rivalled for our daughter. What, in the least,
Will you require in present dower with her,
Or cease your quest of love ?
  Bur.   Most royal majesty,
I crave no more than hath your highness offered,
Nor will you tender less.
  Lear.   Right noble Burgundy,
When she was dear to us, we did hold her so ;
But now her price is fall'n. Sir, there she stands :
If aught within that little-seeming substance,
Or all of it, with our displeasure pieced,
And nothing more, may fitly like your grace,
She 's there, and she is yours.
  Bur.   I know no answer.
  Lear. Will you, with those infirmities she owes,
Unfriended, new adopted to our hate,
Dowered with our curse, and strangered with our oath,
Take her, or leave her ?
  Bur.   Pardon me, royal sir ;
Election makes not up on such conditions.
  Lear. Then leave her, sir ; for, by the power that made me,
I tell you all her wealth.—[*To* FRANCE.] For you, great king,
I would not from your love make such a stray,
To match you where I hate : therefore, beseech you
To avert your liking a more worthier way
Than on a wretch whom Nature is ashamed
Almost to acknowledge hers.
  France.   This is most strange,
That she who even but now was your best object,
The argument of your praise, balm of your age,
Most best, most dearest, should in this trice of time

Commit a thing so monstrous, to dismantle
So many folds of favour. Sure, her offence
Must be of such unnatural degree,
That monsters it, or your fore-vouched affection
Fall into taint, which to believe of her,
Must be a faith that reason without miracle
Could never plant in me.
  Cor.   I yet beseech your majesty
If for I want that glib and oily art,
To speak and purpose not; since what I well intend,
I'll do 't before I speak; that you make known
It is no vicious blot, murder, or foulness,
No unchaste action, or dishonoured step,
That hath deprived me of your grace and favour;
But even for want of that for which I am richer,
A still-soliciting eye, and such a tongue
That I am glad I have not, though not to have it
Hath lost me in your liking.
  Lear.   Better thou
Hadst not been born, than not to have pleased me better.
  France. Is it but this? a tardiness in nature,
Which often leaves the history unspoke
That it intends to do?—My Lord of Burgundy,
What say you to the lady? Love's not love,
When it is mingled with regards that stand
Aloof from the entire point. Will you have her?
She is herself a dowry.
  Bur.   Royal king,
Give but that portion which yourself proposed,
And here I take Cordelia by the hand,
Duchess of Burgundy.
  Lear. Nothing. I have sworn: I am firm.
  Bur. I am sorry, then, you have so lost a father
That you must lose a husband.
  Cor.   Peace be with Burgundy!
Since that respects of fortune are his love,
I shall not be his wife.
  France. Fairest Cordelia, that art most rich, being poor;
Most choice, forsaken; and most loved, despised;
Thee and thy virtues here I seize upon:

Be it lawful I take up what's cast away.
Gods, gods! 't is strange, that from their cold'st neglect
My love should kindle to inflamed respect.
Thy dowerless daughter, king, thrown to my chance,
Is Queen of us, of ours, and our fair France :
Not all the dukes of waterish Burgundy
Shall buy this unprized precious maid of me.
Bid them farewell, Cordelia, though unkind :
Thou losest here, a better where to find.
 Lear. Thou hast her, France : let her be thine ; for we
Have no such daughter, nor shall ever see
That face of hers again. Therefore, be gone
Without our grace, our love, our benison.—
Come, noble Burgundy.
      [*Exeunt* LEAR, BURGUNDY, CORNWALL,
      ALBANY, GLOSTER, *and Attendants.*

 France. Bid farewell to your sisters.
 Cor. The jewels of our father, with washed eyes
Cordelia leaves you. I know you what you are,
And, like a sister, am most loath to call
Your faults as they are named. Love well our father :
To your professéd bosoms I commit him ;
But yet, alas, stood I within his grace,
I would prefer him to a better place.
So farewell to you both.
 Reg. Prescribe not us our duty.
 Gon.   Let your study
Be, to content your lord, who hath received you
At fortune's alms : you have obedience scanted,
And well are worth the want that you have wanted.
 Cor. Time shall unfold what pleated cunning hides ;
Who cover faults, at last shame them derides.
Well may you prosper !
 France.   Come, my fair Cordelia.

Hamlet, Prince of Denmark.
Act V., Scene II.—A Hall in the Castle.
Enter Hamlet *and* Horatio.

Ham. So much for this, sir : now let me see the other ;
You do remember all the circumstance ?
Hor. Remember it, my lord ?
Ham. Sir, in my heart there was a kind of fighting,
That would not let me sleep : methought, I lay
Worse than the mutines in the bilboes.   Rashly,
And praise be rashness for it, let us know,
Our indiscretion sometimes serves us well,
When our deep plots do pall ; and that should teach us,
There's a divinity that shapes our ends,
Rough-hew them how we will—
Hor.   That is most certain.
Ham. Up from my cabin,
My sea-gown scarf'd about me, in the dark
Grop'd I to find out them : had my desire ;
Finger'd their packet ; and, in fine, withdrew
To mine own room again : making so bold,
My fears forgetting manners, to unseal
Their grand commission ; where I found, Horatio,
O royal knavery ! an exact command,
Larded with many several sorts of reason,
Importing Denmark's health, and England's too,
With, ho ! such bugs and goblins in my life,
That, on the supervise, no leisure bated,
No, not to stay the grinding of the axe,
My head should be struck off.
Hor.   Is't possible ?
Ham. Here's the commission ; read it at more leisure.
But wilt thou hear me how I did proceed ?
Hor. Ay, 'beseech you.
Ham. Being thus be-netted round with villanies,
Ere I could make a prologue to my brains,
They had begun the play—I sat me down ;
Devised a new commission ; wrote it fair :
I once did hold it, as our statists do,

A baseness to write fair, and labour'd much
How to forget that learning ; but, sir, now
It did me yeoman's service. Wilt thou know
The effects of what I wrote ?
    Hor.   Ay, good my lord.
    Ham. An earnest conjuration from the king,—
As England was his faithful tributary ;
As love between them as the palm should flourish ;
As peace should still her wheaten garland wear,
And stand a comma 'tween their amities :
And many such like as's of great charge,—
That on the view and know of these contents,
Without debatement further, more or less,
He should the bearers put to sudden death,
Not shriving-time allow'd.
    Hor.   How was this sealed ?
    Ham. Why, even in that was heaven ordinant ;
I had my father's signet in my purse,
Which was the model of that Danish seal :
Folded the writ up in form of the other ;
Subscrib'd it ; gave 't the impression ; placed it safely,
The changeling never known—Now, the next day
Was our sea-fight ; and what to this was sequent
Thou know'st already.
    Hor. So Guildenstern and Rosencrantz go to 't.
    Ham. Why, man, they did make love to this employment ;
They are not near my conscience ; their defeat
Does by their own insinuation grow :
'Tis dangerous, when the baser nature comes
Between the pass and fell incensed points
Of mighty opposites.
    Hor.   Why, what a king is this !
    Ham. Does it not, think thee, stand me now upon ?
He that hath kill'd my king, and wed my mother ;
Popp'd in between the election and my hopes ;
Thrown out his angle for my proper life,
And with such cozenage ; is't not perfect conscience
To quit him with this arm ? and is't not to be damn'd
To let this canker of our nature come
In further evil ?

Hor. It must be shortly known to him from England,
What is the issue of the business there.
  Ham. It will be short : the interim is mine ;
And a man's life's no more than to say, 'one.'
But I am very sorry, good Horatio,
That to Laertes I forgot myself ;
For by the image of my cause, I see
The portraiture of his : I'll count his favours ;
But, sure, the bravery of his grief did put me
Into a towering passion.
  Hor.   Peace ! who comes here ?

Enter OSRIC.

  Osr. Your lordship is right welcome back to Denmark.
  Ham. I humbly thank you, sir.—Dost know this water-fly?
  Hor. No, my good lord.
  Ham. Thy state is the more gracious ; for 'tis a vice to know him.
  Osr. Sweet lord, if your lordship were at leisure, I should impart a thing to you from his majesty.
  Ham. I will receive it with all diligence of spirit. Put your bonnet to his right use ; 'tis for the head.
  Osr. I thank your lordship, 'tis very hot.
  Ham. No, believe me, 'tis very cold ; the wind is northerly.
  Osr. It is indifferent cold, my lord, indeed.
  Ham. But yet methinks it is very sultry and hot, for my complexion.
  Osr. Exceedingly, my lord ; it is very sultry,—as 'twere,— I cannot tell how.—But, my lord, his majesty bade me signify to you, that he has laid a great wager on your head : Sir, this is the matter.
  Ham. I beseech you, remember—

   [HAMLET *moves him to put on his hat.*

  Osr. Nay, in good faith ; for mine ease, in good faith. Sir, here is newly come to court, Laertes : believe me, an absolute gentleman, full of most excellent differences, of very soft society, and great showing : Indeed, to speak feelingly of him, he is the card or calendar of gentry, for you shall find in him the continent of what part a gentleman would see.
  Ham. Sir, his definement suffers no perdition in you ;

though, I know, to divide him inventorially, would dizzy the arithmetic of memory; and yet but yaw neither, in respect of his quick sail. But, in the verity of extolment, I take him to be a soul of great article.

Osr. Your lordship speaks most infallibly of him.

Ham. The concernancy, sir? why do we wrap the gentleman in our more rawer breath?

Osr. Sir?

Hor. Is't not possible to understand in another tongue? You will do't, sir, really.

Ham. What imports the nomination of this gentleman?

Osr. Of Laertes?

Hor. His purse is empty already; all his golden words are spent.

Ham. Of him, sir.

Osr. I know you are not ignorant—

Ham. I would you did, sir; yet, in faith, if you did, it would not much approve me.—Well, sir.

Osr. You are not ignorant of what excellence Laertes is—

Ham. I dare not confess that, lest I should compare with him in excellence; but, to know a man well, were to know himself.

Osr. I mean, sir, for his weapon; but in the imputation laid on him by them, in his meed he's unfellowed.

Ham. What's his weapon?

Osr. Rapier and dagger.

Ham. That's two of his weapons: but, well.

Osr. The king, sir, hath wagered with him six Barbary horses: against the which he has imponed, as I take it, six French rapiers and poniards, with their assigns, as girdle, hangers, or so: Three of the carriages, in faith, are very dear to fancy, very responsive to the hilts, most delicate carriages, and of very liberal conceit.

Ham. What call you the carriages?

Hor. I knew you must be edified by the margent, ere you had done.

Osr. The carriages, sir, are the hangers.

Ham. The phrase would be more german to the matter, if we could carry cannon by our sides: I would it might be hangers till then. But, on: Six Barbary horses against six French swords, their assigns, and three liberal-conceited carriages; that's the French bet, against the Danish. Why is this 'imponed,' as you call it?

Osr. The king, sir, hath laid, that in a dozen passes between yourself and him, he shall not exceed you three hits; he hath laid on twelve for nine; and that would come to immediate trial, if your lordship would vouchsafe the answer.

Ham. How, if I answer 'no'?

Osr. I mean, my lord, the opposition of your person in trial.

Ham. Sir, I will walk here in the hall. If it please his majesty, it is the breathing time of day with me: let the foils be brought, the gentleman willing, and the king hold his purpose, I will win for him, if I can; if not, I will gain nothing but my shame, and the odd hits.

Osr. Shall I re-deliver you e'en so?

Ham. To this effect, sir; after what flourish your nature will.

Osr. I commend my duty to your lordship. [*Exit.*

Ham. Yours, yours. He does well to commend it himself; there are no tongues else for's turn.

Hor. This lapwing runs away with the shell on his head.

Ham. Thus has he (and many more of the same bevy, that, I know, the drossy age dotes on) only got the tune of the time, and outward habit of encounter; a kind of yesty collection, which carries them through and through the most fond and winnowed opinions; and do but blow them to their trials, the bubbles are out.

Enter a LORD.

Lord. My lord, his majesty commended him to you by young Osric, who brings back to him, that you attend him in the hall: he sends to know, if your pleasure hold to play with Laertes, or that you will take longer time.

Ham. I am constant to my purposes, they follow the king's pleasure; if his fitness speaks, mine is ready; now, or whensoever, provided I be so able as now.

Lord. The king, and queen, and all are coming down.

Ham. In happy time.

Lord. The queen desires you to use some gentle entertainment to Laertes, before you go to play.

Ham. She well instructs me. [*Exit* Lord.
Hor. You will lose this wager, my lord.
Ham. I do not think so; since he went into France, I have been in continual practice: I shall win at the odds. But thou wouldst not think how ill all's here about my heart: but it is no matter.
Hor. Nay, good my lord,—
Ham. It is but foolery; but it is such a kind of gaingiving as would, perhaps, trouble a woman.
Hor. If your mind dislike anything, obey: I will forestall their repair hither, and say, you are not fit.
Ham. Not a whit, we defy augury; there's a special providence in the fall of a sparrow. If it be now, 'tis not to come; if it be not to come, it will be now; if it be not now, yet it will come: the readiness is all: since no man has aught of what he leaves, what is 't to leave betimes?

SOLILOQUIES AND SPEECHES.

Queen Mab.

O, then, I see, Queen Mab hath been with you.
She is the fairies' midwife; and she comes
In shape no bigger than an agate stone
On the fore-finger of an alderman,
Drawn with a team of little atomies
Athwart men's noses as they lie asleep:
Her wagon-spokes made of long spinner's legs;
The cover, of the wings of grasshoppers;
The traces, of the smallest spider's web;
The collars of the moonshine's watery beams;
Her whip, of cricket's bone; the lash of film:
Her wagoner, a small grey-coated gnat,
Not half so big as a round little worm
Pricked from the lazy finger of a maid:
Her chariot is an empty hazel-nut,
Made by the joiner Squirrel, or old Grub,
Time out of mind the fairies' coach-makers,
And in this state she gallops night by night

Through lovers' brains, and then they dream of love:
On courtiers' knees, that dream on court'sies straight:
O'er lawyers' fingers, who straight dream on fees:
O'er ladies' lips, who straight on kisses dream.
Sometimes she gallops o'er a courtier's nose,
And then dreams he of smelling out a suit:
And sometimes comes she with a tithe-pig's tail,
Tickling a parson as he lies asleep—
Then dreams he of another benefice:
Sometimes she driveth o'er a soldier's neck,
And then dreams he of cutting foreign throats,
Of breaches, ambuscadoes, Spanish blades,
Of healths five-fathom deep; and then anon
Drums in his ear; at which he starts, and wakes;
And, being thus frighted, swears a prayer or two,
And sleeps again.

Gloster's Soliloquy.

Now is the winter of our discontent
Made glorious summer by this sun of York;
And all the clouds, that lower'd upon our house,
In the deep bosom of the ocean buried.
Now are our brows bound with victorious wreaths;
Our bruisèd arms hung up for monuments;
Our stern alarums chang'd to merry meetings;
Our dreadful marches to delightful measures.
Grim-visag'd war hath smooth'd his wrinkled front;
And now,—instead of mounting barbèd steeds,
To fright the souls of fearful adversaries,—
He capers nimbly in a lady's chamber,
To the lascivious pleasing of a lute.
But I,—that am not shaped for sportive tricks,
Nor made to court an amorous looking-glass;
I, that am rudely stamp'd, and want love's majesty,
To strut before a wanton ambling nymph;
I, that am curtail'd of this fair proportion,
Cheated of features by dissembling nature,
Deform'd, unfinish'd, sent before my time

Into this breathing world, scarce half made up,
And that so lamely and unfashionable,
That dogs bark at me, as I halt by them ;—
Why I, in this weak piping time of peace,
Have no delight to pass away the time
Unless to see my shadow in the sun,
And descant on mine own deformity :
And therefore, since I cannot prove a lover,
To entertain these fair well-spoken days,
I am determinèd to prove a villain,
And hate the idle pleasures of these days.
Plots have I laid, inductions dangerous,
By drunken prophecies, libels, and dreams,
To set my brother Clarence and the king
In deadly hate the one against the other.
And, if king Edward be as true and just
As I am subtle, false, and treacherous,
This day should Clarence closely be mew'd up,
About a prophecy, which says, that G
Of Edward's heirs the murderer shall be.
The king is sickly, weak, and melancholy,
And his physicians fear him mightily.
He cannot live, I hope, and must not die,
Till George be pack'd with posthorse up to heaven.
I'll in, to urge his hatred more to Clarence,
With lies well steel'd with weighty arguments ;
And, if I fail not in my deep intent,
Clarence hath not another day to live :
Which done, God take king Edward to his mercy,
And leave the world for me to bustle in !
For then I'll marry Warwick's youngest daughter.
What though I kill'd her husband and her father,
The readiest way to make the wench-amends,
Is to become her husband, and her father :
The which will I ; not all so much for love,
As for another secret close intent,
By marrying her, which I must reach unto.
But yet I run before my horse to market :
Clarence still breathes ; Edward still lives and reigns :
When they are gone, then must I count my gains.

Henry V.
BEFORE THE BATTLE OF AGINCOURT.

What's he that wishes men from England? you, cousin Westmoreland?—No, my fair cousin: if we are marked to die, we are enough to do our country loss; and if to live, the fewer men, the greater share of honour. I pray thee, cousin, wish not one man more. By Jove, I am not covetous for gold: nor care I who doth feed upon my cost; it yearns me not, if men my garments wear; such outward things dwell not in my desires! But, if it be a sin to covet honour, I am the most offending soul alive. No, 'faith, my coz, wish not a man from England: I would not lose so great an honour, as one man more, methinks would share from me, for the best hope I have! Oh do not wish one more: rather proclaim it, Westmoreland, throughout my host, that he who hath no stomach to this fight may straight depart: his passport shall be made, and crowns of convoy put into his purse: we would not die in that man's company, that fears his fellowship to die with us. This day is call'd the feast of Crispian: he that outlives this day, and comes safe home, will stand a tip-toe when this day is named, and rouse him at the name of Crispian: he that shall live this day, and see old age, will yearly on the vigil feast his friends, and say—"To-morrow is Saint Crispian:" then will he strip his sleeve, and show his scars and say,— "These wounds I had on Crispin's day." Old men forget; yet shall not all forget, but they'll remember with advantages, what feats they did that day. Then shall our names, familiar in their mouths as household words, Harry the king, Bedford, and Exeter, Warwick, and Talbot, Salisbury, and Gloster, be in their flowing cups freshly remember'd: this story shall the good man teach his son; and Crispin Crispian shall ne'er go by from this day to the ending of the world, but we in it shall be remembered: we few, we happy few, we band of brothers; for he to-day that sheds his blood with me, shall be my brother! be he ne'er so vile, this day shall gentle his condition: and gentlemen in England now a-bed, shall think themselves accurs'd they were not here! and hold their manhoods cheap, while any speaks that fought with us upon Saint Crispin's day. All things are ready if our minds be so. You know your places: God be with you all!

MISCELLANEOUS DIALOGUES.

Scene from "The Hunchback."

HELEN.   MODUS.

Helen. I'm weary wandering from room to room;
A castle after all is but a house—
The dullest one when lacking company.
Were I at home, I could be company
Unto myself.   I see not Master Walter.
He's ever with his ward.   I see not her.
By Master Walter will she bide, alone.
My father stops in town.   I can't see him.
My cousin makes his books his company.
I'll go to bed and sleep.   No—I'll stay up
And plague my cousin into making love!
For, that he loves me, shrewdly I suspect.
How dull he is, that hath not sense to see
What lies before him, and he'd like to find!
I'll change my treatment of him.   Cross him, where
Before I used to humour him.   He comes,
Poring upon a book.   What's that you read?

Enter MODUS.

Mod. Latin, sweet cousin.
Helen. 'T is a naughty tongue,
I fear, and teaches men to lie.
Mod. To lie!
Helen. You study it.   You call your cousin sweet,
And treat her as you would a crab.   As sour
'T would seem you think her, so you covet her!
Why how the monster stares, and looks about!
You construe Latin, and can't construe that!
Mod. I never studied women.
Helen. No; nor men.
Else would you better know their ways; nor read
In presence of a lady.   [*Strikes the book from his hand.*
Mod. Right you say,

And well you served me, cousin, so to strike
The volume from my hand. I own my fault;
So please you may I pick it up again?
I'll put it in my pocket!
  Helen. Pick it up.
He fears me as I were his grandmother!
What is the book?
  Mod. 'T is Ovid's Art of Love.
  Helen. That Ovid was a fool!
  Mod. In what?
  Helen. In that!
To call that thing an art, which art is none.
  Mod. And is not love an art?
  Helen. Are you a fool
As well as Ovid? Love an art! No art
But taketh time and pains to learn. Love comes
With neither! Is't to hoard such grain as that
You went to college? Better stay at home,
And study homely English!
  Mod. Nay, you know not
The argument.
  Helen. I don't? I know it better
Than ever Ovid did! The face,—the form,—
The heart,—the mind we fancy, cousin! that's
The argument! Why, cousin, you know nothing!
Suppose a lady were in love with thee,
Couldst thou by Ovid, cousin, find it out?
Couldst find it out, wert thou in love, thyself?
Could Ovid, cousin, teach thee to make love?
I could, that never read him! You begin
With melancholy; then to sadness; then
To sickness; then to dying—but not die!
She would not let thee, were she of my mind!
She'd take compassion on thee. Then for hope;
From hope to confidence; from confidence
To boldness;—then you'd speak; at first entreat;
Then urge; then flout; then argue; then enforce;
Make prisoner of her hand; besiege her waist;
Threaten her lips with storming; keep thy word
And carry her! My sampler 'gainst thy Ovid!

Why, cousin, are you frighten'd, that you stand
As you were stricken dumb? The case is clear,
You are no soldier! You'll ne'er win a battle,
You care too much for blows!
   Mod. You wrong me there.
At school I was the champion of my form;
And since I went to college——
   Helen. That for college!
   Mod. Nay, hear me!
   Helen. Well? What, since you went to college?
You know what men are set down for, who boast
Of their own bravery? Go on, brave cousin:
What, since you went to college? Was there not
One Quentin Halworth there? You know there was,
And that he was your master?
   Mod. He my master?
Thrice was he worsted by me!
   Helen, Still was he
Your master.
   Mod. He allow'd I had the best!
Allow'd it, mark me! nor to me alone,
But twenty I could name.
   Helen. And master'd you
At last! Confess it, cousin, 't is the truth!
A proctor's daughter you did both affect—
Look at me and deny it!—Of the twain
She more affected you;—I've caught you now,
Bold cousin! Mark you! opportunity
On opportunity she gave you, sir,—
Deny it if you can!—but though to others,
When you discoursed of her, you were a flame,
To her you were a wick that would not light,
Though held in the very fire! And so he won her—
Won her, because he woo'd her like a man;
For all your cuffings, cuffing you again
With most usurious interest! Now, sir,
Protest that you are valiant!
   Mod. Cousin Helen!
   Helen. Well, sir?
   Mod. The tale is all a forgery!

Helen. A forgery!
Mod. From first to last; ne'er spoke I
To a proctor's daughter, while I was at college.
Helen. Well, 'twas a scrivener's, then—or somebody's.
But what concerns it whose? Enough, you loved her!
And, shame upon you, let another take her!
Mod. Cousin, I tell you, if you'll only hear me,
I loved no woman while I was at college—
Save one, and her I fancied ere I went there.
Helen. Indeed! Now I'll retreat, if he's advancing.
Comes he not on! O what a stock 's the man!
Well, cousin?
Mod. Well! What more wouldst have me say?
I think I've said enough.
Helen. And so think I.
I did but jest with you. You are not angry?
Shake hands! Why, cousin, do you squeeze me so?
Mod. [*Letting her go.*] I swear I squeezed you not.
Helen. You did not?
Mod. No.
May I die if I did!
Helen. Why then you did not, cousin.
So let's shake hands again—[*He takes her hand as before.*]—O
go! and now
Read Ovid! Cousin, will you tell me one thing:
Wore lovers ruffs in master Ovid's time?
Behoved him teach them, then, to put them on;
And that you have to learn. Hold up your head!
Why, cousin, how you blush! Plague on the ruff!
I cannot give 't a set. You're blushing still!
Why do you blush, dear cousin? So!—'t will beat me!
I'll give it up.
Mod. Nay, prithee don't—try on!
Helen. And if I do, I fear you'll think me bold.
Mod. For what?
Helen. To trust my face so near to thine.
Mod. I know not what you mean!
Helen. I'm glad you don't!
Cousin, I own right well-behaved you are,
Most marvellously well-behaved! They've bred

You well at college.   With another man
My lips would be in danger!   Hang the ruff!
   Mod. Nay, give it up, nor plague thyself, dear cousin.
   Helen. Dear fool!   [*Throws the ruff on the ground.*]
I swear the ruff is good for just
As little as its master!   There!—'T is spoil'd—
You'll have to get another!   Hie for it,
And wear it in the fashion of a wisp,
Ere I adjust it for thee!   Farewell, cousin!
You'd need to study Ovid's Art of Love!
                                            [HELEN *goes out.*
   Mod. Went she in anger?   I will follow her,—
No, I will not!   Heigho!   I love my cousin!
O would that she loved me!   Why did she taunt me
With backwardness in love?   What could she mean?
Sees she I love her, and so laughs at me,
Because I lack the front to woo her?   Nay,
I'll woo her, then!   Her lips shall be in danger,
When next she trusts them near me!   Look'd she at me
To-day, as never did she look before!
A bold heart, Master Modus!   'T is a saying,
A faint one never won fair lady yet!
I'll woo my cousin, come what will on 't.   Yes:
             [*Begins reading again, throws down the book.*
Hang Ovid's Art of Love!   I'll woo my cousin!

     *   *   *   *   *   *

                  Enter HELEN.

   Helen. Why, cousin Modus?   What, will you stand by
And see me forced to marry?   Cousin Modus?
Have you not got a tongue?   Have you not eyes?
Do you not see I'm very—very ill,
And not a chair in all the corridor?
   Mod. I'll find one in the study.
   Helen. Hang the study!
   Mod. My room's at hand.   I'll fetch one thence.
   Helen. You shan't!
I'd faint ere you came back!
   Mod. What shall I do?
   Helen. Why don't you offer to support me?   Well?

Give me your arm—be quick! [MODUS *offers his arm.*
Is that the way
To help a lady when she's like to faint?
I'll drop unless you catch me! [MODUS *supports her.*
That will do.
I'm better now—[MODUS *offers to leave her*] don't leave me!
  Is one well
Because one's better? Hold my hand. Keep so.
I'll soon recover, so you move not. Loves he— [*Aside.*
Which I'll be sworn he does, he'll own it now.
Well, cousin Modus?
  Mod. Well, sweet cousin!
  Helen. Well?
You heard what Master Walter said?
  Mod. I did.
  Helen. And would you have me marry? Can't you speak?
Say yes, or no.
  Mod. No, cousin!
  Helen. Bravely said!
And why, my gallant cousin?
  Mod. Why?
  Helen. Ay, why?
Women, you know, are fond of reasons—Why
Would you not have me marry? How you blush!
Is it because you do not know the reason?
You mind me of a story of a cousin
Who once her cousin such a question ask'd—
He had not been to college, though—for books,
Had pass'd his time in reading ladies' eyes,
Which he could construe marvellously well,
Though writ in language all symbolical.
Thus stood they once together, on a day—
As we stand now—discours'd as we discourse,—
But with this difference,—fifty gentle words
He spoke to her, for one she spoke to him!—
What a dear cousin! Well, as I was saying,
As now I question'd thee, she question'd him.
And what was his reply? To think of it
Sets my heart beating—'T was so kind a one!
So like a cousin's answer—a dear cousin!

A gentle, honest, gallant, loving cousin !
What did he say ?—A man might find it out
Though never read he Ovid's Art of Love—
What did he say ?   He'd marry her himself !
How stupid are you, cousin !   Let me go !
   Mod. You are not well yet ?
   Helen. Yes.
   Mod. I'm sure you're not !
   Helen. I'm sure I am.
   Mod. Nay, let me hold you, cousin !
I like it.
   Helen. Do you ?   I would wager you
You could not tell me why you like it.   Well ?
You see how true I know you !   How you stare !
What see you in my face to wonder at ?
   Mod. A pair of eyes !
   Helen. At last he'll find his tongue—   [*Aside.*
And saw you ne'er a pair of eyes before ?
   Mod. Not such a pair.
   Helen. And why ?
   Mod. They are so bright !
You have a Grecian nose.
   Helen. Indeed.
   Mod. Indeed !
   Helen. What kind of mouth have I ?
   Mod. A handsome one.
I never saw so sweet a pair of lips !
I ne'er saw lips at all till now, dear cousin !
   Helen. Cousin, I'm well,—You need not hold me now.
Do you not hear ?   I tell you I am well !
I need your arm no longer—take 't away !
So tight it locks me, 't is with pain I breathe !
Let me go, cousin !   Wherefore do you hold
Your face so close to mine ?   What do you mean ?
   Mod. You've question'd me, and now I'll question you.
   Helen. What would you learn ?
   Mod. The use of lips.
   Helen. To speak.
   Mod. Nought else ?
   Helen. How bold my modest cousin grows !

Why, other use know you?
Mod. I do!
Helen. Indeed!
You're wondrous wise! And pray what is it?
Mod. This! [*Attempts to kiss her.*
Helen. Soft! my hand thanks you, cousin—for my lips
I keep them for a husband!—Nay, stand off!
I'll not be held in manacles again!
Why do you follow me?
Mod. I love you, cousin.
'T is out at last. [*Aside.*
Helen. You love me! Love me, cousin!
O cousin, mean you so? That's passing strange!
Falls out most crossly—is a dire mishap—
A thing to sigh for, weep for, languish for,
And die for!
Mod. Die for!
Helen. Yes, with laughter, cousin,
For, cousin, I love you!
Mod. And you'll be mine?
Helen. I will.
Mod. Your hand upon it.
Helen. Hand and heart.
Hie to thy dressing-room, and I'll to mine—
Attire thee for the altar—so will I.
Whoe'er may claim me, thou'rt the man shall have me.
Away! Despatch! But hark you, ere you go,
Ne'er brag of reading Ovid's Art of Love!
Mod. And cousin! stop—One little word with you.
[*She returns—he snatches a kiss.*

The Rivals.

LYDIA LANGUISH.—*From* ACT I., SCENE I.

Enter MRS. MALAPROP *and* SIR ANTHONY ABSOLUTE.

Mrs. Mal. There, Sir Anthony, there sits the deliberate simpleton who wants to disgrace her family, and lavish herself on a fellow not worth a shilling.

Lyd. Madam, I thought you once—

Mrs. Mal. You thought, miss! I don't know any business you have to think at all—thought does not become a young woman. But the point we would request of you is, that you will promise to forget this fellow—to illiterate him, I say, quite from your memory.

Lyd. Ah, madam! our memories are independent of our wills. It is not so easy to forget.

Mrs. Mal. But I say it is, miss; there is nothing on earth so easy as to forget, if a person chooses to set about it. I'm sure I have as much forgot your poor dear uncle as if he had never existed—and I thought it my duty so to do; and let me tell you, Lydia, these violent memories don't become a young woman.

Sir Anth. Why sure she won't pretend to remember what she's ordered not!—ay, this comes of her reading!

Lyd. What crime, madam, have I committed to be treated thus?

Mrs. Mal. Now don't attempt to extirpate yourself from the matter; you know I have proof controvertible of it.— But tell me, will you promise to do as you're bid? Will you take a husband of your friends' choosing?

Lyd. Madam, I must tell you plainly, that had I no preference for any one else, the choice you have made would be my aversion.

Mrs. Mal. What business have you, miss, with preference and aversion? They don't become a young woman; and you ought to know, that as both always wear off, 'tis safest in matrimony to begin with a little aversion. I am sure I hated your poor dear uncle before marriage as if he'd been a blackamoor—and yet, miss, you are sensible what a wife I made!—and when it pleased Heaven to release me from him, 'tis unknown what tears I shed!—But suppose we were going to give you another choice, will you promise us to give up this Beverley?

Lyd. Could I belie my thoughts so far as to give that promise, my actions would certainly as far belie my words.

Mrs. Mal. Take yourself to your room.—You are fit company for nothing but your own ill-humours.

Lyd. Willingly, ma'am—I cannot change for the worse.

[*Exit.*

Mrs. Mal. There's a little intricate hussy for you!

Sir Anth. It is not to be wondered at, ma'am,—all this is the natural consequence of teaching girls to read. Had I a thousand daughters, by Heavens! I'd as soon have them taught the black art as their alphabet!

Mrs. Mal. Nay, nay, Sir Anthony, you are an absolute misanthropy.

Sir Anth. In my way hither, Mrs. Malaprop, I observed your niece's maid coming forth from a circulating library!—She had a book in each hand—they were half-bound volumes, with marble covers!—From that moment I guessed how full of duty I should see her mistress!

Mrs. Mal. Those are vile places, indeed!

Sir Anth. Madam, a circulating library in a town is as an evergreen tree of diabolical knowledge! It blossoms through the year!—and depend on it, Mrs. Malaprop, that they who are so fond of handling the leaves, will long for the fruit at last.

Mrs. Mal. Fy, fy, Sir Anthony! you surely speak laconically.

Sir Anth. Why, Mrs. Malaprop, in moderation now, what would you have a woman know?

Mrs. Mal. Observe me, Sir Anthony. I would by no means wish a daughter of mine to be a progeny of learning; I don't think so much learning becomes a young woman; for instance, I would never let her meddle with Greek, or Hebrew, or algebra, or simony, or fluxions, or paradoxes, or such inflammatory branches of learning—neither would it be necessary for her to handle any of your mathematical, astronomical, diabolical instruments.—But, Sir Anthony, I would send her, at nine years old, to a boarding school, in order to learn a little ingenuity and artifice. Then, sir, she should have a supercilious knowledge in accounts;—and as she grew up, I would have her instructed in geometry, that she might know something of the contagious countries;—but above all, Sir Anthony, she should be mistress of orthodoxy, that she might not mis-spell, and mis-pronounce words so shamefully as girls usually do; and likewise that she might reprehend the true meaning of what she is saying. This, Sir Anthony, is what I would have a woman know;—and I don't think there is a superstitious article in it.

Sir Anth. Well, well, Mrs. Malaprop, I will dispute the point no further with you ; though I must confess, that you are a truly moderate and polite arguer, for almost every third word you say is on my side of the question. But, Mrs. Malaprop, to the more important point in debate—you say you have no objection to my proposal?

Mrs. Mal. None, I assure you. I am under no positive engagement with Mr. Acres, and as Lydia is so obstinate against him, perhaps your son may have better success.

Sir Anth. Well, madam, I will write for the boy directly. He knows not a syllable of this yet, though I have for some time had the proposal in my head. He is at present with his regiment.

Mrs. Mal. We have never seen your son, Sir Anthony; but I hope no objection on his side.

Sir Anth. Objection!—let him object if he dare!—No, no, Mrs. Malaprop, Jack knows that the least demur puts me in a frenzy directly. My process was always very simple—in their younger days, 'twas "Jack, do this;"—if he demurred, I knocked him down—and if he grumbled at that, I always sent him out of the room.

Mrs. Mal. Ay, and the properest way, o' my conscience!— nothing is so conciliating to young people as severity.—Well, Sir Anthony, I shall give Mr. Acres his discharge, and prepare Lydia to receive your son's invocations;—and I hope you will represent her to the captain as an object not altogether illegible.

Sir Anth. Madam, I will handle the subject prudently.— Well, I must leave you ; and let me beg you, Mrs. Malaprop, to enforce this matter roundly to the girl.—Take my advice— keep a tight hand : if she rejects this proposal, clap her under lock and key ; and if you were just to let the servants forget to bring her dinner for three or four days, you can't conceive how she'd come about. [*Exit.*

She Stoops to Conquer.

From ACT II., SCENE I.—HASTINGS, MARLOW, MISS NEVILLE.
Enter MISS HARDCASTLE.

Hast. [*Introducing Marlow.*] Miss Hardcastle—Mr. Marlow. I'm proud of bringing two persons of such merit together, that only want to know, to esteem each other.

Miss Hard. [*Aside.*] Now, for meeting my modest gentleman with a demure face, and quite in his own manner. [*After a pause, in which he appears to be very uneasy and disconcerted.*] I'm glad of your safe arrival, sir. I'm told you had some accidents by the way.

Marl. Only a few, madam. Yes, we had some. Yes, madam, a good many accidents; but should be sorry—madam—or rather glad of any accidents—that are so agreeably concluded. Hem!

Hast. [*To him.*] You never spoke better in your whole life. Keep it up, and I'll ensure you the victory.

Miss Hard. I'm afraid you flatter, sir. You, that have seen so much of the finest company, can find little entertainment in an obscure corner of the country.

Marl. [*Gathering courage.*] I have lived, indeed, in the world, madam; but I have kept very little company. I have been but an observer upon life, madam, while others were enjoying it.

Miss Nev. But that, I am told, is the way to enjoy it at last.

Hast. [*To him.*] Cicero never spoke better. Once more, and you are confirmed in assurance for ever.

Marl. [*To him.*] Hem! Stand by me, then; and when I'm down, throw in a word or two, to set me up again.

Miss Hard. An observer, like you, upon life, were, I fear, disagreeably employed, since you must have had much more to censure than to approve.

Marl. Pardon me, madam. I was always willing to be amused. The folly of most people is rather an object of mirth than uneasiness.

Hast. [*To him.*] Bravo, bravo! Never spoke so well in

your whole life. Well! [*To* Miss Hard.] Miss Hardcastle,
I see that you and Mr. Marlow are going to be very good
company. I believe our being here will but embarrass the
interview.

Marl. Not in the least, Mr. Hastings. We like your company of all things. [*To him.*] Zounds! George, sure you won't go—how can you leave us?

Hast. Our presence will but spoil conversation, so we'll retire to the next room. [*To him.*] You don't consider, man, that we are to manage a little tête-à-tête of our own.
[*Exeunt.*]

Miss Hard. [*After a pause.*] But you have not been wholly an observer, I presume, sir: the ladies, I should hope, have employed some part of your addresses.

Marl. [*Relapsing into timidity.*] Pardon me, madam, I—I—I as yet have studied—only—to—deserve them.

Miss Hard. And that, some say, is the very worst way to obtain them.

Marl. Perhaps so, madam. But I love to converse only with the more grave and sensible part of the sex. But I'm afraid I grow tiresome.

Miss Hard. Not at all, sir; there is nothing I like so much as grave conversation myself; I could hear it for ever. Indeed, I have often been surprised how a man of *sentiment* could ever admire those light, airy pleasures, where nothing reaches the heart.

Marl. It's—a disease—of the mind, madam. In the variety of tastes there must be some, who, wanting a relish —for—um-a-um.

Miss Hard. I understand you, sir. There must be some, who, wanting a relish for refined pleasures, pretend to despise what they are incapable of tasting.

Marl. My meaning, madam, but infinitely better expressed. And I can't help observing—a——

Miss Hard. [*To him.*] You were going to observe, sir——

Marl. I was observing, madam—I protest, madam, I forget what I was going to observe.

Miss Hard. [*Aside.*] I vow, and so do I. [*To him.*] You were observing, sir, that in this age of hypocrisy—something about hypocrisy, sir.

Marl. Yes, madam; in this age of hypocrisy there are few who, upon strict inquiry, do not—a—a—a——

Miss Hard. I understand you perfectly, sir.

Marl. [*Aside.*] Indeed! and that's more than I do myself.

Miss Hard. You mean that, in this hypocritical age, there are few that do not condemn in public what they practise in private.

Marl. True, madam; those who have most virtue in their mouths have least of it in their bosoms. But I'm sure I tire you, madam.

Miss Hard. Not in the least, sir; there's something so agreeable, and spirited, in your manner; such life and force—pray, sir, go on.

Marl. Yes, madam; I was saying—that there are some occasions—when a total want of courage, madam, destroys all the—and puts us—upon a—a—a——

Miss Hard. I agree with you entirely; a want of courage upon some occasions, assumes the appearance of ignorance, and betrays us when we most want to excel. I beg you'll proceed.

Marl. Yes, madam; morally speaking, madam—But I see Miss Neville expecting us in the next room. I would not intrude for the world.

Miss Hard. I protest, sir, I never was more agreeably entertained in all my life. Pray go on.

Marl. Yes, madam; I was—but she beckons us to join her. Madam, shall I do myself the honour to attend you?

Miss Hard. Well then, I'll follow.

Marl. [*Aside.*] This pretty smooth dialogue has done for me. [*Exit.*

MISS HARDCASTLE.

Miss Hard. Ha! ha! ha! Was there ever such a sober, sentimental interview? I'm certain he scarce looked in my face the whole time. Yet the fellow, but for his unaccountable bashfulness, is pretty well too. He has good sense; but then so buried in his fears, that it fatigues one more than ignorance. If I could teach him a little confidence, it would be doing somebody, that I know of, a piece of service. But who is that somebody?—that is a question I can scarce answer. [*Exit.*

Bubbles of the Day.
Adapted for Recital.

Sir Phenix Clearcake. I come with a petition to you—a petition, not parliamentary, but charitable. We propose, my lord, a fancy fair in Guildhall; its object so benevolent, and more than that, so respectable.

Lord Skindeep. Benevolence and respectability! Of course, I'm with you. Well, the precise object?

Sir P. It is to remove a stain—a very great stain—from the city; to give an air of maiden beauty to a most venerable institution; to exercise a renovating taste at a most inconsiderable outlay; to call up, as it were, the snowy beauty of Greece in the coal-smoke atmosphere of London; in a word, my lord—but as yet 'tis a profound secret—it is to paint St. Paul's! To give it a virgin outside—to make it so truly respectable.

Lord S. A gigantic effort!

Sir P. The fancy fair will be on a most comprehensive and philanthropic scale. Every alderman takes a stall; and to give you an idea of the enthusiasm of the city—but this also is a secret—the Lady Mayoress has been up three nights making pincushions.

Lord S. But you don't want me to take a stall—to sell pincushions?

Sir P. Certainly not, my lord. And yet your philanthropic speeches in the House, my lord, convince me that, to obtain a certain good, you would sell anything.

Lord S. Well, well; command me in any way; benevolence is my foible. (*Enter* CAPT. SMOKE.)

Captain Smoke. We are about to start a company to take on lease Mount Vesuvius for the manufacture of lucifer matches.

Sir P. A stupendous speculation! I should say that, when its countless advantages are duly numbered, it will be found a certain wheel of fortune to the enlightened capitalist.

Smoke. Now, sir, if you would but take the chair at the first meeting—(*Aside to Chatham:* We shall make it all right about the shares)—if you would but speak for two or three hours on the social improvement conferred by the lucifer-match, with the monopoly of sulphur secured to the company—a monopoly which will suffer no man, woman, or child to strike a light without our permission.

Chatham. Truly, sir, in such a cause, to such an auditory— I fear my eloquence.

Smoke. Sir, if you would speak well anywhere, there's nothing like first grinding your eloquence on a mixed meeting. Depend upon it, if you can only manage a little humbug with a mob, it gives you great confidence for another place.

Lord Skin. Smoke, never say humbug; it's coarse.

Sir P. And not respectable.

Smoke. Pardon me, my lord, it *was* coarse. But the fact is, humbug has received such high patronage, that now it's quite classic.

Chat. But why not embark his lordship in the lucifer question?

Smoke. I can't; I have his lordship in three companies already. Three. First, there's a company—half a million capital—for extracting civet from assafœtida. The second is a company for a trip all round the world. We propose to hire a three-decker of the lords of the Admiralty, and fit her up with every accommodation for families. We've already advertised for nurses and maids-of-all-work.

Sir P. A magnificent project! And then the fittings up will be so respectable. A delightful billiard-table in the ward-room; with, for the humbler classes, skittles on the orlop-deck. Swings and archery for the ladies, trap-ball and cricket for the children, whilst the marine sportsman will find the stock of gulls unlimited. Weippert's quadrille band is engaged, and—

Smoke. For the convenience of lovers, the ship will carry a parson.

Chat. And the object?

Smoke. Pleasure and education. At every new country we shall drop anchor for at least a week, that the children may go to school and learn the language. The trip must answer: 'twill occupy only three years, and we've forgotten nothing to make it delightful—nothing from hot rolls to cork jackets.

Brown. And now, sir, the third venture?

Smoke. That, sir, is a company to buy the Serpentine River for a Grand Junction Temperance Cemetery.
Brown. What! so many watery graves?
Smoke. Yes, sir, with floating tombstones. Here's the prospectus. Look here; surmounted by a hyacinth—the very emblem of temperance—a hyacinth flowering in the limpid flood. Now, if you don't feel equal to the lucifers—I know his lordship's goodness—he'll give you up the cemetery. (*Aside to Chatham*: A family vault as a bonus to the chairman.)
Sir P. What a beautiful subject for a speech! Water-lilies and aquatic plants gemming the translucent crystal, shells of rainbow brightness, a constant supply of gold and silver fish, with the right of angling secured to shareholders. The extent of the river being necessarily limited, will render lying there so select, so very respectable.

NARRATIVE (POETRY).

Little Golden-Hair.

Little Golden-hair was watching, in the window broad and high,
    For the coming of her father, who had gone the foe to fight:
He had left her in the morning, and had told her not to cry,
    But to have a kiss all ready when he came to her at night.
        She had wandered all the day,
        In her simple childish way,
        And had asked, as time went on,
        Where her father could have gone:
She had heard the muskets firing, she had counted every one,
    Till the number grew so many that it was too great a load;
Then the evening fell upon her, clear of sound of shot or gun,
    And she gazed with wistful waiting down the dusty Concord road.

Little Golden-hair had listened, not a single week before,
    While the heavy sand was falling on her mother's coffin-lid;
And she loved her father better for the loss that then she bore,
    And thought of him, and yearned for him, whatever else she did.

So she wondered all the day
What could make her father stay,
And she cried a little too,
As he told her not to do ;

And the sun sank slowly downward, and went grandly out of sight,
And she had the kiss all ready on his lips to be bestowed ;
But the shadows made one shadow, and the twilight grew to night,
And she looked, and looked, and listened, down the dusty Concord road.

Then the night grew lighter and lighter, and the moon rose full and round,
In the little sad face peering, looking piteously and mild ;
Still upon the walks of gravel there was heard no welcome sound,
And no father came there, eager for the kisses of his child.

Long and sadly did she wait,
Listening at the cottage gate ;
Then she felt a quick alarm,
Lest he might have come to harm.

With no bonnet but her tresses, no companion but her fears,
And no guide except the moonbeams that the pathway dimly showed,
With a little sob of sorrow, quick she threw away her tears,
And alone she bravely started down the dusty Concord road.

And for many a mile she struggled, full of weariness and pain,
Calling loudly for her father, that her voice he might not miss ;
Till at last, among a number of the wounded and the slain,
Was the white face of the soldier, waiting for his daughter's kiss.

Softly to his lips she crept,
Not to wake him as he slept ;
Then, with her young heart at rest,
Laid her head upon his breast.

And upon the dead face smiling, with the living one near by,
  All the night a golden streamlet of the moonbeams gently
  flowed ;
One to live a lonely orphan, one beneath the sod to lie—
  They found them in the morning on the dusty Concord road.

A Legend of Bregenz.

(Verse printed as Prose.)

Girt round with rugged mountains the fair Lake Constance lies ; in her blue heart reflected, shine back the starry skies. Midnight is there ; and Silence, enthroned in heaven, looks down upon her own calm mirror, upon a sleeping town : for Bregenz, that quaint city upon the Tyrol shore, has stood above Lake Constance a thousand years and more.

Mountain and lake and valley a sacred legend know of how the town was saved one night three hundred years ago. Far from her home and kindred a Tyrol maid had fled, to serve in the Swiss valleys, and toil for daily bread ; and every year that fleeted so silently and fast, seemed to bear farther from her the memory of the past. And so she dwelt : the valley more peaceful year by year ; when suddenly strange portents of some great deed seemed near.

One day, out in the meadow, with strangers from the town some secret plan discussing, the men walked up and down. At eve they all assembled ; then care and doubt were fled ; with jovial laugh they feasted ; the board was nobly spread. The elder of the village rose up, his glass in hand, and cried, ' We drink the downfall of an accursed land ! The night is growing darker ; ere one more day is flown, Bregenz, our foeman's stronghold, Bregenz, shall be our own ! '

The women shrank in terror (yet pride, too, had her part), but one poor Tyrol maiden felt death within her heart. Nothing she heard around her (though shouts rang forth again) ; gone were the green Swiss valleys, the pasture and the plain ; before her eyes one vision, and in her heart one cry that said, ' Go forth ! save Bregenz, and then, if need be, die ! ' With trembling haste and breathless, with noiseless step, she sped ;

horses and weary cattle were standing in the shed ; she loosed the strong, white charger, that fed from out her hand ; she mounted, and she turned his head towards her native land.

Out—out into the darkness—faster, and still more fast—the smooth grass flies behind her, the chestnut wood is passed. 'Faster!' she cries, 'oh, faster!' Eleven the church-bells chime. 'Oh God,' she cries, 'help Bregenz, and bring me there in time!' But louder than bells' ringing, or lowing of the kine, grows nearer in the midnight the rushing of the Rhine. She strives to pierce the blackness, and looser throws the rein ; her steed must breast the waters that dash above his mane. How gallantly, how nobly, he struggles through the foam, and see—in the far distance shine out the lights of home! They reach the gates of Bregenz just as the midnight rings, and out come serf and soldier to meet the news she brings.

Bregenz is saved! Ere daylight her battlements are manned ; defiance greets the army that marches on the land. Three hundred years are vanished, and yet upon the hill an old stone gateway rises to do her honour still. And there, when Bregenz women sit spinning in the shade, they see in quaint old carving the charger and the maid. And when, to guard old Bregenz by gateway, street, and tower, the warder paces all night long and calls each passing hour ; ' Nine,' ' ten,' 'eleven,' he cries aloud. And then (oh, crown of fame!), when midnight pauses in the skies, he calls the maiden's name!

Grace Darling.

All night the storm had raged, nor ceased, nor paused,
When, as day broke, the Maid, through misty air,
Espies far off a Wreck, amid the surf,
Beating on one of those disastrous isles—
Half of a Vessel, half—no more ; the rest
Had vanished, swallowed up with all that there
Had for the common safety striven in vain,
Or thither thronged for refuge. With quick glance
Daughter and Sire through optic-glass discern,

Clinging about the remnant of this Ship,
Creatures—how precious in the Maiden's sight !
For whom, belike, the old Man grieves still more
Than for their fellow-sufferers engulfed
Where every parting agony is hushed,
And hope and fear mix not in further strife.
" But courage, Father ! let us out to sea—
A few may yet be saved." The Daughter's words,
Her earnest tone, and look beaming with faith,
Dispel the Father's doubts : nor do they lack
The noble-minded Mother's helping hand
To launch the boat; and with her blessing cheered,
And inwardly sustained by silent prayer
Together they put forth, Father and Child !
Each grasps an oar, and struggling on they go—
Rivals in effort; and, alike intent
Here to elude and there surmount, they watch
The billows lengthening, mutually crossed
And shattered, and re-gathering their might ;
As if the tumult, by the Almighty's will
Were, in the conscious sea, roused and prolonged,
That woman's fortitude—so tried, so proved—
May brighten more and more !

                    True to the mark,
They stem the current of that perilous gorge,
Their arms still strengthening with the strengthening heart,
Though danger, as the Wreck is near'd, becomes
More imminent. Not unseen do they approach ;
And rapture, with varieties of fear
Incessantly conflicting, thrills the frames
Of those who, in that dauntless energy,
Foretaste deliverance ; but the least perturbed
Can scarcely trust his eyes, when he perceives
That of the pair—tossed on the waves to bring
Hope to the hopeless, to the dying, life—
One is a Woman, a poor earthly sister,
Or, be the Visitant other than she seems,
A guardian Spirit sent from pitying Heaven,
In woman's shape. But why prolong the tale,

Casting weak words amid a host of thoughts
Armed to repel them? Every hazard faced
And difficulty mastered, with resolve
That no one breathing should be left to perish,
This last remainder of the crew are all
Placed in the little boat, then o'er the deep
Are safely borne, landed upon the beach
And, in fulfilment of God's mercy, lodged
Within the sheltering Lighthouse.

Bishop Hatto.

The summer and autumn had been so wet,
That in winter the corn was growing yet;—
'Twas a piteous sight to see all around
The grain lie rotting on the ground.

Every day the starving poor
Crowded around Bishop Hatto's door,—
For he had a plentiful last year's store,
And all the neighbourhood could tell
His granaries were furnished well.

At last Bishop Hatto appointed a day
To quiet the poor without delay;
He bade them to his great barn repair,
And they should have food for the winter there.

Rejoiced such tidings good to hear,
The poor folk flocked from far and near;
The great barn was full, as it could hold—
Of women and children, and young and old.

Then when he saw it could hold no more,
Bishop Hatto he made fast the door;
And while for mercy on Christ they call,
He set fire to the barn and burnt them all.

"I' faith, 'tis an excellent bonfire," quoth he,
"And the country is greatly obliged to me,
For ridding it in these times forlorn
Of rats, that only consume the corn."

So then to his palace returnèd he,
And he sat down to supper merrily,
And he slept that night like an innocent man ;
But Bishop Hatto never slept again.

In the morning, as he entered the hall,
Where his picture hung against the wall,
A sweat like death all over him came,
For the rats had eaten it out of the frame.

As he looked there came a man from the farm,
He had a countenance white with alarm ;
"My lord, I opened your granaries this morn,
And the rats had eaten all your corn."

Another came running presently,
And he was pale as pale could be,
"Fly, my Lord Bishop, fly," quoth he,
"Ten thousand rats are coming this way—
And the Lord forgive you for yesterday !"

"I'll go to my tower on the Rhine," replied he,
"'Tis the safest place in Germany ;
The walls are high, and the shores are steep,
And the stream is strong, and the water deep."

Bishop Hatto fearfully hastened away,
And he crossed the Rhine without delay,
And reached his tower, and barred with care
All the windows, doors, and loopholes there.

He laid him down, and closed his eyes,
But soon a scream made him arise ;—
He started, and saw two eyes of flame
On his pillow from whence the screaming came.

He listened and looked ; it was only the cat ;
But the Bishop he grew more fearful for that,
For she sat screaming, mad with fear,
At the army of rats that was drawing near.

For they have swum over the river so deep,
And they have climbed the shores so steep,
And up the tower their way is bent
To do the work for which they were sent.

They are not to be told by the dozen or score,
By thousands they come, and by myriads and more ;
Such numbers have never been heard of before,
Such a judgment had never been witnessed of yore.

Down on his knees the Bishop fell,
And faster and faster his beads did he tell,
As louder and louder drawing near
The gnawing of their teeth he could hear.

And in at the windows, and in at the door,
And through the walls helter-skelter they pour,
And down from the ceiling, and up through the floor,
From the right and the left, from behind and before,
From within and without, from above and below,
And all at once to the Bishop they go.

Sir Richard Grenville's Last Fight.

Our second Richard Grenville
   In days of great Queen Bess,
He did this deed, he played this part
   With true old nobleness
And wrath heroic that was nursed
To bear the fiercest battle-burst,
When maddened foes should wreak their worst.

Signalled the English Admiral,
   "Weigh or cut anchors." For
A Spanish fleet bore down, in all
   The majesty of war
Athwart our tack for many a mile
As there we lay off Florez Isle,
With crews half sick, all tired of toil.

Eleven of our twelve ships escaped ;
   Sir Richard stood alone !
Though there were three and fifty sail—
   A hundred men to one—
The old Sea-Rover would not run,
So long as he had man or gun ;
But he could die when all was done.

"The Demon 's broken loose, my lads,
   He comes from swarthy Spain ;
And we must sink him in the sea,
   Or hound him home again.
Now, you old War-dogs, show your paws !
Have at them tooth and nail and claws !"
And then his long, bright blade he draws.
"Push home ; my hardy pikemen,
   For we play a desperate part ;
To-day, my gunners, let them feel
   The pulse of England's heart !
They shall remember long that we
Once lived ; and think how shamefully
We shook them !—One to fifty-three."
With face of one who cheerily goes
   To meet his doom that day,
Sir Richard sprang upon his foes
   The foremost gave him way :
His round shot smashed them through and through,
At every flash white splinters flew :
And madder grew his fighting few.
They clasp the little ship Revenge
   As in the arms of fire ;
They run aboard her, six at once,
   Hearts beat, hot guns leap higher;
Through gory gaps the boarders swarm,
But still our English stay the storm,
The bulwark in their breast is firm.
Ship after ship, like broken waves
   That wash up on a rock,
Those mighty galleons fall back foiled,
   And shattered from the shock.
With fires she answers all their blows ;
Again, again, in pieces strews
The girdle round her as they close.
Some know not they are wounded till
   'Tis slippery where they stand ;
Then each one tighter grips his steel
   As 'twere Salvation's hand.

Grim faces glow through lurid night
With sweat of spirit shining bright:
Only the dead on deck turn white.

At daybreak the flame-picture fades
  In blackness and in blood ;
There, after fifteen hours of fight,
  The unconquered Sea-king stood
Defying all the powers of Spain :
Fifteen armadas hurled in vain,
And fifteen hundred foemen slain.

About that little bark Revenge
  The baffled Spaniards ride
At distance. Two of their good ships
  Were sunken at her side ;
The rest lie round her in a ring
As round the dying Lion-king,
The dogs, afraid of his death-spring.

Our pikes all broken, powder spent,
  Sails, masts, to shivers blown,
And with her dead and wounded crew
  The ship was going down !
Sir Richard's wounds were hot and deep ;
Then cried he with a proud pale lip,
"Ho ! Master Gunner, sink the ship !

"Make ready now, my Mariners,
  To go aloft with me,
That nothing to the Spaniard
  May remain of victory.
They cannot take us, nor we yield ;
So let us leave our battle-field,
Under the shelter of God's shield."

They had not heart to dare fulfil
  The stern Commander's word :
With swelling hearts, and welling eyes,
  They carried him aboard
The Spaniard's ship ; and round him stand
The warriors of his wasted band :
Then said he, feeling death at hand :

"Here die I, Richard Grenville,
  With a joyful and quiet mind;
I reach a Soldier's end, I leave
  A Soldier's fame behind,
Who for his Queen and Country fought,
For Honour and Religion wrought,
And died as a true Soldier ought."
Old heroes who could grandly do,
  As they could greatly dare,
A vesture, very glorious,
  Their shining spirits wear
Of noble deeds! God give us grace,
That we may see such face to face,
In our great day that comes apace.

The Singing of the Magnificat.
(By permission of the Author.)

In midst of wide green pasture lands, cut through
  By lines of alders bordering deep-banked streams,
Where bulrushes and yellow iris grew,
  And rest, and peace, and all the flower of dreams,
The Abbey stood—so still, it seemed a part
Of the marsh country's almost pulseless heart.

Where grey-green willows fringed the stream and pool,
  The lazy meek-faced cattle strayed to graze;
Sheep in the meadows cropped the grasses cool,
  And silver fish shone through the watery ways;
And many a load of fruit and load of corn
Into the Abbey storehouses was borne.

Yet though so much they had of life's good things,
  The monks but held them as a sacred trust,
Lent from the storehouse of the King of kings
  Till they, his stewards, should crumble back to dust.
"Not as our own," they said, "but as the Lord's,
All that the stream yields, or the land affords."

And all the villages and hamlets near
  Knew the monks' wealth, and how that wealth was spent.

In tribulation, sickness, want, or fear,
 First to the Abbey all the peasants went,
Certain to find a welcome, and to be
Helped in the hour of their extremity.

When plague or sickness smote the people sore,
 The Brothers prayed beside the dying bed,
And nursed the sick back into health once more,
 And through the horror and the danger said:
" How good is God, Who has such love for us,
He lets us tend His suffering children thus."

They in their simple ways and works were glad :
 Yet all men must have sorrows of their own.
And so a bitter grief the Brothers had,
 Nor mourned for others' heaviness alone.
This was the secret of their sorrowing,
That not a monk in all the house could sing !

Was it the damp air from the lovely marsh,
 Or strain of scarcely intermitted prayer,
That made their voices, when they sang, as harsh
 As any frog's that croaks in evening air—
That made less music in their hymns to lie
Than in the hoarsest wildfowl's hoarsest cry ?

If love could sweeten voice to sing a song,
 Theirs had been sweetest song was ever sung :
But their hearts' music reached their lips all wrong,
 The soul's intent foiled by the traitorous tongue
That marred the chapel's peace, and seemed to scare
The rapt devotion lingering in the air.

The birds that in the chapel built their nests,
 And in the stone-work found their small lives fair,
Flew thence with hurried wings and fluttering breasts
 When rang the bell to call the monks to prayer.
" Why will they sing," they twittered, " Why at all ?
In heaven their silence must be festival ! "

The Brothers prayed with penance and with tears,
 That God would let them give some little part
Out for the solace of their own sad ears
 Of all the music crowded in their heart.

Their nature and the marsh-air had their way,
And still they sang more vilely every day.
And all their prayers and fasts availing not
    To give them voices sweet, their souls' desire,
The Abbot said, "Gifts He did not allot
    God at our hands will not again require.
The love He gives us He will ask again
In love to Him and to our fellow-men.

"Praise Him we must, and since we cannot praise
    As we would choose, we praise Him as we can.
In heaven we shall be taught the angels' ways
    Of singing—we afford to wait a span.
In singing, as in toil, do ye your best;
God will adjust the balance—do the rest!"

But one good Brother, anxious to remove
    This, the reproach now laid on them so long,
Rejected counsel, and for very love
    Besought a Brother, skilled in art of song,
To come to them—his cloister far to leave—
And sing *Magnificat* on Christmas Eve.

So when each brown monk duly sought his place,
    By two and two, slow pacing to the choir,
Shrined in his dark oak stall, the strange monk's face
    Shone with a light as of devotion's fire.
Good, young and fair, his seemed a form wherein
Pure beauty left no room at all for sin.

And when the time for singing it had come,
    '*Magnificat*,' face raised, and voice, he sang:
Each in his stall the monks stood glad and dumb,
    As through the chancel's dusk his voice outrang,
Pure, clear, and perfect—as the thrushes sing
Their first impulsive welcome of the spring.

At the first notes the Abbot's heart spoke low:
"O God, accept this singing, seeing we,
Had we the power, would ever praise Thee so—
    Would ever, Lord, Thou know'st, sing thus for Thee;
Thus in our hearts Thy hymns are ever sung,
As he Thou blessest sings them with his tongue."

But as the voice rose higher and more sweet,
    The Abbot's heart said, "Thou hast heard us grieve,
And sent an angel from beside Thy feet,
    To sing *Magnificat* on Christmas Eve ;
To ease our ache of soul and let us see
How we some day in heaven shall sing to Thee."

Through the cold Christmas night the hymn rang out,
    In perfect cadence, clear as sunlit rain—
Such heavenly music that the birds without
    Beat their warm wings against the window pane,
Scattering the frosted crystal snow outspread
Upon the stone-lace and the window-lead.

The white moon through the window seemed to gaze
    On the pure face and eyes the singer raised ;
The storm-wind hushed the clamour of its ways,
    God seemed to stoop to hear Himself thus praised,
And breathless all the Brothers stood, and still
Reached longing souls out to the music's thrill.

Old years came back, and half remembered hours,
    Dreams of delight that never was to be,
Mothers' remembered kiss, the funeral flowers
    Laid on the grave of life's felicity ;
An infinite dear passion of regret
Swept through their hearts, and left their eyelids wet.

The birds beat ever at the window, till—
    They broke the pane, and so could entrance win ;
Their slender feet clung to the window-sill,
    And though with them the bitter air came in,
The monks were glad that the birds too should hear,
Since to God's creatures all, His praise is dear.

The lovely music waxed and waned, and sank,
    And brought less conscious sadness in its train,
Unrecognized despair that thinks to thank
    God for a joy renounced, a chosen pain—
And deems that peace which is but stifled life
Dulled by a too-prolonged unfruitful strife.

When, service done, the Brothers gathered round
    To thank the singer—modest-eyed, said he :

"Not mine the grace, if grace indeed abound ;
   God gave the power, if any power there be ;
If I in hymn or psalm clear voice can raise,
   As His the gift, so His be all the praise !"
That night—the Abbot, lying on his bed—
   A sudden flood of radiance on him fell,
Poured from the crucifix above his head,
   And cast a stream of light across his cell—
And in the fullest fervour of the light
An Angel stood, glittering, and great, and white.

His wings of thousand rainbow clouds seemed made,
   A thousand lamps of love shone in his eyes,
The light of dawn upon his brows was laid,
   Odours of thousand flowers of Paradise
Filled all the cell, and through the heart there stirred
A sense of music that could not be heard.

The Angel spoke—his voice was low and sweet
   As the sea's murmur on low-lying shore—
Or whisper of the wind in ripened wheat :
   "Brother," he said, "the God we both adore
Has sent me down to ask, is all not right ?—
Why was *Magnificat* not sung to-night ?"

Tranced in the joy the Angel's presence brought,
   The Abbot answered : "All these weary years
We have sung our best—but always have we thought
   Our voices were unworthy heavenly ears ;
And so to-night we found a clearer tongue,
And by it the *Magnificat* was sung."

The Angel answered, " All these happy years
   In heaven has your *Magnificat* been heard ;
This night alone, the Angels' listening ears
   Of all its music caught no single word.
Say, who is he whose goodness is not strong
Enough to bear the burden of his song ?"

The Abbot named his name.   "Ah, why," he cried,
   "Have angels heard not what we found so dear ?"
"Only pure hearts," the Angel's voice replied,
   "Can carry human songs up to God's ear ;

To-night in heaven was missed the sweetest praise
That ever rises from earth's mud-stained maze.
"The monk who sang *Magnificat* is filled
   With lust of praise, and with hypocrisy ;
He sings for earth—in heaven his notes are stilled
   By muffling weight of deadening vanity ;
His heart is chained to earth, and cannot bear
His singing higher than the listening air !
" From purest hearts most perfect music springs,
   And while you mourned your voices were not sweet,
Marred by the accident of earthly things,—
   In heaven, God, listening, judged your song complete.
The sweetest of earth's music came from you,
The music of a noble life and true ! "

The Story of the Faithful Soul

The fettered Spirits linger
   In purgatorial pain,
With penal fires effacing
   Their last faint earthly stain,
Which life's imperfect sorrow
   Had tried to cleanse in vain.

Yet, on each feast of Mary
   Their sorrow finds release,
For the great Archangel Michael
   Comes down and bids it cease ;
And the name of these brief respites
   Is called " Our Lady's Peace."

Yet once—so runs the Legend—
   When the Archangel came,
And all these holy spirits
   Rejoiced at Mary's name ;
One voice alone was wailing,
   Still wailing on the same.

And though a great Te Deum
   The happy echoes woke,
This one discordant wailing
   Through the sweet voices broke ;

So when St. Michael questioned,
    Thus the poor spirit spoke :—
" I am not cold or thankless,
    Although I still complain ;
I prize our Lady's blessing,
    Although it comes in vain
To still my bitter anguish,
    Or quench my ceaseless pain.

" On earth a heart that loved me
    Still lives and mourns me there,
And the shadow of his anguish
    Is more than I can bear ;
All the torment that I suffer
    Is the thought of his despair.

" The evening of my bridal
    Death took my Life away ;
Not all Love's passionate pleading
    Could gain an hour's delay ;
And he I left has suffered
    A whole year since that day.

" If I could only see him,—
    If I could only go
And speak one word of comfort
    And solace,—then, I know
He would endure with patience,
    And strive against his woe."

Thus the Archangel answered :—
    " Your time of pain is brief,
And soon the peace of Heaven
    Will give you full relief ;
Yet if his earthly comfort
    So much outweighs your grief,

" Then through a special mercy
    I offer you this grace,—
You may seek him who mourns you
    And look upon his face,
And speak to him of comfort
    For one short minute's space.

"But when that time is ended,
 Return here, and remain
A thousand years in torment,
 A thousand years in pain:
Thus dearly must you purchase
 The comfort he will gain."

. . . .

The Lime-trees' shade at evening
 Is spreading broad and wide;
Beneath their fragrant arches,
 Pace slowly, side by side,
In low and tender converse,
 A Bridegroom and his Bride.

The night is calm and stilly,
 No other sound is there
Except their happy voices:
 What is that cold bleak air
That passes through the Lime-trees
 And stirs the Bridegroom's hair?

While one low cry of anguish,
 Like the last dying wail
Of some dumb, hunted creature,
 Is borne upon the gale:—
Why does the Bridegroom shudder
 And turn so deathly pale?

. . . .

Near Purgatory's entrance
 The radiant Angels wait;
It was the great St. Michael
 Who closed that gloomy gate
When the poor wandering spirit
 Came back to meet her fate.

"Pass on," thus spoke the Angel:
 "Heaven's joy is deep and vast;
Pass on, pass on, poor Spirit,
 For Heaven is yours at last;
In that one minute's anguish
 Your thousand years have passed."

Paul Revere's Ride.
(Verse printed as Prose.)

Listen, my children, and you shall hear of the midnight ride of Paul Revere, on the eighteenth of April, in 'Seventy-five; hardly a man is now alive who remembers that famous day and year. . . . . He said to his friend, "If the British march by land or sea from the town to-night, hang a lantern aloft in the belfry-arch of the North Church tower as a signal light,—one, if by land, and two, if by sea; and I on the opposite shore will be, ready to ride and spread the alarm through every Middlesex village and farm, for the country-folk to be up and to arm." Then he said, "Good night!" and, with muffled oar, silently rowed to the Charlestown shore, just as the moon rose over the bay, where swinging wide at her moorings lay the *Somerset*, British man-of-war; a phantom-ship, with each mast and spar across the moon like a prison bar, and a huge black hulk, that was magnified by its own reflection in the tide.

Meanwhile, his friend, through alley and street, wanders and watches with eager ears, till in the silence around him he hears the muster of men at the barrack-door, the sound of arms, and the tramp of feet, and the measured tread of the grenadiers marching down to their boats on the shore. Then he climbed to the tower of the Old North Church, up the wooden stairs, with stealthy tread, to the belfry-chamber over-head, and startled the pigeons from their perch on the sombre rafters, that round him made masses and moving shapes of shade,—up the trembling ladder, steep and tall, to the highest window in the wall, where he paused to listen and look down a moment on the roofs of the town, and the moonlight flowing over all. Beneath, in the churchyard, lay the dead, in their night-encampment on the hill, wrapped in silence so deep and still that he could hear, like a sentinel's tread, the watchful night-wind as it went creeping along from tent to tent, and seeming to whisper, "All is well!" A moment only he feels the spell of the place and the hour, and the secret dread of the lonely belfry and the dead; for suddenly all his thoughts are bent on a shadowy something far away, where the river widens to meet the bay,—a line of black that bends and floats on the rising tide, like a bridge of boats.

Meanwhile, impatient to mount and ride, booted and spurred, with a heavy stride on the opposite shore walked Paul Revere. Now he patted his horse's side, now gazed at the landscape far and near, then, impetuous, stamped the earth, and turned and tightened his saddle-girth; but mostly he watched with eager search the belfry tower of the Old North Church, as it rose above the graves on the hill, lonely and spectral, and sombre and still.   And lo ! as he looks, on the belfry's height a glimmer, and then a gleam of light! He springs to the saddle, the bridle he turns, but lingers and gazes, till full on his sight a second lamp in the belfry burns !   .   .   .   .   A hurry of hoofs in a village street, a shape in the moonlight, a bulk in the dark, and beneath, from the pebbles, in passing, a spark struck out by a steed flying fearless and fleet; that was all ! And yet, through the gloom and the light, the fate of a nation was riding that night ; and the spark struck out by that steed in his flight, kindled the land into flame with its heat.

It was twelve by the village clock when he crossed the bridge into Medford town. He heard the crowing of the cock and the barking of the farmer's dog, and felt the damp of the river fog, that rises after the sun goes down.   .   .   .   .   It was one by the village clock when he galloped into Lexington. He saw the gilded weathercock swim in the moonlight as he passed, and the meeting-house windows, blank and bare, gaze at him with a spectral glare, as if they already stood aghast at the bloody work they would look upon.   .   .   .   .   It was two by the village clock when he came to the bridge in Concord town. He heard the bleating of the flock and the twitter of birds among the trees, and felt the breath of the morning breeze blowing over the meadows brown. And one was safe and asleep in his bed who at the bridge would be first to fall, who that day would be lying dead, pierced by a British musket-ball.

You know the rest. In the books you have read how the British Regulars fired and fled,—how the farmers gave them ball for ball, from behind each fence and farmyard wall, chasing the red-coats down the lane, then crossing the field to emerge again under the trees at the turn of the road, and only pausing to fire and load. So through the night rode

Paul Revere; and so through the night went his cry of alarm to every Middlesex village and farm,—a cry of defiance and not of fear; a voice in the darkness, a knock at the door, and a word that shall echo for evermore! For, borne on the night-wind of the Past, through all our history, to the last, in the hour of darkness and peril and need the people will waken and listen to hear the hurrying hoof-beats of that steed, and the midnight message of Paul Revere.

The Feast of Belshazzar.
(Abridged.)

(Verse printed as Prose.)

High on a throne of ivory and gold, from crown to footstool clad in purple fold, Lord of the East from sea to distant sea—the King, Belshazzar, feasteth royally: vessels of silver, cups of crusted gold, blush with a brighter red than all they hold; pendulous lamps, like planets of the night, fling on the diadems a fragrant light. No lack of goodly company was there, no lack of laughing eyes to light the cheer.

It seemed, no summer-cloud of passing woe could fling its shadow on so fair a show; it seemed the gallant forms that feasted there were all too high for woe, too great for care. Whence then the anxious eye, the altered tone, the dull presentiment no heart would own? It is not that they know the spoiler waits, harnessed for battle, at the brazen gates; it is not that they hear the watchman's call mark the slow minutes on the leagured wall: the clash of quivers and the ring of spears make pleasant music in a soldier's ears; and not a scabbard hideth sword to-night, that hath not glimmered in the front of fight.—May not the blood in every beating vein have quick fore-knowledge of some coming pain? even as the prisoned silver, dead and dumb, shrinks at cold Winter's foot-fall ere he come.

The King is troubled, and his heart's unrest heaves the broad purple of his belted breast: sudden he speaks—"What! doth the beaded juice savour like hyssop, that ye scorn its use? wear ye so pitiful and sad a soul that tramp of foemen scares ye from the bowl? Think ye the gods, on yonder starry floor, tremble for terror when the thunders roar? Are we not gods? have we not fought with God? and shall we shiver at a robber's nod? No!—let them batter till the brazen bars ring merry mocking of their idle wars; their fall is fated for to-morrow's sun; the lion rouses when his feast is done:—crown me a cup—and fill the bowls we brought from Judah's temple when the fight was fought:—drink, till the merry madness fills the soul, to Salem's conqueror, in Salem's bowl!"

His eager lips are on the jewelled brink—hath the cup poison that he doubts to drink? is there a spell upon the sparkling gold, that so his fevered fingers quit their hold? Whom sees he where he gazes? What is there—freezing his vision into fearful stare? . . .

There cometh forth a Hand!—upon the stone graving the symbols of a speech unknown; fingers like mortal fingers!—leaving there the blank wall flashing characters of fear;—and still it glideth silently and slow, and still beneath the spectral letters grow!—now the scroll endeth—now, the seal is set—the Hand is gone!—the record tarries yet.

With wand of ebony and sable stole, Chaldæa's wisest scan the spectral scroll: strong in the lessons of a lying art, each comes to gaze, but gazes to depart; and still, for mystic sign and muttered spell, the graven letters guard their secret well; gleam they for warning?—glare they to condemn?—God speaketh,—but He speaketh not for them.

Oh! ever; when the happy laugh is dumb, all the joy gone, and all the anguish come;—when strong adversity and subtle pain wring the sad soul and rack the throbbing brain;—when friends once faithful, hearts once all our own, leave us to weep, to bleed, and die alone;—when fears and cares the lonely thought employ, and clouds of sorrow hide the sun of joy;—when weary life, breathing reluctant breath, hath no hope sweeter than the hope of death;—then, the best counsel and the best relief to cheer the spirit or to cheat the grief,—the only calm, the only comfort heard, comes in the music of a Woman's word:—like beacon-bell, on some wild island-shore, silvery ringing in the tempest's roar, whose sound, borne shipward through the midnight gloom, tells of the path, and turns her from her doom.

So, in the silence of that awful hour, when baffled magic mourned its parted power—when Kings were pale and Satraps shook for fear—a Woman speaketh—and the wisest hear. She—the high daughter of a thousand thrones, telling, with trembling lip and timid tones, of him—the Captive,—in the feast forgot, who readeth visions—him, whose wondrous lot sends him to lighten doubt and lessen gloom, and gaze undazzled on the days to come—Daniel the Hebrew,—such his name and race, held by a monarch highest in his grace, he may declare—oh !—bid them quickly send !—so may the mystery have happy end !

Calmly and silent—as the fair full moon comes sailing upward in the sky of June—so through the hall the Prophet passed along, so from before him fell the festal throng. His lip was steady and his accent clear, "The King hath needed me, and I am here."

"Art thou the Prophet? read me yonder scroll whose undeciphered horror daunts my soul :—there shall be guerdon for the grateful task, fitted for me to give, for thee to ask ;— a chain to deck thee, and a robe to grace,—thine the third throne, and thou the third in place."

"Keep for thyself the guerdon and the gold—what God hath graved, God's Prophet shall unfold ! Could not thy father's crime, thy father's fate, teach thee this terror thou hast learnt too late ? Hast thou not read the lesson of his life, 'Who wars with God shall strive a losing strife ?' Ay! when his heart was hard, his spirit high, God drove him from his kingly majesty, far from the brotherhood of fellow-men, to seek for dwelling in the desert den : where bitter-biting frost and dews of night schooled him in sorrow, till he knew the right—that God is ruler of the rulers still, and setting up as sovereign whom He will. Oh ! hadst thou treasured, in repentant breast, thy father's pride, fall, penitence and rest, and bowed submissive to Jehovah's will, then had thy sceptre been a sceptre still. But thou hast mocked the majesty of heaven, and shamed the vessels to its service given ; and thou hast fashioned idols of thine own—idols of gold, of silver, and of stone : to them hast bowed the knee, and breathed the breath, and they must help thee in the hour of death. Woe for the sign unseen, the sin forgot ! God was among ye, and ye knew it not! Hear what He writeth there :—'Thy race is run ; thy years are numbered, and thy days are done : thy soul hath mounted in the scale of fate ; the Lord hath weighed thee, and thou lackest weight! Now, in thy palace-porch, the spoilers stand, to seize thy sceptre, to divide thy land.'"

That night they slew him on his father's throne, the deed unnoticed, and the hand unknown :—crownless and sceptreless, Belshazzar lay—a robe of purple round a form of clay!

Baby in Church.

Aunt Nellie had fashioned a dainty thing,
    Of hamburg and ribbon and lace,
And Mamma had said, as she settled it 'round
    Our beautiful Baby's face,
Where the dimples play and the laughter lies
Like sunbeams hid in her violet eyes :
"If the day is pleasant and Baby is good,
She may go to church and wear her new hood."

Then Ben, aged six, began to tell,
    In elder-brotherly way,
How very, very good she must be
    If she went to church next day.
He told of the church, the choir and the crowd,
And the man up in front who talked so loud ;
But she must not talk nor laugh nor sing,
But just sit as quiet as anything.

And so, on a beautiful Sabbath in May,
    When the fruit-buds burst into flowers
(There wasn't a blossom on bush or tree
    So fair as this blossom of ours),
All in her white dress, dainty and new,
Our Baby sat in the family pew.
The grand, sweet music, the reverent air,
The solemn hush and the voice of prayer,

Filled all her baby soul with awe,
    As she sat in her little place,

And the holy look that the angels wear
    Seemed pictured upon her face.
And the sweet words uttered so long ago
Came into my mind with a rhythmic flow :
" Of such is the Kingdom of Heaven," said He,
And I knew that He spake of such as she.
The sweet-voiced organ pealed forth again,
    The collection-box came round,
And Baby dropped her penny in,
    And smiled at the chinking sound.
Alone in the choir Aunt Nellie stood,
Waiting the close of the soft prelude,
To begin her solo. High and strong
She struck the first note, clear and long.
She held it, and all were charmed but one,
    Who, with all the might she had,
Sprang to her little feet and cried :
    "*Aunt Nellie, you's being bad !*"
The audience smiled, the minister coughed,
The little boys in the corner laughed,
The tenor-man shook like an aspen leaf
And hid his face in his handkerchief.
And poor Aunt Nellie never could tell
    How she finished that terrible strain,
But says that nothing on earth would tempt
    Her to go through the scene again.
So, we have decided, perhaps 'tis best,
For her sake, ours, and all the rest,
That we wait, maybe for a year or two,
Ere our Baby re-enter the family pew.

Mary Queen of Scots.

I look'd far back into other years, and lo ! in bright array,
I saw, as in a dream, the forms of ages passed away.
    It was a stately convent, with its old and lofty walls,
And gardens with their broad green walks, where soft the
    footstep falls ;

And o'er the antique dial-stone the creeping shadow passed,
And all around the noon-day sun a drowsy radiance cast.
No sound of busy life was heard, save, from the cloister dim,
The tinkling of the silver bell, or the sisters' holy hymn.
And there five noble maidens sat beneath the orchard trees,
In that first budding spring of youth, when all its prospects please;
And little recked they, when they sang, or knelt at vesper prayers,
That Scotland knew no prouder names—held none more dear than theirs:
And little even the loveliest thought, before the holy shrine,
Of royal blood and high descent from the ancient Stuart line:
Calmly her happy days flew on, uncounted in their flight,
And as they flew, they left behind a long-continuing light.

 The scene was changed. It was the court, the gay court of Bourbon,
And 'neath a thousand silver lamps, a thousand courtiers throng;
And proudly kindles Henry's eye—well pleased, I ween, to see
The land assemble all its wealth of grace and chivalry:—
But fairer far than all the rest who bask on fortune's tide,
Effulgent in the light of youth, is she, the new-made bride!
The homage of a thousand hearts—the fond, deep love of one—
The hopes that dance around a life whose charms are but begun,—
They lighten up her chestnut eye, they mantle o'er her cheek,
They sparkle on her open brow, and high-souled joy bespeak:
Ah! who shall blame, if scarce that day, through all its brilliant hours,
She thought of that quiet convent's calm, its sunshine and its flowers?

 The scene was changed. It was a bark that slowly held its way,
And o'er its lee the coast of France in the light of evening lay;
And on its deck a Lady sat, who gazed with tearful eyes
Upon the fast receding hills, that dim and distant rise.
No marvel that the Lady wept,—there was no land on earth
She loved like that dear land, although she owed it not her birth:

It was her mother's land, the land of childhood and of friends,—
It was the land where she had found for all her griefs amends,—
The land where her dead husband slept—the land where she
    had known
The tranquil convent's hushed repose, and the splendours of a
    throne :
No marvel that the Lady wept—it was the land of France—
The chosen home of chivalry—the garden of romance !
The past was bright, like those dear hills so far behind her
    bark ;
The future, like the gathering night, was ominous and dark !
One gaze again—one long, last gaze,—" Adieu, fair France, to
    thee ! "
The breeze comes forth—she is alone on the unconscious sea !

    The scene was changed. It was an eve of raw and surly
    mood,
And in a turret-chamber high of ancient Holyrood
Sat Mary, listening to the rain, and sighing with the winds,
That seemed to suit the stormy state of men's uncertain
    minds.
The touch of care had blanched her cheek—her smile was
    sadder now,
The weight of royalty had pressed too heavy on her brow ;
And traitors to her councils came, and rebels to the field,
The Stuart SCEPTRE well she swayed, but the SWORD she could
    not wield.
She thought of all her blighted hopes—the dreams of youth's
    brief day,
And summoned Rizzio with his lute, and bade the minstrel
    play
The songs she loved in early years—the songs of gay Navarre,
The songs perchance that erst were sung by gallant Chatelar ;
They half beguiled her of her cares, they soothed her into
    smiles,
They won her thoughts from bigot zeal, and fierce domestic
    broils :—
But hark ! the tramp of armed men ! the Douglas' battle-cry !
They come—they come !—and lo ! the scowl of Ruthven's
    hollow eye !

And swords are drawn, and daggers gleam, and tears and words are vain—
The ruffian steel is in his heart—the faithful Rizzio's slain!
Then Mary Stuart dashed aside the tears that trickling fell:
"Now for my father's arm!" she said; "my woman's heart, farewell!"

The scene was changed. It was a lake, with one small lonely isle,
And there, within the prison-walls of its baronial pile,
Stern men stood menacing their queen, till she should stoop to sign
The traitorous scroll that snatched the crown from her ancestral line:—
"My lords, my lords!" the captive said, "were I but once more free,
With ten good knights on yonder shore, to aid my cause and me,
That parchment would I scatter wide to every breeze that blows,
And once more reign a Stuart-queen o'er my remorseless foes!"
A red spot burned upon her cheek—streamed her rich tresses down,
She wrote the words—she stood erect—a queen without a crown!

The scene was changed. A royal host a royal banner bore,
And the faithful of the land stood round their smiling queen once more;—
She stayed her steed upon a hill—she saw them marching by—
She heard their shouts—she read success in every flashing eye.—
The tumult of the strife begins—it roars—it dies away;
And Mary's troops and banners now, and courtiers—where are they?
Scattered and strown, and flying far, defenceless and undone;—
Alas! to think what she has lost, and all that guilt has won!
—Away! away! thy gallant steed must act no laggard's part;
Yet vain his speed—for thou dost bear the arrow in thy heart!

The scene was changed. Beside the block a sullen headsman stood,
And gleamed the broad axe in his hand, that soon must drip with blood.

With slow and steady step there came a Lady through the hall,
And breathless silence chained the lips, and touched the hearts of all.
I knew that queenly form again, though blighted was its bloom,—
I saw that grief had decked it out—an offering for the tomb!
I knew the eye, though faint its light, that once so brightly shone ;
I knew the voice, though feeble now, that thrilled with every tone ;
I knew the ringlets, almost gray, once threads of living gold ;
I knew that bounding grace of step—that symmetry of mould!
Even now I see her far away, in that calm convent aisle,
I hear her chant her vesper hymn, I mark her holy smile,—
Even now I see her bursting forth, upon the bridal morn,
A new star in the firmament, to light and glory born!
Alas! the change!—she placed her foot upon a triple throne,
And on the scaffold now she stands—beside the block —ALONE!
The little dog that licks her hand—the last of all the crowd
Who sunned themselves beneath her glance, and round her footsteps bowed!
—Her neck is bared—the blow is struck—the soul is passed away!
The bright—the beautiful—is now a bleeding piece of clay!
The dog is moaning piteously ; and, as it gurgles o'er,
Laps the warm blood that trickling runs unheeded to the floor!
The blood of beauty, wealth, and power—the heart-blood of a queen—
The noblest of the Stuart race—the fairest earth has seen,—
Lapped by a dog!—a solemn text!—Go, think of it alone ;
Then weigh, against a grain of sand, the glories of a throne!

The Last Shot:

A TALE OF THE INDIAN MUTINY.

Three to ride and to save, one to ride and be saved—
That's the key of my tale, boys, deep on my heart engraved.

With death before and behind, through dangers many and nigh,
Four to ride together, and three of the four to die.
There was the Captain's daughter, a young and delicate girl,
With her childlike face and shining eyes, and hair of sunniest curl;
She looked like a beautiful flower, too slight to be even caressed,
Yet never had hero braver heart than beat in that girlish breast.

And then there was Sergeant Gray, a martinet old and grim;
The biggest tyrant that ever lived was a lamb compared to him;
Ne'er-dae-weel Douglas next, a Borderer born and bred,
With a sin on his soul for every hair that grew on his handsome head.
And then there was Fighting Denis—Denis, the stout of heart,
Foremost in every row and brawl, and skilled in the "manly art;"
Take the three altogether, the truth is, old and young,
They were three o' the greatest scamps, boys, that ever deserved to be hung.

What was *she* doing, you ask, alone with fellows like these,
Down by the Ganges' bank, hid 'mong the mango trees?
Well, she couldn't help herself, could only wait and pray,
And they—they were doing their duty as well as they knew the way.

Slowly the red moon rose, and then the sergeant spoke—
" Pat, look to the horses' girths; Graham, give the lady this cloak.
Now, miss, be your father's daughter, our lads are close below,
The horses are fresh, the road is clear, and we've only five miles to go."

Then spoke the Captain's daughter, and her voice was weak but clear—
" I want you to promise, brave friends, while we're together here,
That you'll keep the last shot for me—when each heart of hope despairs;
Better to die by hands like yours than be left alive in theirs."

The sergeant cleared his throat, and turned his face away ;
Denis, the stout of heart, had never a word to say ;
And Douglas grasped his hilt with a look and gesture grim,
While he looked on the face o' the girl with eyes grown
    suddenly blurred and dim.

"Oh, you'll promise me, will you not?" the weak voice pleaded
    again,
"You will not leave me to them—you—soldiers—my father's
    men?
For the sake of my mother in Heaven—and God and death so
    near—
Oh, father, father, you would, I know, if only you were here."

"I promise." "And I." "And I." The voices were hoarse
    and low,
And each man prayed, I ween, that the task *he* might not
    know,
As out on the plain they rode swiftly and silently—
Four to ride together, and three o' the four to die.

The sergeant's charger led with a long and raking stride,
And her Arab's lighter bound kept the lady by his side,
While hanging on either flank, the watchers, steady and strong,
Swept on through the clouds of dust that rose as the leaders
    hastened along.

Fire to the right and left, fire in front and rear,
As the dusky demons broke from their lurking ambush near.
"Noo, Denis, boot tae boot—keep close between, ye twa—
We've cut her a way through waur than this, an'—"Charge!"
"Hurroo!" "Hurrah!"

As the lightning cleaves the cloud, as the tempest rends the oak,
The comrades' headlong rush the gathering miscreants broke ;
Unharmed through the yelling horde the Captain's daughter
    fled,
While thick and fast in fierce pursuit the Sirdar's horsemen sped.

Up on the crest o' the rise where Cawnpore's curse of blood
Hushes with horror yet the wide and rolling flood,
Douglas reeled in his saddle, and whispered brokenly—
"Gray, dinna let her ken, but it's near a' ower wi' me."

"Hit?" "Ay, here in the side." "Bad?" "Ay, bad, but a—h!
I'll face yon hounds on the brae, it may gain ye a minute or twa—
Tak' my horse—ye may need it for her. Steady, there!—woa, there, Gem!
Dinna forget your promise—yon lassie's no for *them*."

An iron grip o' the hands—mist o'er the sergeant's sight,
As he swiftly wheeled the horses, and vanished in the night;
Then round to the nearing foe, under the starry sky,
Alone with his God and his own brave heart, Grahame Douglas turned to die.

On came Hamed, the boastful—who so sure as he,
With his Siva-charmed sword, keen-edged, against the Feringhee?
Woe for Hamed, the boastful! woe the mistake he made,
When he matched his sword 'gainst a Border arm and the sweep of a Border blade!

Then fighting it, thrust for thrust, and fighting it, blow for blow,
Till at last, where the bank fell sheer to the dusky stream below,
He fell—a groan—a plunge—wave circles eddying wide—
And the ne'er-dae-weel was still at last 'neath the river's turbid tide.

On and over all,—over nullah and stream;
On, where the serpents hiss, where the leopards' eyeballs gleam;
On and on like the wind, faster and faster yet,
While the iron fingers clutch the hilt, and the grinding teeth are set.

"Stretch to it, gallant Selim! leap to it, Ned and Dan!
Well done, brave brutes! Hurrah! Let them catch us now who can!"
On and on for life—for a higher, dearer stake—
For true men's chivalry—for a helpless woman's sake!

A splutter of fire on the right, a flame of fire in the rear,
And Gem leaped up and fell—another, and all too near
The hissing bullets came, and then the sergeant knew
His blood and life were ebbing away with every breath he drew.

Sore and deep the wound, but never a moan he made,
And, rising up in his saddle, erect as when on parade—
"Pat, if you get in, report that Douglas and I are dead ;
Tell them we did our duty, and mind—your promise," he said.

The maiden checked her horse with a quick, wild scream of pain—
"O Heaven, have pity!" she sobbed, as Denis seized her rein.
Then giving his last command—"Ride on!" with impatient frown,
True British soldier to the last, the brave old man went down.

Oh, pale the maiden's face, but her brow was calm and clear,
Though never had woman yet such awful cause for fear;
And Denis, the stout of heart, in his saddle turned to rise,
With the lurid glare of maddened rage in his kindly Irish eyes.

Swiftly he aimed and fired—every shot was sure,
And fierce the yells that hailed the fall of each dusky blackamoor,
Till sudden the maiden's voice came shrill in agony—
"Oh, Denis, brave Denis, you promised you would keep the last for me!"

Was that the glint of steel that flashed from yonder wood?
Rose there hoarse commands in voices stern and rude?
"On, on—O God! so near—so near, and to fail at last!
On, on—in vain—our brave brutes fail us—hope is past!"

Oh, pale was the maiden's face, and her white lips moved in prayer;
Then with never a sign of fear, for the hero soul was there;
With the Virgin martyr's glory lighting her bonny brow,
She laid her hand on Denis' arm, and gently whispered, "Now!"

The strong man shook 'neath the touch of those tiny finger-tips,
And "Say you forgive me, Miss," broke hoarse from his ashen lips.
"Forgive you! Again and again! You see I do not fear!
God bless you, gallant soldier! Now, straight and sure—aim here!"

She laid one hand on her heart, then clasped them o'er her head,
And into the darkened sky her latest look she sped ;

And Denis raised his arm with slow and deadly aim—
When all hell seemed leaping to meet them in thunder and cloud and flame.

'Mid the smoke—'mid splintering shells that glare and shriek and grate—
'Mid the battery's bursting blaze—'mid the rifle's flashing hate—
'Mid the pibroch's savage swell—'mid the trumpet's madd'ning alarms—
The Captain's daughter fainted, safe in her frantic father's arms.

While with hurricane-roar, and rush, with clang of hoof and steel,
With flame in each rider's eyes, and fire at each charger's heel,
With shouts that rose to the sky on vengeance-laden breath,
The British squadrons thundered by to the carnival of death.

Sabres reddened and gleamed, pistols and carbines rang,
Lances shook and flashed, bullets hissed and sang.
Full the payment then of a black and damning debt—
They frighten their dusky babes with tales of that midnight murder yet.

Prone on his back lay Denis—Denis, the stout of heart,—
Still as she for whom he had played a hero's part.
Dying—alone! Unheeded! What matter? The fight was won.
He was only a common soldier—besides, his work was done.

The sounds o' the vengeful strife aroused death's drowsy ear,
He listened—rose on his elbow, and then with a whispered cheer—
" Ho, Douglas, Gray—we've beaten that murderin' son of a thafe !
I'm going—What matter?—Hurroo! Sure, the Captain's daughter's safe ! "

.   .   .   .   .   .

Only three common soldiers, only three common men,
Giving their lives for a woman, as men have again and again ;
Only doing their duty, teaching *this* lesson anew—
Where'er true woman points the way, true man will dare and do.

N

Then here's to the gallant three—reckless and rough and brave!
And here's to the Captain's daughter, the girl they died to save!
And here's to all true women, where'er they are under the sun—
Worthy the toast they well must be for whom such deeds are done.

The Singing Leaves.
A BALLAD.

I.

"What fairings will ye that I bring?"
   Said the King to his daughters three;
"For I to Vanity Fair am boun',
   Now say what shall they be?"
Then up and spake the eldest daughter,
   That lady tall and grand:
"Oh, bring me pearls and diamonds great,
   And gold rings for my hand."
Thereafter spake the second daughter,
   That was both white and red:
"For me bring silks that will stand alone,
   And a gold comb for my head."
Then came the turn of the least daughter,
   That was whiter than thistle-down,
And among the gold of her blithesome hair
   Dim shone the golden crown.
"There came a bird this morning,
   And sang 'neath my bower eaves,
Till I dreamed, as his music made me,
   'Ask thou for the Singing Leaves.'"
Then the brow of the King swelled crimson
   With a flush of angry scorn:
"Well have ye spoken, my two eldest,
   And chosen as ye were born;
"But she, like a thing of peasant race,
   That is happy binding the sheaves;"
Then he saw her dead mother in her face,
   And said, "Thou shalt have thy leaves."

II.

He mounted and rode three days and nights
    Till he came to Vanity Fair,
And 'twas easy to buy the gems and the silk,
    But no Singing Leaves were there.

Then deep in the greenwood rode he,
    And asked of every tree,
"Oh, if you have ever a Singing Leaf,
    I pray you give it me!"

But the trees all kept their counsel,
    And never a word said they,
Only there sighed from the pine-tops
    A music of seas far away.

Only the pattering aspen
    Made a sound of growing rain,
That ever fell faster and faster,
    Then faltered to silence again.

"Oh where shall I find a little foot-page
    That would win both hose and shoon,
And will bring to me the Singing Leaves,
    If they grow under the moon?"

Then lightly turned him Walter the page,
    By the stirrup as he ran:
"Now pledge you me the truesome word
    Of a king and gentleman,

"That you will give me the first, first thing
    You meet at your castle-gate,
And the princess shall get the Singing Leaves,
    Or mine be a traitor's fate."

The King's head dropt upon his breast
    A moment, as it might be;
'Twill be my dog, he thought, and said,
    "My faith I plight to thee."

Then Walter took from next his heart
    A packet small and thin,
"Now give you this to the Princess Anne,
    The Singing Leaves are therein."

III.

As the King rode in at his castle-gate,
   A maiden to meet him ran,
And "Welcome, father!" she laughed and cried
   Together, the Princess Anne.

"Lo, here the Singing Leaves," quoth he,
   "And woe, but they cost me dear!"
She took the packet, and the smile
   Deepened down beneath the tear.

It deepened down till it reached her heart,
   And then gushed up again,
And lighted her tears as the sudden sun
   Transfigures the summer rain.

And the first Leaf, when it was opened,
   Sang: "I am Walter the page,
And the songs I sing 'neath thy window
   Are my only heritage."

And the second Leaf sang: "But in the land
   That is neither on earth or sea,
My lute and I are lords of more
   Than thrice this kingdom's fee."

And the third Leaf sang: "Be mine! Be mine!"
   And ever it sang, "Be mine!"
Then sweeter it sang and ever sweeter,
   And said, "I am thine, thine, thine!"

At the first Leaf she grew pale enough,
   At the second she turned aside,
At the third, 'twas as if a lily flushed
   With a rose's red heart's tide.

"Good counsel gave the bird," said she,
   "I have my hope thrice o'er,
For they sing to my very heart," said she,
   "And it sings to them evermore."

She brought to him her beauty and truth,
   But and broad earldoms three,
And he made her queen of the broader lands
   He held of his lute in fee.

Barbara Frietchie.

(Verse printed as Prose.)

Up from the meadows rich with corn, clear in the cool September morn, the clustered spires of Frederick stand green-walled by the hills of Maryland. Round about them orchards sweep, apple and peach-tree fruited deep,—fair as a garden of the Lord to the eyes of the famished rebel horde. On that pleasant morn of the early fall, when Lee marched over the mountain wall,—over the mountains winding down, horse and foot, into Frederick Town—forty flags with their silver stars, forty flags with their crimson bars, flapped in the morning wind: the sun of noon looked down, and saw not one.—Up rose old Barbara Frietchie then, bowed with her fourscore years and ten; bravest of all in Frederick Town, she took up the flag the men hauled down: in her attic window the staff she set, to show that one heart was loyal yet. . . . Up the street came the rebel tread, Stonewall Jackson riding ahead. Under his slouched hat, left and right, he glanced: the old flag met his sight. "Halt!"—the dust-brown ranks stood fast. "Fire!"—out blazed the rifle-blast. It shivered the window, pane and sash; it rent the banner with seam and gash. Quick, as it fell from the broken staff, Dame Barbara snatched the silken scarf; she leaned far out on the window-sill, and shook it forth with a royal will. "Shoot, if you must, this old grey head,—but spare your country's flag!" she said.

A shade of sadness, a blush of shame, over the face of the leader came; the nobler nature within him stirred to life at that woman's deed and word. "Who touches a hair of yon gray head, dies like a dog! March on!" he said. . . . All day long through Frederick Street sounded the tread of marching feet; all day long that free flag tossed over the heads of the rebel host. Ever its torn folds rose and fell on the loyal winds that loved it well; and, through the hill-gaps, sunset light shone over it with a warm good-night.

Barbara Frietchie's work is o'er, and the rebel rides on his raids no more. Honour to her!—and let a tear fall, for her sake, on Stonewall's bier. Over Barbara Frietchie's grave, flag of Freedom and Union wave! Peace, and order, and beauty, draw round thy symbol of light and law; and ever the stars above look down on thy stars below in Frederick Town!

Maud Müller.

(Verse printed as Prose.)

Maud Müller, on a summer's day, raked the meadow sweet with hay. Beneath her torn hat glowed the wealth of simple beauty and rustic health. Singing, she wrought, and her merry glee the mock-bird echoed from his tree. But, when she glanced to the far-off town, white from its hill-slope looking down, the sweet song died; and a vague unrest and a nameless longing filled her breast—a wish, that she hardly dared to own, for something better than she had known!

The Judge rode slowly down tne lane, smoothing his horse's chestnut mane. He drew his bridle in the shade of the apple-trees, to greet the Maid, and ask a draught, from the spring that flowed through the meadows across the road.—She stooped where the cool spring bubbles up, and filled for him her small tin cup; and blushed as she gave it, looking down on her feet so bare, and her tattered gown. "Thanks!" said the Judge, "a sweeter draught from a fairer hand was never quaffed." He spoke of the grass, and flowers, and trees, of the singing birds, and the humming bees; then talked of the haying, and wondered whether the cloud in the west would bring foul weather. And Maud forgot her briar-torn gown, and her graceful ankles bare and brown; and listened, while a pleased surprise looked from her long-lashed hazel eyes,—At last, like one who for delay seeks a vain excuse, he rode away!

Maud Müller looked and sighed: "Ah me! that I the Judge's bride might be! He would dress me up in silks so fine, and praise and toast me at his wine. My father should wear a broad-cloth coat; my brother should sail a painted boat. I'd dress my mother so grand and gay! and the baby should have a new toy each day. And I'd feed the hungry, and clothe the poor, and all should bless me who left our door."

The Judge looked back as he climbed the hill, and saw Maud Müller standing still. "A form more fair, a face more sweet, ne'er hath it been my lot to meet. And her modest answer and graceful air, show her wise and good as she is fair. Would she were mine! and I to-day, like her, a harvester of hay: no doubtful balance of rights and wrongs, and weary lawyers with endless tongues; but low of cattle, and song of birds, and health of quiet and loving words." Then he thought of his sisters, proud and cold; and his mother, vain of her rank and gold. So, closing his heart, the Judge rode on, and Maud was left in the field alone. But the lawyers smiled that afternoon, when he hummed in court an old love tune;—and the young girl mused beside the well, till the rain on the unraked clover fell.

He wedded a wife of richest dower, who lived for fashion, as he for power. Yet oft in his marble hearth's bright glow, he watched a picture come and go: and sweet Maud Müller's hazel eyes looked out in their innocent surprise. Oft when the wine in his glass was red, he longed for the wayside-well instead; and closed his eyes on his garnished rooms, to dream of meadows and clover blooms. And the proud man sighed, with a secret pain: " Ah! that I were free again! free as when I rode that day, where the barefoot maiden raked her hay."

She wedded a man unlearn'd and poor, and many children played round her door. But care and sorrow, and household pain, left their traces on heart and brain. And oft, when the summer-sun shone hot on the new-mown hay in the meadow lot, in the shade of the apple-tree, again she saw a Rider draw his rein: and, gazing down with timid grace, she felt his pleased eyes read her face. Sometimes her narrow kitchen walls stretched away into stately halls; the weary wheel to a spinnet turned, the tallow candle an astral burned; and, for him who sat by the chimney lug, dozing and grumbling o'er pipe and mug, a manly form at her side she saw,—and joy was duty, and love was law! . . . Then, she took up her burden of life again, saying only, " It might have been!"

Alas for Maiden! alas for Judge! for rich repiner and household drudge! God pity them both! and pity us all, who vainly the dreams of youth recall. For, of all sad words of tongue or pen, the saddest are these: " It might have been!" Ah, well for us all some sweet hope lies deeply buried from human eyes; and, in the Hereafter, angels may roll the stone from its grave away!

"Ginevra."

(Verse printed as Prose.)

She was an only child—her name Ginevra, the joy, the pride of an indulgent sire ; and in her fifteenth year became a bride, marrying an only son, Francesco Doria, her playmate from her birth, and her first love. She was all gentleness, all gaiety, her pranks the favourite theme of every tongue. But now the day was come, the day, the hour ; now, frowning, smiling, for the hundredth time, the nurse, that ancient lady, preached decorum ; and Ginevra, in the lustre of her youth, gave her hand, with her heart in it, to Francesco. Great was the joy ; but, at the nuptial feast, when all sat down, the bride was wanting there, nor was she to be found ! Her father cried, " 'Tis but to make a trial of our love !" and filled his glass to all ; but his hand shook, and soon from guest to guest the panic spread. 'Twas but that instant she had left Francesco, laughing, and looking back, and flying still—her ivory tooth imprinted on his finger. But now, alas ! she was not to be found ; nor from that hour could any thing be guessed, but that she was not !

Weary of his life, Francesco flew to Venice, and forthwith flung it away in battle with the Turk. Orsini lived : and long mightst thou have seen an old man wandering as in quest of something, something he could not find—he knew not what. When he was gone, the house remained awhile silent and tenantless—then went to strangers.

Full fifty years were past, and all forgot ; when on an idle day,—a day of search 'mid the old lumber in the gallery,—that mouldering chest was noticed ; and 'twas said by one as young, as thoughtless as Ginevra, " Why not remove it from its lurking place ?" 'Twas done as soon as said ; but, on the way, it burst, it fell ; and lo ! a skeleton, with here and there a pearl, an emerald-stone, a golden clasp, clasping a shred of gold ! All else had perished—save a nuptial-ring, and a small seal, her mother's legacy, engraven with a name, the name of both—" Ginevra." There then had she found a grave ! Within that chest had she concealed herself, fluttering with joy, the happiest of the happy ; when a spring-lock, that lay in ambush there, closed, and fastened her down for ever !

Paradise and the Peri.
From " Lalla Rookh."
(Verse printed as Prose.)

One morn a Peri at the gate of Eden stood, disconsolate; and as she listen'd to the Springs of Life within, like music flowing, and caught the light upon her wings through the half-open portal glowing, she wept to think her recreant race should e'er have lost that glorious place! "How happy," exclaimed this child of air, "are the holy Spirits who wander there, 'mid flowers that never shall fade or fall; though mine are the gardens of earth and sea, and the stars themselves have flowers for me, one blossom of Heaven out-blooms them all!

"Go, wing thy flight from star to star, from world to luminous world, as far as the universe spreads its flaming wall: Take all the pleasures of all the spheres, and multiply each through endless years, one minute of Heaven is worth them all!" The glorious Angel, who was keeping the gates of Light, beheld her weeping; and, as he nearer drew and listen'd to her sad song, a tear-drop glisten'd within his eye-lids, like the spray from Eden's fountain, when it lies on the blue flow'r, which—Bramins say—blooms nowhere but in Paradise! "Nymph of a fair but erring line!" gently he said—"One hope is thine. 'Tis written in the Book of Fate, *the Peri yet may be forgiven who brings to this Eternal gate the Gift that is most dear to Heaven!* Go seek it, and redeem thy sin—'tis sweet to let the Pardon'd in!"

. . . .

Cheer'd by this hope she bends her thither;—still laughs the radiant eye of Heaven, nor have the golden bowers of Even in the rich West begun to wither;—when, o'er the vale of Balbec winging slowly, she sees a child at play, among the rosy wild-flowers singing, as rosy and as wild as they; chasing, with eager hands and eyes, the beautiful blue damsel-flies, that flutter'd round the jasmine stems, like winged flowers or flying gems:—and, near the boy, who tir'd with play, now nestling 'mid the roses lay, she saw a wearied man dismount from his hot steed, and on the brink of a small imaret's rustic fount impatient fling him down to drink. Then swift his haggard brow he turn'd to the fair child, who fearless sat, though never yet hath day-beam burn'd upon a brow more fierce than

that,—sullenly fierce—a mixture dire, like thunder-clouds, of
gloom and fire ! in which the Peri's eyes could read dark tales
of many a ruthless deed; the ruin'd maid—the shrine pro-
fan'd—oaths broken—and the threshold stain'd with blood of
guests !—*there* written, all, black as the damning drops that
fall from the denouncing Angel's pen, ere Mercy weeps them
out again !

Yet tranquil now that man of crime, (as if the balmy
evening time soften'd his spirit,) look'd and lay, watching the
rosy infant's play.

But hark ! the vesper call to prayer, as slow the orb of daylight sets, is rising sweetly on the air, from Syria's thousand
minarets! The boy has started from the bed of flowers, where
he had laid his head, and down upon the fragrant sod kneels,
with his forehead to the south, lisping the eternal name of
God from purity's own cherub mouth, and looking, while his
hands and eyes are lifted to the glowing skies, like a stray babe
of Paradise, just lighted on that flowery plain, and seeking for
its home again ! Oh, 'twas a sight—that Heav'n—that Child
—a scene, which might have well beguil'd ev'n haughty Eblis
of a sigh for glories lost and peace gone by !

And how felt *he*, the wretched Man reclining there—while
memory ran o'er many a year of guilt and strife, flew o'er the
dark flood of his life, nor found one sunny resting-place, nor
brought him back one branch of grace ! "There *was* a time,"
he said, in mild, heart-humbled tones—"thou blessed child !
when young and haply pure as thou, I look'd and pray'd like
thee—but now "—he hung his head—each nobler aim and
hope and feeling, which had slept from boyhood's hour, that
instant came fresh o'er him, and he wept—he wept !

Blest tears of soul-felt penitence ! in whose benign, redeem-
ing flow is felt the first, the only sense of guiltless joy that
guilt can know. "There's a drop," said the Peri, "that down
from the moon falls through the withering airs of June upon
Egypt's land, of so healing a power, so balmy a virtue, that
ev'n in the hour that drop descends, contagion dies, and health
reanimates earth and skies ! Oh, is it not thus, thou man of
sin, the precious tears of repentance fall? Though foul thy
fiery plagues within, one heavenly drop hath dispell'd them
all !" And now—behold him kneeling there by the child's

side, in humble prayer, while the same sunbeam shines upon the guilty and the guiltless one, and hymns of joy proclaim through Heaven the Triumph of a soul Forgiven!

'Twas when the golden orb had set, while on their knees they linger'd yet, there fell a light, more lovely far than ever came from sun or star, upon the tear that, warm and meek, dew'd that repentant sinner's cheek : to mortal eye this light might seem a northern flash or meteor beam—but well the enraptured Peri knew 'twas a bright smile the Angel threw from Heaven's gate, to hail that tear her harbinger of glory near!

"Joy, joy for ever! my task is done—the Gates are pass'd, and Heaven is won! Oh, am I not happy? I am, I am. To thee, sweet Eden! how dark and sad are the diamond turrets of Shadukiam, and the fragant bowers of Amberabad!

"Farewell, ye odours of Earth, that die, passing away like a lover's sigh; my feast is now of the Tooba Tree, whose scent is the breath of Eternity!

"Farewell, ye vanishing flowers, that shone in my fairy wreath, so bright and brief,—oh! what are the brightest that e'er have blown, to the lote-tree, springing by Alla's Throne, whose flowers have a soul in every leaf! Joy, joy for ever! my task is done—the Gates are pass'd, and Heaven is won!"

LYRICS, IDYLLS, AND BALLADS.

Sandalphon.

Have you read in the Talmud of old,
In the Legends the Rabbins have told
  Of the limitless realms of the air,—
Have you read it,—the marvellous story
Of Sandalphon, the Angel of Glory,
  Sandalphon, the Angel of Prayer?

How, erect, at the outermost gates
Of the City Celestial he waits,
  With his feet on the ladder of light
That, crowded with angels unnumbered
By Jacob was seen, as he slumbered
  Alone in the desert at night?

The Angels of Wind and of Fire
Chant only one hymn, and expire
   With the song's irresistible stress ;
Expire in their rapture and wonder,
As harp-strings are broken asunder
   By music they throb to express.

But serene in the rapturous throng,
Unmoved by the rush of the song
   With eyes unimpassioned and slow,
Among the dead angels, the deathless
Sandalphon stands listening breathless
   To sounds that ascend from below ;—

From the spirits on earth that adore,
From the souls that entreat and implore
   In the fervour and passion of prayer ;
From the hearts that are broken with losses,
And weary with dragging the crosses
   Too heavy for mortals to bear.

And he gathers the prayers as he stands,
And they change into flowers in his hands,
   Into garlands of purple and red ;
And beneath the great arch of the portal,
Through the streets of the City Immortal
   Is wafted the fragrance they shed.

It is but a legend, I know,—
A fable, a phantom, a show,
   Of the ancient Rabbinical lore ;
Yet the old mediæval tradition,
The beautiful, strange superstition,
   But haunts me and holds me the more.

When I look from my window at night,
And the welkin above is all white,
   All throbbing and panting with stars,
Among them majestic is standing
Sandalphon the angel, expanding
   His pinions in nebulous bars.

And the legend, I feel, is a part
Of the hunger and thirst of the heart,
The frenzy and fire of the brain,
That grasps at the fruitage forbidden,
The golden pomegranates of Eden,
To quiet its fever and pain.

The Captain of the "Northfleet."

So often is the proud deed done by men like this at duty's call :
So many are the honours won for us, we cannot wear them all !
They make the heroic commonplace and dying thus the natural way ;
And yet, our world-wide English race feels nobler, for that death, to-day !
It stirs us with a sense of wings that strive to lift the earthiest soul ;
It brings the thoughts that fathom things to anchor fast where billows roll.
Love was so new, and life so sweet, but at the call he left the wine,
And sprang full-statured to his feet, responsive to the touch divine.
Nay, Dear, I cannot see you die. For me, I have my work to do Up here. Down to the boat. Good-bye. God bless you. I shall see it through.
We read, until the vision dims and drowns ; but, ere the pang be past,
A tide of triumph overbrims and breaks with light from heaven at last.
Through all the blackness of that night a glory streams from out the gloom ;
His steadfast spirit lifts the light that shines till night is overcome.
The sea will do its worst, and life be sobbed out in a bubbling breath ;
But firmly in the coward strife there stands a man who has conquered Death !

A soul that masters wind and wave, and towers above a sinking
    deck ;
A bridge across the gaping wave, a rainbow rising o'er the wreck.
Others he saved ; he saved the name unsullied that he gave his
    wife :
And dying with so pure an aim, he had no need to save his life !
Lord, how they shame the life we live, these sailors of our sea-
    girt isle,
Who cheerily take what Thou mayst give, and go down with a
    heavenward smile !
The men who sow their lives to yield a glorious crop in lives
    to be :
Who turn to England's harvest-field the unfruitful furrows of
    the sea.
With such a breed of men so brave, the Old Land has not had
    her day ;
But long her strength, with crested wave, shall ride the Seas
    the proud old way.

The Maids of Attitash.

In sky and wave the white clouds swam,
And the blue hills of Nottingham
   Through gaps of leafy green
   Across the lake were seen,—
When, in the shadow of the ash,
That dreams its dream in Attitash,
   In the warm summer weather,
   Two maidens sat together.

They sat and watched in idle mood
The gleam and shade of lake and wood,—
   The beach the keen light smote,
   The white sail of a boat,—
Swan flocks of lilies shoreward lying,
In sweetness, not in music, dying,—
   Hardhack, and virgin's-bower,
   And white-spiked clethra-flower.

With careless ears they heard the plash
And breezy wash of Attitash,

The wood-bird's plaintive cry,
The locust's sharp reply.
And teased the while, with playful hand,
The shaggy dog of Newfoundland,
   Whose uncouth frolic spilled
   Their baskets berry-filled.
Then one, the beauty of whose eyes
Was evermore a great surprise,
   Tossed back her queenly head,
   And, lightly laughing, said,—
" No bridegroom's hand be mine to hold
That is not lined with yellow gold ;
   I tread no cottage-floor ;
   I own no lover poor.
" My love must come on silken wings,
With bridal lights of diamond rings,—
   Not foul with kitchen smirch,
   With tallow-dip for torch."
The other, on whose modest head
Was lesser dower of beauty shed,
   With look for home-hearths meet,
   And voice exceeding sweet,
Answered,—" We will not rivals be;
Take thou the gold, leave love to me ;
   Mine be the cottage small,
   And thine the rich man's hall.
" I know, indeed, that wealth is good;
But lowly roof and simple food,
   With love that hath no doubt,
   Are more than gold without."
Hard by a farmer hale and young
His cradle in the rye-field swung,
   Tracking the yellow plain
   With windrows of ripe grain.
And still, whene'er he paused to whet
His scythe, the sidelong glance he met
   Of large dark eyes, where strove
   False pride and secret love.

Be strong, young mower of the grain :
That love shall overmatch disdain,
   Its instincts soon or late
   The heart shall vindicate.

In blouse of grey, with fishing-rod,
Half screened by leaves, a stranger trod
   The margin of the pond,
   Watching the group beyond.

The supreme hours unnoted come ;
Unfelt the turning tides of doom ;
   And so the maids laughed on,
   Nor dreamed what Fate had done,—

Nor knew the step was Destiny's
That rustled in the birchen trees,
   As, with their lives forecast,
   Fisher and mower passed.

Erelong by lake and rivulet side
The summer roses paled and died,
   And Autumn's fingers shed
   The maple's leaves of red.

Through the long gold-hazed afternoon,
Alone, but for the diving loon,
   The partridge in the brake,
   The black duck on the lake,

Beneath the shadow of the ash
Sat man and maid by Attitash ;
   And earth and air made room
   For human hearts to bloom.

Soft spread the carpets of the sod
And scarlet-oak and golden-rod
   With blushes and with smiles
   Lit up the forest aisles.

The mellow light the lake aslant,
The pebbled margin's ripple-chant
   Attempered and low-toned,
   The tender mystery owned.

And through the dream the lovers dreamed
Sweet sounds stole in and soft lights streamed ;
   The sunshine seemed to bless,
   The air was a caress.

Not she who lightly laughed is there,
With scornful toss of midnight hair,
   Her dark, disdainful eyes,
   And proud lip worldly-wise.

Her haughty vow is still unsaid,
But all she dreamed and coveted
   Wears, half to her surprise,
   The youthful farmer's guise!

With more than all her old-time pride
She walks the rye-field at his side,
   Careless of cot or hall,
   Since love transfigures all.

Rich beyond dreams, the vantage-ground
Of life is gained ; her hands have found
   The talisman of old
   That changes all to gold.

While she who could for love dispense,
With all its glittering accidents,
   And trust her heart alone,
   Finds love and gold her own.

What wealth can buy or art can build
Awaits her ; but her cup is filled
   Even now unto the brim ;
   Her world is love and him!

The Lost Found.
From " Evangeline."

In that delightful land which is washed by the Delaware's waters,
Guarding in sylvan shades the name of Penn the apostle,
Stands on the banks of its beautiful stream the city he founded.
There all the air is balm, and the peach is the emblem of beauty,

And the streets still re-echo the names of the trees of the forest,
As if they fain would appease the Dryads whose haunts they
    molested.
There from the troubled sea had Evangeline landed, an exile,
Finding among the children of Penn a home and a country.
There old René Leblanc had died ; and when he departed,
Saw at his side only one of all his hundred descendants.
Something at least there was in the friendly streets of the city,
Something that spake to her heart, and made her no longer a stranger ;
And her ear was pleased with the Thee and Thou of the Quakers,
For it recalled the past, the old Acadian country,
Where all men were equal, and all were brothers and sisters.
So, when the fruitless search, the disappointed endeavour,
Ended, to recommence no more upon earth, uncomplaining,
Thither, as leaves to the light, were turned her thoughts and her
    footsteps.
As from a mountain's top the rainy mists of the morning
Roll away, and afar we behold the landscape below us,
Sun-illumined, with shining rivers and cities and hamlets,
So fell the mists from her mind, and she saw the world far below her,
Dark no longer, but all illumined with love ; and the pathway
Which she had climbed so far, lying smooth and fair in the distance.
Gabriel was not forgotten. Within her heart was his image,
Clothed in the beauty of love and youth, as last she beheld him,
Only more beautiful made by his death-like silence and absence.
Into her thoughts of him time entered not, for it was not.
Over him years had no power ; he was not changed, but transfigured;
He had become to her heart as one who is dead, and not absent ;
Patience and abnegation of self, and devotion to others,
This was the lesson a life of trial and sorrow had taught her.
So was her love diffused, but, like to some odorous spices,
Suffered no waste nor loss, though filling the air with aroma.
Other hope had she none, nor wish in life, but to follow
Meekly, with reverent steps, the sacred feet of her Saviour.
Thus many years she lived as a Sister of Mercy ; frequenting
Lonely and wretched roofs in the crowded lanes of the city,
Where distress and want concealed themselves from the sunlight,
Where disease and sorrow in garrets languished neglected.
Night after night, when the world was asleep, as the watchman
    repeated
Loud, through the gusty streets, that all was well in the city,
High at some lonely window he saw the light of her taper.
Day after day, in the grey of the dawn, as slow through the suburbs
Plodded the German farmer, with flowers and fruits of the market,
Met he that meek, pale face, returning home from its watchings.

Then it came to pass that a pestilence fell on the city,
Presaged by wondrous signs, and mostly by flocks of wild pigeons,
Darkening the sun in their flight, with naught in their craws but an acorn.
And, as the tides of the sea arise in the month of September,
Flooding some silver stream, till it spreads to a lake in the meadow,
So death flooded life, and, o'erflowing its natural margin,
Spread to a brackish lake, the silver stream of existence.
Wealth had no power to bribe, nor beauty to charm, the oppressor;
But all perished alike beneath the scourge of his anger;—
Only, alas! the poor, who had neither friends nor attendants,
Crept away to die in the almshouse, home of the homeless.
Then in the suburbs it stood, in the midst of meadows and woodlands;—
Now the city surrounds it; but still, with its gateway and wicket
Meek, in the midst of splendour, its humble walls seem to echo
Softly the words of the Lord—" The poor ye always have with you."
Thither, by night and by day, came the Sister of Mercy. The dying
Looked up into her face, and thought, indeed, to behold there
Gleams of celestial light encircle her forehead with splendour,
Such as the artist paints o'er the brows of saints and apostles,
Or such as hangs by night o'er a city seen at a distance.
Unto their eyes it seemed the lamps of the city celestial,
Into whose shining gates ere long their spirits would enter.

Thus, on a Sabbath morn, through the streets, deserted and silent,
Wending her quiet way, she entered the door of the almshouse.
Sweet on the summer air was the odour of flowers in the garden;
And she paused on her way to gather the fairest among them,
That the dying once more might rejoice in their fragrance and beauty.
Then, as she mounted the stairs to the corridors, cooled by the east wind,
Distant and soft on her ear fell the chimes from the belfry of Christ Church,
While, intermingled with these, across the meadows were wafted
Sounds of psalms, that were sung by the Swedes in their Church at Wicaco.
Soft as descending wings fell the calm of the hour on her spirit;
Something within her said—"At length thy trials are ended;"
And, with light in her looks, she entered the chambers of sickness.
Noiselessly moved about the assiduous, careful attendants,
Moistening the feverish lip and the aching brow, and in silence
Closing the sightless eyes of the dead, and concealing their faces,
Where on their pallets they lay, like drifts of snow by the road-side.
Many a languid head, upraised as Evangeline entered,
Turned on its pillow of pain to gaze while she passed, for her presence

Fell on their hearts like a ray of the sun on the walls of a prison.
And, as she looked around, she saw how Death, the consoler,
Laying his hand upon many a heart, had healed it for ever.
Many familiar forms had disappeared in the night-time ;
Vacant their places were, or filled already by strangers.

   Suddenly, as if arrested by fear or a feeling of wonder,
Still she stood, with her colourless lips apart, while a shudder
Ran through her frame, and, forgotten, the flow'rets dropped from
    her fingers,
And from her eyes and cheeks the light and bloom of the morning.
Then there escaped from her lips a cry of such terrible anguish,
That the dying heard it, and started up from their pillows.
On the pallet before her was stretched the form of an old man.
Long, and thin, and grey were the locks that shaded his temples ;
But, as he lay in the morning light, his face for a moment
Seemed to assume once more the forms of its earlier manhood ;
So are wont to be changed the faces of those who are dying.
Hot and red on his lips still burned the flush of the fever,
As if life, like the Hebrew, with blood had besprinkled its portals,
That the Angel of Death might see the sign, and pass over.
Motionless, senseless, dying, he lay, and his spirit exhausted
Seemed to be sinking down through infinite depths in the darkness,
Darkness of slumber and death, for ever sinking and sinking.
Then through those realms of shade, in multiplied reverberations,
Heard he that cry of pain, and through the hush that succeeded
Whispered a gentle voice, in accents tender and saint-like,
"Gabriel ! O my beloved !" and died away into silence.
Then he beheld, in a dream, once more the home of his childhood ;
Green Acadian meadows, with sylvan rivers among them,
Village, and mountain, and woodlands ; and, walking under their
    shadow,
As in the days of her youth, Evangeline rose in his vision.
Tears came into his eyes ; and as slowly he lifted his eyelids,
Vanished the vision away, but Evangeline knelt by his bedside.
Vainly he strove to whisper her name, for the accents unuttered
Died on his lips, and their motion revealed what his tongue would
    have spoken.
Vainly he strove to rise ; and Evangeline, kneeling beside him,
Kissed his dying lips, and laid his head on her bosom.
Sweet was the light of his eyes ; but it suddenly sank into darkness,
As when a lamp is blown out by a gust of wind at a casement.

   All was ended now, the hope, and the fear, and the sorrow,
All the aching of heart, the restless, unsatisfied longing,
All the dull, deep pain, and constant anguish of patience !
And, as she pressed once more the lifeless head to her bosom,
Meekly she bowed her own, and murmured, " Father, I thank thee !"

The Song of the Camp.

"Give us a song!" the soldiers cried,
   The outer trenches guarding,
When the heated guns of the camps allied
   Grew weary of bombarding.

The dark Redan in silent scoff
   Lay grim and threatening under—
The tawny mound of the Malakoff
   No longer belched its thunder.

There was a pause—the guardsman said,
   "We storm the forts to-morrow;
Sing while we may; another day
   Will bring enough of sorrow."

They lay along the battery's side,
   Below the smoking cannon—
Brave hearts from Severn, and from Clyde,
   And from the banks of Shannon.

They sang of love and not of fame,
   Forgot was Britain's glory;
Each heart recalled a different name,
   But all sang "Annie Laurie."

Voice after voice caught up the song,
   Until its tender passion
Rose like an anthem, rich and strong—
   Their battle-eve confession.

Dear girl! her name he dared not speak;
   Yet as the song grew louder,
Something upon the soldier's cheek
   Washed off the stain of powder.

Beyond the darkening ocean burned
   The bloody sunset's embers,
While the Crimean valleys learn'd
   How English love remembers.

And once again a fire of hell
   Rained on the Russian quarters,
With scream of shot and burst of shell,
   And bellowing of the mortars.

Sweet Irish Nora's eyes are dim
  For a singer dumb and gory;
And English Mary mourns for him
  Who sang of " Annie Laurie."

Oh, soldiers ! to your honoured rest
  Your truth and valour bearing—
The bravest are the tenderest,
  The loving are the daring."

The Forlorn.

The night is dark, the stinging sleet,
  Swept by the bitter gusts of air,
Drives whistling down the lonely street,
  And glazes on the pavement bare.

The street-lamps flare and struggle dim
  Through the gray sleet-clouds as they pass,
Or, governed by a boisterous whim,
  Drop down and rustle on the glass.

One poor, heart-broken, outcast girl
  Faces the east-wind's searching flaws,
And, as about her heart they whirl,
  Her tattered cloak more tightly draws.

The flat brick walls look cold and bleak,
  Her bare feet to the sidewalk freeze;
Yet dares she not a shelter seek,
  Though faint with hunger and disease.

The sharp storm cuts her forehead bare,
  And, piercing through her garments thin,
Beats on her shrunken breast, and there
  Makes colder the cold heart within.

She lingers where a ruddy glow
  Streams outward through an open shutter,
Adding more bitterness to woe,
  More loneness to desertion utter.

One half the cold she had not felt
  Until she saw this gush of light

Spread warmly forth, and seem to melt
    Its slow way through the deadening night.
She hears a woman's voice within,
    Singing sweet words her childhood knew,
And years of misery and sin
    Furl off, and leave her heaven blue.

Her freezing heart, like one who sinks
    Outwearied in the drifting snow,
Drowses to deadly sleep and thinks
    No longer of its hopeless woe :
Old fields, and clear blue summer days,
    Old meadows, green with grass, and trees
That shimmer through the trembling haze
    And whiten in the western breeze,
Old faces, all the friendly past
    Rises within her heart again,
And sunshine from her childhood cast
    Makes summer of the icy rain.

Enhaloed by a mild, warm glow,
    From man's humanity apart,
She hears old footsteps wandering slow
    Through the lone chambers of the heart.

Outside the porch before the door,
    Her cheek upon the cold, hard stone,
She lies, no longer foul and poor,
    No longer dreary and alone.

Next morning something heavily
    Against the opening door did weigh,
And there, from sin and sorrow free,
    A woman on the threshold lay.

A smile upon the wan lips told
    That she had found a calm release,
And that, from out the want and cold,
    The song had borne her soul in peace.

For, whom the heart of man shuts out,
    Sometimes the heart of God takes in,
And fences them all round about
    With silence mid the world's loud din ;

And one of His great charities
  Is Music, and it doth not scorn
To close the lids upon the eyes
  Of the polluted and forlorn;
Far was she from her childhood's home,
  Farther in guilt had wandered thence,
Yet thither it had bid her come
  To die in maiden innocence.

The First Snow-fall.

The snow had begun in the gloaming,
  And busily all the night
Had been heaping field and highway
  With a silence deep and white.

Every pine and fir and hemlock
  Wore ermine too dear for an earl,
And the poorest twig on the elm-tree
  Was ridged inch deep with pearl.

From sheds new-roofed with Carrara
  Came Chanticleer's muffled crow,
The stiff rails were softened to swan's-down,
  And still fluttered down the snow.

I stood and watched by the window
  The noiseless work of the sky,
And the sudden flurries of snow-birds,
  Like brown leaves whirling by.

I thought of a mound in sweet Auburn,
  Where a little headstone stood;
How the flakes were folding it gently,
  As did robins the babes in the wood.

Up spoke our own little Mabel,
  Saying, "Father, who makes it snow?"
And I told of the good All-Father
  Who cares for us here below.

Again I looked at the snow-fall,
  And thought of the leaden sky

That arched o'er our first great sorrow,
  When that mound was heaped so high.
I remembered the gradual patience
  That fell from that cloud like snow,
Flake by flake, healing and hiding
  The scar of our deep-plunged woe.

And again to the child I whispered,
  "The snow that husheth all,
Darling, the merciful Father
  Alone can make it fall!"
Then, with eyes that saw not, I kissed her;
  And she, kissing back, could not know
That *my* kiss was given to her sister,
  Folded close under deepening snow.

"Rock of Ages."

"Rock of Ages cleft for me,"
  Thoughtlessly the maiden sung,
Fell the words unconsciously
  From her girlish gleeful tongue,
Sang as little children sing,
  Sang as do the birds in June,
Fell the words like light leaves down
  On the current of the tune.
"Rock of ages cleft for me,
  Let me hide myself in Thee."

"Let me hide myself in Thee"—
  Felt her soul no need to hide;
Sweet the song as song could be,
  And she had no thought beside;
All the words unheedingly
  Fell from lips untouched by care,
Dreaming not that each might be
  On some other lips a prayer.
"Rock of Ages cleft for me,
  Let me hide myself in Thee."

"Rock of Ages cleft for me"—
'Twas a woman sang them now,
Pleadingly and prayerfully,
   Every word her heart did know;
Rose the song, as storm-tossed bird
   Beats with weary wing the air,
Every note by sorrow stirred,
   Every syllable a prayer.
"Rock of Ages cleft for me,
   Let me hide myself in Thee."

"Rock of Ages cleft for me,"
   Lips grown aged sung the hymn
Trustingly and tenderly,
   Voice grown weak and eyes grown dim;
"Let me hide myself in Thee,"
   Trembling tho' the voice and low,
Ran the sweet strain peacefully,
   Like a river in its flow;
Sung as only they can sing
   Who life's thorny paths have pressed,
Sung as only they can sing
   Who behold the promised rest.
"Rock of Ages cleft for me,
   Let me hide myself in Thee."

"Rock of Ages cleft for me,"
   Sung above a coffin lid,
Underneath all restfully,
   All life's joys and sorrows hid.
Never more, oh! storm-tossed soul,
   Never more from wind and tide,
Never more from billows' roll,
   Wilt thou need thyself to hide:
Could those sightless sunken eyes,
   Closed beneath the soft gray hair
Could those mute and stiffened lips
   Move again in pleading prayer,
Still, aye still the words would be,
   "Let me hide myself in Thee."

At Last.

When on my day of life the night is falling,
    And, in the winds from unsunned spaces blown,
I hear far voices out of darkness calling
    My feet to paths unknown,

Thou who hast made my home of life so pleasant,
    Leave not its tenant when its walls decay ;
O Love Divine, O Helper ever present,
    Be Thou my strength and stay!

Be near me when all else is from me drifting:
    Earth, sky, home's pictures, days of shade and shine,
And kindly faces to my own uplifting
    The love which answers mine.

I have but Thee, my Father! let Thy spirit
    Be with me then to comfort and uphold ;
No gate of pearl, no branch of palm I merit,
    Nor street of shining gold.

Suffice it if—my good and ill unreckoned,
    And both forgiven through Thy abounding grace—
I find myself by hands familiar beckoned
    Unto my fitting place.

Some humble door among Thy many mansions,
    Some sheltering shade where sin and striving cease,
And flows for ever through heaven's green expansions
    The river of Thy peace.

There, from the music round about me stealing,
    I fain would learn the new and holy song,
And find at last, beneath Thy trees of healing,
    The life for which I long.

In School-Days.

Still sits the school-house by the road,
    A ragged beggar sunning ;
Around it still the sumachs grow,
    And blackberry-vines are running.

Within, the master's desk is seen,
    Deep scarred by raps official ;

The warping-floor, the battered seats,
  The jack-knife's carved initial;
The charcoal frescoes on its wall;
  Its door's worn sill, betraying
The feet that, creeping slow to school,
  Went storming out to playing!

Long years ago a winter sun
  Shone over it at setting;
Lit up its western window-panes,
  And low eaves' icy fretting.

It touched the tangled golden curls,
  And brown eyes full of grieving,
Of one who still her steps delayed
  When all the school were leaving.

For near her stood the little boy
  Her childish favour singled:
His cap pulled low upon a face
  Where pride and shame were mingled.

Pushing with restless feet the snow
  To right and left, he lingered;—
As restlessly her tiny hands
  The blue-checked apron fingered.

He saw her lift her eyes; he felt
  The soft hand's light caressing,
And heard the tremble of her voice,
  As if a fault confessing.

"I'm sorry that I spelt the word:
  I hate to go above you,
Because,"—the brown eyes lower fell,—
  "Because, you see, I love you!"

Still memory to a grey-haired man
  That sweet child-face is showing.
Dear girl! the grasses on her grave
  Have forty years been growing!

He lives to learn, in life's hard school,
  How few who pass above him
Lament their triumph and his loss,
  Like her,—because they love him.

The Minister's Daughter.

In the minister's morning sermon
    He had told of the primal fall,
And how thenceforth the wrath of God
    Rested on each and all.

And how, of His will and pleasure,
    All souls, save a chosen few,
Were doomed to the quenchless burning,
    And held in the way thereto.

Yet never by faith's unreason
    A saintlier soul was tried,
And never the harsh old lesson
    A tenderer heart belied.

And, after the painful service
    On that pleasant Sabbath day,
He walked with his little daughter
    Through the apple-bloom of May.

Sweet in the fresh green meadows
    Sparrow and blackbird sung;
Above him their tinted petals
    The blossoming orchards hung.

Around on the wonderful glory
    The minister looked and smiled;
"How good is the Lord who gives us
    These gifts from His hand, my child.

"Behold in the bloom of apples
    And the violets in the sward
A hint of the old, lost beauty
    Of the Garden of the Lord!"

Then up spake the little maiden,
    Treading on snow and pink:
"O father! these pretty blossoms
    Are very wicked, I think.

"Had there been no Garden of Eden
    There never had been a fall;
And if never a tree had blossomed
    God would have loved us all."

"Hush, child!" the father answered,
  "By His decree man fell;
His ways are in clouds and darkness,
  But He doeth all things well.

"And whether by His ordaining
  To us cometh good or ill,
Joy or pain, or light or shadow,
  We must fear and love Him still."

"Oh, I fear Him!" said the daughter,
  "And I try to love Him, too;
But I wish He was good and gentle,
  Kind and loving as you."

The minister groaned in spirit
  As the tremulous lips of pain
And wide, wet eyes uplifted
  Questioned his own in vain.

Bowing his head he pondered
  The words of the little one;
Had he erred in his life-long teaching?
  Had he wrong to his Master done?

To what grim and dreadful idol
  Had he lent the holiest name?
Did his own heart, loving and human,
  The God of his worship shame?

And lo! from the bloom and greenness,
  From the tender skies above,
And the face of his little daughter,
  He read a lesson of love.

No more as the cloudy terror
  Of Sinai's mount of law,
But as Christ in the Syrian lilies
  The vision of God he saw.

And, as when, in the clefts of Horeb,
  Of old was His presence known,
The dread Ineffable Glory
  Was Infinite Goodness alone.

Thereafter his hearers noted
  In his prayers a tenderer strain,
And never the gospel of hatred
  Burned on his lips again.

And the scoffing tongue was prayerful,
  And the blinded eyes found sight,
And hearts, as flint aforetime,
  Grew soft in his warmth and light.

The Bivouac Fire.

(Verse printed as Prose.)

Round the bivouac fire, at midnight, lay the weary soldier-band; bloody were their spears with slaughter, gory was each hero's hand, for the ghastly strife was ended: From each soul a whisper came—"God of battles, we have triumphed; hallowed be Thy holy name!" It was beautiful, at midnight, when the bloody war was done, when the battle clashed no longer, and no longer blazed the sun, calmly, in the balmy starlight, to repose outwearied limbs; not a sound to stir the stillness, save the sound of holy hymns: "Thou hast given us the glory: Thou hast bade our troubles cease: Thou art great as God of battles: Thou art best as God of peace!"

Pensive, by the gleaming firelight, mute one lonely Soldier stood; in his hand he grasped a paper, scrawled in letters large and crude—in his gory hands he grasped it; and the tender childlike tear, from his manful bosom welling, bathed the blood upon his spear! Then the gory paper oped he, scrawled in letters crude and wild—"Little news from England, comrades; 'tis a letter from my child!"

"O my father! what hath kept you? You are nigh three years away; it was snowtime when you left us—this is morn of new year's day. 'Good-bye, baby, until summer, or till Christmas-time,' you said: O my father! what hath kept you? summer, Christmas, twice have fled. Mother says your war is holy—that you bear a noble name—that you fight for God and honour, and to shield our home from shame; yet I often hear her praying: 'Make all war, O God, to cease: Thou art great as God of battles: Thou art best as God of peace.' Night and morn I pray for father; in the sunny morning hours I am often in the garden; I have sown your name in flowers—like your coat, in flowers of scarlet, all in tulips soldier-red. Come, before the flowers are faded—come, before your name is dead!

Little brother died at Christmas—mother told me not to tell—but I think it better, father, for you said, 'The dead are well.' He was buried side o' Mary; mother since has never smiled. Till we meet, good-bye, dear father . . . from your LOVING LITTLE CHILD."

Silent wore the night to morning—silent, at their soul's desire, lay the soldiers, lost in dreaming, round the dying bivouac fire: home were they again in England! miles were they from war's alarms!.. Hark! the sudden bugle sounding! hark! the cry, "To arms! to arms!" Out from ambush, out from thicket, charged the foemen through the plain; "Up, my warriors! arm, my heroes! strike for God and home again!—for our homes, our babes, our country!" and the ruddy morning light flared on brandished falchions, bloody still with gore of yesternight.

Purple grew the plain with slaughter, steed and rider side by side; and the crimson day of carnage in a crimson sunset died: shuddering on the field of battle glimpsed the starlight overhead; and the moonlight, ghostlike, glimmered on the dying and the dead. Faint and few around the firelight were the laid outwearied limbs—faint and few the hero-voices that uprose in holy hymns; few the warriors left to whisper, "Thou hast cast our foes to shame: God of battles, we have triumphed; hallowed be Thy mighty name!"

On the purple plain of slaughter, who is this that smiles in rest, with a shred of gory paper lying on his mangled breast? nought remaining save a fragment, scrawled in letters crude and wild—"Till we meet, good-bye, dear father, from your loving little child!" Raise him softly, lift him gently; staunch his life-blood ebbing slow; he is breathing! he is whispering! What is this he mutters low? "Saved! my child—my home—my country! FATHER, give my pangs release: Thou art great as God of battles: Thou art best as God of peace."

The Three Preachers.

(Verse printed as Prose.)

There are Three Preachers, ever preaching, filled with eloquence and power:—one is old, with locks of white, skinny as an anchorite: and he preaches, every hour, with a

shrill fanatic voice, and a bigot's fiery scorn :—"Backward !
ye presumptuous nations ; man to misery is born ! born to
drudge, and sweat, and suffer—born to labour and to pray !
Backward, ye presumptuous nations—back ! be humble, and
obey !"

The Second is a milder Preacher; soft he talks, as if he
sung ; sleek and slothful in his look, and his words, as from a
book, issue glibly from his tongue. With an air of self-
content high he lifts his fair white hands : " Stand ye still, ye
restless nations, and be happy, all ye lands ! Fate is law, and
law is perfect; if ye meddle, ye will mar ; change is rash, and
ever was so : we are happy as we are !"

Mightier is the Younger Preacher ; genius flashes from his
eyes ; and the crowds who hear his voice give him, while their
souls rejoice, throbbing bosoms for replies. Awed they listen,
yet elated, while his stirring accents call : " Forward ! ye
deluded nations ; Progress is the rule of all : Man was made
for healthful effort ; Tyranny has crushed him long: he shall
march from good to better, and do battle with the wrong.

"Standing still is childish folly, going backward is a crime :
none should patiently endure any ill that he can cure. Onward ! keep the march of Time ! Onward ! While a wrong
remains to be conquered by the right ; while Oppression lifts
a finger to affront us by his might ; while an error clouds the
reason of the universal heart, or a slave awaits his freedom—
action is the wise man's part.

"Lo ! the world is rich in blessings ; Earth and Ocean,
Flame and Wind, have unnumbered secrets still, to be ran
sacked, when you will, for the service of mankind : Science is
a child, as yet ; but her power and scope shall grow, and her
triumphs in the future shall diminish toil and woe ; shall
extend the bounds of pleasure with an ever-widening ken ; and,
of woods and wildernesses, make the homes of happy men.

"Onward !—there *are* ills to conquer ; daily, wickedness is
wrought ; Tyranny is swoln with Pride, Bigotry is deified,
Error intertwined with Thought ; Vice and Misery ramp and
crawl : root them out, their day has passed ; Goodness is alone
immortal, Evil was not made to last : Onward ! and all Earth
shall aid us ere our peaceful flag be furled !"—And the
preaching of this Preacher stirs the pulses of the world.

The Red Thread of Honour.

Eleven men of England
    A breast-work charged in vain ;
Eleven men of England
    Lie stripped, and gashed, and slain.
Slain ; but of foes that guarded
    Their rock-built fortress well,
Some twenty had been mastered,
    When the last soldier fell.

Whilst Napier piloted his wondrous way
    Across the sand-waves of the desert sea,
Then flashed at once, on each fierce clan, dismay,
    Lord of their wild Truckee.
These missed the glen to which their steps were bent,
    Mistook a mandate, from afar half heard,
And, in that glorious error, calmly went
    To death without a word.

The robber chief mused deeply,
    Above those daring dead ;
"Bring here," at length he shouted,
    "Bring quick, the battle thread.
Let Eblis blast for ever
    Their souls, if Allah will :
But we must keep unbroken
    The old rules of the Hill.

"Before the Ghiznee tiger
    Leapt forth to burn and slay ;
Before the holy Prophet
    Taught our grim tribes to pray :
Before Secunder's lances
    Pierced through each Indian glen :
The mountain laws of honour
    Were framed for fearless men.

"Still when a chief dies bravely,
    We bind with green one wrist—
Green for the brave, for heroes
    One crimson thread we twist.

Say ye, oh gallant Hillmen,
    For these, whose life has fled,
Which is the fitting colour,
    The green one, or the red?"
" Our brethren, laid in honoured graves, may wear
    Their green reward," each noble savage said ;
" To these, whom hawks and hungry wolves shall tear,
    Who dares deny the red?"
Thus conquering hate, and steadfast to the right,
    Fresh from the heart that haughty verdict came ;
Beneath a waning moon, each spectral height
    Rolled back its loud acclaim.
Once more the chief gazed keenly
    Down on those daring dead ;
From his good sword their hearts' blood
    Crept to that crimson thread.
Once more he cried, " The judgment,
    Good friends, is wise and true,
But though the red be given,
    Have we not more to do?
" These were not stirred by anger,
    Nor yet by lust made bold ;
Renown they thought above them,
    Nor did they look for gold,
To them their leader's signal
    Was as the voice of God :
Unmoved, and uncomplaining,
    The path it showed they trod.
" As, without sound or struggle,
    The stars unhurrying march,
Where Allah's finger guides them,
    Through yonder purple arch,
These Franks, sublimely silent,
    Without a quickened breath,
Went, in the strength of duty,
    Straight to their goal of death.
" If I were now to ask you
    To name our bravest man

Ye all at once would answer,
　They called him Mehrab Khan.
He sleeps among his fathers,
　Dear to our native land,
With the bright mark he bled for
　Firm round his faithful hand.
" The songs they sing of Roostrum
　Fill all the past with light ;
If truth be in their music,
　He was a noble knight.
But were those heroes living,
　And strong for battle still,
Would Mehrab Khan or Roostrum
　Have climbed, like these, the Hill ? "

And they replied, " Though Mehrab Khan was brave
　As chief, he chose himself what risks to run ;
Prince Roostrum lied, his forfeit life to save,
　Which these had never done."

" Enough ! " he shouted fiercely ;
　" Doomed though they be to hell,
Bind fast the crimson trophy
　Round *both* wrists—bind it well.
Who knows but that great Allah
　May grudge such matchless men,
With none so decked in heaven,
　To the fiends' flaming den ? "

Then all those gallant robbers
　Shouted a stern " Amen ! "
They raised the slaughtered sergeant,
　They raised his mangled ten.
And when we found their bodies
　Left bleaching in the wind,
Around *both* wrists in glory
　That crimson thread was twined.

Then Napier's knightly heart, touched to the core,
　Rung like an echo, to that knightly deed ;
He bade its memory live for evermore,
　That those who run may read.

The Singers.

God sent his Singers upon earth
With songs of sadness and of mirth,
That they might touch the hearts of men,
And bring them back to heaven again.

The first, a youth, with soul of fire,
Held in his hand a golden lyre;
Through groves he wandered, and by streams,
Playing the music of our dreams.

The second, with a bearded face,
Stood singing in the market-place,
And stirred with accents deep and loud
The hearts of all the listening crowd.

A grey old man, the third and last,
Sang in cathedrals dim and vast,
While the majestic organ rolled
Contrition from its mouths of gold.

And those who heard the Singers three,
Disputed which the best might be;
For still their music seemed to start
Discordant echoes in each heart.

But the great Master said, "I see
No best in kind, but in degree;
I gave a various gift to each,
To charm, to strengthen, and to teach.

"These are the three great chords of might,
And he whose ear is tuned aright
Will hear no discord in the three,
But the most perfect harmony."

Above and Below.

I.

O dwellers in the valley-land,
  Who in deep twilight grope and cower,
Till the slow mountain's dial-hand
  Shortens to noon's triumphal hour,

While ye sit idle, do ye think
    The Lord's great work sits idle too?
That light dare not o'erleap the brink
    Of morn, because 'tis dark with you?

Though yet your valleys skulk in night,
    In God's ripe fields the day is cried,
And reapers, with their sickles bright,
    Troop, singing, down the mountain-side:
Come up and feel what health there is
    In the frank Dawn's delighted eyes,
As bending with a pitying kiss,
    The night-shed tears of earth she dries!

The Lord wants reapers: Oh, mount up,
    Before Night comes, and says, " Too late!"
Stay not for taking scrip or cup,
    The Master hungers while ye wait;
'Tis from these heights alone, your eyes
    The advancing spears of day can see,
That o'er the eastern hill-tops rise,
    To break your long captivity.

II.

Lone watcher on the mountain height,
    It is right precious to behold
The first long surf of climbing light
    Flood all the thirsty east with gold;
But we, who in the shadow sit,
    Know also when the day is nigh,
Seeing thy shining forehead lit
    With His inspiring prophecy.

Thou hast thine office; we have ours;
    God lacks not early service here,
But what are thine eleventh hours
    He counts with us for morning cheer;
Our day, for Him, is long enough,
    And when He giveth work to do,
The bruisèd reed is amply tough
    To pierce the shield of error through.

But not the less do thou aspire
  Light's earlier messages to preach ;
Keep back no syllable of fire,
  Plunge deep the rowels of thy speech.
Yet God deems not thine aeried sight
  More worthy than our twilight dim ;
For meek Obedience, too, is Light,
  And following that is finding Him.

A Song for Stout Workers.

Onward, brave men, onward go,
Place is none for rest below ;
He who laggeth faints and fails,
He who presses on prevails!

Monks may nurse their mouldy moods
Caged in musty solitudes ;
Men beneath the breezy sky
March to conquer or to die!

Work and live—this only charm
Warms the blood and nerves the arm,
As the stout pine stronger grows
By each gusty blast that blows.

On high throne or lowly sod,
Fellow-workers we with God ;
Then most like to Him when we
March through toil to victory.

If there be who sob and sigh,
Let them sleep or let them die ;
While we live we strain and strive,
Working most when most alive!

Where the fairest blossom grew,
There the spade had most to do ;
Hearts that bravely serve the Lord,
Like St. Paul, must wear the sword!

Onward, brothers, onward go !
Face to face to find the foe !
Words are weak, and wishing fails,
But the well-aimed blow prevails.

David Livingstone.

Droop, half-mast colours ! bow, bare-headed crowds !
   As this plain coffin o'er the side is slung,
To pass by woods of masts and ratlined shrouds,
   As erst by Afric's trunks liana-hung.

'Tis the last mile, of many thousands trod
   With failing strength, but *never*-failing will,
By the worn frame, now at its rest with God,
   That never rested from its fight with ill.

Or if the ache of travel and of toil
   Would sometimes wring a short sharp cry of pain,
From agony of fever, blain, and boil,
   'Twas but to crush it down, and on again !

He knew not that the trumpet he had blown,
   Out of the darkness of that dismal land,
Had reached, and roused an army of its own,
   To strike the chains from the Slave's fettered hand.

Now, we believe, he knows, sees all is well :
   How God had stayed his will, and shaped his way,
To bring the light to those that darkling dwell,
   With gains that life's devotion *well* repay.

Open the Abbey doors, and bear him in
   To sleep with king and statesman, chief, and sage,
The Missionary, come of weaver-kin,
   But great by work that brooks no lower wage.

He needs *no* epitaph to guard a name
   Which men shall prize while worthy work is known ;
He lived and died for *good*—be that his fame :
   Let marble crumble : this is Living-stone.

UNCLASSIFIED POETRY.

"The Great Renunciation."
From "The Light of Asia."

Then in her tears she slept, but sleeping sighed—
As if that vision passed again—"The time!
The time is come!" Whereat Siddârtha turned,
And, lo! the moon shone by the Crab! the stars
In that same silver order long foretold
Stood ranged to say, "This is the night!—choose thou
The way of greatness or the way of good:
To reign a King of kings, or wander lone,
Crownless and homeless, that the world be helped."
Moreover, with the whispers of the gloom,
Came to his ears again that warning song,
As when the Devas spoke upon the wind:
And surely Gods were round about the place
Watching our Lord, who watched the shining stars.

"I will depart," he spake; "the hour is come!
Thy tender lips, dear Sleeper, summon me
To that which saves the earth but sunders us;
And in the silence of yon sky I read
My fated message flashing. Unto this
Came I, and unto this all nights and days
Have led me; for I will not have that crown
Which may be mine: I lay aside those realms
Which wait the gleaming of my naked sword:
My chariot shall not roll with bloody wheels
From victory to victory, till earth
Wears the red record of my name. I choose
To tread its paths with patient, stainless feet,
Making its dust my bed, its loneliest wastes
My dwelling, and its meanest things my mates;
Clad in no prouder garb than outcasts wear,
Fed with no meats save what the charitable
Give of their will, sheltered by no more pomp
Than the dim cave lends or the jungle-bush.

This will I do because the woful cry
Of life and all flesh living cometh up
Into my ears, and all my soul is full
Of pity for the sickness of this world;
Which I will heal, if healing may be found
By uttermost renouncing and strong strife.
For which of all the great and lesser gods
Have power or pity? Who hath seen them—who?
What have they wrought to help their worshippers?
How hath it steaded man to pray, and pay
Tithes of the corn and oil, to chant the charms,
To slay the shrieking sacrifice, to rear
The stately fane, to feed the priests, and call
On Vishnu, Shiva, Surya, who save
None—not the worthiest—from the griefs that teach
Those litanies of flattery and fear
Ascending day by day, like wasted smoke?
Hath any of my brothers 'scaped thereby
The aches of life, the stings of love and loss,
The fiery fever and the ague-shake,
The slow, dull, sinking into withered age,
The horrible dark death—and what beyond
Waits—till the whirling wheel comes up again,
And new lives bring new sorrows to be borne,
New generations for the new desires
Which have their end in the old mockeries?
Hath any of my tender sisters found
Fruit of the fast or harvest of the hymn.
Nay; it may be some of the Gods are good
And evil some, but all in action weak;
Both pitiful and pitiless, and both—
As men are—bound upon this wheel of change,
Knowing the former and the after lives.
For so our scriptures truly seem to teach,
That—once, and wheresoe'er, and whence begun—
Life runs its rounds of living, climbing up
From mote, and gnat, and worm, reptile, and fish,
Bird and shagged beast, man, demon, deva, God,
To clod and mote again; so are we kin
To all that is; and thus, if one might save

Man from his curse, the whole wide world should share
The lightened horror of this ignorance
Whose shadow is still fear, and cruelty
Its bitter pastime. Yea, if one might save!
And means must be! There must be refuge! Men
Perished in winter-winds till one smote fire
From flint-stones coldly hiding what they held,
The red spark treasured from the kindling sun.
They gorged on flesh like wolves, till one sowed corn,
Which grew a weed, yet makes the life of man;
They mowed and babbled till some tongue struck speech,
And patient fingers framed the lettered sound.
What good gift have my brothers, but it came
From search and strife and loving sacrifice?
If one, then, being great and fortunate,
Rich, dowered with health and ease, from birth designed
To rule—if he would rule—a King of kings;
If one, not tired with life's long day but glad
I' the freshness of its morning, one not cloyed
With love's delicious feasts, but hungry still;
If one not worn and wrinkled, sadly sage,
But joyous in the glory and the grace
That mix with evils here, and free to choose
Earth's loveliest at his will: one even as I,
Who ache not, lack not, grieve not, save with griefs
Which are not mine, except as I am man;—
If such a one, having so much to give,
Gave all, laying it down for love of men,
And thenceforth spent himself to search for truth,
Wringing the secret of deliverance forth,
Whether it lurk in hells or hide in heavens,
Or hover, unrevealed, nigh unto all:
Surely at last, far off, sometime, somewhere,
The veil would lift for his deep-searching eyes,
The road would open for his painful feet,
That should be won for which he lost the world,
And Death might find him conqueror of death.
This will I do, who have a realm to lose,
Because I love my realm, because my heart
Beats with each throb of all the hearts that ache,

Known and unknown, these that are mine and those
Which shall be mine, a thousand million more
Saved by this sacrifice I offer now.

Robert of Lincoln.

(Verse printed as Prose.)

Merrily swinging on brier and weed, near to the nest of his little dame, over the mountain-side or mead, Robert of Lincoln is telling his name :—" Bob-o'-link ! bob-o'-link ! spink, spank, spink ! Snug and safe is that nest of ours, hidden among the summer flowers, chee, chee, chee ! chink ! "

Robert of Lincoln is gaily dressed, wearing a bright black wedding-coat ; white are his shoulders and white his crest. Hear him call his merry note :—" Bob-o'-link ! bob-o'-link ! spink, spank, spink ! Look, what a nice new coat is mine ! Sure there never was a bird so fine ! Chee, chee, chee ! chink ! "

Robert of Lincoln's Quaker wife, pretty and quiet, with plain brown wings, passing at home a patient life, broods in the grass while her husband sings :—" Bob-o'-link ! bob-o'-link ! spink, spank, spink ! Brood, kind creature ; you need not fear thieves and robbers while I am here. Chee, chee, chee ! chink ! "

Modest and shy as a nun is she, one weak chirp is her only note ; braggart and prince of braggarts is he, pouring boasts from his little throat :—" Bob-o'-link ! bob-o'-link ! spink, spank, spink ! Never was I afraid of man ; catch me, cowardly knaves, if you can,—chee, chee, chee ! chink ! "

Six white eggs on a bed of hay, freckled with purple,—a pretty sight ! there, as the Mother sits all day, Robert is singing with all his might :—" Bob-o'-link ! bob-o'-link ! spink, spank, spink ! Nice good wife, that never goes out, keeping house while I frolic about. Chee, chee, chee ! chink ! "

As soon as the little ones chip the shell, six wide mouths are open for food ; Robert of Lincoln bestirs him well, gathering seed for the hungry brood. " Bob-o'-link ! bob-o'-link ! spink, spank, spink ! This new life is likely to be hard for a gay young fellow like me. Chee, chee, chee ! chink ! "

Robert of Lincoln at length is made sober with work and silent with care ; off is his holiday garment laid, half forgotten that merry air :—" Bob-o'-link ! bob-o'-link ! spink, spank, spink ! Nobody knows, but my mate and I, where our nest and our nestlings lie. Chee, chee, chee ! chink ! "

Summer wanes ; the children are grown ; fun and frolic no more he knows ; Robert of Lincoln's a humdrum crone ; off he flies, and *we* sing as he goes :—" Bob-o'-link ! bob-o'-link ! spink, spank, spink ! When you can pipe that merry old strain, Robert of Lincoln, come back again ! Chee, chee, chee ! chink ! "

The Creed of the Bells.

(Verse printed as Prose.)

How sweet the chime of Sabbath bells !—Each one its Creed in music tells, in tones that float upon the air as soft as song, as pure as prayer ! And I will put in simple rhyme the language of each golden chime : my happy heart with rapture swells, responsive to the bells—sweet bells !

" In deeds of love, excel ! excel ! " chimed out, from ivied towers, a bell ; " Oh ! heed the Church—not based on sands,—emblem of one not built with hands : its forms and sacred rites revere ! Come worship here ! Come worship here ! In rituals and faith excel ! "—chimed out the " Episcopalian " bell !

" Oh ! heed the ancient landmarks well ! " in solemn tones exclaimed a bell. "No progress made by mortal man can change the just eternal plan : with God there can be nothing new ; ignore the false, embrace the true, while all is well !—is well ! —is well ! "—pealed out the " Presbyterian " bell !

" Ye purifying waters, swell ! " in mellow tones rang out a bell. " Though trust alone in Christ can save, man must be plunged beneath the wave, to show the world unfaltering faith in what the sacred Scripture saith : oh, swell ! ye rising waters, swell ! "—pealed out the clear-toned " Baptist " bell.

" Not faith alone, but works as well, must test the soul ! " said a soft bell. " Come here, and cast aside your load ; and work your way along the road, with faith in God, and faith in man, and hope in Christ—where hope began : do well ! do well ! do well ! do well ! "—rang out the friendly " Quaker " bell.

" Farewell ! farewell ! base world farewell ! " in touching tones exclaimed a bell. " Life is a boon to mortals given, to fit the soul for bliss in heaven; do not invoke the avenging rod; come here, and learn the way to God! Say to the world, 'Farewell! farewell!'"—pealed forth the solemn "Cloister" bell!

"To all, the truth we tell! we tell!" shouted, in ecstacies, a bell. "Come, all ye weary wanderers, see! our LORD has made salvation free! repent, believe, have faith!—and then be saved, and praise the Lord! Amen! Salvation's free, we tell! we tell!"—shouted the "Methodistic" bell!

"In after-life there is no hell!" in raptures rang a hopeful bell. "Look up to heaven this holy day, where angels wait to lead the way: there are no fires, no fiends, to blight the future life: be just and right: No hell! no hell! no hell! no hell!" rang out the "Universalist" bell!

"The Pilgrim Fathers heeded well my cheerful voice," pealed forth a bell. "No fetters here, to clog the soul: no arbitrary forms control the free heart and progressive mind, that leave the dusky past behind. Speed well! speed well! speed well! speed well!"—pealed out the "Independent" bell!

"No rigid creeds to doom to hell!" in solemn joy rang out a bell. "Great men have stamped their fervent zeal upon all hearts, which truly feel that loyalty to God will be the fealty that makes men free! God's praise alone still tell! still tell!" rang out the "Unitarian" bell!

"All hail, ye saints in heaven that dwell close by the Cross!" exclaimed a bell. "Lean o'er the battlements of bliss, and deign to bless a world like this: let mortals kneel before this shrine —adore the water and the wine! All hail, ye saints! the chorus swell!"—chimed out the grand old "Catholic" bell!

"Ye workers all, who toil so well to save the race!" said a sweet bell, "with varied badge, and banner, come,—each brave heart beating like a drum; be royal men of noble deeds, for love is holier than creeds; in faith, hope, charity, excel!" —sang forth each creed— rang forth each bell!

The Old Schoolmaster.

He sat at his desk at the close of day, for he felt the weight of
 his many years.—
His form was bent and his hair was grey, and his eyes were
 dim with the falling tears.

The school was out and his task was done, and the house seemed
  now so strangely still,
As the red beam of the setting sun stole silently over the
  window-sill,—
Stole silently into the twilight gloom, and the deepening
  shadows fell athwart
The vacant seats and the vacant room, and the vacant place
  in the old man's heart—
For his school had been all in all to him, who had no wife,
  child, land, nor gold ;
But his frame was weak, and his eyes were dim, and the fiat
  was issued at last—" Too old."

He bowed his head on his trembling hands a moment, as one
  might bend to pray;
" Too old ! " they say, and the school demands a wiser and
  younger head to-day.
" Too old ! too old ! " these men forget it was I who guided
  their tender years ;
Their hearts were hard, and they pitied not my trembling lips
  and my falling tears.

" Too old ! too old ! " it was all they said ; I looked in their
  faces one by one,
But they turned away, and my heart was lead : " Dear Lord,
  it is hard, but Thy will be done."
The night stole on and a blacker gloom was over the vacant
  benches cast ;
The master sat in the silent room, but his mind was back in
  the days long past.

And he smiled as his kindly glances fell on the well beloved
  faces there—
John, Rob, and Will, and laughing Nell, and blue-eyed Bess,
  with golden hair,
And Tom, and Charley, and Ben, and Paul, who stood at the
  head of the spelling class—
All in their places—and yet they all were lying under the
  graveyard grass.

Thus all night long, till the morning came, and the darkness
  folded her robe of gloom,

And the sun looked in with his eye of flame, on the vacant
    seats of the silent room,
And the wind stole over the window-sill, and swept through
    the aisles in a merry rout;
But the face of the master was white and still—his work was
    finished, his school was out.

A Character.

So noble that he cannot see
    He stands in aught above the rest,
But does his greatness easily,
    And mounts his scaffold with a jest:

Not vaunting any daily death,
    Because he scorns the thing that dies,
And not in love with any breath
    That might proclaim him grand or wise.

Not much concerned with schemes that show
    The counterchange of weak with strong,
But never passing by a woe,
    Nor sitting still to watch a wrong.

Of all hearts careful save his own :
    Most tender when he suffers most;
Wont, if a foe must be o'erthrown,
    To count, but never grudge the cost.

Sharp insight, severing with a glance
    Greater from less, from substance shade ;
Faith, in gross darkness, of mischance
    Unable to be much afraid ;

Out-looking eyes that seek and scan,
    Ready to love what they behold ;
Quick reverence for his brother man ;
    Quick sense where gilding is not gold.

Such impulse of his self-control,
    It seems a voluntary grace,
The careless grandeur of a soul
    That holds no mirror to his face.

True sympathy, a light that grows
    And broadens like the summer morn's,
And hope that trusts before it knows,
    Being out of tune with all the scorns.

On-moving, temperately intent
    On radiant ends by means as bright,
And never cautious, but content
    With all the bitter fruits of right.

Under this shade the tired may lie,
    Worn with the greatness of their way;
Under this shield the brave may die,
    Aware that they have won the day.

For such a leader lifts his times
    Out of the limits of the night,
And, falling grandly, while he climbs,
    Falls with his face toward the height.

Only a Wee Bit Bairn.

Only a wee bit bairn, but 'tis bitterly hard to miss
The tread of her toddling feet, the balm of her loving kiss,
The grasp of her gentle hand, the touch of her soft, warm cheek;
Blue eyes beaming with love, that the young tongue could not
    speak.
They say she has gone before us, where little children go,
To dwell in a garden of lilies, in garments white as snow.
But we envy the angels our treasure, and wish her back once
    more,
Her small, sweet face at the window, her laugh at the open door.

Only a wee bit bairn, with soft, blue, bonny eyes;
Ready to dance with fun, or laugh with the light of surprise;
Hands ever ready for mischief, mouth ever ready for glee,
Voice like a cherub—at least so it seemed to her mother and me.
Seraphs have given her welcome, coaxed her to enter the fold,
Where lambs that are missed on earth are gathered and lovingly
    told.

But our ears were so used to her bleating, we hear what no
    others can hear,
The cry of a lost little child from some distant, unseen sphere.

Only a wee bit bairn, with lamb-like innocent ways,
But the lilt of her little voice will be heard to the end of our
    days,
Blithe as a bee was our baby, and sweet as the flowers in May ;
Now she sleeps under the daisies with which she delighted to
    play.
They bid us be patient and faithful, that God brings all things
    right,
But we pine for her prattle by day, and her dear little form at
    night.
They say she is singing to angels—we want her to sing to us
    here ;
Could we tire of such music as hers in little less than a year?

Only a wee little bairn, with pinky hands and toes,
Teeth like the purest of pearls, lips and cheeks like a rose,
Beautiful glossy hair, that curled like the shoots of a vine,
And bound with a magic clasp her mother's heart and mine.
They say she is happy—we feel it! but think that it hardly
    can be—
Torn from her brothers and sisters, her loving mother and me.
We gaze at the stars above us, and bow to the weight of our load;
Perchance the same Hand that has scattered will gather the
    thorns from our road.

The Fool's Prayer.

The royal feast was done; the king
Sought some new sport to banish care,
And to his jester cried, "Sir Fool,
Kneel down and make for us a prayer!"

The jester doffed his cap and bells,
And stood the mocking court before:
They could not see the bitter smile
Behind the painted grin he wore.

He bowed his head and bent his knee
Upon the monarch's silken stool;
His pleading voice arose, "O Lord,
Be merciful to me, a fool!

"No pity, Lord, could change the heart
From red with wrong to white as wool,
The rod must heal the sin; but, Lord,
Be merciful to me, a fool!

"'Tis not by guilt the onward sweep
Of truth and right, O Lord, we stay;
'Tis by our follies that so long
We hold the earth from Heaven away.

"These clumsy feet still in the mire,
Go crushing blossoms without end;
These hard well-meaning hands, we thrust
Among the heart-strings of a friend.

"The ill-timed truth we might have kept,
Who knows how sharp it pierced and stung;
The word we had not sense to say,
Who knows how grandly it had rung!

"Our faults no tenderness should ask,
The chastening stripes must cleanse them all
But for our blunders: Oh, in shame,
Before the eyes of Heaven we fall.

"Earth bears no balsam for mistakes:
Men crown the knave, and scourge the tool
That did his will; but Thou, O Lord,
Be merciful to me, a fool."

The room was hushed; in silence rose
The king, and sought his gardens cool,
And walked apart, and murmured low,
"Be merciful to me, a fool."

Marit and I.

Marit at the brookside sitting, rosy, dimpled, merry-eyed,
Saw her lovely visage trembling in the mirror of the tide,
While between her pretty teeth a golden coil of hair she held;
Like a shining snake it quivered in the tide, and shrunk and swelled.

And she dipped her dainty fingers deftly in the chilly brook ;
Scarce she minded how her image with the ripples curved and shook ;
Stooping with a tiny shudder, dashed the water in her face ;
O'er her brow and cheeks the dew-drops glistening rolled and fell
    apace.
Breathless sat I, safely hidden in the tree-top dense and green ;
For a maid is ne'er so sweet as when she thinks herself unseen ;
And I saw her with a scarlet ribbon tie her braid of hair,
And it seemed to me that moment I had ne'er seen aught so fair.
Now, if you will never breathe it, I will tell you something queer—
Only step a little nearer ; let me whisper in your ear ;
If you think it was the first time that in this sequestered dell
I beheld the little Marit—well, 'tis scarcely fair to tell.
There within my leafy bower sat I, happy as a king,
And two anxious wrens were flitting round about me twittering,
While I gazed at Marit's image framed in heaven's eternal blue,
While the clouds were drifting past it, and the birds across it flew.
But anon the smile that hovered in the water stole away,
Though the sunshine through the birch leaves flung of light its shim-
    mering spray,
And a breath came floating upward as if some one gently sighed,
And at just the self-same moment sighed the image in the tide.
Then I heard a mournful whisper : "O thou poor, thou pretty face !
Without gold what will avail thee, bloom of beauty, youth and grace ?
For a maid who has no dower—" and her curly head she shook :
It was little Marit speaking to her image in the brook.
More I heard not, for the whisper in a shivering sigh expired,
And the image in the water looked so sad and sweet and tired.
Full of love and full of pity, down I stooped her plaint to hear :
I could almost touch the ringlets curling archly round her ear.
Nearer, still a little nearer, forth I crept along the bough.
Tremblingly her lips were moving, and a cloud rose on her brow,
" Precious darling," thought I, "grieve not that thou hast no lover
    found—"
Crash the branch went, and, bewildered, down I tumbled on the
    ground.
Up then sprang the little Marit with a cry of wild alarm,
And she gazed as if she dreaded I had come to do her harm.
Swift she darted through the bushes, and with stupid wonder mute
Stood I staring blankly after ere I started in pursuit.
And a merry chase I gave her through the underbush and copse :
Over fallen trunks and boulders on she fled with skips and hops ;
Glancing sharply o'er her shoulder when she heard my footsteps
    sound,
Dashing on with reckless terror like a deer before the hound.

Hot with zeal I broke my pathway where the clustered boughs were dense,
For I wanted to assure her I intended no offence ;
And at last, exhausted, fell she on the green-sward quivering,
Sobbing, panting, pleading, weeping, like a wild, unreasoning thing.
" Marit," said I, stooping down, " I hardly see why you should cry :
There is scarce in all the parish such a harmless lad as I ;
And you know I always liked you "—here my voice was soft and low.
" No, indeed," she sobbed, in answer—" no, indeed, I do not know."
But methought that in her voice there was a touch of petulance ;
Through the glistening tears I caught a little shy and furtive glance.
Growing bolder then, I clasped her dainty hand full tenderly,
Though it made a mock exertion, struggling faintly to be free.
" Little Marit," said I, gently, " tell me what has grieved you so,
For I heard you sighing sorely at the brook a while ago."
" O," she said, her sobs subduing, with an air demure and meek—
" O, it was that naughty kitten ; he had scratched me on the cheek."
" Nothing worse ?" I answered, gayly, while I strove her glance to catch.
" Let me look ; my kiss is healing. May I cure the kitten's scratch ? "
And I kissed the burning blushes on her cheeks in heedless glee,
Though the marks of Pussy's scratches were invisible to me.
" O thou poor, thou pretty darling ! " cried I, frantic with delight,
While she gazed upon me smiling, yet with eyes that tears made bright,
" Let thy beauty be thy dower, and be mine to have and hold ;
For a face as sweet as thou hast needs, in sooth, no frame of gold."

Scandal.

A woman to a holy father went ;
Confession of her sins was her intent ;
And so her misdemeanors, great and small,
She faithfully rehearsed them all ;
And chiefest in her catalogue of sin,
She owned that she a tale-bearer had been,
And borne a bit of scandal up and down
To all the long-tongued gossips in the town.
The holy father for her other sins
Granted the absolution asked of him ;
But while for all the rest he pardon gave,
He told her this offence was very grave,

And that to do fit penance she must go
Out by the wayside, where the thistles grow,
And gathering the largest, ripest one,
Scatter its seeds, and that when this was done
She must come back again another day
To tell him; his commands she must obey.

. . . .

Feeling right glad she had escaped so well,
Next day but one she went the priest to tell;
The priest sat still and heard her story through,
Then said : " There's something still for you to do ;
Those little thistle-seeds which you have sown
I bid you to re-gather, every one."
The woman said : " But, father, 'twould be vain
To try to gather up those seeds again ;
The winds have scattered them both far and wide
O'er the meadowed vale and mountain side."
The father answered : " May I hope from this
The lesson I have taught, you will not miss ? '
You cannot gather back the scattered seeds,
Which far and wide will grow to noxious weeds,
Nor can the mischief once by scandal sown
By any penance be again undone.

The Charming Woman.

So Miss Myrtle is going to marry?
   What a number of hearts she will break !
There's Lord George and Tom Brown and Sir Harry,
   Are dying of love for her sake !
'Tis a match that we all must approve,
   Let the gossips say all that they can !
For indeed she's a *charming* woman,
   And he's a most fortunate man.
Yes, indeed, she's a *charming* woman,
   And she reads both Latin and Greek ;
And I'm told that she solved a problem
   In Euclid, before she could speak !
Had she been but a daughter of mine,
   I'd have taught her to hem and to sew,

But her mother—a *charming* woman—
  Couldn't think of such trifles, you know !
Oh, she's really a *charming* woman !
  But I think she's a little too thin ;
And no wonder such very late hours
  Should ruin her beautiful skin !
Her shoulders are rather too bare,
  And her dress might be longer, they say ;
But I'm told that those *charming* women
  May dress in this scant sort of way.

Yes, she's really a *charming* woman !
  But have you observed, by the bye,
A something that's rather uncommon,
  In the flash of that very bright eye ?
It may be a fancy of mine,
  Though her voice *has* a rather sharp tone ;
But I'm told that those *charming* women
  Are apt to have wills of their own !

She sings like a bulfinch or linnet,
  And she talks like an archbishop, too ;
She can play you a rubber, and *win* it,
  If she's got nothing better to do !
She can chatter of poor laws and tithes,
  And the value of labour and land ;
'Tis a pity when *charming* women
  Talk of things they don't understand !

I'm told that she hasn't a penny,
  Yet her gowns would make Mr. Worth stare,
And I fear that her bills must be many—
  But, you know, that's her husband's affair !
Such husbands are very uncommon,
  So regardless of prudence and pelf ;
But they say such a *charming* woman
  Is a fortune, you know, in *herself !*

She has brothers and sisters by dozens,
  And all *charming* people, they say !
And she's several tall Irish cousins,
  Whom she loves—in a sisterly way.

Oh, young men! if you'd take my advice,
You will find it an excellent plan—
Don't marry a *charming* woman,
If you are a *sensible* man!

SATIRE AND HUMOUR.

Aunt Tabitha.

(Verse printed as Prose.)

Whatever I do and whatever I say, Aunt Tabitha tells me that isn't the way; when *she* was a girl (forty summers ago), Aunt Tabitha tells me they never did so.—Dear aunt! If I only would take her advice—but I like my own way, and I find it *so* nice! and besides, I forget half the things I am told, but they all will come back to me—when I am old.—If a youth passes by, it may happen, no doubt, he may chance to look in as I chance to look out; *she* would never endure an impertinent stare, it is *horrid*, she says, and I mustn't sit there.—A walk in the moonlight has pleasures, I own, but it isn't quite safe to be walking alone; so I take a lad's arm,—just for safety, you know,—but Aunt Tabitha tells me, *they* didn't do so.—How wicked we are, and how good they were then! They kept at arm's length those detestable men; what an era of virtue she lived in!—but stay—were the men all such rogues in Aunt Tabitha's day?—If the men *were* so wicked—I'll ask my papa how he dared to propose to my darling mamma? Was he like the rest of them? Goodness! who knows? and what shall *I* say if a wretch should propose? —I am thinking if aunt knew so little of sin, what a wonder Aunt Tabitha's *aunt* must have been! and her *great-aunt*—it scares me—how shockingly sad that we girls of to-day are so frightfully bad!—A martyr will save us, and nothing else can; let *me* perish to rescue some wretched young man! Though when to the altar a victim I go, Aunt Tabitha 'll tell me *she* never did so!

Trouble in the 'Amen Corner.'

(Verse printed as Prose.)

'Twas a stylish congregation, that of Theophrastus Brown, and its organ was the finest and the biggest in the town, and the chorus—all the papers favourably commented on it, for 'twas said each female member had a forty-dollar bonnet. Now in the 'amen corner' of the church sat Brother Eyer, who persisted every Sabbath-day in singing with the choir; he was poor, but genteel-looking, and his heart as snow was white, and his old face beamed with sweetness when he sang with all his might. His voice was cracked and broken, age had touched his vocal chords, and nearly every Sunday he would mispronounce the words of the hymns: and 'twas no wonder; he was old and nearly blind, and the choir rattling onward always left him far behind. The chorus stormed and blustered, Brother Eyer sang too slow, and then he used the tunes in vogue a hundred years ago; at last the storm-cloud burst, and the church was told, in fine, that the brother must stop singing, or the choir would resign.

Then the pastor called together in the lecture-room one day seven influential members who subscribe more than they pay, and having asked God's guidance in a printed prayer or two, they put their heads together to determine what to do. They debated, thought, suggested, till at last 'dear Brother York,' who last winter made a million on a sudden rise in pork, rose and moved that a committee wait at once on Brother Eyer, and proceed to rake him lively 'for disturbin'' of the choir.' Said he: 'In that 'ere organ I've invested quite a pile, and we'll sell it if we cannot worship in the latest style. Our Philadelphy tenor tells me 'tis the hardest thing fer to make God understand him when the brother tries to sing. We've got the biggest organ, the best-dressed choir in town, we pay the steepest sal'ry to our pastor, Brother Brown; but if we must humour ignorance because it's blind and old—if the choir's to be pestered, I will seek another fold.'

Of course the motion carried, and one day a coach and four, with the latest style of driver, rattled up to Eyer's door; and the sleek, well-dressed committee, Brothers Sharkey, York, and Lamb, as they crossed the humble portal took good care to miss the jamb. They found the choir's great trouble sitting in his old arm-chair, and the summer's golden sunbeams lay upon his thin white hair; he was singing 'Rock of Ages' in a voice both cracked and low, but the angels understood him, 'twas all he cared to know.

Said York : 'We're here, dear brother, with the vestry's approbation, to discuss a little matter that affects the congregation.' 'And the choir, too,' said Sharkey, giving Brother York a nudge. 'And the choir, too!" he echoed with the graveness of a judge. 'It was the understanding when we bargained for the chorus, that it was to relieve us, that is, do the singing for us; if we rupture the agreement, it is very plain, dear brother, it will leave our congregation and be gobbled by another. We don't want any singing except that what we've bought! The latest tunes are all the rage; the old ones stand for naught; and so we have decided—are you listening, Brother Eyer?—that you'll have to stop your singin', for it flurrytates the choir.'

The old man slowly raised his head, a sign that he did hear, and on his cheek the trio caught the glitter of a tear; his feeble hands pushed back the locks white as the silky snow, as he answered the committee in a voice both sweet and low. 'I've sung the psalms of David for nearly eighty years; they've been my staff and comfort, and calmed life's many fears. I'm sorry I disturb the choir, perhaps I'm doing wrong; but when my heart is filled with praise, I can't keep back a song. 'I wonder if beyond the tide that's breaking at my feet, in the far-off heavenly temple, where the Master I shall greet—yes, I wonder, when I try to sing the songs of God up higher, if the angel band will church me for disturbing heaven's choir.'

A silence filled the little room; the old man bowed his head; the carriage rattled on again, but Brother Eyer was dead! Yes, dead! his hand had raised the veil the future hangs before us, and the Master dear had called him to the everlasting chorus. The choir missed him for a while, but he was soon forgot, a few church-goers watched the door; the old man entered not. Far away, his voice no longer cracked, he sings his heart's desires, where there are no church committees and no fashionable choirs!

The Little Quaker Sinner.

A little Quaker maiden, with dimpled cheek and chin,
Before an ancient mirror stood, and viewed her form within—

She wore a gown of sober grey, a cape demure and prim,
With only simple fold and hem, yet dainty, neat, and trim.
Her bonnet, too, was grey and stiff; its only line of grace
Was in the lace, so soft and white, shirred round her rosy face.
Quoth she, "Oh, how I hate this hat ! I hate this gown and cape !
I do wish all my clothes were not of such outlandish shape ;
The children passing by to school have ribbons on their hair ;
The little girl next door wears blue ; oh, dear, if I could dare,
I know what I should like to do !"—(The words were whispered low,
Lest such tremendous heresy should reach her aunts below.)
Calmly reading in the parlour sat the good aunts, Faith and Peace,
Little dreaming how rebellious throbbed the heart of their young niece.
All their prudent, humble teaching wilfully she cast aside,
And, her mind now fully conquered by sad vanity and pride,
She, with trembling heart and fingers, on a hassock sat her down,
And this little Quaker sinner *sewed a tuck into her gown !*
"Little Patience, art thou ready? Fifth-day meeting-time has come,
Mercy Jones and Goodman Elder with his wife have left their home."
'Twas Aunt Faith's sweet voice that called her, and the naughty little maid—
Gliding down the dark old stairway—hoped their notice to evade,
Keeping shyly in their shadow as they went out at the door,
Ah, never little Quakeress a guiltier conscience bore !
Dear Aunt Faith walked looking upward ; all her thoughts were pure and holy ;
And Aunt Peace walked gazing downward, with a humble mind and lowly.
But "tuck—*tuck !*" chirped the sparrows at the little maiden's side ;
And, in passing Farmer Watson's, where the barn-door opened wide,
Every sound that issued from it, every grunt and every cluck,
Seemed to her affrightened fancy like "a tuck !" "a tuck !" "a tuck !"

In meeting Goodman Elder spoke of pride and vanity,
While all the Friends seemed looking round that dreadful tuck
   to see.
How it swelled in its proportions, till it seemed to fill the air,
And the heart of little Patience grew heavier with her care.
Oh, the glad relief to her, when, prayers and exhortations ended,
Behind her two good aunties her homeward way she wended.

The pomps and vanities of life she'd seized with eager arms,
And deeply she had tasted of the world's alluring charms,—
Yea, to the dregs had drained them, and only this to find:
All was vanity of spirit and vexation of the mind.
So repentant, saddened, humbled, on her hassock she sat down,
And this little Quaker sinner *ripped the tuck out of her gown!*

On the Door-Step.

The conference-meeting through at last,
　　We boys around the vestry waited
To see the girls come tripping past,
　　Like snow-birds willing to be mated.

Not braver he that leaps the wall
　　By level musket flashes bitten,
Than I, who stepped before them all,
　　Who longed to see me get the mitten.

But no! she blushed and took my arm:
　　We let the old folks have the highway,
And started toward the Maple Farm
　　Along a kind of lovers' by-way.

I can't remember what we said—
　　'Twas nothing worth a song or story;
Yet that rude path by which we sped
　　Seemed all transformed and in a glory.

The snow was crisp beneath our feet,
　　The moon was full, the fields were gleaming;
By hood and tippet sheltered sweet,
　　Her face with youth and health was beaming.

The little hand outside her muff—
　　O sculptor! if you could but mould it!—

So slightly touched my jacket cuff,
  To keep it warm I had to hold it.
To have her with me there alone—
  'Twas love and fear and triumph blended.
At last we reached the foot-worn stone
  Where that delicious journey ended.

The old folks, too, were almost home :
  Her dimpled hand the latches fingered,
We heard the voices nearer come,
  Yet on the doorstep still we lingered.

She shook her ringlets from her hood,
  And with a 'Thank you, Ned !' dissembled ;
But yet I knew she understood
  With what a daring wish I trembled.

A cloud passed kindly overhead,
  The moon was slyly peeping through it,
Yet hid its face, as if it said,
  'Come, now or never ! do it ! *do it !'*

My lips till then had only known
  The kiss of mother and of sister,
But somehow full upon her own
  Sweet rosy darling mouth—I kissed her !

Perhaps 'twas boyish love, yet still,
  O listless woman ! weary lover !
To feel once more that fresh, wild thrill,
  I'd give—but who can live youth over ?

The Nine Suitors.

(Verse printed as Prose.)

A British ship at anchor lay in the harbour of New York : the stevedores were packing her with Yankee beef and pork. Nine slim Young Men went up the plank, and they were tall and good ; but none of them had ever loved—they said they never would ! But whether they wouldn't,—or whether they couldn't,—or their mothers said they shouldn't,—the world will never know !

The passengers were all on board : the vessel got up steam, and floated down the river, like the—ah—something—of a dream. A pretty Girl came up on deck, and near the railing stood; she never loved a fellow-man, and said she never would. But whether she couldn't,—or whether she wouldn't,—or her Father said she shouldn't,—the world will never know!

The Nine Young Men came up on deck, each in his Sunday clothes, and went abaft the wheel-house, in order to propose. The Lady had no preference, but said that, if she could, she'd marry every one of them,—but it wasn't any good! Now whether she couldn't,—or whether she wouldn't,—or that custom said she shouldn't,—the world will never know!

The Lady asked the Captain how she ever should decide. Said he, "The love of those young men should certainly be tried." So, when they all were present, she fell into the sea; and eight of them jumped after her, the ninth—oh! where was he? Now whether he couldn't (jump),—or whether he wouldn't (swim),—or the Captain said he shouldn't (try),—the world will never know!

Once fairly out of the water, she went up to him, and said, "Dear sir, you are a solid man, and have a level head; so, without further parley, or hint of a pretence, I agree to marry you, sir, for you have common sense." So her Father said he couldn't,—and her Mother said she wouldn't,—and the Captain said he shouldn't,—refuse to give consent!

John Day.

John Day he was the biggest man
  Of all the coachman kind,
With back too broad to be conceived
  By any narrow mind.

The very horses knew his weight
  When he was in the rear,
And wished his box a Christmas-box
  To come but once-a-year.

Alas! against the shafts of love
  What armour can avail?
Soon Cupid sent an arrow through
  His scarlet coat of mail.

The barmaid of the Crown he loved,
   From whom he never ranged ;
For though he changed his horses there,
   His love he never changed.
He thought her fairest of all fares,
   So fondly love prefers ;
And often, among twelve outsides,
   Deemed no outside like hers.
One day, as she was sitting down
   Beside the porter-pump,
He came, and knelt with all his fat,
   And made an offer plump.
Said she, " My taste will never learn
   To like so huge a man,
So I must beg you will come here
   As little as you can."
But still he stoutly urged his suit,
   With vows, and sighs, and tears,
It could not pierce her heart, although
   He drove the " Dart " for years.
In vain he wooed, in vain he sued ;
   The maid was cold and proud,
And sent him off to Coventry,
   While on his way to Stroud.
He fretted all the way to Stroud,
   And thence all back to town ;
The course of love was never smooth,
   So his went up and down.
At last her coldness made him pine
   To merely bones and skin,
But still he loved like one resolved
   To love through thick and thin.
" O Mary! view my wasted back,
   And see my dwindled calf ;
Though I have never had a wife,
   I've lost my better half."
Alas ! in vain he still assailed,
   Her heart withstood the dint ;

Though he had carried sixteen stone,
    He could not move a flint.
Worn out, at last he made a vow
    To break his being's link ;
For he was so reduced in size
    At nothing he could shrink.
Now some will talk in water's praise,
    And waste a deal of breath,
But John, though he drank nothing else,
    He drank himself to death.
The cruel maid that caused his love
    Found out the fatal close,
For, looking in the butt, she saw
    The butt end of his woes.
Some say his spirit haunts the Crown,
    But that is only talk—
For after riding all his life,
    His ghost objects to walk.

A Lay of Real Life.

Who ruined me ere I was born,
Sold every acre, grass or corn,
And left the next heir all forlorn?
                  My Grandfather.

Who said my mother was no nurse,
And physicked me and made me worse,
Till infancy became a curse?
                  My Grandmother.

Who left me in my seventh year
A comfort to my mother dear,
And Mr. Pope, the overseer?
                  My Father.

Who let me starve, to buy her gin,
Till all my bones came through my skin,
Then called me "ugly little sin?"
                  My Mother.

Who said my mother was a Turk,
And took me home—and made me work,
But managed half my meals to shirk?
                    My Aunt.

Who " of all earthly things " would boast,
" He hated others' brats the most,"
And therefore made me feel my post?
                    My Uncle.

Who got in scrapes, an endless score,
And always laid them at my door,
Till many a bitter bang I bore?
                    My Cousin.

Who took me home when mother died,
Again with father to reside,
Black shoes, clean knives, run far and wide?
                    My Stepmother.

Who marred my stealthy urchin joys,
And when I played cried " What a noise !"
Girls always hector over boys—
                    My Sister.

Who used to share in what was mine,
Or took it all, did he incline,
'Cause I was eight, and he was nine?
                    My Brother.

Who stroked my head, and said "Good lad,"
And gave me sixpence, "all he had,"
But at the stall the coin was bad?
                    My Godfather.

Who, gratis, shared my social glass,
But when misfortune came to pass,
Referr'd me to the pump? Alas !
                    My Friend.

Through all this weary world, in brief,
Who ever sympathised with grief,
Or shared my joy—my sole relief?
                    Myself.

R

The Philosopher and her Father.

(Verse printed as Prose.)

A sound came booming through the air—" What is that sound ? " quoth I. My blue-eyed pet, with golden hair, made answer presently, " Papa, you know it very well—that sound —it was Saint Pancras bell." " My own Louise, put down that cat, and come and stand by me ; I'm sad to hear you talk like that, where's your philosophy ? That sound—attend to what I tell—that sound was *not* Saint Pancras bell. Sound is the name the sage selects for the concluding term of a long series of effects, of which the blow's the germ. The following brief analysis shows the interpolations, miss. The blow which, when the clapper slips, falls on your friend, the bell, changes its circle to ellipse (a word you'd better spell), and then comes elasticity, restoring what it used to be. Nay, making it a little more, the circle shifts about, as much as it shrunk in before the bell, you see, swells out ; and so a new ellipse is made (you're not attending I'm afraid). This change of form disturbs the air, which in its turn behaves in like elastic fashion there, creating waves on waves ; these press each other onward, dear, until the outmost finds your ear." " And then, papa, I hear the sound, exactly what I said ; you're only talking round and round, just to confuse my head. All that you say about the bell my Uncle George would call a 'sell.'" " Not so, my child, my child, not so, sweet image of your sire ! a long way further we must go before it's time to tire ; this wondrous, wandering wave, or tide, has only reached your ear's outside. Within that ear the surgeons find a *tympanum*, or drum, which has a little bone behind,—*malleus* it's called by some ; but those not proud of Latin grammar humbly translate it as the hammer. The wave's vibrations this transmits, on to the *incus* bone (*incus* means anvil, which it hits), and this transfers the tone to the small *os, orbiculare*, the tiniest bone that people carry. The *stapes* next—the name recalls a stirrup's form, my daughter—joins, three half-circular canals, each fill'd with limpid water ; their curious lining, you'll observe, made of the auditory nerve. This vibrates next—and then we find the mystic work is crown'd, for there my daughter's gentle mind first recognises sound. See what a host of causes swell to make up what you call 'the bell.'" Awhile she paused, my bright Louise, and ponder'd on the case; then, settling that he meant to tease, she slapp'd her father's face: "You bad old man to sit and tell such gibberybosh about a bell!"

The True Story of Little Boy Blue.

Little Boy Blue, so the story goes,
   One morning while reading fell fast asleep,
When he should have been, as every one knows,
   Watching the cows and sheep.

All of you children remember what
   Came of the nap on that summer morn;
How the sheep got into the meadow-lot,
   The cows got into the corn.

Neglecting a duty is wrong, of course,
   But I've always felt, if we could but know,
That the matter was made a great deal worse
   Than it should have been; and so

I find, in my sifting, that there was one
   More to blame than Little Boy Blue.
I'm anxious to have full justice done,
   And so I know are you.

The one to blame I have found to be,
   I'm sorry to say it, Little Bo-Peep;
But you will remember, perhaps, that she
   Had trouble about her sheep.

Well, Little Bo-Peep came tripping along,
   The sheep she tended were running at large;
Little Boy Blue sat singing a song,
   Faithfully minding his charge.

Said Little Bo-Peep, "It's a burning shame
   That you should sit here from week to week;
Just leave your work, and we'll play a game
   Oh!—well, of hide and seek."

It was dull work, and he liked to play
   Better, I'm sure, than to eat or sleep;

He liked the bloom of the summer day ;
  He liked—he liked Bo-Peep.
And so, with many a laugh and shout,
  They hid from each other—now here, now there ;
And whether the cows were in or out
  Bo-Peep had never a care.
" I will hide once more," said the little maid.
  " You shall not find me this time, I say—
Shut your eyes up tight " (Boy Blue obeyed)—
  " Under this stack of hay."
" Now, wait till I call," said Miss Bo-Peep,
  And over the meadows she slipped away,
With never a thought for cows or sheep—
  Alas ! alas ! the day.
And long and patiently waited he
  For the blithesome call from her rosy lip.
He waited in vain—quite like, you see,
  The boy on the burning ship.
She let down the bars, did Miss Bo-Peep—
  Such trifles as bars she held in scorn—
And into the meadows went the sheep,
  And the cows went into the corn.
By and by, when they found Boy Blue
  In the merest doze, he took the blame.
It was very fine, I think, don't you,
  Not to mention Bo-Peep's name ?
Thus it has happened that all these years
  He has borne the blame she ought to share.
Since I know the truth of it, it appears
  To me to be only fair
To tell the story from shore to shore,
  From sea to sea, and from sun to sun,
Because, as I think I said before,
  I like to see justice done.
And whatever you've read or seen or heard,
  Believe me, children, I tell the true
And only genuine (take my word)
  Story of Little Boy Blue.

Our Village.

Our village, that's to say not Miss Mitford's village, but our village of Bullock Smithy,
Is come into by an avenue of trees, three oak pollards, two elders, and a withy;
And in the middle, there's a green of about not exceeding an acre and a half;
It's common to all, and fed off by nineteen cows, six ponies, three horses, five asses, two foals, seven pigs, and a calf!
Besides a pond in the middle, as is held by a similar sort of common law lease,
And contains twenty ducks, six drakes, three ganders, two dead dogs, four drown'd kittens, and twelve geese.
Of course the green's cropt very close, and does famous for bowling when the little village boys play at cricket;
Only some horse, or pig, or cow, or great jackass is sure to come and stand right before the wicket.
There's fifty-five private houses, let alone barns and workshops, and pig-sties, and poultry huts, and such-like sheds;
With plenty of public-houses—two Foxes, one Green Man, three Bunch of Grapes, one Crown, and six King's Heads.
The Green Man is reckon'd the best, as the only one that for love or money can raise
A postillion, a blue jacket, two deplorable lame white horses, and a ramshackled "neat post-chaise."
There's one parish church for all the people, whatsoever may be their ranks in life or their degrees,
Except one very damp, small, dark, freezing-cold little Methodist chapel of Ease;
And close by the church-yard, there's a stone-mason's yard, that when the time is seasonable
Will furnish with afflictions sore and marble urns and cherubims very low and reasonable.
There's a cage, comfortable enough; I've been in it with Old Jack Jeffrey and Tom Pike;
For the Green Man next door will send you in ale, gin, or anything else you like.
I can't speak of the stocks, as nothing remains of them but the upright post;

But the pound is kept in repairs for the sake of Cob's horse,
  as is always there almost.
There's a smithy of course, where that queer sort of a chap in
  his way, Old Joe Bradley,
Perpetually hammers and stammers, for he stutters and shoes
  horses very badly.
There's a shop of all sorts, that sells every thing, kept by the
  widow of Mr. Task ;
But when you go there it's ten to one she's out of every thing
  you ask.
You'll know her house by the swarm of boys, like flies, about
  the old sugary cask.
There are six empty houses, and not so well papered inside as
  out,
For bill-stickers won't beware, but sticks notices of sales and
  election placards all about.
That's the Doctor's with a green door, where the garden pots
  in the windows is seen ;
A weakly monthly rose that don't blow, and a dead geranium,
  and a tea-plant with five black leaves and one green.
As for hollyoaks at the cottage doors, and honeysuckles and
  jasmines, you may go and whistle ;
But the Tailor's front gardens grow two cabbages, a dock, a
  ha'porth of pennyroyal, two dandelions, and a thistle.
There are three small orchards—Mr. Busby's the schoolmaster's
  is the chief—
With two pear-trees that don't bear ; one plum and an apple,
  that every year is stripped by a thief.
There's another small day-school, too, kept by the respectable
  Mrs. Gaby ;
A select establishment, for six little boys and one big, and
  four little girls and a baby.
There's a rectory, with pointed gables and strange odd chim-
  neys that never smokes,
For the rector don't live on his living like other Christian
  sort of folks ;
There's a barber's, once a-week well filled with rough black-
  bearded shock-headed churls,
And a window with two feminine men's heads, and two
  masculine ladies in false curls ;

There's a butcher's and a carpenter's and a plumber's and a small green-grocer's, and a baker,
But he won't bake on a Sunday, and there's a sexton that's a coal-merchant besides, and an undertaker ;
And a toy-shop, but not a whole one, for a village can't compare with the London shops ;
One window sells drums, dolls, kites, carts, bats, Clout's balls, and the other sells malt and hops.
And Mrs. Brown, in domestic economy not to be a bit behind her betters,
Lets her house to a milliner, a watchmaker, a rat-catcher, a cobbler, lives in it herself, and it's the post-office for letters.
Now I've gone through all the village—ay, from end to end, save and except one more house,
But I haven't come to that—and I hope I never shall—and that's the Village Poor-House !

The Owl Critic.
(Verse printed as Prose.)

"Who stuffed that white owl?" No one spoke in the shop ! the barber was busy, and he couldn't stop ! the customers, waiting their turns, were all reading the *Daily*, the *Herald*, the *Post*, little heeding the young man who blurted out such a blunt question ; not one raised a head or even made a suggestion ; and the barber kept on shaving.—"Don't you see, Mister Brown," cried the youth with a frown, "how wrong the whole thing is, how preposterous each wing is, how flattened the head is, how jammed down the neck is—in short, the whole owl, what an ignorant wreck 'tis ! I make no apology, I've learned owleology, I've passed days and nights in a hundred collections, and cannot be blinded to any deflections arising from unskilful fingers that fail to stuff a bird right, from his beak to his tail. Mister Brown ! Mister Brown ! Do take that bird down, or you'll soon be the laughing-stock all over town !" And the barber kept on shaving.—"I've *studied* owls, and other night fowls, and I tell you what I know to be true ; an owl cannot roost with his limbs so unloosed. No owl in this world ever had his claws curled, ever had his legs slanted, ever had his bill canted, ever had his neck screwed into that attitude. He can't *do* it, because 'tis against all bird laws ; anatomy teaches, ornithology preaches, an owl has a toe that *can't* turn out so ! I've made the white owl my study for years, and to see such a job almost moves me to tears ! Mister Brown, I'm amazed you should be so gone crazed as to put up a bird in that posture absurd ! To *look* at that owl really brings on a dizziness ; the man who stuffed him don't half know his business!" And the barber kept on shaving.— "Examine those eyes, I'm filled with surprise taxidermists should pass off on you such poor glass ; so unnatural they seem they'd make Audubon scream, and John Burroughs laugh to encounter such chaff. Do take that bird down: have him stuffed again, Brown!" And the barber kept on shaving. "With some sawdust and bark I could stuff in the dark an owl better than that. I could make an old hat look more like an owl than that horrid fowl. Stuck up there so stiff like a side of coarse leather, in fact, about *him* there's not one natural feather."—Just then, with a wink and a sly normal lurch, the owl, very gravely, got down from his perch, walked round, and regarded his fault-finding critic (who thought he was stuffed) with a glance analytic. And then fairly hooted, as if he should say : " Your learning's at fault this time, anyway ; don't waste it again on a live bird, I pray. I'm an owl ; you're another, Sir Critic, good day !" And the barber kept on shaving.

In Nevada.

(Verse printed as Prose.)

Like an awful alligator breathing fire and screeching *wildly*, with a pack of hounds behind him, as if hunted by the *furies*, came the smoking locomotive, followed by the cars and tender, down among the mountain gorges, till it stopped before a village as the starry night came on.—Just before a mountain village, where there was a howling shindy, just around a brannew gallows, with a roaring blazing bonfire, casting a red light upon it, while a crowd of roughest rowdies shouted, " Cuss him ! *tear* his vitals ! bust him ! sink him ! burn him ! skin him ! "—evidently much excited as the starry night came on.—On the gallows stood a culprit shrieking painfully for mercy. As the train and engine halted, louder yelled the gasping victim. Then out cried the grim conductor, "What in thunder is the matter? What's ye doin' with that feller? Why've ye got both fire and gallows?" And unto him some one answered, as the starry night came on :—" This all-fired, skunk-eyed villain, whom you see upon the gallows, lately stole the loveliest mewel that you ever sot your peeps on, for a hundred shiny dollars, went and sold it to the Greasers. But, as you perceive, we've nailed him, and at present we're debatin' whether we had better hang him, or else roast him like an Injun, ere the starry night comes on.—And I think ez ther ar' ladies here to grace this gay occasion, in the train, and quite convenient, we had better take and burn him. 'Twould be kinder interestin', or, as folks might say, romantic, to behold an execution, as we do 'em here in *this* town, in the real frontier fashion, ere the starry night comes on."—Up from all the assembled ladies, and from all the passengeros, went a scream of protestation,—" What ! for nothing but a mewel ! only for a hundred dollars roast alive a fine young fellow ! never, never, never, ne—ver ! " Falling on her knees, a damsel begged the maddened crowd to spare him ! and to her replied the spokesman, as the starry night came on :—" Since a lady begs it of us, and as we ar' galiant fellers, we will smash the tail of Jestis, and will spare this orful miscrint, ef you'll raise a hundred dollars to replace the vanished mewel. Then this fiend, unwhipped, undamaged, may go wanderin' to thunder, soon as he tarnation pleases, ere the starry night comes on." Straight among the pitying ladies, and the other passengeros, went the hat around in circle. Dollars, quarters, halves, and greenbacks rained into it till the hundred was accomplished, and the ransom paid unto Judge Lynch in person, who received it very gracious, and at once released the prisoner, sternly bidding him to squaddle, just as fast as he could make it, ere the starry night came on. And the lady who by kneeling had destroyed the path of justice, seized upon the fine young fellow, he who had the mulomania, or who was a kleptomuliac ; and she led him by the halter, while the reckless population made atrocious puns upon it ; and she stowed him in the Pullman as the safest sanctuary, as the starry night came on. It was over. Loud the whistle blew a signal of departure ; still the dying bonfire flickering showed on high the ghastly gallows, seeming like some hungry monster disappointed of a victim, gasping as in fitful anger, pouring out unto the gallows or the sympathetic scaffold, all the story of its sorrow, as the clouds passed o'er the moon-face, as the starry night came on.—Soon the train and those within it reached and passed a second station, and was speeding ever onward, when at once a shriek came ringing— 'twas an utterance from the lady who by tears had baffled justice; loud she cried, "Where is my hero? where, oh, where's the handsome prisoner?" And the affable conductor searched the train from clue to ear-ring, but they could not find the captive. He had clearly just evaded at the station just behind them, as the starry night came on.—Then outspoke a man unnoted hitherto: "I heard the fellow say just now to the conductor, ere we reached the second deapot, that he reckoned he must hook it this here time a little sooner, if he hoped to get his portion of the hundred, since the last time he came awful nigh to lose it; for it might be anted off all 'fore he got a chance to strike it, ere the starry night came on."— And the unknown thus continued: "They hev hed that gallows standin' all the summer and the people mostly git ther livin' from it, for they take ther turns in being mournful victims who hev stolen every one a lovely mewel; and they always every evenin' hev the awful death-fire kindled, and the ghastly captive ready. It's the fourth time I hev seen it, comin' through and never missed it, only for a variation now and then they hire a nigger for the people from New England, as the starry night comes on.—And they find that fire and gallows just as good as a bonanza, for they got the Legislater lately to incopperate it; and I hear the stock is risin' up like prairie smoke in autumn. Yes, in this world men diskiver cur'ous ways to make a livin', ez you'll find when you hev tried it for a year or so about here." And the passengers in silence mused upon this new experience, most of all the fine young lady, as the dragon darted onward, and the starry night came on.

Little Dora's Soliloquy.

I tan't see what our baby boy is dood for anyway:
He don't know how to walk or talk, he don't know how to play;

He tears up ev'ry single zing he posser-bil-ly tan,
An' even tried to break, one day, my mamma's bestest fan.
He's al'ays tumblin' 'bout ze floor, an' gives us awful scares,
An' when he goes to bed at night, he never says his prayers.
On Sunday, too, he musses up my go-to-meetin' clothes,
An' once I foun' him hard at work a-pinc'in' Dolly's nose ;
An' ze uzzer day zat naughty boy (now what you s'pose you zink ?)
Upset a dreat big bottle of my papa's writin' ink ;
An', 'stead of kyin' dood an' hard, as course he ought to done,
He laughed, and kicked his head 'most off, as zough he zought 'twas fun.
He even tries to reach up high, an' pull zings off ze shelf,
An' he's al'ays wantin' you, of course, jus' when you wants you'self.
I rather dess, I really do, from how he pulls my turls,
Zey all was made a-purpose for to 'noy us little dirls ;
An' I wish zere wasn't no such zing as naughty baby boys——
Why—why, zat's him a-kyin' now ; he makes a drefful noise,
I dess I better run and see, for if he has—boo-hoo !—
Felled down ze stairs and killed his-self, whatever s-s-s'all I do !

Altruism.

The *Lovely Mary*, on her way
From Singapore to Boston Bay,
Had cloudless skies and glorious weather,
With favouring winds for days together ;
And everything was going well,
When, near the Cape, it so befell
That, with a most decided shock,
The *Lovely Mary*—struck a rock.

She sank ; but as the night was clear,
The ocean calm, an island near,
All who could keep themselves afloat
With cask, spar, life-preserver, boat—
In short, whatever came to hand—
Put off, and safely reached the land ;
Leaving the gallant ship to sleep
Beneath the waves nine fathoms deep.

Now, as it chanced, upon that ship,
Returning from an Eastern trip,
Two scholars sailed, of great renown,
Jones, and the yet more famous Brown ;
And when 'twas plain that naught could save
The vessel from a watery grave,
As Fate or Chance would have it, each
Espied within convenient reach
Something that both desired to own,—
A life-preserver, which, 'tis known,
Can never be relied upon
To hold up safely more than *one*.
Yet on this life-preserver *both*
Seized in an instant, nothing loath ;
And all of it Brown couldn't clasp
Was quickly locked in Jones's grasp ;
And Jones's keen, determined eye
In grim resolve was equalled by
The stern, uncompromising frown
Upon the lofty brow of Brown.

But, lest you think that selfish thought
In those two noble bosoms wrought,
I will relate, from first to last,
The high, heroic words that passed
From Brown to Jones, and Jones to Brown,
While the good ship was going down,
Dear Reader, bear them well in mind,
And think more nobly of your kind !

Quoth Jones : " Dear Brown, pray do not think
'Tis selfish fear that makes me shrink
From yielding up this wretched breath
To save a fellow-man from death,
I long to cry, ' Dear friend, oh take
This life-preserver for my sake !'
But this, alas ! I cannot do :
I am not free, dear Brown, like you,—
You may enjoy the bliss divine
Of giving up your life for mine ;
But ah ! 'tis different with *me !*

I have a wife and children three;
And, for their sake, I must control
The generous impulse of my soul.
Yet trust me, Brown, most willingly,
Nay, with unfeigned alacrity,
This life-preserver I'd resign,
Were my case yours, or your case mine!"
"Dear Jones, your reasons," Brown replied,
"Are good, and cannot be denied.
All that your words imply is true:
I have no wife nor child like you.
But, Jones, I have a tie to life
Far stronger—do not start—than wife
Or child, though dear, could ever be:
I mean my great 'Cosmogony,'
Of which, as you have doubtless heard,
One volume is to come—the third.
Oh, were that mighty task complete
Down to the last corrected sheet,
Believe me, Jones, to save your life
To your dear family and wife,
I'd yield to you, unmurmuring,
This frail support to which we cling!
But what are wife and children three
Compared with a Cosmogony?
Or what—confess it, dearest Jones—
Are many wives' and children's moans
To that loud cry of grief and woe
With which the learned world shall know
That it can never hope to see
The long expected Volume Three?"

"Quite true," sighed Jones; "and yet—and yet—
I think, dear Brown, that you forgot
The theory of average
As held in this enlightened age.
Had all the mighty men of old—
Kings, scholars, statesmen, heroes bold—
Suffered untimely taking off
With measles, croup, or whooping-cough,

Think you that this great earth would then
Have nourished only common men ?
Had Homer died a stripling lad,
Should we have lost the *Iliad?*
Would Shakespeare's early, timeless death
Have cost us *Hamlet, Lear, Macbeth?*
The voice of reason answers, 'No ;
Wrong not prolific Nature so !'
Now, if this theory is true,
It must apply, dear Brown, to you ;
And fearless, you may leave behind
This master-product of your mind
(Though all unfinished, as you say),
Assured that at no distant day,
Another will be found to do
The work so well begun by you ;
But I——"

" Allow me !" struck in Brown,
" The ship is plainly going down ;
And ere she sinks beneath us, I
Would most decidedly deny
The theory of which you speak ;
It is ingenious, but weak—
A vain though pleasing fallacy,
That never has deluded me.
Besides, the theory, if true,
Applies with equal force to you ;
For, dearest Jones, if you are drowned,
Doubtless *another* will be found
To comfort your dear wife, and be
A father to your children three !"

" Nay, nay !" cried Jones, " you jest, dear Brown—"
But at this point the ship went down ;
The arguments of both, you see,
Balanced to such a nicety,
So fine, so subtle, so profound,
They both held on,—and both were drowned.

Catching the Cat.
(Verse printed as Prose.)

The mice had met in council, they all looked haggard and worn, for affairs had become too terrible to be any longer borne. Not a family out of mourning—there was crape on every hat. They were desperate—something *must* be done, and done at once, to the cat.

An elderly member rose and said :—"It might prove a possible thing to set the trap which they set for us—that one with the awful spring!" The suggestion was applauded loudly by one and all, till somebody squeaked, "That trap would be about ninety-five times too small!"

Then a medical mouse suggested—a little under his breath—they should confiscate the very first mouse that died a natural death, and he'd undertake to poison the cat if they'd let him prepare that mouse. "There's not been a natural death," they cried, "since that cat came into the house!"

The smallest mouse in the council arose with a solemn air, and, by way of increasing his stature, rubbed up his whiskers and hair. He waited until there was silence all along the pantry shelf, and then he said with dignity :—"*I* will catch that cat myself! When next I hear her coming, instead of running away, I shall turn and face her boldly, and pretend to be at play; she will not see her danger, poor creature! I suppose; but as *she* stoops to catch *me*, *I* shall catch *her* by the nose!"

The mice began to look hopeful, yes, even the old ones; when a grey-haired sage said slowly, "and what will you do with her then?" The champion, disconcerted, replied with dignity—"Well, I think, if you'll excuse me, 'twill be wiser not to tell! We all have our inspirations,"—this produced a general smirk—"but we are not all at liberty to explain just how they'll work. I ask you, then, to trust me; you need have no further fears; consider our enemy done for!"—the council gave three cheers.

"I do believe she is coming!" said a small mouse nervously. "Run if you like," said the champion, "but *I* shall wait and see!" And sure enough she *was* coming—the mice all scampered away, except the noble champion who had made up his mind to stay.

The mice had faith, of course they had—they were all of them noble souls; but a sort of general feeling kept them safely in their holes until some time in the evening; then the boldest ventured out, and saw in the hazy distance the cat prance gaily about!

There was dreadful consternation, till some one at last said, "Oh, he's not had time to do it, let us not prejudge him so!" "I believe in him, of course I do," said the nervous mouse with a sigh, "but the cat looks suspiciously happy, and I wish I *did* know why!"

The cat, I regret to acknowledge, still prances about that house, and no message, letter, or telegram has come from the champion mouse. The mice are a little discouraged, the demand for crape goes on; they feel they'd be happier if they knew where the champion mouse has gone.

This story has a moral—it is very short, you'll see; so, of course, you all will listen to it, for fear of offending me. It is well to be courageous and valiant and all that, but—if you are mice—you'd better think twice 'ere you try to catch the cat.

PROSE.

(A) SERIOUS.

The Blank Bible.

I thought I was at home, and that, on taking up my Bible one morning, I found, to my surprise, what seemed to be the old familiar book was a total blank: not a character was inscribed in it or upon it. On going into the street, I found everyone complaining in similar perplexity of the same loss; and before night it became evident that a great and wonderful miracle had been wrought in the world: the hand which had written its awful menace on the walls of Belshazzar's palace had reversed the miracle, and expunged from our Bibles every syllable they contained:—thus reclaiming the most precious gift that Heaven had bestowed, and ungrateful man had abused.

I was curious to watch the effects of this calamity on the varied characters of mankind. There was, however, universally, an interest in the Bible, now it was lost, such as had never attached to it while it was possessed. Some, to whom the Sacred Book had been a blank for twenty years, and who never would have known of their loss but for the lamentations of their neighbours, were not the least vehement in their expressions of sorrow. The calamity not only stirred the feelings of men, but it immediately stimulated their ingenuity to repair the loss. It was very early suggested that the whole Bible had again and again been quoted piecemeal in one book or other; that it had impressed its image on human literature, and had been reflected on its surface, as the stars on a stream. But alas! on inspection, it was found that every text, every phrase which had been quoted, whether in books of theology, poetry, or fiction, had been remorselessly obliterated.

It was with trembling hand that some made the attempt to transcribe the erased text from memory. They feared that the *writing* would surely fade away; but, to their unspeakable joy, they found the impression durable; and people at length came to the conclusion, that God left them at liberty, if they could, to reconstruct the Bible for themselves out of their collective remembrances of its contents. Some obscure individuals who had studied nothing else but the Bible, but who had well studied that, came to be objects of reverence among Christians and booksellers; and he who could fill up a chasm by the restoration of words which were only partially remembered, was regarded as a public benefactor.

At length, a great movement was projected amongst the divines of all denominations, to collate the results of these partial recoveries of the Sacred Text. But here it was curious to see the variety of different readings of the same passages insisted on by conflicting theologians. No doubt the worthy men were generally unconscious of the influence of prejudice; yet somehow the memory was seldom so clear in relation to texts which told against, as in relation to those which told for, their several theories.

It was curious, too, to see by what odd associations, sometimes of contrast, sometimes of resemblance, obscure texts were recovered. A miser contributed a maxim of prudence, which he recollected principally from having systematically abused. All the ethical maxims were soon collected; for though, as usual, no one recollected his own peculiar duties or infirmities, every one kindly remembered those of his neighbours. As for Solomon's "times for everything," few could recall the whole, but everybody remembered some. Undertakers said there was "a time to mourn"; and comedians said there was "a time to laugh"; young ladies innumerable remembered there was "a time to love"; and people of all kinds, that there was "a time to hate"; everybody knew there was "a time to speak"; and a worthy Quaker added, that there was also "a time to keep silence."

But the most amusing thing of all was, to see the variety of speculations which were entertained respecting the object and design of this strange event. Many gravely questioned whether it could be right to attempt the reconstruction of a Book of which God Himself had so manifestly deprived the world; and some, who were secretly glad to be relieved of so troublesome a monitor, were particularly pious on this head, and exclaimed bitterly against this rash attempt to counteract the decrees of Heaven. Some even maintained that the visitation was not in judgment, but in mercy; that God, in compassion, and not in indignation, had taken away a book which men had regarded with an extravagant admiration and idolatry; and that, if a rebuke at all was intended, it was a rebuke to a rampant Bibliolatry. This last reason, which assigned, as a cause of God's resumption of His own gift, an extravagant admiration and reverence of it on the part of mankind—it being so notorious that even the best of those who professed belief in its Divine origin and authority had so grievously neglected it—struck me as so exquisitely ludicrous, that I broke into a fit of laughter—which awoke me!

The morning sun was streaming in at the window, and shining upon the open Bible which lay on the table; and it was with joy that my eyes rested on these words, which I read through grateful tears,—"The gifts of God are without repentance."

The Colonel's Death-Bed.

Clive, and the boy sometimes with him, used to go daily to Grey Friars, where the Colonel still lay ill. After some days, the fever, which had attacked him, left him; but left him so weak and enfeebled that he could only go from his bed to the chair by his fireside. The season was exceedingly bitter, the chamber which he inhabited was warm and spacious; it was considered unadvisable to move him until he had attained greater strength, and till warmer weather. The medical men of the House hoped he might rally in spring. My friend, Dr. Goodenough, came to him; he hoped too: but not with a hopeful face. A chamber, luckily vacant, hard by the Colonel's, was assigned to his friends, where we sat when we were too many for him. Besides his customary attendant, he had two dear and watchful nurses, who were almost always with him—Ethel, and Madame de Florac, who had passed many a faithful year by an old man's bedside; who would have come, as to a work of religion, to any sick couch, much more to this one, where he lay for whose life she would once gladly have given her own.

But our Colonel, we all were obliged to acknowledge, was no more our friend of old days. He knew us again, and was good to every one round him, as his wont was; especially when Boy came, his old eyes lighted up with simple happiness, and, with eager trembling hands, he would seek under his bedclothes, or the pockets of his dressing-gown, for toys or cakes, which he had caused to be purchased for his grandson. There was a little, laughing, red-cheeked, white-headed gown-boy of the school, to whom the old man had taken a great fancy. One of the symptoms of his returning consciousness and recovery, as we hoped, was his calling for this child, who pleased our friend by his archness and merry ways; and who, to the old gentleman's unfailing delight, used to call him 'Codd Colonel.' 'Tell little F—— that Codd Colonel wants to see him!' and the little gown-boy was brought to him; and the Colonel would listen to him for hours, and hear all about his lessons and his play; and prattle, almost as childishly, about Dr. Raine and his own early school-days. The boys of the school, it must be said, had heard the noble old gentleman's touching history, and had all got to know and love him. They came every day to hear news of him;

sent him in books and papers to amuse him; and some benevolent young souls—God's blessing on all honest boys, say I—painted theatrical characters, and sent them in to Codd Colonel's grandson. The little fellow was made free of gown-boys, and once came thence to his grandfather in a little gown, which delighted the old man hugely. Boy said he would like to be a little gown-boy; and I make no doubt, when he is old enough, his father will get him that post, and put him under the tuition of my friend Dr. Senior.

So weeks passed away, during which our dear old friend still remained with us. His mind was gone at intervals, but would rally feebly; and with his consciousness returned his love, his simplicity, his sweetness. He would talk French with Madame de Florac, at which time his memory appeared to awaken with surprising vividness, his cheek flushed, and he was a youth again—a youth all love and hope—a stricken old man, with a beard as white as snow covering the noble careworn face. At such times he called her by her Christian name of Léonore; he addressed courtly old words of regard and kindness to the aged lady; anon he wandered in his talk, and spoke to her as if they still were young. Now, as in those early days, his heart was pure; no anger remained in it; no guile tainted it; only peace and good-will dwelt in it.

The days went on, and our hopes, raised sometimes, began to flicker and fail. One evening the Colonel left his chair for his bed in pretty good spirits, but passed a disturbed night, and the next morning was too weak to rise. Then he remained in his bed, and his friends visited him there. One afternoon he asked for his little gown-boy, and the child was brought to him, and sat by the bed with a very awe-stricken face; and then gathered courage, and tried to amuse him by telling him how it was a half-holiday, and they were having a cricket-match with the St. Peter's boys in the green, and Grey Friars was in and winning. The Colonel quite understood about it; he would like to see the game; he had played many a game on that green when he was a boy. He grew excited; Clive dismissed his father's little friend, and put a sovereign into his hand; and away he ran to say that Codd Colonel had come into a fortune, and to buy tarts, and to see the match out. *I, curre*, little white-haired gown-boy! Heaven speed you, little friend.

After the child had gone, Thomas Newcome began to wander more and more. He talked louder; he gave the word of command, spoke Hindustani as if to his men. Then he spoke words in French rapidly, seizing a hand that was near him, and crying, 'Toujours, toujours!' But it was Ethel's hand which he took. Ethel and Clive and the nurse were in the room with him; the latter came to us who were sitting in the adjoining compartment; Madame de Florac was there, with my wife and Bayham.

At the look in the woman's countenance, Madame de Florac started up. 'He is very bad, he wanders a great deal,' the nurse whispered. The French lady fell instantly on her knees, and remained rigid in prayer.

Some time afterwards, Ethel came in with a scared face to our pale group. 'He is calling for you again, dear lady,' she said, going up to Madame de Florac, who was still kneeling; 'and just now he said he wanted Pendennis to take care of his boy. He will not know you.' She hid her tears as she spoke.

She went into the room, where Clive was at the bed's foot; the old man within it talked on rapidly for a while: then again he would sigh and be still: once more I heard him say hurriedly: 'Take care of him when I'm in India;' and then with a heart-rending voice he called out, 'Léonore, Léonore!' She was kneeling by his side now. The patient's voice sank into faint murmurs; only a moan now and then announced that he was not asleep.

At the usual evening hour the chapel bell began to toll, and Thomas Newcome's hands outside the bed feebly beat a time. And just as the last bell struck, a peculiar sweet smile shone over his face, and he lifted up his head a little, and quickly said 'Adsum!' and fell back. It was the word we used at school, when names were called; and lo, he, whose heart was as that of a little child, had answered to his name, and stood in the presence of The Master.

A Lifeboat Episode.
(By kind permission of the Author.)

One night in January, 1881, during a tremendous storm, a brig struck on the sunken reefs within the southern arm of Robin Hood's Bay. The crew got out the jolly boat, and made her fast with a rope to the mast of the wreck. All night long they fought with the waves, the people on shore being entirely ignorant of their calamity.

Early in the morning the quarter-board of the vessel, driven ashore, was seen by the coastguardsmen, who gave the alarm, and it was then discovered that the brig had foundered during the night, and that the crew were still tossing about in their boat in the midst of a furious gale, a blinding snowstorm, and a heavy sea.

Now, at that time, the lifeboat at Robin Hood's Bay was old and unseaworthy. To put out in her was to incur swift and certain death. Neither could the brig's boat possibly make shore through the terrible breakers, even had her crew known the lay of the reefs, through which there are but two narrow channels where a boat can pass.

What was to be done? The good people of Robin Hood's Bay could not let the shipwrecked sailors drown before their eyes, and no ordinary boat could live in such a sea. There was but one chance—the telegraph. They wired to Whitby, requesting that the lifeboat might be sent at once.

The Whitby men received this message after having been out five times during the night. They held a consultation.

The first suggestion was that the lifeboat should be towed round to Robin Hood's Bay, about ten miles, by a steam tug; but this was impossible, as no tug could weather such a storm as then was raging.

The next suggestion was to man the lifeboat and pull round. This was put to the vote, and unanimously negatived. With the ebb tide and the furious gale against them, no boat's crew in the world could have taken the boat to the wreck, even if there had been a hope of living in that tremendous storm. The brave men of Whitby looked at the great cauldron of the sea, where the swirling water and the shrieking spray and flying snow were blent in one great seething hell-broth, and shook their heads despairingly.

And all this time the crew of the foundered ship, cut off from all communication with the shore, were fighting their hopeless battle for life, looking to the land they could not reach, and praying for the aid which could not come. And then—then when all hope of going to the rescue by the sea had been abandoned, out spoke some hero of the Lifeboat Council on the Whitby beach, and said : *We will take her overland.*

They would take the lifeboat overland ! Do you realise the magnitude of the task ? The heroic audacity of the idea. Between Whitby and Robin Hood's Bay there are six long miles of hilly country. A lifeboat is a huge and ponderous vessel. A terrific storm was raging. There was a hard frost, and the roads were deep with snow !

On the face of it, the project looked like madness. But there was a boat's crew of sailors hoping against hope amongst the breakers ; and British fishermen, having made up their minds to do a thing, bring desperate courage to face desperate emergencies.

The men of Whitby would take their lifeboat overland ! The rumour spread. The crowd increased. The enthusiasm began to blaze. Old men, women, and children—the fathers, mothers, wives, daughters, and sons of fishermen—came out into the storm. The coxswain led the way to the boathouse, which was waist-deep in water, and the approach to which was swept every minute by the furious charges of the seas which rushed up the slip and over the pier.

Oh ! it was a marvellous sight ! The boat was dragged out. Ropes were made fast to it. A hundred, two hundred, three hundred men seized the ropes ; a great crowd followed, pushing the carriage or turning the wheels. Through the falling snow and crackling ice, the flying spume and spray, the lifeboat was dragged down the street and over the bridge. At the turn of the road a couple of horses were yoked on ; a few yards up the hill a couple more ; a few yards farther a couple more ; and so as the procession went were men and horses added to win the way against wind and weather.

One mile out a couple of travellers met the party, vowed the enterprise was hopeless ; told how the roads were one mass of ice and snow ; how they themselves had left their traps and horses half buried in the drifts ; to get to the bay, they said, was quite impossible.

Impossible ! Whitby was aroused. Whitby had got its blood up, the blood of the Vikings, who feared neither steel, nor storm, nor fire ! Impossible ! Whitby laughed.

What, ho! A score of men! Two, three score of men there quickly, with axes and bars and shovels. We will see about this snow, we men of Whitby; we will go, though the skies should fall.

The men were there—a hundred men with spades and axes; a hundred more with ropes and lanterns. They hewed the ice and cut the snow from the track; they grew more fierce and resolute the greater grew the obstacles.

At every hamlet, at every farm and cross-road they picked up volunteers. Farmers and carriers met them with their cattle. Soon they had thirty horses, and of men a regiment. They dragged the great boat by main force up the steep hills, and through the ruts and puddles. They hacked their way through drifts and hedges; they pulled up gates and broke down walls, and so, panting, straining, heaving like giants, they hauled the lifeboat into the crowd at the top of the winding and abrupt declivity which leads to the beach of the bay.

Howl, demoniacal winds; rage, hungry waves, around the fainting seamen in their broken boat! The Vikings are upon you, the men who brought the lifeboat overland.

The steep road down on to the shore is a mass of ice; the horses cannot stand upon it; the seas break fiercely over the wall. The men of Robin Hood's Bay come forward. They are Vikings, too. They lash the hind wheels of the carriage. They seize the ropes, the boat, the wheels, the sides, nine hundred lusty men, and they dash the thing down to the water with one mighty rush.

Then no time is lost. Swiftly the men of the crew are dressed, the boat is launched, and with a lurch and a plunge leaps bodily into the storm.

But all is not yet over. The sea is something tremendous; the coast is a mass of hidden reefs; and in a few minutes the lifeboat is hurled back, beaten, to the shore, with all the oars on one side broken, and half the crew exhausted or disabled.

It is three hours now since the men of Whitby formed their grand and daring resolution. All that time the crew of the sunken vessel have been holding on in hopeless desperation, knowing nothing of the efforts made on their behalf; hearing nothing but the shrieks of the tempest and the thunder of the waves; seeing nothing but the vast, dark hillsides of water, the misty loom of the land, and the baffling veil of eddying snowflakes, whirling, whirling.

Eight men of the lifeboat's crew are out of action; eight volunteers take their places. Eight oars are shattered; eight more are shipped from the damaged boat belonging to the Bay. A pilot also, a fisherman of the village, goes aboard, and again the boat is rushed into the billows.

Rescue or death these men will win. The boat must go, shall go; the blood of the Vikings is on fire; they would in their present temper fetch their comrades ashore though hell itself should gape.

Out again into the mirk and fury. Out in the boat they have carried overland. Out under the eyes of all the gallant men and brave women of the village. Out in the teeth of the tempest, into the roaring, rolling black-green valleys of the shadow of death. Now rising on the crest of some huge roller, now hidden from sight in some fearful hissing pit, now hurled upon its beam ends by the sudden impact of a heavy sea, the Whitby boat fights its way towards the men who *shall* be rescued.

Not till the lifeboat was close upon them had those desperate clinging wretches any knowledge of the succour so heroically brought. Fainting with fatigue, perished with cold, still they hold on—stubborn, but hopeless. They cannot see the lifeboat, they cannot see the shore.

And now, now comes the glorious moment. We are upon them; we shall save them. No; they are giving way, they will be lost, and we within a hundred yards of them. The crisis is bitter in its intensity. The coxswain of the Whitby boat, Henry Freeman, turns to his crew, and in his great, deep voice cries, " Now, my lads, give them a rousing cheer; " and over the scream of the gale, and over the roar of the sea, and over the hiss of the brine, goes up the Vikings' shout, the shout of victory!

Oh, it was a glorious day! a strife of giants! a triumph of heroes! Imagine the delighted enthusiasm, the frantic excitement of the crowd when the shipwrecked crew were landed on that dangerous rocky shore, snatched from the very jaws of death—saved, saved to a man!—saved by the dauntless courage and magnificently heroic devotion of the fishermen of Whitby, who brought their lifeboat overland.

Noble Revenge.

A young officer (in what army no matter) had so far forgotten himself, in a moment of irritation, as to strike a private soldier, full of personal dignity (as sometimes happens in all ranks), and distinguished for his courage. The inexorable laws of military discipline forbade to the injured soldier any practical redress—he could look for no retaliation by acts. Words only were at his command, and, in a tumult of indignation, as he turned away, the soldier said to his officer that he would 'make him repent it.' This, wearing the shape of a menace, naturally rekindled the officer's anger, and intercepted any disposition which might be rising within him toward a sentiment of remorse; and thus the irritation between the two young men grew hotter than before.

Some weeks after this a partial action took place with the enemy. Suppose yourself a spectator, and looking down into a valley occupied by the two armies. They are facing each other, you see, in martial array. But it is no more than a skirmish which is going on; in the course of which, however, an occasion suddenly arises for a desperate service. A redoubt which has fallen into the enemy's hands must be recaptured at any price, and under circumstances of all but hopeless difficulty.

A strong party has volunteered for the service; there is a cry for somebody to head them; you see a soldier step out from the ranks to assume this dangerous leadership: the party moves rapidly forward; in a few minutes it is swallowed up from your eyes in clouds of smoke; for one half-hour, from behind these clouds you receive hieroglyphic reports of bloody strife—fierce repeating signals, flashes from the guns, rolling musketry, and exulting hurrahs advancing or receding, slackening or redoubling.

At length all is over; the redoubt has been recovered; that which was lost is found again; the jewel which had been made captive is ransomed with blood. Crimsoned with glorious gore, the wreck of the conquering party is relieved, and at liberty to return. From the river you see it ascending. The plume-crested officer in command rushes forward, with his left hand raising his hat in homage to the blackened fragments of what was once a flag, whilst with his right he seizes that of the leader, though no more than a private from the ranks. *That* perplexes you not; mystery you see none in *that*. For distinctions of order perish, ranks are confounded; 'high and low' are words without a meaning, and to wreck goes every notion or feeling that divides the noble from the noble, or the brave man from the brave.

But wherefore is it that now, when suddenly they wheel into mutual recognition, suddenly they pause? This soldier, this officer—who are they? O reader! once before they had stood face to face—the soldier that was struck, the officer that struck him. Once again they are meeting; and the gaze of armies is upon them. If for a moment a doubt divides them, in a moment the doubt has perished. One glance exchanged between them publishes the forgiveness that is sealed for ever.

As one who recovers a brother whom he has accounted dead, the officer sprang forward, threw his arms around the neck of the soldier, and kissed him, as if he were some martyr glorified by that shadow of death from which he was returning; whilst, on his part, the soldier, stepping back, and carrying his open hand through the beautiful motions of the military salute to a superior, makes this immortal answer—that answer which shut up for ever the memory of the indignity offered to him, even while for the last time alluding to it: 'Sir,' he said, 'I told you before, that I would make you repent it.'

The Long Path.

Yes, that was my last walk with the *schoolmistress*. It happened to be the end of a term; and before the next began, a very nice young woman, who had been her assistant, was announced as her successor, and she was provided for elsewhere. So it was no longer the schoolmistress that I walked with, but——Let us not be in unseemly haste. I shall call her the schoolmistress still; some of you love her under that name.

When it became known among the boarders that two of their number had joined hands to walk down the long path of life side by side, there was, as you may suppose, no small sensation. I confess I pitied our landlady. It took her all of a suddin,— she said. Had not known that we was keepin' company, and

never mistrusted anything partic'lar. Ma'am was right to
better herself. Didn't look very rugged to take care of a femily,
but could get hired haälp, she calc'lated.—The great maternal
instinct came crowding up in her soul just then, and her eyes
wandered until they settled on her daughter.

No, poor, dear woman,—that could not have been. But I
am dropping one of my internal tears for you, with this pleasant
smile on my face all the time.

The great mystery of Providence is the permitted crushing
out of flowering instincts. Life is maintained by the respiration of oxygen and of sentiments. In the long catalogue of
scientific cruelties there is hardly anything quite so painful to
think of as that experiment of putting an animal under the
bell of an air-pump and exhausting the air from it. [I never
saw the accursed trick performed. *Laus Deo !*] There comes
a time when the souls of human beings, women, perhaps, more
even than men, begin to faint for the atmosphere of the affections they were made to breathe. Then it is that Society
places its transparent bellglass over the young woman who is
to be the subject of one of its fatal experiments. The element
by which only the heart lives is sucked out of her crystalline
prison. Watch her through its transparent walls ;—her bosom
is heaving, but it is in a vacuum. Death is no riddle, compared
to this. I remember a poor girl's story in the *Book of Martyrs*.
The "dry-pan and the gradual fire" were the images that
frightened her most. How many have withered and wasted
under as slow a torment in the walls of that larger Inquisition
which we call Civilisation.

Yes, my surface-thought laughs at you, you foolish, plain,
over-dressed, mincing, cheaply-organised, self-saturated young
person, whoever you may be, now reading this,—little thinking
you are what I describe, and in blissful unconsciousness that
you are destined to the lingering asphyxia of soul which is the
lot of such multitudes worthier than yourself. But it is only
my surface-thought which laughs. For that great procession of
the UNLOVED who not only wear the crown of thorns, but must
hide it under the locks of brown or gray,—under the snowy
cap, under the chilling turban,—hide it even from themselves,
—perhaps never know they wear it, though it kills them,—
there is no depth of tenderness in my nature that Pity has not

sounded. Somewhere,—somewhere,—love is in store for them,—the universe must not be allowed to fool them so cruelly. What infinite pathos in the small, half-unconscious artifices by which unattractive young persons seek to recommend themselves to the favour of those towards whom our dear sisters, the unloved, like the rest, are impelled by their Heaven-given instincts!

Read what the singing-women—one to ten thousand of the suffering women—tell us, and think of the griefs that die unspoken! Nature is in earnest when she makes a woman; and there are women enough lying in the next churchyard with very commonplace blue slate-stones at their head and feet, for whom it was just as true that "all sounds of life assumed one tone of love," as for Letitia Landon, of whom Elizabeth Browning said it; but she could give words to her grief, and they could not.—Will you hear a few stanzas of mine?

THE VOICELESS.

We count the broken lyres that rest
  Where the sweet wailing singers slumber,—
But o'er their silent sister's breast
  The wild flowers who will stoop to number?
A few can touch the magic string,
  And noisy Fame is proud to win them;—
Alas for those that never sing,
  But die with all their music in them!

Nay, grieve not for the dead alone,
  Whose song has told their hearts' sad story,—
Weep for the voiceless, who have known
  The cross without the crown of glory!
Not where Leucadian breezes sweep
  O'er Sappho's memory-haunted billow,
But where the glistening night-dews weep
  On nameless sorrow's churchyard pillow.

Oh, hearts that break and give no sign
  Save whitening lip and fading tresses,
'Till death pours out his cordial wine,
  Slow-dropped from Misery's crushing presses,
If singing breath or echoing chord
  To every hidden pang were given,
What endless melodies were poured,
  As sad as earth, as sweet as heaven!

So the last day of summer came. It was our choice to go
to the church, but we had a kind of reception at the boarding-
house. The presents were all arranged, and among them none
gave more pleasure than the modest tributes of our fellow-
boarders,—for there was not one, I believe, who did not send
something. The landlady would insist on making an elegant
bride-cake with her own hands ; to which Master Benjamin
Franklin wished to add certain embellishments out of his
private funds, namely, a Cupid in a mouse-trap, done in white
sugar, and two miniature flags with the stars and stripes,
which had a very pleasing effect, I assure you. The landlady's
daughter sent a richly bound copy of Tupper's *Poems*. On a
blank leaf was the following, written in a very delicate and
careful hand :—

>Presented to . . . by . . .
>On the eve ere her union in holy matrimony.
>May sunshine ever beam o'er her !

Even the poor relative thought she must do something, and
sent a copy of *The Whole Duty of Man*, bound in very attractive variegated sheepskin, the edges nicely marbled. From the
divinity-student came the loveliest English edition of Keble's
Christian Year. I opened it, when it came, to the *Fourth
Sunday in Lent*, and read that angelic poem, sweeter than
any thing I can remember since Xavier's "My God, I love
Thee."—I am not a Churchman,—I don't believe in planting
oaks in flowerpots,—but such a poem as "The Rosebud"
makes one's heart a proselyte to the culture it grows from.
Talk about it as much as you like,—one's breeding shows itself nowhere more than in his religion. A man should be a
gentleman in his hymns and prayers ; the fondness for "scenes,"
among vulgar saints, contrasts so meanly with that—

>"God only and good angels look
>Behind the blissful scene,"—

and that other,—

>"He could not trust his melting soul
>But in his Maker's sight."—

that I hope some of them will see this, and read the poem and
profit by it.

My laughing and winking young friend undertook to procure and arrange the flowers for the table, and did it with immense zeal. I never saw him look happier than when he came in, his hat saucily on one side, and a cheroot in his mouth, with a huge bunch of tea-roses which he said were for "Madam."

One of the last things that came was an old square box, smelling of camphor, tied and sealed. It bore in faded ink, the marks, "Calcutta, 1805." On opening it, we found a white cashmere shawl, with a very brief note from the dear old gentleman opposite, saying that he had kept this some years, thinking he might want it, and many more, not knowing what to do with it,—that he had never seen it unfolded since he was a young supercargo,—and now, if she would spread it on her shoulders it would make him feel young to look at it.

Poor Bridget, or Biddy, our red-armed maid-of-all-work! What must she do but buy a small copper breast-pin and put it under "Schoolma'am's" plate that morning, at breakfast? And Schoolma'am would wear it,—though I made her cover it, as well as I could, with a tea-rose.

It was my last breakfast as a boarder, and I could not leave them in utter silence.

"Good-bye,"—I said,—"my dear friends, one and all of you! I have been long with you, and I find it hard parting. I have to thank you for a thousand courtesies, and above all for the patience and indulgence with which you have listened to me when I have tried to instruct or amuse you. My friend the Professor (who, as well as my friend the Poet, is unavoidably absent on this interesting occasion) has given me reason to suppose that he would occupy my empty chair about the first of January next. If he comes among you, be kind to him, as you have been to me. May the Lord bless you all!"—And we shook hands all round the table.

Half an hour afterwards the breakfast-things and the cloth were gone. I looked up and down the length of the bare boards over which I had so often uttered my sentiments and experiences—and—yes, I am a man, like another.

All sadness vanished, as, in the midst of these old friends of mine, whom you know, and others a little more up in the world, perhaps, to whom I have not introduced you, I took the schoolmistress before the altar from the hands of the old gentleman who used to sit opposite, and who would insist on giving her away.

And now we two are walking the long path in peace together. The "schoolmistress" finds her skill in teaching called for again, without going abroad to seek little scholars. Those visions of mine have all come true.

I hope you all love me none the less for anything I have told you. Farewell!

The Chariot Race.

When the dash for position began, Ben-Hur, as we have seen, was on the extreme left of the six. For a moment, like the others, he was half blinded by the light in the arena; yet he managed to catch sight of his antagonists and divine their purpose. At Messala, who was more than an antagonist to him, he gave one searching look. The air of passionless hauteur characteristic of the fine patrician face was there as of old, and so was the Italian beauty, which the helmet rather increased; but more—it may have been a jealous fancy, or the effect of the brassy shadow in which the features were at that moment cast, still the Israelite thought he saw the soul of the man as through a glass, darkly: cruel, cunning, desperate; not so excited as determined—a soul in a tension of watchfulness and fierce resolve.

In a time not longer than was required to turn to his four again, Ben-Hur felt his own resolution harden to a like temper. At whatever cost, at all hazards, he would humble this enemy! Prize, friends, wagers, honour—everything that can be thought of as a possible interest in the race was lost in the one deliberate purpose. Regard for life even should not hold him back. Yet there was no passion, on his part; no blinding rush of heated blood from heart to brain, and back again; no impulse to fling himself upon Fortune: he did not believe in Fortune; far otherwise. He had his plan, and, confiding in himself, he settled to the task never more observant, never more capable. The air about him seemed aglow with a renewed and perfect transparency.

When not half-way across the arena, he saw that Messala's rush would, if there was no collision, and the rope fell, give him the wall; that the rope would fall, he ceased as soon to doubt; and, further, it came to him, a sudden flash-like insight, that Messala knew it was to be let drop at the last moment (pre-arrangement with the editor could safely reach that point in the contest); and it suggested, what more Roman-like than for the official to lend himself to a countryman who, besides being so popular, had also so much at stake? There could be no other accounting for the confidence with which Messala pushed his four forward the instant his competitors were prudentially checking their fours in front of the obstruction—no other except madness.

It is one thing to see a necessity and another to act upon it. Ben-Hur yielded the wall for the time.

The rope fell, and all the fours but his sprang into the course under the urgency of voice and lash. He drew head to the right, and, with all the speed of his Arabs, darted across the trails of his opponents, the angle of movement being such as to lose the least time and gain the greatest possible advance. So, while the spectators were shivering at the Athenian's mishap, and the Sidonian, Byzantine, and Corinthian were striving, with such skill as they possessed, to avoid involvement in the ruin, Ben-Hur swept around and took the course neck and neck with Messala, though on the outside. The marvellous skill shown in making the change thus from the extreme left across to the right without appreciable loss did not fail the sharp eyes upon the benches: the Circus seemed to rock and rock again with prolonged applause. Then Esther clasped her hands in glad surprise; then Sanballat, smiling, offered his hundred sestertii a second time without a taker; and then the Romans began to doubt, thinking that Messala might have found an equal, if not a master, and that in an Israelite!

And now, racing together side by side, a narrow interval between them, the two neared the second goal. The pedestal of the three pillars there, viewed from the west, was a stone wall in the form of a half-circle, around which the course and opposite balcony were bent in exact parallelism. Making this turn was considered in all respects the most telling test of a charioteer; it was, in fact, the very feat in which Orestes failed. As an involuntary admission of interest on the part of the spectators, a hush fell over all the Circus, so that for the

T

first time in the race the rattle and clang of the cars plunging after the tugging steeds were distinctly heard. Then, it would seem, Messala observed Ben-Hur, and recognized him; and at once the audacity of the man flamed out in an astonishing manner.

"Down Eros, up Mars!" he shouted, whirling his lash with practised hand—"Down Eros, up Mars!" he repeated, and caught the well-doing Arabs of Ben-Hur a cut the like of which they had never known.

The blow was seen in every quarter, and the amazement was universal. The silence deepened; up on the benches behind the consul the boldest held his breath, waiting for the outcome. Only a moment thus: then, involuntarily, down from the balcony, as thunder falls, burst the indignant cry of the people.

The four sprang forward affrighted. No hand had ever been laid upon them except in love: they had been nurtured ever so tenderly; and as they grew, their confidence in man became a lesson to men beautiful to see. What should such dainty natures do under such indignity but leap as from death?

Forward they sprang as with one impulse, and forward leaped the car. Past question, every experience is serviceable to us. Where got Ben-Hur the large hand and mighty grip which helped him now so well? Where but from the oar with which so long he fought the sea? And what was this spring of the floor under his feet to the dizzy eccentric lurch with which in the old time the trembling ship yielded to the beat of the staggering billows, drunk with their power? So he kept his place, and gave the four free rein, and called to them in soothing voice, trying merely to guide them round the dangerous turn; and before the fever of the people began to abate he had back the mastery. Nor that only: on approaching the first goal, he was again side by side with Messala, bearing with him the sympathy and admiration of every one not a Roman. So clearly was the feeling shown, so vigorous its manifestation, that Messala, with all his boldness, felt it unsafe to trifle further.

As the cars whirled round the goal, Esther caught sight of Ben-Hur's face—a little pale, a little higher raised, otherwise calm, even placid.

Immediately a man climbed on the entablature at the west

end of the division wall, and took down one of the conical wooden balls. A dolphin on the east entablature was taken down at the same time.

In like manner, the second ball and second dolphin disappeared.

And then the third ball and third dolphin.

Three rounds concluded : still Messala held the inside position ; still Ben-Hur moved with him side by side ; still the other competitors followed as before. The contest began to have the appearance of one of the double races which became so popular in Rome during the later Cæsarean period—Messala and Ben-Hur, in the first, the Corinthian, Sidonian, and Byzantine in the second. Meantime the ushers succeeded in returning the multitude to their seats, though the clamour continued to run the rounds, keeping as it were, even pace with the rivals in the course below.

In the fifth round the Sidonian succeeded in getting a place outside Ben-Hur, but lost it directly.

The sixth round was entered upon without change of relative position.

Gradually the speed had been quickened—gradually the blood of the competitors warmed with the work. Men and beasts seemed to know alike that the final crisis was near, bringing the time for the winner to assert himself.

The interest which from the beginning had centered chiefly in the struggle between the Roman and the Jew, with an intense and general sympathy for the latter, was fast changing to anxiety on his account. On all the benches the spectators bent forward motionless, except as their faces turned following the contestants. Ilderim quitted combing his beard, and Esther forgot her fears.

"A hundred sestertii on the Jew !" cried Sanballat to the Romans under the consul's awning.

There was no reply.

"A talent—or five talents, or ten : choose ye !"

He shook his tablets at them defiantly.

"I will take thy sestertii," answered a Roman youth, preparing to write.

"Do not so," interposed a friend.

"Why ?"

"Messala hath reached his utmost speed. See him lean over his chariot-rim, the reins loose as flying ribbons. Look then at the Jew."
The first one looked.
"By Hercules!" he replied, his countenance falling. "The dog throws all his weight on the bits. I see, I see! If the gods help not our friend, he will be run away with by the Israelite. No, not yet. Look! Jove with us, Jove with us!"
The cry, swelled by every Latin tongue, shook the *velaria* over the consul's head.
If it were true that Messala had attained his utmost speed, the effort was with effect; slowly but certainly he was beginning to forge ahead. His horses were running with their heads low down; from the balcony their bodies appeared actually to skim the earth; their nostrils showed blood-red in expansion; their eyes seemed straining in their sockets. Certainly the good steeds were doing their best! How long could they keep the pace? It was but the commencement of the sixth round. On they dashed. As they neared the second goal, Ben-Hur turned in behind the Roman's car.
The joy of the Messala faction reached its bound: they screamed and howled, and tossed their colours; and Sanballat filled his tablets with wagers of their tendering.
Malluch, in the lower gallery over the Gate of Triumph, found it hard to keep his cheer. He had cherished the vague hint dropped to him by Ben-Hur of something to happen in the turning of the western pillars. It was the fifth round, yet the something had not come; and he had said to himself, the sixth will bring it; but, lo! Ben-Hur was hardly holding a place at the tail of his enemy's car.
Over in the east end, Simonides' party held their peace. The merchant's head was bent low. Ilderim tugged at his beard, and dropped his brows till there was nothing of his eyes but an occasional sparkle of light. Esther scarcely breathed. Iras alone appeared glad.
Along the home-stretch—six round—Messala leading, next him Ben-Hur, and so close it was the old story:

"First flew Eumelus on Pheretian steeds;
  With those of Tros bold Diomed succeeds;

> Close on Eumelus' back they puff the wind,
> And seem just mounting on his car behind;
> Full on his neck he feels the sultry breeze,
> And, hovering o'er, their stretching shadow sees."

Thus to the first goal and round it. Messala, fearful of losing his place, hugged the stony wall with perilous clasp; a foot to the left, and he had been dashed to pieces; yet, when the turn was finished, no man, looking at the wheel tracks of the two cars, could have said, here went Messala, there the Jew. They left but one trace behind them.

As they whirled by, Esther saw Ben-Hur's face again, and it was whiter than before.

Simonides, shrewder than Esther, said to Ilderim the moment the rivals turned into the course, "I am no judge, good sheik, if Ben-Hur be not about to execute some design. His face hath that look."

To which Ilderim answered, "Saw you how clean they were and fresh? By the splendour of God, friend, they have not been running! But now watch!"

One ball and one dolphin remained on the entablatures; and all the people drew a long breath, for the beginning of the end was at hand.

First, the Sidonian gave the scourge to his four, and, smarting with fear and pain, they dashed desperately forward, promising for a brief time to go to the front. The effort ended in promise. Next the Byzantine and Corinthian each made the trial with like result, after which they were practically out of the race. Thereupon, with a readiness perfectly explicable, all the factions except the Romans joined hope in Ben-Hur, and openly indulged their feeling.

"Ben-Hur! Ben-Hur!" they shouted, and the blent voices of the many rolled overwhelmingly against the consular stand.

From the benches above him as he passed, the favour descended in fierce injunctions.

"Speed thee, Jew!"

"Take the wall now!"

"On! loose the Arabs! Give them rein and scourge!"

"Let him not have the turn on thee again. Now or never!"

Over the balustrade they stooped low, stretching their hands imploringly to him.

Either he did not hear, or could not do better, for half-way round the course and he was still following; at the second goal even still no change!

And now, to make the turn, Messala began to draw in his left-hand steeds, an act which necessarily slackened their speed. His spirit was high; more than one altar was richer of his vows; the Roman genius was still president. On the three pillars only six hundred feet away were fame, increase of fortune, promotions, and a triumph ineffably sweetened by hate, all in store for him! That moment Malluch, in the gallery, saw Ben-Hur lean forward over his Arabs and give them the reins. Out flew the many-folded lash in his hand; over the backs of the startled steeds it writhed and hissed, and hissed and writhed again and again; and though it fell not, there was both sting and menace in its quick report; and as the man passed thus from quiet to resistless action, his face suffused, his eyes gleaming, along the reins he seemed to flash his will; and instantly not one, but the four as one, answered with a leap that landed them alongside the Roman's car. Messala, on the perilous edge of the goal, heard, but dared not look to see what the awakening portended. From the people he received no sign. Above the noises of the race there was but one voice, and that was Ben-Hur's. In the old Aramaic, as the sheik himself, he called to the Arabs, "On, Atair! On, Rigel! What, Antares! dost thou linger now! Good horse—oho, Aldebaran! I hear them singing in the tents. I hear the children singing and the women—singing of the stars, of Atair, Antares, Rigel, Aldebaran, victory!—and the song will never end. Well done! Home to-morrow, under the black tent—home! On, Antares! The tribe is waiting for us, and the master is waiting! 'Tis done! 'tis done! Ha, ha! We have overthrown the proud. The hand that smote us is in the dust. Ours the glory! Ha, ha!—steady! the work is done—soho! Rest!"

There had never been anything of the kind more simple; seldom anything so instantaneous.

At the moment chosen for the dash, Messala was moving in a circle round the goal. To pass him, Ben-Hur had to cross the track, and good strategy required the movement to be in a forward direction; that is, on a like circle limited to the least possible increase. The thousands on the benches understood it all : they saw the signal given—the magnificent response ; the four close outside Messala's outer wheel, Ben-Hur's inner wheel behind the other's car—all this they saw. Then they heard a crash loud enough to send a thrill through the Circus, and, quicker than thought, out over the course a spray of shining white and yellow flinders, flew. Down on its right side toppled the bed of the Roman's chariot. There was a rebound as of the axle hitting the hard earth ; another and another ; then the car went to pieces ; and Messala, entangled in the reins, pitched forward headlong.

To increase the horror of the sight by making death certain, the Sidonian, who had the wall next behind, could not stop or turn out. Into the wreck full speed he drove ; then over the Roman, and into the latter's four, all mad with fear. Presently, out of the turmoil, the fighting of horses, the resound of blows, the murky cloud of dust and sand, he crawled in time to see the Corinthian and Byzantine go on down the course after Ben-Hur, who had not been an instant delayed.

The people arose, and leaped upon the benches, and shouted and screamed. Those who looked that way caught glimpses of Messala, now under the trampling of the fours, now under the abandoned cars. He was still ; they thought him dead ; but far the greater number followed Ben-Hur in his career. They had not seen the cunning touch of the reins by which, turning a little to the left, he caught Messala's wheel with the iron-shod point of his axle, and crushed it ; but they had seen the transformation of the man, and themselves felt the heat and glow of his spirit, the heroic resolution, the maddening energy of action with which, by look, word, and gesture, he so suddenly inspired his Arabs. And such running ! It was rather the long leaping of lions in harness ; but for the lumbering chariot, it seemed the four were flying. When the Byzantine and Corinthian were half way down the course, Ben-Hur turned the first goal.

And the race was won !

A Tale of Terror.

The following story I had from the lips of a well-known aëronaut, and nearly in the same words.

It was on one of my ascents from Vauxhall, and a gentleman of the name of Mavor had engaged himself as a companion in my aërial excursion. But when the time came his nerves failed him, and I looked vainly around for the person who was to occupy the vacant seat in the car. Having waited for him till the last possible moment, and the crowd in the gardens becoming impatient, I prepared to ascend alone; and the last cord that attached me to the earth was about to be cast off, when suddenly a strange gentleman pushed forward, and volunteered to go up with me into the clouds. He pressed the request with so much earnestness, that, having satisfied myself by a few questions of his respectability, and received his promise to submit in every point to my directions, I consented to receive him in lieu of the absentee; whereupon he stepped with evident eagerness and alacrity into the machine. In another minute we were rising above the trees; and, in justice to my companion, I must say that, in all my experience, no person at a first ascent had ever shown such perfect coolness and self-possession.

The sudden rise of the machine, the novelty of the situation, the real and exaggerated dangers of the voyage, and the cheering of the spectators, are apt to cause some trepidation, or at any rate excitement in the boldest individuals; whereas the stranger was as composed and comfortable as if he had been sitting quite at home in his library chair. A bird could not have seemed more at ease, or more in its element, and yet he solemnly assured me, upon his honour, that he had never been up before in his life. Instead of exhibiting any alarm at our great height from the earth, he evinced the liveliest pleasure whenever I emptied one of my bags of sand, and even once or twice urged me to part with more of my ballast. In the meantime the wind, which was very light, carried us gently along in a north-east direction; and the day being particularly bright and clear, we enjoyed a delightful bird's-eye view of the great metropolis and the surrounding country. My companion listened with great interest while I pointed out to him the various objects over which we passed, till I happened casually to observe that the balloon must be directly over Hoxton. My fellow-traveller then for the first time betrayed some uneasiness, and anxiously inquired whether I thought we could be recognised by anyone at our then distance from the earth. It was, I told him, quite impossible. Nevertheless, he continued very uneasy, frequently repeating, "I hope they don't see me," and entreating me earnestly to discharge more ballast. It then flashed upon me for the first time that his offer to ascend with me had been a whim of the moment, and that he feared the being seen at that perilous elevation by any member of his own family. I therefore asked him if he resided at Hoxton, to which he replied in the affirmative; urging again, and with great vehemence, the emptying of the remaining sand-bags.

This, however, was out of the question, considering the altitude of the balloon, the course of the wind, and the proximity of the sea-coast. But my comrade was deaf to these reasons—he insisted on going higher; and on my refusal to discharge more ballast, deliberately pulled off and threw his hat, coat, and waistcoat overboard.

"Hurrah, that lightened her!" he shouted; "but it's not enough yet," and he began unloosening his cravat.

"Nonsense," said I, "my good fellow, nobody can recognise you at this distance, even with a telescope."

"Don't be too sure of that," he retorted rather simply; "they have sharp eyes at Miles's."

"At where?"

"At Miles's Madhouse!"

Gracious Heaven!—the truth then flashed upon me in an instant. I was sitting in the frail car of a balloon, at least a mile above the earth, with a Lunatic. The horrors of the situation, for a minute, seemed to deprive me of my own senses. A sudden freak of a distempered fancy—a transient fury—the slightest struggle, might send us both, at a moment's notice, into eternity! In the meantime the Maniac, still repeating his insane cry of "Higher, higher, higher," divested himself, successively, of every remaining article of clothing, throwing each portion, as soon as taken off, to the winds. The inutility of remonstrance, or rather the probability of its producing a fatal irritation, kept one silent during these operations, but judge of my terror when, having thrown his stockings overboard, I heard him say, "We are not yet high enough by 10,000 miles—one of us must throw out the other."

To describe my feelings at this speech is impossible. Not only the awfulness of my position, but its novelty, conspired to bewilder me—for certainly no flight of imagination—no, not the wildest nightmare dream, had ever placed me in so forlorn and desperate a situation. It was horrible! horrible! Words, pleadings, remonstrances, were useless, and resistance would be certain destruction.

I had better have been unarmed, in an American wilderness, at the mercy of a savage Indian! And now, without daring to stir a hand in opposition, I saw the Lunatic deliberately heave first one, and then the other bag of ballast from the car, the balloon of course rising with proportionate rapidity. Up, up, up it soared—to an altitude I had never even dared to contemplate—the earth was lost to my eyes, and nothing but the huge clouds rolled beneath us! The world was gone, I felt, for ever! The Maniac was still dissatisfied with our ascent, and again began to mutter.

"Have you a wife and children?" he asked abruptly. Prompted by a natural instinct, and with a pardonable deviation from truth, I replied that I was married, and had 14 young ones who depended on me for their bread.

"Ha! ha! ha!" laughed the Maniac, with a sparkling of his eyes that chilled my very marrow. "I have 300 wives and 5,000 children; and if the balloon had not been so heavy by carrying double, I should have been home to them by this time."

"And where do they live?" I asked, anxious to gain time by any question that first occurred to me.

"In the Moon," replied the Maniac; "and when I have lightened the car I shall be there in no time."

I heard no more, for, suddenly approaching me, and throwing his arms around my body,——

(B) HUMOROUS.

The Stage-Coach.

In the course of a December tour in Yorkshire, I rode for a long distance in one of the public coaches, on the day preceding Christmas. The coach was crowded both inside and out with passengers, who by their talk seemed principally bound to the mansions of relations or friends to eat the Christmas dinner. It was loaded also with hampers of game, and baskets and boxes of delicacies; and hares hung dangling their long ears about the coachman's box, presents from distant friends for the impending feast. I had three fine rosy-cheeked schoolboys for my fellow-passengers inside, full of the buxom health and manly spirit which I have observed in the children of this country. They were returning home for the holidays in high glee, and promising themselves a world of enjoyment. It was delightful to hear the gigantic plans of pleasure of the little rogues, and the impracticable feats they were to perform during their six weeks' emancipation from the abhorred thraldom of book, birch, and pedagogue. They were full of anticipations of the meeting with the family and household, down to the very cat and dog; and of the joy they were to give their little sisters by the presents with which their pockets were crammed: but the meeting to which they seemed to look forward with the greatest impatience was with Bantam, which I found to be a pony, and, according to their talk, possessed of more virtues than any steed since the days of Bucephalus. How he could trot! how he could run! and then such leaps as he could take—there was not a hedge in the whole country that he could not clear.

They were under the particular guardianship of the coachman, to whom, whenever an opportunity presented, they addressed a host of questions, and pronounced him one of the best fellows in the whole world. Indeed, I could not but notice the more than ordinary air of bustle and importance of the coachman, who wore his hat a little on one side, and had a large bunch of Christmas greens stuck in the button-hole of his coat. He is always a personage full of mighty care and business; but he is particularly so during this season, having so many commissions to execute in consequence of the great interchange of presents. And here, perhaps, it may not be unacceptable to my untravelled readers to have a sketch that may serve as a general representation of this very numerous and important class of functionaries, who have a dress, a manner, a language, an air, peculiar to themselves, and prevalent throughout the fraternity; so that whenever an English stage-coachman may be seen, he cannot be mistaken for one of any other craft or mystery.

He has commonly a broad, full face, curiously mottled with red, as if the blood had been forced by hard feeding into every vessel of the skin; he is swelled into jolly dimensions by frequent potations of malt liquors, and his bulk is still further increased by a multiplicity of coats, in which he is buried like a cauliflower, the upper one reaching to his heels. He wears a broad-brimmed, low-crowned hat; a huge roll of coloured handkerchief about his neck, knowingly knotted and tucked in at the bosom; and has in summer time a large bouquet of flowers in his button-hole. His waistcoat is commonly of some bright colour, striped; and his small-clothes extend far below the knees, to meet a pair of jockey boots which reach about half-way up his legs.

All this costume is maintained with much precision; he has a pride in having his clothes of excellent materials; and, notwithstanding the seeming grossness of his appearance, there is still discernible that neatness and propriety of person which is almost inherent in an Englishman. He enjoys great consequence and consideration along the road; has frequent conferences with the village housewives, who look upon him as a man of great trust and dependence; and he seems to have a good understanding with every bright-eyed country lass. The moment he arrives where the horses are to be changed, he throws down the reins with something of an air, and abandons the cattle to the care of the ostler : his duty being merely to drive from one stage to another. When off the box, his hands are thrust in the pockets of his great coat, and he rolls about the inn-yard with an air of the most absolute lordliness. Here he is generally surrounded by an admiring throng of ostlers, stable-boys, shoe-blacks, and those nameless hangers-on that infest inns and taverns, and run errands, and do all kinds of odd jobs, for the privilege of battening on the drippings of the kitchen, and the leakage of the tap-rooms. These all look up to him as an oracle; treasure up his cant phrases; echo his opinions about horses and other topics of jockey lore; and, above all, endeavour to imitate his air and carriage.

Perhaps it might be owing to the pleasing serenity that reigned in my own mind, that I fancied I saw cheerfulness in every countenance throughout the journey. A stage-coach, however, carries animation always with it, and puts the world in motion as it wheels along. The horn, sounded at the entrance of a village, produces a general bustle. Some hasten forth to meet friends; some with bundles and band-boxes to secure places, and in the hurry of the moment can hardly take leave of the group that accompanies them. In the meantime, the coachman has a world of small commissions to execute. Sometimes he delivers a hare or pheasant; sometimes jerks a small parcel or newspaper to the door of a public-house; and sometimes, with knowing look and words of sly import, hands to some half-blushing, half-laughing housemaid, an odd-shaped billet-doux from some rustic admirer. As the coach rattles through the village, every one runs to the window, and you have glances on every side of fresh country faces, and blooming, giggling girls. At the corners are assembled juntas of village idlers and wise men, who take their station there for the important purpose of seeing company pass; but the sagest knot is generally at the blacksmith's, to whom the passing of the coach is an event fruitful of much speculation. The smith, with the horse's heel in his lap, pauses as the vehicle rolls by; the Cyclops round the anvil suspend their ringing hammers, and suffer the iron to grow cool; and the sooty spectre in brown paper cap, labouring at the bellows, leans on the handle for a moment, and permits the asthmatic engine to heave a long-drawn sigh, while he glares through the murky smoke and sulphurous gleams of the smithy.

Perhaps the impending holiday might have given a more than usual animation to the country, for it seemed to me as if everybody was in good looks and good spirits; game, poultry, and other luxuries of the table, were in brisk circulation in the villages; the grocers', butchers', and fruiterers' shops were thronged with customers. The housewives were stirring briskly about, putting their dwellings in order; and the glossy branches of holly, with their bright red berries, began to appear at the windows. The scene brought to my mind an old writer's account of Christmas preparations :—" Now capons and hens, besides turkeys, geese, and ducks, with beef and mutton, must all die, for in twelve days a multitude of people will not be fed with a little."

I was roused from this fit of luxurious meditation by a shout from my little travelling companions. They had been looking out of the coach windows for the last few miles, recognising every tree and cottage as they approached home, and now there was a general burst of joy :—" There's John! and there's old Carlo! and there's Bantam!" cried the happy little rogues, clapping their hands.

At the end of a lane there was an old sober-looking servant in livery waiting for them; he was accompanied by a superannuated pointer, and by the redoubtable Bantam, a little old rat of a pony, with a shaggy mane and long rusty tail, who stood dozing quietly by the road side, little dreaming of the bustling times that awaited him.

I was pleased to see the fondness with which the little fellows leaped about the steady old footman, and hugged the pointer, who wriggled his whole body for joy. But Bantam was the great object of interest; all wanted to mount at once; and it was with some difficulty that John arranged that they should ride by turns, and the eldest should ride first.

Off they set at last, one on the pony, with the dog bounding and barking before him, and the others holding John's hands; both talking at once, and overpowering him by questions about home, and with school anecdotes. I looked after them with a feeling in which I do not know whether pleasure or melancholy predominated; for I was reminded of those days when, like them, I had neither known care nor sorrow, and a holiday was the summit of earthly felicity. We stopped a few moments afterwards to water the horses, and on resuming our route a turn of the road brought us in sight of a neat country seat. I could just distinguish the forms of a lady and two young girls in the portico, and I saw my little comrades, with Bantam, and Carlo, and old John, trooping along the carriage road; I leaned out of the coach window, in hopes of witnessing the happy meeting, but a grove of trees shut it from my sight.

In the evening we reached a village where I had determined to pass the night. As we drove into the great gateway of the inn, I saw on one side the light of a rousing kitchen fire beaming through a window; I entered, and admired, for the hundredth time, that picture of convenience, neatness, and broad, honest enjoyment, the kitchen of an English inn. It was of spacious dimensions, hung round with copper and tin vessels highly polished, and decorated here and there with a Christmas green. Hams, tongues, and flitches of bacon, were suspended from the ceiling; a smoke-jack made its ceaseless clacking beside the fireplace, and a clock ticked in one corner, a well-scoured deal table extended along one side of the kitchen, with a cold round of beef, and other hearty viands, upon it, over which two foaming tankards of ale seemed mounting guard. Travellers of inferior order were preparing to attack this stout repast, while others sat smoking and gossiping over their ale on two high-backed oaken seats beside the fire. Trim housemaids were hurrying backwards and forwards under the directions of a fresh, bustling landlady; but still seizing an occasional moment to exchange a merry word, and have a rallying laugh, with the group round the fire.

The Artless Prattle of Childhood.

We always did pity the man who does not love children. There is something morally wrong with such a man. If his tender sympathies are not awakened by their innocent prattle, if his heart does not echo their merry laughter, if his whole nature does not reach out in ardent longing after their pure thoughts and unselfish motives, he is a crusty, crabbed old stick, and a world full of children has no use for him. And what a pleasure it is to talk with them! Ah! yes, to be sure.

One day a lady friend who was down in the city shopping came into the sanctum with her little boy, a dear little tid-toddler of five summers, and begged us to amuse him while she pursued some duties which called her down town. Such a pretty boy; so delightful it was to talk to him. We can never forget the blissful half-hour we spent getting that prodigy up in his centennial history.

"Now, listen, Clary," we said—his name was Clarence Fitzherbert Alençon de Marchemont Carruthers,—"and learn about George Washington."

"Who's he?" inquired Clarence.

"Listen," we said, "he was the father of his country."

"Whose country?"

"Ours—yours and mine: the confederated union of the American people, cemented with the life-blood of the men of '76, poured out upon the altars of our country. The dearest libations her votaries could offer."

"Who did?" asked Clarence.

There is a peculiar tact in talking to children that very few people possess. Now most people would have grown impatient when little Clarence asked so many irrelevant questions, but we did not. We knew that however careless he might appear at first, we could soon interest him in the story. And so, smiling, we went on. "Well, one day George's father—"

"George who?" asked Clarence.

"George Washington—he was a little boy then just like you. One day his father—"

"Whose father?" demanded Clarence, with an encouraging expression of anxiety.

"George Washington, this great man we were telling you of. One day George Washington's father gave him a little hatchet for—"

"Gave who a little hatchet?" the dear child interrupted with a gleam of bewitching intelligence. Most men would have betrayed signs of impatience, but we did not. We know how to talk to children, so we went on.

"George Washington; his—"

"Who gave him the little hatchet?"

"His father. And his father—"

"Whose father?"

"George Washington's."

"Oh!"

"Yes, George Washington. And his father told him—"

"Told who?"

"Told George."

"Oh yes! George."

And we went on. We took up the story where the boy interrupted; for we could see he was just crazy to hear the end of it. We said:

"And he told him that—"
"Who told him what!" Clarence broke in.
"Why, George's father told George."
"What did he tell him?"
"Why, that is just what I'm going to tell you. He told him—"
"George told him?"
"No; his father told George—"
"Oh!"
"Yes; told him that he must be careful with the hatchet—"
"Who must be careful?"
"George must."
"Oh!"
"Yes, must be careful with the hatchet—"
"What hatchet?"
"Why, George's."
"Oh!"
"Yes, with the hatchet, and not cut himself with it, or drop it in the cistern, or leave it out on the grass at night. So George went round cutting everything he could reach with his hatchet. At last he came to a splendid cherry-tree, his father's favourite, and he cut it down, and—"
"Who cut it down?"
"George did."
"Oh!"
"And his father came home, and saw it the first thing, and—"
"Saw the hatchet?"
"No, saw the cherry-tree. And he said: 'Who has cut down my favourite cherry-tree?'"
"What cherry-tree?"
"George's father's. And everybody said they did not know anything about it, and—"
"Anything about what?"
"The cherry-tree."
"Oh!"
"—And George came up and heard them talking about it."
"Heard who talking about it?"
"Heard his father and his men."

"What was they talking about?"
"About this cherry-tree."
"What cherry-tree?"
"The favourite cherry-tree that George cut down."
"George who?"
"George Washington."
"Oh!"
"So George came up and heard them talking about it, and he—"
"What did he cut it down for?"
"Just to try his little hatchet."
"Whose little hatchet?"
"Why, his own. The one his father gave to him."
"Gave who?"
"Why, George Washington."
"Who gave it to him?"
"His father did."
"Oh!"
"So George came up, and he said: 'Father, I cannot tell a lie. I—'"
"Who could not tell a lie?"
"Why, George Washington. He said: 'Father, I cannot tell a lie. It was—'"
"His father could not?"
"Why, no. George could not."
"Oh, George; oh, yes!"
"'It was I cut down your cherry-tree. I did—'"
"His father did?"
"No, no! it was George said this."
"Said he cut his father?"
"No, no, no! Said he cut down his cherry-tree."
"George's cherry-tree?"
"No, no! His father's."
"Oh!"
"He said—"
"His father said?"
"No, no, no! George said: 'Father, I cannot tell a lie. I did it with my little hatchet.' And his father said: 'Noble boy, I would rather lose a thousand trees than have you tell a lie.'"

" George did ? "
" No, his father said that."
" Said he would rather have a thousand cherry-trees ? "
" No, no, no ! Said he would rather lose a thousand cherry-trees than—"
"Said he would rather George would ? "
" No ! said he would rather he would than have him lie."
" Oh ! George would rather have his father lie ? "
We are patient and love children, but if Mrs. Carruthers had not come and got her prodigy, we do not believe all Burlington Street could have brought us out of the snarl. And as Clarence Fitzherbert Alençon de Marchemont Carruthers trotted downstairs we heard him telling his mother about a boy " who had a father named George, and he told him to cut down a cherry-tree, and he said he would rather tell a thousand lies than cut down one apple-tree."

Briary Villas.

I'm number one : Vidler is number two Briary Villas, Plimliville.

Now, I am not a violent man, and I never make use of bad language, but I must say something when I mention Vidler's name, if it's only " Boil Vidler."

We were just settling down when he arrived, and the very first night his servant came and knocked at our door with " master's compliments, and he had left his last house on account of the horgans, and would we leave off playing the pyhanner."

That was a sample, for every day there was something the nasty little, fat, round, bald-headed old bachelor, or his pealike sister had to complain about.

At last the troubles culminated one cold February evening, and that trouble cost me fifty pounds, and made Vidler my sworn enemy for life.

Binny and I were just having a quiet chat in the sitting-room, and all was cosy, when suddenly I sniffed. Then Binny sniffed. Then we both sniffed together.

" What a smell of soot ! " I exclaimed.

"It's that odious old Vidler's chimney smoking," said Binny. "Oh, Charlie, do let's move, they are such disagreeable people. The old woman actually made faces at me to-day as I sat by the window."

At this moment there was a knock at the door, and "Our Emma" appeared. Cook calls her "Our Emma," to distinguish her, I suppose, from the next door servant, whose name is Jane.

"Well, Emma?"

"Oh, if you please, mum, will you come down, please!"

"Is anything the matter, Emma?"

"No, mum, there's nothink the matter; but I made up a good fire, as you told me, in the dining-room, and it will keep on a-roaring so."

"Why, you've set the chimney on fire!" I shouted.

"Well, sir, that's what cook says; but I don't think it is."

I ran downstairs to find that not only was the fire roaring away, but great pats of burning soot were tumbling down the chimney. I seized the salt-cellars and emptied them on the fire. That seemed no good; so calling to the maids to bring a couple of pails, I had them filled and carried upstairs, climbed the ladder, and got on the roof. "It will make a horrible mess," I thought, as I looked at the smoke pouring up from the long narrow chimney stack. "But better a dirty fender," I continued aloud, "than five pounds for a fire-engine."

As I spoke I raised the pail of water and poured it down the smoking chimney. Then I took a full can from Emma, whose head appeared upon the scene.

"No fire-engines to-night," I chuckled; and as a rumbling, gurgling noise came up the chimney, I poured down the second pailful and descended. "How is the dining-room, Binny?" I asked, when I got down.

"It's left off roaring, dear," she replied; and on going in, to my surprise I found the fire burning brightly, while the roaring noise had ceased, and all was beautiful and clean.

"Why, my dear Binny!" I exclaimed; and then the roaring noise began again—not in the chimney this time, but at the front door, which somebody seemed determined to batter down.

"I'll go, Emma," I said; "it's the engine." Going to the door then I opened it cautiously, but only to be driven in and followed by a hideous little object in the shape of Vidler—round, fierce, blackened with soot, drenched with water, and foaming at the mouth. I was not afraid of him, but of the dirt, as he chased me into the dining-room, where I kept him at bay with the legs of a chair.

"You atrocious scoundrel!" he panted, from the midst of his strangely blackened face, as he tore with sooty hand at his wet black shirt-front and white kerseymere waistcoat. "You villain, this is one of your cursed practical jokes; but I'll have an action—I'll have an action!"

"Perhaps, sir, as plaintiff, you will explain upon what grounds," I said blandly.

"Grounds, sir! grounds! you smooth-tongued, insulting blackguard. Why, sir, five minutes ago I was standing, as is my wont, reading my paper and warming my back, when an avalanche, a cataract—a dirty, abominable fall of Niagara, sir, came rushing down my chimney, sir, deluging me, my Turkey carpet and my hearth-rug, and putting out my fire. As soon as I could recover from my astonishment, sir, I thrust my head up the chimney, sir, and roared out to you to cease, when, sir, a second avalanche came down, and—and—hang it all, sir, just look at me!"

I did look, and he certainly was a guy.

"Now, sir, what does this mean?"

"Mean, sir," I replied, "well, I'm afraid I poured the water down the wrong chimney."

A Discussion at the "Rainbow."

(Adapted.)

The conversation, which was now at a high pitch of animation, had, as usual, been slow and intermittent when the company first assembled. The pipes began to be puffed in a silence which had an air of severity; the more important customers, who drank spirits and sat nearest the fire, staring at each other as if a bet were depending on the first man who winked; while the beer drinkers, chiefly men in fustian jackets and smock-frocks, kept their eyelids down and rubbed their hands across their mouths, as if their draughts of beer were a funereal duty attended with embarrassing sadness. At last, Mr. Snell, the landlord, a man of a neutral disposition, accustomed to stand aloof from human differences as those of beings who were all alike in need of liquor, broke silence, by saying in a doubtful tone to his cousin the butcher—

"Some folks 'ud say that was a fine beast you druv in yesterday, Bob?"

The butcher, a jolly, smiling, red-haired man, was not disposed to answer rashly. He gave a few puffs before he spat and replied, "And they wouldn't be fur wrong, John."

After this feeble delusive thaw, the silence set in as severely as before.

"Was it a red Durham?" said the farrier, taking up the thread of discourse after the lapse of a few minutes.

The farrier looked at the landlord, and the landlord looked at the butcher, as the person who must take the responsibility of answering.

"Red it was," said the butcher, in his good-humoured husky treble—"and a Durham it was."

"Then you needn't tell *me* who you bought it of," said the farrier, looking round with some triumph; "I know who it is has got the red Durhams o' this country-side. And she'd a white star on her brow, I'll bet a penny?" The farrier leaned forward with his hands on his knees as he put this question, and his eyes twinkled knowingly.

"Well, yes—she might," said the butcher, slowly, considering that he was giving a decided affirmative. "I don't say contrairy."

"I knew that very well," said the farrier, throwing himself backward again, and speaking defiantly; "if *I* don't know Mr. Lammeter's cows, I should like to know who does—that's all. And as for the cow you've bought, bargain or no bargain, I've been at the drenching of her—contradick me who will."

The farrier looked fierce, and the mild butcher's conversational spirit was roused a little.

"I'm not for contradicking no man," he said; "I'm for peace and quietness. Some are for cutting long ribs—I'm for cutting 'em short myself; but *I* don't quarrel with 'em. All I say is, it's a lovely carkiss—and anybody as was reasonable, it 'ud bring tears into their eyes to look at it."

"Well, it's the cow as I drenched, whatever it is," pursued

the farrier, angrily; "and it was Mr. Lammeter's cow, else you told a lie when you said it was a red Durham."

"I tell no lies," said the butcher, with the same mild huskiness as before, "and I contradick none—not if a man was to swear himself black: he's no meat o' mine, nor none o' my bargains. All I say is, it's a lovely carkiss. And what I say I'll stick to; but I'll quarrel wi' no man."

"No," said the farrier, with bitter sarcasm, looking at the company generally; and p'rhaps you aren't pig-headed; and p'rhaps you didn't say the cow was a red Durham; and p'rhaps you didn't say she'd got a star on her brow—stick to that, now you're at it."

"Come, come," said the landlord; "let the cow alone. The truth lies atween you: you're both right and both wrong, as I allays say. And as for the cow's being Mr. Lammeter's, I say nothing to that; but this I say, as the Rainbow's the Rainbow. And for the matter o' that, if the talk is to be o' the Lammeter's, *you* know the most upo' that head, eh, Mr. Macey; you remember when first Mr. Lammeter's father come into these parts, and took the Warrens?"

Mr. Macey, tailor and parish-clerk, the latter of which functions rheumatism had of late obliged him to share with a small-featured young man who sat opposite him, held his white head on one side, and twirled his thumbs with an air of complacency, slightly seasoned with criticism. He smiled pityingly, in answer to the landlord's appeal, and said—

"Ay, ay; I know, I know; but I let other folks talk. I've laid by now, and gev up to the young uns. Ask them as have been to school at Tarley: they've learnt pernouncing; that's come up since my day."

"If you're pointing at me, Mr. Macey," said the deputy-clerk, with an air of anxious propriety, "I'm nowise a man to speak out of my place. As the psalm says—

'I know what's right, nor only so,
But also practise what I know.'"

"Well, then, I wish you'd keep hold o' the tune, when it's set for you; if you're for prac*tis*ing, I wish you'd prac*tise* that," said a large jocose-looking man, an excellent wheelwright in his week-day capacity, but on Sundays leader of the choir. He winked, as he spoke, at two of the company, who were known officially as the "bassoon" and the "key-bugle," in the confidence that he was expressing the sense of the musical profession in Raveloe.

Mr. Tookey, the deputy-clerk, who shared the unpopularity common to deputies, turned very red, but replied, with careful moderation—" Mr. Winthrop, if you'll bring me any proof as I'm in the wrong, I'm not the man to say I won't alter. But there's people set up their own ears for a standard, and expect the whole choir to follow 'em. There may be two opinions, I hope."

" Ay, ay," said Mr. Macey, who felt very well satisfied with this attack on youthful presumption ; " you're right there, Tookey : there's allays two 'pinions ; there's the 'pinion a man has of himsen, and there's the 'pinion other folks have on him. There'd be two 'pinions about a cracked bell, if the bell could hear itself."

" Well, Mr. Macey," said poor Tookey, serious amidst the general laughter, " I undertook to partially fill up the office of parish-clerk by Mr. Crackenthorp's desire, whenever your infirmities should make you unfitting ; and it's one of the rights thereof to sing in the choir—else why have you done the same yourself ? "

" Ah ! but the old gentleman and you are two folks," said Ben Winthrop. "The old gentleman's got a gift. Why, the Squire used to invite him to take a glass, only to hear him sing the 'Red Rovier ;' didn't he, Mr. Macey ? It's a nat'ral gift. There's my little lad Aaron, he's got a gift—he can sing a tune off straight, like a throstle. But as for you Master Tookey, you'd better stick to your 'Amens :' your voice is well enough when you keep it up in your nose. It's your inside as isn't right made for music : it's no better nor a hollow stalk."

This kind of unflinching frankness was the most piquant form of joke to the company at the Rainbow, and Ben Winthrop's insult was felt by everybody to have capped Mr. Macey's epigram.

" I see what it is plain enough," said Mr. Tookey, unable to keep cool any longer. "There's a conspiracy to turn me out o' the choir, as I shouldn't share the Christmas money—that's where it is. But I shall speak to Mr. Crackenthorp ; I'll not be put upon by no man."

"Nay, nay, Tookey," said Ben Winthrop. "We'll pay you your share to keep out of it—that's what we'll do. There's things folks 'ud pay to be rid on, besides varmin."

"Come, come," said the landlord, who felt that paying people for their absence was a principle dangerous to society; "a joke's a joke. We're all good friends here, I hope. We must give and take. You're both right and you're both wrong, as I say. I agree wi' Mr. Macey here, as there's two opinions; and if mine was asked, I should say they're both right. Tookey's right and Winthrop's right, and they've only got to split the difference and make themselves even."

The farrier was puffing his pipe rather fiercely, in some contempt at this trivial discussion. He had no ear for music himself, and never went to church, as being of the medical profession, and likely to be in requisition for delicate cows. But the butcher, having music in his soul, had listened with a divided desire for Tookey's defeat, and for the preservation of the peace.

"To be sure," he said, following up the landlord's conciliatory view, "we're fond of our old clerk; it's nat'ral, and him used to be such a singer, and got a brother as is known for the first fiddler in this country-side. Eh, it's a pity but what Solomon lived in our village, and could give us a tune when we liked; eh, Mr. Macey? I'd keep him in liver and lights for nothing—that I would."

"Ay, ay," said Mr. Macey, in the height of complacency; "our family's been known for musicianers as far back as anybody can tell. But them things are dying out, as I tell Solomon every time he comes round; there's no voices like what there used to be, and there's nobody remembers what we remember, if it isn't the old crows."

"Ay, you remember when first Mr. Lammeter's father come into these parts, don't you, Mr. Macey?" said the landlord.

"I should think I did," said the old man, who had now gone through that complimentary process necessary to bring him up to the point of narration; "and a fine old gentleman he was—as fine, and finer nor the Mr. Lammeter as now is. He came from a bit north'ard, so far as I could ever make out. But there's nobody rightly knows about those parts: only it couldn't be far north'ard, nor much different from this country, for he brought a fine breed of sheep with him, so there must be pastures there, and everything reasonable. We heared tell as he'd sold his own land to come and take the Warrens, and that seemed odd for a man as had land of his own, to come and rent a farm in a strange place. But they said it was along of his wife's dying; though there's reasons in things as nobody knows on—that's pretty much what I've made out; yet some folks are so wise, they'll find you fifty reasons straight off, and all the while the real reason's winking at 'em in the corner, and they niver see't. Howsomever, it was soon seen as we'd got a new parish'ner as know'd the rights and customs o' things, and kep a good house, and was well looked on by everybody. And the young man—that's the Mr. Lammeter as now is, for he'd niver a sister—soon begun to court Miss Osgood, that's the sister o' the Mr. Osgood as now is, and a fine handsome lass she was—eh, you can't think—they pretend this young lass is like her, but that's the way wi' people as don't know what come before 'em. *I* should know, for I helped the old rector, Mr. Drumlow as was, I helped him marry 'em."

Here Mr. Macey paused; he always gave his narrative in instalments, expecting to be questioned according to precedent.

"Ay, and a partic'lar thing happened, didn't it, Mr. Macey, so as you were likely to remember that marriage?" said the landlord, in a congratulatory tone.

"I should think there did—a *very* partic'lar thing," said Mr. Macey, nodding sideways. "For Mr. Drumlow—poor old gentleman, I was fond on him, though he'd got a bit confused in his head, what wi' age and wi' taking a drop o' summat warm when the service come of a cold morning. And young Mr. Lammeter, he'd have no way but he must be married in Janiwary, which, to be sure, 's a unreasonable time to be married in, for it isn't like a christening or a burying, as you can't help; and so Mr. Drumlow—poor old gentleman, I was fond on him—but when he come to put the questions, he put 'em by the rule o' contrairy, like, and he says, 'Wilt thou have this man to thy wedded wife?' says he, and then he says, 'Wilt thou have this woman to thy wedded husband?' says he. But the partic'larest thing of all is, as nobody took any notice on it but me, and they answered straight off 'yes,' like as if it had been me saying 'Amen' i' the right place, without listening to what went before."

"But *you* knew what was going on well enough, didn't you, Mr. Macey? You were live enough, eh?" said the butcher.

"Lor bless you!" said Mr. Macey, pausing, and smiling in pity at the impotence of his hearer's imagination—"why, I was all of a tremble: it was as if I'd been a coat pulled by the two tails, like; for I couldn't stop the parson, I couldn't take upon me to do that; and yet I said to myself, I says, 'Suppose they shouldn't be fast married, 'cause the words are contrairy?' and my head went working like a mill, for I was allays uncommon for turning things over and seeing all round 'em; and I says to myself, 'Is't the meanin' or the words as makes folks fast i' wedlock?' For the parson meant right, and the bride and bridegroom meant right. But then, when I come to think on it, meanin' goes but a little way i' most things, for you may mean to stick things together and your glue may be bad, and then where are you? And so I says to mysen, 'It isn't the meanin', it's the glue.' And I was worreted as if I'd got three bells to pull at once, when we went into the vestry, and they begun to sign their names. But where's the use o' talking?—you can't think what goes on in a 'cute man's inside."

"But you held in for all that, didn't you, Mr. Macey?" said the landlord.

"Ay, I held in tight till I was by mysen wi' Mr. Drumlow, and then I out wi' everything, but respectful, as I allays did. And he made light on it, and he says, 'Pooh, pooh, Macey, make yourself easy,' he says; 'it's neither the meaning nor the words—it's the re*gi*ster does it—that's the glue.' So you see he settled it easy; for parsons and doctors know everything by heart, like, so as they aren't worreted wi' thinking what's the rights and wrongs o' things, as I'n been many and many's the time. And sure enough the wedding turned out all right, on'y poor Mrs. Lammeter—that's Miss Osgood as was—died afore the lasses was growed up; but for prosperity and everything respectable, there's no family more looked on."

Every one of Mr. Macey's audience had heard this story many times, but it was listened to as if it had been a favourite tune, and at certain points the pulling of the pipes was momentarily suspended, that the listeners might give their whole minds to the expected words.

Mr. Gregsbury and the Deputation.

"Gentlemen," said Mr. Gregsbury, "you are welcome. I am rejoiced to see you."

For a gentleman who was rejoiced to see a body of visitors, Mr. Gregsbury looked as uncomfortable as might be; but perhaps this was occasioned by senatorial gravity, and a statesmanlike habit of keeping his feelings under control. He was a tough, burly, thick-headed gentleman, with a loud voice, a pompous manner, a tolerable command of sentences with no meaning in them, and in short, every requisite for a very good member indeed.

"Now, gentlemen," said Mr. Gregsbury, tossing a great bundle of papers into a wicker basket at his feet, and throwing himself back in the chair with his arms over the elbows, "you are dissatisfied with my conduct, I see by the newspapers."

"Yes, Mr. Gregsbury, we are," said a plump old gentleman in a violent heat, bursting out of the throng, and planting himself in the front.

"Do my eyes deceive me," said Mr. Gregsbury, looking towards the speaker, "or is that my old friend Pugstyles?"

"I am that man, and no other, sir," replied the plump old gentleman.

"Give me your hand, my worthy friend," said Mr. Gregsbury. "Pugstyles, my dear friend, I am very sorry to see you here."

"I am very sorry to be here, sir," said Mr. Pugstyles; "but your conduct, Mr. Gregsbury, has rendered this deputation from your constituents imperatively necessary."

"My conduct, Pugstyles," said Mr. Gregsbury, looking round upon the deputation with gracious magnanimity—"my conduct has been, and ever will be, regulated by a sincere regard for the true and real interests of this great and happy country. Whether I look at home or abroad, whether I behold the peaceful industrious communities of our island home, her rivers covered with steamboats, her roads with locomotives, her streets with cabs, her skies with balloons of a power and magnitude hitherto unknown in the history of aeronautics in this or any other nation—I say, whether I look merely at home, or stretching my eyes further, contemplate the boundless prospect of conquest and possession—achieved by British perseverance and British valour—which is outspread before me, I clasp my hands, and turning my eyes to the broad expanse above my head, exclaim, "Thank Heaven I am a Briton!'"

The time had been when this burst of enthusiasm would have been cheered to the very echo; but now the deputation received it with chilling coldness. The general impression seemed to be, that as an explanation of Mr. Gregsbury's political conduct, it did not enter quite enough into detail, and one gentleman in the rear did not scruple to remark aloud, that for his purpose it savoured rather too much of a 'gammon' tendency.

"The meaning of that term—gammon," said Mr. Gregsbury, "is unknown to me. If it means that I grow a little too fervid, or perhaps even hyperbolical, in extolling my native land, I admit the full justice of the remark. I *am* proud of this free and happy country. My form dilates, my eye glistens, my breast heaves, my heart swells, my bosom burns, when I call to mind her greatness and her glory."

"We wish, sir," remarked Mr. Pugstyles, calmly, "to ask you a few questions."

"If you please, gentlemen; my time is yours—and my country's—and my country's," said Mr. Gregsbury.

This permission being conceded, Mr. Pugstyles put on his spectacles, and referred to a written paper which he drew from his pocket, whereupon nearly every other member of the deputation pulled a written paper from *his* pocket, to check Mr. Pugstyles off, as he read the questions.

This done, Mr. Pugstyles proceeded to business.

"Question number one.—Whether, sir, you did not give a voluntary pledge previous to your election, that in the event of your being returned you would immediately put down the practice of coughing and groaning in the House of Commons? And whether you did not submit to be coughed and groaned down in the very first debate of the session, and have since made no effort to effect a reform in this respect? Whether you did not also pledge yourself to astonish the government, and make them shrink in their shoes? And whether you have astonished them and made them shrink in their shoes, or not?"

"Go on to the next one, my dear Pugstyles," said Mr. Gregsbury.

"Have you any explanation to offer with reference to that question, sir?" asked Mr. Pugstyles.

"Certainly not," said Mr. Gregsbury.

The members of the deputation looked fiercely at each other, and afterwards at the member, and "dear Pugstyles" having taken a very long stare at Mr. Gregsbury over the tops of his spectacles, resumed his list of inquiries.

"Question number two.—Whether, sir, you did not likewise give a voluntary pledge that you would support your colleague on every occasion; and whether you did not, the night before last, desert him and vote upon the other side, because the wife of a leader on that other side had invited Mrs. Gregsbury to an evening party?"

"Go on," said Mr. Gregsbury.

"Nothing to say on that either, sir?" asked the spokesman.

"Nothing whatever," replied Mr. Gregsbury. The deputation, who had only seen him at canvassing or election time, were struck dumb by his coolness. He didn't appear like the same man; then he was all milk and honey—now he was all starch and vinegar. But men *are* so different at different times!

"Question number three—and last," said Mr. Pugstyles, emphatically. "Whether, sir, you did not state upon the hustings, that it was your firm and determined intention to oppose everything proposed; to divide the house upon every question, to move for returns on every subject, to place a motion on the books every day, and, in short, in your own memorable words, to play the devil with everything and everybody?" With this comprehensive inquiry Mr. Pugstyles folded up his list of questions, as did all his backers.

Mr. Gregsbury reflected, blew his nose, threw himself further back in his chair, came forward again, leaning his elbows on the table, made a triangle with his two thumbs and his two forefingers, and tapping his nose with the apex thereof, replied (smiling as he said it), "I deny everything."

At this unexpected answer a hoarse murmur arose from the deputation; and the same gentleman who had expressed an opinion relative to the gammoning nature of the introductory speech, again made a monosyllabic demonstration, by growling out "Resign;" which growl being taken up by his fellows, swelled into a very earnest and general remonstrance.

"I am requested, sir, to express a hope," said Mr. Pugstyles, with a distant bow, "that on receiving a requisition to that effect from a great majority of your constituents, you will not object at once to resign your seat in favour of some candidate whom they think they can better trust."

To which Mr. Gregsbury read the following reply, which, anticipating the request, he had composed in the form of a letter, whereof copies had been made to send round to the newspapers.

'MY DEAR PUGSTYLES,

'Next to the welfare of our beloved island—this great and free and happy country, whose powers and resources are, I sincerely believe, illimitable—I value that noble independence which is an Englishman's proudest boast, and which I fondly hope to bequeath to my children untarnished and unsullied. Actuated by no personal motives, but moved only by high and great constitutional considerations which I will not attempt to explain, for they are really beneath the comprehension of those who have not made themselves masters, as I have, of the intricate and arduous study of politics, I would rather keep my seat, and intend doing so.

'Will you do me the favour to present my compliments to the constituent body, and acquaint them with this circumstance?

'With great esteem,
'My dear Pugstyles,
'etc., etc.'

"Then you will not resign, under any circumstances?" asked the spokesman.

Mr. Gregsbury smiled, and shook his head.

"Then good morning, sir," said Pugstyles, angrily.

"God bless you," said Mr. Gregsbury. And the deputation, with many growls and scowls, filed off as quickly as the narrowness of the staircase would allow of their getting down.

The last man being gone, Mr. Gregsbury rubbed his hands and chuckled, as merry fellows will, when they think they have said or done a more than commonly good thing.

Examination of Mr. Winkle and Sam Weller.

Judge. What is the first case on the file, Brother Buzfuz?
Buzfuz. Bardell *versus* Pickwick, my Lud.
Judge. Who is your first witness?
Buz. Samuel Weller, my Lud.

Judge. Call Samuel Weller.

Sam Weller, upon hearing his name, stepped briskly into the witness-box, put his hat on the floor, his arms on the rail, and took a bird's-eye view of the assembled Court.

Judge. What's your name, sir?

Sam. Sam. Weller, my Lord.

Judge. Do you spell it with a V or a W?

Sam. That depends upon the taste and fancy of the speller, my Lord. I never had occasion to spell it more than once or twice in my life, but I spells it with a V.

Here a voice in the gallery exclaimed aloud—"Quite right, too, Samivel; quite right. Put it down a we, my Lord, put it down a we."

Judge. Do you know who that is who has dared to address the Court?

Sam. I rayther suspect it is my father, my Lord.

Judge. Do you see him here now?

Sam. "No, I don't, my Lord," replied Sam, staring right up into the lantern in the roof of the court.

Judge. If you could have pointed him out, I would have committed him instantly.

Sam bowed his acknowledgments, and turned with unimpaired cheerfulness of countenance towards Serjeant Buzfuz.

Buz. Now, Mr. Weller.

Sam. Now, sir.

Buz. I believe you are in the service of Mr. Pickwick? Speak up, if you please, Mr. Weller.

Sam. I mean to speak up, sir; I am in the service of that 'ere gen'l'man, and a wery good service it is.

Buz. Little to do, and plenty to get, I suppose?

Sam. Oh, quite enough to get, sir, as the soldier said ven they ordered him three hundred and fifty lashes.

Judge. You must not tell us what the soldier, or any other man, said, sir; it's not evidence.

Sam. Wery good, my Lord.

Buz. Do you recollect anything particular happening on the morning when you were first engaged by the defendant? Eh, Mr. Weller?

Sam. Yes, I do, sir.

Buz. Have the goodness to tell the jury what it was.

Sam. I had a reg'lar new fit out o' clothes that mornin', gen'l'men of the jury, and that was a wery partickler and uncommon circumstance vith me in those days.

Judge. You had better be careful, sir.

Sam. So Mr. Pickwick said at the time, my Lord, and I was wery careful o' that 'ere suit o' clothes; wery careful, indeed, my Lord.

The Judge looked sternly at Sam for full two minutes, but Sam's features were so perfectly calm and serene that the Judge said nothing, and motioned Serjeant Buzfuz to proceed.

Buz. Do you mean to tell me, Mr. Weller—do you mean to tell me, that you saw nothing of the fainting on the part of the plaintiff in the arms of the defendant?

Sam. Certainly not. I was in the passage till they called me up, and then the old lady wasn't there.

Buz. Now, attend, Mr. Weller. You were in the passage till they called you up, and yet saw nothing of what was going forward. Have you a pair of eyes, Mr. Weller?

Sam. Yes, I have a pair o' eyes, and that's just it. If they was a pair o' patent double million magnifyin' gas microscopes of hextra power, p'raps I might be able to see through a flight o' stairs, and a deal-door; but bein' only eyes, you see, my wision's limited.

Buz. It's perfectly useless, my Lud, attempting to get at any evidence, through the impenetrable stupidity of this witness. Stand down, sir.

Sam. Would any other gen'l'man like to ask me anythin'?

Buz. Go down, sir!!!

Sam went down accordingly.

Judge. Who is your next witness, Brother Buzfuz?

Buz. Nathaniel Winkle, my Lud.

Judge. Call Nathaniel Winkle.

Mr. Winkle entered the witness-box, and bowed to the Judge.

Judge. Don't look at me, sir; look at the jury.

Mr. Winkle obeyed the mandate.

Judge. What's your name, sir?

Winkle. W-Winkle.

Judge. What's your Christian name, sir?

Winkle. Na-thaniel, sir.

Judge. Daniel—any other name?
Winkle. Na-thaniel, sir.
Judge. Nathaniel Daniel—or Daniel Nathaniel?
Winkle. No, my Lord, only Na-thaniel—not Daniel at all.
Judge. Why did you tell me it was Daniel, then?
Winkle. I d-didn't, my Lord.
Judge. You did, sir; how could I have got Daniel in my notes, unless you had told me so?
Buz. Now, Mr. Winkle, attend to me, if you please. I believe you are a particular friend of Mr. Pickwick, are you not?
Winkle. I—I have known Mr. Pickwick, now—as well as I can recollect at this moment, nearly—
Buz. Pray, Mr. Winkle, do not evade the question. Are you, or are you not, a particular friend of Mr. Pickwick?
Winkle. I—I was just about to say, that ——
Buz. Will you, or will you not, answer my question?
Judge. If you don't answer the question, sir, you'll be committed.
Buz. Come, sir, yes or no, if you please.
Winkle. Y-Yes—I am.
Buz. Yes, you are!! And why couldn't you say so at once, sir? Perhaps you know Mrs. Bardell, too—eh, Mr. Winkle?
Winkle. I—I don't know her—I—I've seen her.
Buz. Oh, you don't know her, but you've seen her. What do you mean by that, Mr. Winkle?
Winkle. I—mean that I am not intimate with her, but that I have seen her, when I went to call upon my friend, Mr. P-Pickwick, in G-Goswell Street.
Judge. Will you stop that stammering, Mr. Winkle!!!
Winkle. My Lord, it's a natural impediment in my sp-speech—which I c-can by no p-possibility g-get over.
Buz. Oh, get down, Mr. Winkle. . . . .

The Art of Proposing.

When Mr. Pickwick descended to the room in which he and Mr. Peter Magnus had spent the preceding evening, he found that gentleman with the major part of the contents of the two bags, the leathern hat-box, and the brown-paper parcel of the night before, displayed to all possible advantage on his person, while he himself was pacing up and down the room in a state of the utmost excitement and agitation.

"Good morning, sir," said Mr. Peter Magnus. "What do you think of this, sir?"

"Very effective indeed," replied Mr. Pickwick, surveying the garments of Mr. Peter Magnus with a good-natured smile.

"Yes, I think it'll do," said Mr. Magnus. "Mr. Pickwick, sir, I have sent up my card."

"Have you?" said Mr. Pickwick.

"And the waiter brought back word that she would see me at eleven—at eleven, sir. It only wants a quarter now."

"Very near the time," said Mr. Pickwick.

"Yes, it is rather near," replied Mr. Magnus, "rather too near to be pleasant—eh! Mr. Pickwick, sir?"

"Confidence is a great thing in these cases," observed Mr. Pickwick.

"I believe it is, sir," said Mr. Peter Magnus. "I am very confident, sir. Really, Mr. Pickwick, I do not see why a man should feel any fear in such a case as this, sir. What is it, sir? There's nothing to be ashamed of: it's a matter of mutual accommodation, nothing more. Husband on one side, wife on the other. That's my view of the matter, Mr. Pickwick."

"It is a very philosophical one," replied Mr. Pickwick. "But breakfast is waiting, Mr. Magnus. Come."

Down they sat to breakfast, but it was evident, notwithstanding the boasting of Mr. Peter Magnus, that he laboured under a very considerable degree of nervousness, of which loss of appetite, a propensity to upset the tea-things, a spectral attempt at drollery, and an irresistible inclination to look at the clock every other second, were among the principal symptoms.

"He—he—he," tittered Mr. Magnus, affecting cheerfulness, and gasping with agitation. "It only wants two minutes, Mr. Pickwick. Am I pale, sir?"

"Not very," replied Mr. Pickwick.

There was a brief pause.

"I beg your pardon, Mr. Pickwick; but have you ever done this sort of thing in your time?" said Mr. Magnus.

"You mean proposing," said Mr. Pickwick.

"Yes."

"Never," said Mr. Pickwick, with great energy; "never."

"You have no idea, then, how it's best to begin?" said Mr. Magnus.

"Why," said Mr. Pickwick, "I may have formed some ideas upon the subject, but, as I have never submitted them to the test of experience, I should be sorry if you were induced to regulate your proceedings by them."

"I should feel very much obliged to you for any advice, sir," said Mr. Magnus, taking another look at the clock, the hand of which was verging on the five minutes past.

"Well, sir," said Mr. Pickwick, with the profound solemnity with which that great man could, when he pleased, render his remarks so deeply impressive, "I should commence, sir, with a tribute to the lady's beauty and excellent qualities; from them, sir, I should diverge to my own unworthiness."

"Very good," said Mr. Magnus.

"Unworthiness for *her* only, mind, sir," resumed Mr. Pickwick; "for to show that I was not wholly unworthy, sir, I should take a brief review of my past life, and present condition. I should argue, by analogy, that to anybody else, I must be a very desirable object. I should then expatiate on the warmth of my love, and the depth of my devotion. Perhaps I might then be tempted to seize her hand."

"Yes, I see," said Mr. Magnus; "that would be a very great point."

"I should then, sir," continued Mr. Pickwick, growing warmer as the subject presented itself in more glowing colours before him : "I should then, sir, come to the plain and simple question, 'Will you have me?' I think I am justified in assuming that upon this she would turn away her head."

"You think that may be taken for granted?" said Mr. Magnus ; "because if she did not do that at the right place it would be embarrassing."

"I think she would," said Mr. Pickwick. "Upon this, sir, I should squeeze her hand, and I think—I *think*, Mr. Magnus— that after I had done that, supposing there was no refusal, I should gently draw away the handkerchief, which my slight knowledge of human nature leads me to suppose the lady would be applying to her eyes at the moment, and steal a respectful kiss. I think I should kiss her, Mr. Magnus; and at this particular point, I am decidedly of opinion that if the lady were going to take me at all, she would murmur into my ears a bashful acceptance."

Ill-bred Hospitality.

Those inferior duties of life, which the French call *les petites morales*, or the smaller morals, are with us distinguished by the name of good manners or breeding. This I look upon, in the general notion of it, to be a sort of artificial good sense, adapted to the meanest capacities, and introduced to make mankind easy in their commerce with each other. Low and little understandings, without some rules of this kind, would be perpetually wandering into a thousand indecencies and irregularities in behaviour; and in their ordinary conversation fall into the same boisterous familiarities that one observes amongst them when a debauch hath quite taken away the use of their reason. In other instances it is odd to consider, that, for want of common discretion, the very end of good breeding is wholly perverted; and civility, intended to make us easy, is employed in laying chains and fetters upon us, in debarring us of our wishes, and in crossing our most reasonable desires and inclinations.

This abuse reigns chiefly in the country, as I found to my vexation, when I was last there, in a visit I made to a neighbour about two miles from my cousin. As soon as I entered the parlour, they put me into the great chair that stood close by a huge fire, and kept me there by force until I was almost stifled. Then a boy came in great hurry to pull off my boots, which I in vain opposed, urging that I must return soon after dinner. In the meantime the good lady whispered her eldest daughter, and slipped a key into her hand; the girl returned instantly with a beer-glass half full of *aqua mirabilis* and syrup of gillyflowers. I took as much as I had a mind for, but madam vowed I should drink it off; for she was sure it would do me good after coming out of the cold air; and I was forced to obey, which absolutely took away my stomach. When dinner came in, I had a mind to sit at a distance from the fire; but

they told me it was as much as my life was worth, and set me
with my back just against it. Although my appetite was quite
gone, I was resolved to force down as much as I could, and
desired the leg of a pullet. 'Indeed, Mr. Bickerstaff (says the
lady), you must eat a wing, to oblige me;' and so put a couple
upon my plate. I was persecuted at this rate during the
whole meal; as often as I called for small beer, the master
tipped the wink, and the servant brought me a brimmer of
October.

Some time after dinner I ordered my cousin's man, who
came with me, to get ready the horses; but it was resolved I
should not stir that night: and when I seemed pretty much
bent upon going, they ordered the stable door to be locked,
and the children hid my cloak and boots. The next question
was, What would I have for supper? I said I never eat anything at night: but was at last, in my own defence, obliged
to name the first thing that came into my head. After three
hours spent chiefly in apologies for my entertainment, insinua-
ting to me, 'That this was the worst time of the year for
provisions; that they were at a great distance from any market;
that they were afraid I should be starved; and that they
knew they kept me to my loss;' the lady went, and left me
to her husband; for they took special care I should never be
alone. As soon as her back was turned, the little misses ran
backwards and forwards every moment, and constantly as they
came in, or went out, made a courtesy directly at me, which,
in good manners, I was forced to return with a bow and Your
humble servant, pretty miss. Exactly at eight the mother
came up, and discovered, by the redness of her face, that
supper was not far off. It was twice as large as the dinner,
and my persecution doubled in proportion. I desired at my
usual hour to go to my repose, and was conducted to my
chamber by the gentleman, his lady, and the whole train of
children. They importuned me to drink something before I
went to bed; and, upon my refusing, at last left a bottle of
stingo as they called it, for fear I should wake and be thirsty
in the night. I was forced in the morning to rise and dress
myself in the dark, because they would not suffer my kins-
man's servant to disturb me at the hour I desired to be called.
I was now resolved to break through all measures to get away;

and, after sitting down to a monstrous breakfast of cold beef, mutton, neats' tongues, venison pasty, and stale beer, took leave of the family. But the gentleman would needs see me part of the way, and carry me a short cut through his own ground, which he told me would save half a mile's riding. This last piece of civility had like to have cost me dear, being once or twice in danger of my neck by leaping over his ditches, and at last forced to alight in the dirt, when my horse, having slipped his bridle, ran away, and took us up more than an hour to recover him again.

Getting into Society.

On the 1st of January, 1838, I was the master of a lovely shop in the neighbourhood of Oxford Market; of a wife, Mrs. Cox; of a business, both in the shaving and cutting line, established three-and-thirty years; of a girl and boy respectively of the ages of eighteen and thirteen; of a three-windowed front, both to my first and second pair; of a young foreman, my present partner, Mr. Orlando Crump; and of that celebrated mixture for the human hair, invented by my late uncle, and called Cox's Bohemian Balsam of Tokay, sold in pots at two-and-three and three-and-nine.

One day—one famous day last January—whirr comes a hackney-coach to the door, from which springs a gentleman in a black coat with a bag.

"Your name is Cox, sir? My name, sir, is Sharpus—Blunt, Hone, and Sharpus, Middle Temple Lane—and I am proud to salute you, sir; happy,—that is to say, sorry to say, that Mr. Tuggeridge, of Portland Place, is dead, and your lady is heiress, in consequence, to one of the handsomest properties in the kingdom."

I handed over the business to Mr. Crump without a single farthing of premium, though Jemmy—my wife—would have made me take four hundred pounds for it; but this I was above: Crump had served me faithfully, and have the shop he should.

We were speedily installed in our fine house; but what's a house without friends? Jemmy made me *cut* all my old acquaintances in the Market, and I was a solitary being; when, luckily, an old lodger of ours, Captain Tagrag, was so kind as to promise to introduce us into distinguished society—aye, and what's more, did.

First he made my wife get an opera-box, and give suppers on Tuesdays and Saturdays. As for me, he made me ride in the Park—me and Jemimarann, with two grooms behind us, who used to laugh all the way, and whose very beards I had shaved.

Well, the horses, the suppers, the opera-box, the paragraphs in the papers about Mr. Coxe Coxe (that's the way; double your name and stick an 'e' to the end of it, and you are a gentleman at once), had an effect in a wonderfully short space of time, and we began to get a very pretty society about us. Some of old Tug's friends brought their wives and daughters to see dear Mrs. Coxe and her charming girl; and when, about the first week in February, we announced a grand dinner and ball for the evening of the 28th, I assure you there was no want of company—no, nor of titles neither; and it always does my heart good even to hear one mentioned.

Let me see. There was, first, my Lord Dunboozle, an Irish peer, and his seven sons, the Honourable Messieurs Trumper (two only to dinner); there was Count Mace, the celebrated French nobleman, and his Excellency Baron von Punter from Baden; there was Lady Blanche Bluenose, the eminent literati, author of "The Distrusted," "The Distorted," "The Disgusted," "The Disreputable One," and other poems; there was the Dowager Lady Max and her daughter, the Honourable Miss Adelaide Blueruin; Sir Charles Codshead from the City; and Field-Marshal Sir Gorman O'Gallagher, K.A., K.B., K.C., K.W., K.X., in the service of the Republic of Guatemala; my friend Tagrag and his fashionable acquaintance, little Tufthunt, made up the party. And when the doors were flung open, and Mr. Hock, in black, with a white napkin, three footmen, coachmen, and a lad whom Mrs. C. had dressed in sugar-loaf buttons and called a page, were seen round the dinner-table, all in white gloves, I promise you I felt a thrill of elation, and thought to myself—Sam Cox, Sam Cox, who ever would have expected to see you here!

After dinner, there was to be, as I have said, an evening party; and to this Messieurs Tagrag and Tufthunt had invited many of the principal nobility that our metropolis had produced. When I mention, among the company to tea, her Grace the Duchess of Zero, her son the Marquis of Fitzurse, and the Ladies North Pole her daughters; when I say that there were yet *others*, whose names may be found in the Blue Book, but sh'n't, out of modesty, be mentioned here, I think I've said enough to show that, in our time, No. 96 Portland Place was the resort of the best of company.

It was our first dinner, and dressed by our new cook, Munseer Cordongblew. I bore it very well; eating, for my share, a filly dysol allameter dotell, a cutlet soubeast, a pully bashymall, and other French dishes; and, for the frisky sweet wine, with tin tops to the bottles, called Champagne, I must say that me and Mrs. Coxe-Tuggeridge Coxe drank a very good share of it (but the Claret and Jonnysberger, being sour, we did not much relish). However, the feed, as I say, went off very well; Lady Blanche Bluenose sitting next to me, and being so good as to put me down for six copies of all her poems; the Count and Baron von Punter engaging Jemimarann for several waltzes, and the Field-Marshal plying my dear Jemmy with Champang, until, bless her! her dear nose became as red as her new crimson satin gown, which, with a blue turban and bird-of-paradise feathers, made her look like an empress, I warrant.

Well, dinner past, Mrs. C. and the ladies went off:—thunder-under-under came the knocks at the door; squeedle-eedle-eedle, Mr. Wippert's fiddlers began to strike up, and, about half-past eleven, me and the gents thought it high time to make our appearance. I felt a *little* squeamish at the thought of meeting a couple of hundred great people; but Count Mace and Sir Gorman O'Gallagher taking each an arm, we reached, at last, the drawing-room.

The young ones in company were dancing, and the Duchess and the great ladies were all seated, talking to themselves very stately, and working away at the ices and macaroons. I looked out for my pretty Jemimarann amongst the dancers, and saw her tearing round the room along with Baron Punter, in what they call a gallypard; then I peeped into the circle of the Duchesses, where, in course, I expected to find Mrs. C.; but she wasn't there! She was seated at the further end of the room, looking very sulky; and I went up and took her arm, and brought her down to the place where the Duchesses were. "Oh, not there!" said Jemmy, trying to break away. "Nonsense, my dear," says I, "you are missis, and this is your place." Then going up to her ladyship the Duchess, says I, "Me and my missis are most proud of the honour of seeing you."

The Duchess (a tall red-haired grenadier of a woman) did not speak.

I went on: "The young ones are all at it, ma'am, you see; and we thought we would come and sit down among the old ones. You and I, ma'am, I think, are too stiff to dance."

"Sir!" says her Grace.

"Ma'am," says I, "don't you know me? My name's Cox. Nobody's introduced me; but, it's my own house, and I may present myself—so give us your hand, ma'am."

And I took her's in the kindest way in the world; but—would you believe it?—the old cat screamed as if my hand had been a hot 'tater. "Fitzurse! Fitzurse!" shouted she, "help! help!" Up scuffled all the other dowagers—in rushed the dancers. "Mamma! mamma!" squeaked Lady Julia North Pole. "Lead me to my mother," howled Lady Aurorer; and both came and flung themselves into her arms. "Wawt's the raw?" said Lord Fitzurse, sauntering up quite stately.

"Protect me from the insults of this man," says her Grace. "Where's Tufthunt? he promised that not a soul in this house should speak to me."

"My dear Duchess," said Tufthunt, very meek.

"Don't Duchess me, sir. Did you not promise they should not speak, and hasn't that horrid tipsy wretch offered to embrace me? Didn't his monstrous wife sicken me with her odious familiarities? Call my people, Tufthunt. Follow me, my children."

"And my carriage," "And mine," "And mine!" shouted twenty more voices. And down they all trooped to the hall, Lady Blanche Bluenose and Lady Max among the very first; leaving only the Field-Marshal and one or two men, who roared with laughter ready to split.

"Oh, Sam," said my wife, sobbing, "why would you take me back to them? they had sent me away before? I only asked the Duchess whether she didn't like rum-shrub better than all your Maxarinos and Curasosos : and—would you believe it ? —all the company burst out laughing ; and the Duchess told me just to keep off, and not to speak till I was spoken to. Imperence ! I'd like to tear her eyes out."

And so I do believe my dearest Jemmy would.

Mr. Flutter goes to a Tea-party.

I have been, am now, and shall always be, a bashful man. I have been told that I am the only bashful man in the world. How that is I cannot say, but should not be sorry to believe that it is so, for I am of too generous a nature to desire any other mortal to suffer the mishaps which have come to me from this distressing complaint. A person can have small-pox, scarlet fever, and measles but once each. But for bashfulness—like mine—there is no first and only attack.

I am a quiet, nice-enough, inoffensive young gentleman, now rapidly approaching my twenty-sixth year. It is unnecessary to state that I am unmarried. I should have been wedded a great many times had not some fresh attack of my malady invariably, and in some new shape, attacked me.

On one memorable day I had, in a weak moment, consented to go to a tea-party. The eventful evening arrived all too quickly.

The thermometer stood at eighty degrees in the shade when I left the store at five o'clock to go to that awful gathering. I was glad the day was warm, for I wanted to wear my white linen suit, with a blue cravat and Panama hat. I felt independent even of Fred Hencoop, as I walked along the street under the shade of the elms ; but, the minute I was inside Widow Jones' gate, and walking up to the door, the thermometer went up to somewhere near 200 degrees. There were something like a dozen heads at each of the parlour windows, and all women's heads at that. Six or eight more were peeping out of the sitting-room, where they were laying the table for tea. Babbletown always did seem to me to have more than its fair share of female population. I think I would like to live in one of those mining towns out in Colorado, where women are as scarce as hairs on the inside of a man's hand. Somebody coughed as I was going up the walk. Did you ever have a girl cough at you?—one of those mean, teasing, expressive little coughs?

I had practised—at home in my own room—taking off my Panama with a graceful, sweeping bow, and saying in calm, well-bred tones: "Good evening, Mrs. Jones. Good evening, ladies. I trust you have had a pleasant as well as a profitable afternoon."

I had *practised* that in the privacy of my chamber. What I really did get off was something like this:—

"Good Jones, Mrs. Evening. I should say, good evening, widows—ladies, I beg your pardon," by which time I was mopping my forehead with my handkerchief, and could just ask, as I sank into the first chair I saw—"Is your mother well, Mrs. Jones?" which was highly opportune, since said mother had been years dead before I was born. As I sat down, a pang sharper than some of those endured by the Spartans ran through my right leg. I was instantly aware that I had plumped down on a needle, as well as a piece of fancy-work, but I had not the courage to rise and extract the excruciating thing.

I turned pale with pain, but by keeping absolutely still I found that I could endure it, and so I sat motionless, like a wooden man, with a frozen smile on my features.

Belle was out in the other room helping to set the table, for which mitigating circumstance I was sufficiently thankful.

Fred Hencoop was on the other side of the room holding a skein of silk for Sallie Brown. He looked across at me, smiling with a malice which made me hate him.

Out of that hate was born a stern resolve—I would conquer my diffidence; I would prove to Fred Hencoop, and any other fellow like him, that I was as good as he was, and could at least equal him in the attractions of my sex.

There was a pretty girl sitting quite near me. I had been introduced to her at the picnic. It seemed to me that she was eyeing me curiously, but I was mad enough at Fred to show him that I could be as cool as anybody, after I got used to it. I hemmed, wiped the perspiration from my face—caused now more by the needle than by the heat—and remarked, sitting stiff as a ramrod, and smiling like an angel:—

"June is my favourite month, Miss Smith—is it yours? When I think of June I always think of strawberries and cream and ro-oh-oh-ses!"

It was the needle. I had forgotten it in the excitement of the subject, and had moved.

"*Is* anything the matter?" Miss Smith tenderly enquired.

"Nothing in the world, Miss Smith. I had a stitch in my side, but it is over now."

"Stitches are very painful," she observed, sympathizingly. "I don't like to trouble you, Mr. Flutter, but I think, I believe, I guess you are sitting on my work. If you will rise, I will try and finish it before tea."

No help for it, and I arose, at the same moment dexterously slipping my hand behind me and withdrawing the thorn in the flesh.

"Oh, dear, where is my needle?" said the young lady, anxiously scrutinising the crushed worsted-work.

I gave it to her with a blush. She burst out laughing.

"I don't wonder you had a stitch in your side," she remarked shyly.

"Hem!" observed Fred very loud, "do you feel sew-sew, John?"

Just then Belle entered the parlour, looking as sweet as a pink, and wearing a sash I had given her. She bowed to me very coquettishly, and announced tea.

"Too bad!" continued Fred; "you have broken the thread of Mr. Flutter's discourse with Miss Smith. But I do not wish to inflict *needle*-less pain, so I will not betray him."

"I hope Mr. Flutter is not in trouble again," said Belle quickly.

"Oh no. Fred is only trying to say something *sharp*," said I.

"Come with me; I will take care of you, Mr. Flutter," said Belle, taking my arm and marching me out into the sitting-room where a long table was heaped full of inviting eatables. She sat me down by her side, and I felt comparatively safe. But Fred and Miss Smith were just opposite, and they disconcerted me.

"Mr. Flutter," said the hostess, when it came to my turn, "will you have tea or coffee?"

"Yes'm," said I.

"Tea or coffee?"
"If you please," said I.
"*Which?*" whispered Belle.
"Oh, excuse me; coffee, ma'am."
"Cream and sugar, Mr. Flutter?"
"I'm not particular which, Mrs. Jones."
"Do you take *both?*" she persisted, with everybody at the table looking my way.
"No, ma'am, only coffee," said I, my face the colour of the beet pickles.

She finally passed me a cup, and in my embarrassment, I immediately took a swallow and burnt my mouth.

"Have you lost any friends lately?" asked that wretched Fred, seeing the tears in my eyes.

I enjoyed that tea-party as geese enjoy *pate de fois gras*. It was a prolonged torment under the guise of pleasure. I refused everything I wanted, and took everything I didn't want. I got a back of the cold chicken; there was nothing on it but bone. I thought I must appear to be eating it; and it slipped out from under my fork and flew into the dish of preserved cherries.

We had strawberries. I am very partial to strawberries and cream. I got a saucer of the berries, and was looking about for the cream when Miss Smith's mother, at my right hand, said:—

"Mr. Flutter, will you have some *whip* with your strawberries?"

Whip with my strawberries! I thought she was making fun of me, and stammered:—

"No, I thank you," and so I lost the delicious frothed cream that I coveted.

The agony of the thing was drawing to a close. I was longing for the time when I could go home and get some cold potatoes out of my mother's cupboard. I hadn't eaten worth a cent.

Pretty soon we all moved back our chairs and rose. I offered my arm to Belle, as I supposed; and in passing through the little dark hall, I squeezed her hand, but on coming into the light, imagine my amazement at seeing that my partner was the widow Jones. I glanced wildly around in search of

Belle; she was hanging on a young lawyer's arm, and not looking at me.

"Now, you needn't colour up so," said the widow, coquettishly, "I know what young men are."

She said it aloud, on purpose for Belle to hear. I felt like killing her. I might have done it, but one thought restrained me—I should be hung for murder, and I was too bashful to submit to so public an ordeal.

I hurried across the room to get rid of her. There was a young fellow standing there who looked about as out-of-place as I felt—I thought I would speak to him.

"Come," said I, "let us take a little promenade outside— the women are too much for me."

He made no answer. I heard giggling and tittering breaking out all round the room, like rash on a baby with the measles.

"Come on," said I; "like as not they're not laughing at us."

"Look-a-here, you shouldn't speak to a fellow till you've been introduced," said that wicked Fred behind me. "Mr. Flutter, allow me to make you acquainted with Mr. Flutter. He's anxious to take a little walk with you."

It was so; I had been talking to myself in a four-foot looking-glass.

I did not feel like staying for the ice-cream and kissing-plays, but had a sly hunt for my hat, and took leave of the tea-party about the eighth of a second afterward.

Amusing Towing Incidents.

(Adapted.)

One sees a good many funny incidents up the river in connection with towing. One of the most common is the sight of a couple of towers, walking briskly along, deep in an animated discussion, while the man in the boat, a hundred yards behind them, is vainly shrieking to them to stop, and making frantic signs of distress with a scull. Something has gone wrong; the rudder has come off, or the boathook has slipped overboard, or his hat has dropped into the water and is floating rapidly down stream. He calls them to stop, quite gently and politely at first.

"Hi! stop a minute, will you?" he shouts cheerily. "I've dropped my hat overboard."

Then: "Hi! Tom—Dick! can't you hear?" not quite so affably this time.

Then: "Hi! Confound *you*, you dunder-headed idiots! Hi! stop! Oh you ——!"

After that he springs up, and dances about, and roars himself red in the face, and curses everything he knows. And the small boys on the bank stop and jeer at him, and pitch stones at him as he is pulled along past them, at the rate of four miles an hour, and can't get out.

Much of this sort of trouble would be saved if those who are towing would keep remembering that they *are* towing, and give a pretty frequent look round to see how their man is getting on. It is best to let one person tow. When two are doing it they get chattering, and forget, and the boat itself, offering, as it does, but little resistance, is of no real service in reminding them of the fact.

As an example of how utterly oblivious a pair of towers can be to their work, George told us, later on in the evening, when we were discussing the subject after supper, of a very curious instance.

He and three other men, so he said, were sculling a very heavily laden boat up from Maidenhead one evening, and a little above Cookham lock they noticed a fellow and a girl, walking along the tow-path, both deep in an apparently interesting and absorbing conversation. They were carrying a boat-hook between them, and attached to the boat-hook was a tow-line, which trailed behind them, its end in the water. No boat was near, no boat was in sight. There must have been a boat attached to that tow-line at some time or other, that was certain; but what had become of it, what ghastly fate had overtaken it, and those who had been left in it, was buried in mystery. Whatever the accident may have been, however, it had in no way disturbed the young lady and gentleman who were towing. They had the boat-hook, and they had the line, and that seemed to be all that they thought necessary to their work.

George was about to call out and wake them up, but, at that moment, a bright idea flashed across him, and he didn't. He got the hitcher instead, and reached over, and drew in the end of the tow-line; and they made a loop in it, and put it over their mast, and then they tidied up the sculls and went and sat down in the stern, and lit their pipes.

And that young man and young woman towed those four hulking chaps and a heavy boat up to Marlow.

George said he never saw so much thoughtful sadness concentrated into one glance before, as when, at the lock, that young couple grasped the idea that, for the last two miles, they had been towing the wrong boat. George fancied that, if it had not been for the restraining influence of the sweet woman at his side, the young man might have given way to violent language.

The maiden was the first to recover from her surprise, and, when she did, she clasped her hands, and said, wildly :

" Oh, Henry, then *where* is auntie ?"

" Did they ever recover the old lady ?" asked Harris.

George replied he did not know.

Another example of the dangerous want of sympathy between tower and towed was witnessed by George and myself once up near Walton. It was where the tow-path shelves gently down into the water, and we were camping on the opposite bank, noticing things in general. By-and-by a small boat came in sight, towed through the water at a tremendous pace by a powerful barge horse, on which sat a very small boy. Scattered about the boat, in dreamy and reposeful attitudes, lay five fellows, the man who was steering having a particularly restful appearance.

" I should like to see him pull the wrong line," murmured George, as they passed. And at that precise moment the man did it, and the boat rushed up the bank with a noise like the ripping up of forty thousand linen sheets. Two men, a hamper, and three oars immediately left the boat on the larboard side, and reclined on the bank, and one and a half moments afterwards, two other men disembarked from the starboard, and sat down among boat-hooks and sails and carpet-bags and bottles. The last man went on twenty yards further, and then got out on his head.

This seemed to sort of lighten the boat, and it went on much easier, the small boy shouting at the top of his voice, and urging his steed into a gallop. The fellows sat up and stared at one another. It was some seconds before they realised what had happened to them, but, when they did, they began to shout lustily for the boy to stop. He, however, was too much occupied with the horse to hear them, and we watched them flying after him, until the distance hid them from view.

I cannot say I was sorry at their mishap. Indeed, I only wish that all the young fools who have their boats towed in this fashion—and plenty do—could meet with similar misfortunes. Besides the risk they run themselves, they become a danger and an annoyance to every other boat they pass. Going at the pace they do, it is impossible for them to get out of anybody else's way, or for anybody else to get out of theirs. Their line gets hitched across your mast, and overturns you, or it catches somebody in the boat, and either throws them into the water, or cuts their face open. The best plan is to stand your ground, and be prepared to keep them off with the butt-end of a mast.

Of all experiences in connection with towing, the most exciting is being towed by girls. It is a sensation that nobody ought to miss. It takes three girls to tow always; two hold the rope, and the other one runs round and round, and giggles. They generally begin by getting themselves tied up. They get the line round their legs, and have to sit down on the path and undo each other, and then they twist it round their necks, and are nearly strangled. They fix it straight, however, at last, and start off at a run, pulling the boat along at quite a dangerous pace. At the end of a hundred yards they are naturally breathless, and suddenly stop, and all sit down on the grass and laugh, and your boat drifts out to mid-stream and turns round, before you know what has happened, or can get hold of a scull. Then they stand up, and are surprised.

"Oh, look!" they say, "he's gone right out into the middle."

They pull on pretty steadily for a bit, after this, and then it all at once occurs to one of them that she will pin up her frock, and they ease up for the purpose, and the boat runs aground.

You jump up and push it off, and you shout to them not to stop.

"Yes. What's the matter?" they shout back.

"Don't stop," you roar.

"Don't what?"

"Don't stop—go on—go on!"

"Go back, Emily, and see what it is they want," says one, and Emily comes back, and asks what it is.

"What do you want?" she says; "anything happened?"

"No," you reply, "it's all right; only go on, you know—don't stop."

"Why not?"

"Why, we can't steer if you keep stopping. You must keep some way on the boat."

"Keep some what?"

"Some way—you must keep the boat moving."

"Oh, all right, I'll tell 'em. Are we doing it all right?"

"Oh, yes, very nicely, indeed, only don't stop."

"It doesn't seem difficult at all. I thought it was so hard."

"Oh, no, it's simple enough. You want to keep on steady at it, that's all."

"I see. Give me out my red shawl, it's under the cushion."

You find the shawl, and hand it out, and by this time another one has come back and thinks she will have hers too, and they take Mary's on chance. Mary does not want it, so they bring it back and have a pocket-comb instead. It is about twenty minutes before they get off again, and, at the next corner they see a cow, and you have to leave the boat to chivy the cow out of their way.

There is never a dull moment in the boat while girls are towing it.

(*By kind permission of the Publishers.*)

Membranous Croup.

(As related by Mr. McWilliams.)

That frightful and incurable disease, membranous croup, was ravaging the town and driving all mothers mad with terror. I called Mrs. McWilliam's attention to little Penelope, and said:—

"Darling, I wouldn't let that child be chewing that pine stick if I were you."

"Precious, where is the harm in it?" said she, but at the same time preparing to take away the stick—for woman cannot receive even the most palpably judicious suggestion without arguing it ; that is, married women.

I replied :—

"Love, it is notorious that pine is the least nutritious wood that a child can eat."

My wife's hand paused, in the act of taking the stick, and returning itself to her lap. She bridled perceptibly, and said,—

"Hubby, you know better than that. You know you do. Doctors *all* say that the turpentine in pine wood is good for weak back and the kidneys."

"Ah...I was under a misapprehension. I did not know that the child's kidneys and spine were affected, and that the family physician had recommended "———

"Who said the child's spine and kidneys were affected?"

"My love, you intimated it."

"The idea. I never intimated anything of the kind."

"Why, my dear, it hasn't been two minutes since you said "———

"Bother what I said! I don't care what I did say. There isn't any harm in the child's chewing a bit of pine stick if she wants to, and you know it perfectly well. And she *shall* chew it, too. So there, now!"

"Say no more, my dear. I now see the force of your reasoning, and I will go and order two or three cords of the best pine wood to-day. No child of mine shall want while I "———

"O *please* go along to your office and let me have some peace. A body can never make the simplest remark but you must take it up and go to arguing and arguing and arguing till you don't know what you are talking about, and you *never* do."

"Very well, it shall be as you say. But there is a want of logic in your last remark which "———

However, she was gone with a flourish before I could finish, and had taken the child with her. That night at dinner she confronted me with a face as white as a sheet.

"O, Mortimer, there's another! Little Georgie Gordon is taken."

"Membranous croup?"

"Membranous croup."

"Is there any hope for him?"

"None in the wide world. O, what is to become of us?"

By-and-by nurse brought in our Penelope, to say good-night, and offer the customary prayer at the mother's knee. In the midst of "Now I lay me down to sleep," she gave a slight cough! My wife fell back like one stricken with death. But the next moment she was up and brimming with the activities which terror inspires.

She commanded that the child's crib be removed from the nursery to our bedroom; and she went along to see the order executed. She took me with her, of course. We got matters arranged with speed. A cot bed was put up in my wife's dressing-room for the nurse. But now Mrs. McWilliams said we were too far away from the other child, and what if *he* were to have the symptoms in the night—and she blanched again, poor thing.

We then restored the crib and the nurse to the nursery, and put up a bed for ourselves in a room adjoining.

Presently, however, Mrs. McWilliams said, "Suppose the baby should catch it from Penelope?" This thought struck a new panic to her heart, and the tribe of us could not get the crib out of the nursery again fast enough to satisfy my wife, though she assisted in her own person and well-nigh pulled the crib to pieces in her frantic hurry.

We moved downstairs; but there was no place there to stow the nurse, and Mrs. McWilliams said the nurse's experience would be an inestimable help. So we returned, bag and baggage, to our own bedroom once more, and felt a great gladness, like storm-buffeted birds that have found their nest again.

Mrs. McWilliams sped to the nursery to see how things were going on there. She was back in a moment with a new dread. She said,—

"What *can* make Baby sleep so?"

I said,—

"Why, my darling, Baby *always* sleeps like a graven image."

"I know, I know; but there's something peculiar about his sleep now. He seems to—to—he seems to breathe so *regularly*. O, this is dreadful."

"But, my dear, he always breathes regularly."

"Oh, I know it, but there's something frightful about it now. His nurse is too young and inexperienced. Maria shall stay there with her, and be on hand if anything happens."

"That is a good idea, but who will help *you*?"

"You can help me all I want. I wouldn't allow anybody to do anything but myself, anyhow, at such a time as this."

I said I would feel mean to lie abed and sleep, and leave her to watch and toil over our little patient all the weary night. But she reconciled me to it. So old Maria departed and took up her ancient quarters in the nursery.

Penelope coughed twice in her sleep.

"Oh, why *don't* that doctor come! Mortimer, this room is too warm. This room is certainly too warm. Turn off the register—quick!"

I shut it off, glancing at the thermometer at the same time, and wondering to myself if 70 *was* too warm for a sick child.

The coachman arrived from down town, now, with the news that our physician was ill and confined to his bed. Mrs. McWilliams turned a dead eye upon me, and said in a dead voice—

"There is a Providence in it. It is foreordained. He never was sick before—Never. We have not been living as we ought to live, Mortimer. Time and time again I have told you so. Now you see the result. Our child will never get well. Be thankful if you can forgive yourself; I never can forgive *my*self."

I said, without intent to hurt, but with heedless choice of words, that I could not see that we had been living such an abandoned life.

"*Mortimer!* Do you want to bring the judgment upon Baby, too?"

Then she began to cry, but suddenly exclaimed,—

"The doctor must have sent medicines!"

I said,—

"Certainly. They are here. I was only waiting for you to give me a chance."

"Well, do give them to me! Don't you know that every moment is precious now? But what was the use in sending medicines, when he *knows* that the disease is incurable?"

I said that while there was life there was hope.

"Hope! Mortimer, you know no more what you are talking about than the child unborn. If you would—As I live, the directions say give one teaspoonful once an hour! Once an hour!—as if we had a whole year before us to save the child in! Mortimer, please hurry. Give the poor perishing thing a tablespoonful, and *try* to be quick!"

"Why, my dear, a tablespoonful might"——

"*Don't* drive me frantic! . . . . . There, there, there, my precious, my own; it's nasty bitter stuff, but it's good for Nelly—good for Mother's precious darling; and it will make her well. There, there, there, put the little head on Mamma's breast and go to sleep, and pretty soon—Oh, I know she can't live till morning! Mortimer, a tablespoonful every half hour will—Oh, the child needs belladonna too; I know she does—and aconite. Get them, Mortimer. Now do let me have my way. You know nothing about these things."

We now went to bed, placing the crib close to my wife's pillow. All this turmoil had worn upon me, and within two minutes I was something more than half asleep! Mrs. McWilliams roused me:

"Darling, is that register turned on?"

"No."

"I thought as much. Please turn it on at once. This room is cold."

I turned it on, and presently fell fast asleep again. I was aroused once more:

"Dearie, would you mind moving the crib to your side of the bed? It is nearer the register."

I moved it, but had a collision with the rug and woke up the child. I dozed off once more, while my wife quieted the sufferer. But in a little while these words came murmuring remotely through the fog of my drowsiness:

"Mortimer, if we only had some goose-grease—will you ring?"

I climbed dreamily out, and stepped on a cat, which responded with a protest and would have got a convincing kick for it if a chair had not got it instead.

"Now, Mortimer, why do you want to turn up the gas and wake up the child again?"

"Because I want to see how much I am hurt, Caroline."

"Well, look at the chair, too—I have no doubt it is ruined. Poor cat, suppose you had"——

"Now I am not going to suppose anything about the cat.

It never would have occurred, if Maria had been allowed to remain here and attend to these duties, which are in her line, and are not in mine."

"Now, Mortimer, I should think you would be ashamed to make a remark like that. It is a pity if you cannot do the few little things I ask of you at such an awful time as this when our child"——

"There, there, I will do anything you want. But I can't raise anybody with this bell. They're all gone to bed. Where is the goose-grease?"

"On the mantlepiece in the nursery. If you'll step there and speak to Maria"——

I fetched the goose-grease and went to sleep again. Once more I was called:

"Mortimer, I so hate to disturb you, but the room is still too cold for me to try to apply this stuff. Would you mind lighting the fire? It is all ready to touch a match to."

I dragged myself out and lit the fire, and then sat down disconsolate.

"Mortimer, don't sit there and catch your death of cold. Come to bed."

As I was stepping in, she said,—

"But wait a moment. Please give the child some more of the medicine."

Which I did. It was a medicine which made a child more or less lively; so my wife made use of its waking interval to strip it and grease it all over with the goose-oil. I was soon asleep once more, but once more I had to get up.

"Mortimer, I feel a draft. I feel it distinctly. There is nothing so bad for this disease as a draft. Please move the crib in front of the fire."

I did it; and collided with the rug again, which I threw in the fire. Mrs. McWilliams sprang out of bed and rescued it and we had some words. I had another trifling interval of sleep, and then got up, by request, and constructed a flax-seed poultice. This was placed upon the child's breast and left there to do its healing work.

A wood fire is not a permanent thing. I got up every twenty minutes and renewed ours, and this gave Mrs. McWilliams the opportunity to shorten the times of giving the medicines by ten minutes, which was a great satisfaction to her. Now and then, between times, I re-organised the flaxseed poultices, and applied sinapisms and other sorts of blisters where unoccupied places could be found upon the child. Well, toward morning the wood gave out and my wife wanted me to go down cellar and get some more. I said,—

" My dear, it is a laborious job, and the child must be nearly warm enough now with her extra clothing. Now, mightn't we put on another layer of poultices and "——

I did not finish, because I was interrupted. I lugged wood up from below for some little time, and then turned in and fell to snoring as only a man can whose strength is all gone and whose soul is worn out. Just at broad daylight I felt a grip on my shoulder that brought me to my senses suddenly. My wife was glaring down upon me and gasping. As soon as she could command her tongue she said,—

" It is all over ! All over ! The child's perspiring ! What *shall* we do ?"

" Mercy, how you terrify me ! *I* don't know what we ought to do. Maybe if we scraped her and put her in the draft again "——

" O, idiot ! There is not a moment to lose ! Go for the doctor. Go yourself. Tell him he *must* come, dead or alive."

I dragged that poor sick man from his bed and brought him. He looked at the child and said she was not dying. This was joy unspeakable to me, but it made my wife as mad as if he had offered her a personal affront. Then he said the child's cough was only caused by some trifling irritation or other in the throat. At this I thought my wife had a mind to show him the door. Now the doctor said he would make the child cough harder and dislodge the trouble. So he gave her something that sent her into a spasm of coughing, and presently up came a little wood splinter or so.

" This child has no membranous croup," said he. " She has been chewing a bit of pine shingle or something of the kind, and got some little slivers in her throat. They won't do her any hurt."

" No," said I, " I can well believe that. Indeed, the turpentine that is in them is very good for certain sorts of disease that are peculiar to children. My wife will tell you so."

But she did not. She turned away in disdain and left the room ; and since that time there is one episode in our life which we never refer to. Hence the tide of our days flows by in deep and untroubled serenity.

My Dentist.
(By kind permission of the Author.)

A highly respectable house in a gloomy looking street. The dentist does not live there—probably because his wife and daughters do not like the observations of their visitors to be interrupted by resounding shrieks proceeding at intervals from the back parlour. He occupies only the ground floor, whereof the first room is used as a waiting-room, and the back-room is used—but I must not anticipate.

Upon the first door is a very neat brass-plate, indicating that Mr. Pullemout is a surgeon-dentist. At the side of the door is a bell which by a somewhat hollow piece of pleasantry has the word "Visitors" written on it. You ring this bell, and are at once conscious, first, that at the moment of doing so the pain in that tooth which has been driving you mad for a fortnight has entirely disappeared, and secondly, that the bell responds to your touch with the most aggravating promptitude —that it gives you no decent time for considering whether after all you will not walk on, and look in next Thursday instead. You are just coming out of this reflection, and are beginning to think that perhaps even now you can get round the corner without being seen, when the door opens and you perceive a sepulchral looking man-servant, dressed in a complete suit of black, who surveys you with the air of one who is saying inwardly, "yet another—the fifteenth to-day. Mine is indeed a painful situation."

You ask whether Mr. Pullemout is in—hoping as you never hoped anything before, that Mr. Pullemout is not in—and the man, with the sense of responsibility of one who is the bearer of evil news, assures you that Mr. Pullemout is in and will soon be disengaged. You take out your watch and ask how soon Mr. Pullemout will be disengaged, with the faint hope that you may hinge on this an excuse for escaping. The words have scarcely left your mouth when a loud yell (accompanied probably by a double tooth), leaves the mouth of a victim at the back of the premises. Whereupon the man-servant, with funereal solemnity, assures you that Mr. Pullemout will be free in a very few minutes, and conducts you into the front room.

In this room you find a round table in the middle, with illustrated books and periodicals upon it, and you observe that it is provided with a large number of chairs. No one about to see Mr. Pullemout has ever been known to look at a book or periodical or sit upon a chair, but people who go into the room merely because they have come with someone else for company, and without any intention of having a personal transaction with that gentleman, may be noticed to maintain the most equable spirits, and to devour the literature and make themselves extremely comfortable on the chairs. This is human nature.

You cannot quite make up your mind whether you hope Mr. Pullemout will really be disengaged soon or not, but you rather think you should like him not to be ready for you just yet. You walk up and down the room, and stand at the window occasionally, to glare out savagely at people who are passing unconcernedly by the door, as if there were no such things as dentists, and a fellow-creature were not about to undergo torments. Your reflections are interrupted occasionally by such incidents as the ringing of a bell at the back of the house, followed by the opening of a door and the muffled sound of a voice which appears to be saying in a tone of authority, "Another jug of warm water," followed in turn by a shuffling of feet along the passage, and then the slamming of the same door. But beyond these tragic indications you are left in the silence of the tomb.

This state of things appears to last many hours—in fact, about fifteen minutes—when the door opens and the sorrowful man-servant enters and informs you that Mr. Pullemout will be "happy" to see you. He says "happy" as if he would like to add, "Poor wretch, I know full well what *your* sentiments are as to seeing *him*."

A minute afterwards and you are seated in a most repulsively comfortable chair, with your head thrown back in a convenient position for Mr. Pullemout to cut it off if so disposed, and a napkin inserted in your mouth in such wise as to preclude the possibility of any utterance but a despairing gurgle. In this helpless situation Mr. Pullemout attacks your mouth with a complicated steel instrument, which he uses to discover where your nerves are, preparatory to playing on them with another instrument. He asks you at intervals to let him know whether he is hurting you, though well aware that he has deprived you of the power of retorting upon him, and at intervals he refers in a light and pleasing manner to current topics of the day.

If the result of this process is to satisfy Mr. Pullemout that the tooth can be stopped, he operates upon it with more instruments, and brings into requisition an apparatus the properties of which appear to lie somewhere midway between those of a coffee-mill and a sewing-machine. This he works with a treadle, and he fastens the end to something which he guides into the recesses of your hapless tooth. During this process you feel as if large splinters were flying from you, and you tingle down to your feet with a sensation of having somehow become a passive part of a buzzing piece of machinery.

If Mr. Pullemout is of opinion that the molar is past stoppage, he says with an airy smile, "I think *we* must have this one out," as if he were going halves with you in the operation, instead of its being perfectly obvious that he will be at the harmless end of the forceps, while you are at its business extremity. And then he rings for a jug of warm water with a pretence of indifference, as if he wanted it for shaving, or washing his hands, or anything but its real horrid purpose. And then he advances upon you with the forceps, which he ostentatiously affects to conceal up his arm, though you can see the instrument perfectly well all the time. And then he puts a gag in your mouth, which makes you feel as if your upper jaw and your lower jaw would never have anything in common again. And then Mr. Pullemout is ready for action, and during the next few minutes he is engaged in a pleasant and stimulating muscular exercise, in which you can only join effectively, to the extent of kicking out your legs, while your feelings are represented by muffled and gagged observations of a most poignant character.

(*From* E. F. Turner's "More T Leaves": Smith, Elder & Co.)

(C) ELOQUENCE.
The Wonders of Creation.

About the time of the invention of the telescope, another instrument was formed which laid open a scene no less wonderful. This was the microscope. The one leads me to see a system in every star. The other leads me to see a world in every atom. The one taught me that this mighty globe, with the whole burden of its people and of its countries, is but a grain of sand on the high field of immensity. The other teaches me that every grain of sand may harbour within it the tribes and the families of a busy population. The one told me of the insignificance of the world I tread upon. The other redeems it from all its insignificance; for it tells me that in the leaves of every forest, and in the flowers of every garden, and in the waters of every rivulet, there are worlds teeming with life, and numberless as are the glories of the firmament. The one has suggested to me that beyond and above all that is visible to man, there may lie fields of creation which sweep immeasurably along, and carry the impress of the Almighty's hand to the remotest scenes of the universe. The other suggests to me, that within and beneath all that minuteness which the aided eye of man has been able to explore, there may lie a region of invisibles; and that could we draw aside the mysterious curtain which shrouds it from our senses, we might there see a theatre of as many wonders as astronomy has unfolded, a universe within the compass of a point so small as to elude all the powers of the microscope, but where the wonder-working God finds room for the exercise of all His attributes, where He can raise another mechanism of worlds, and fill and animate them all with the evidences of His glory.

By the telescope we have discovered that no magnitude, however vast, is beyond the grasp of the Divinity. But by the microscope we have also discovered that no minuteness, however shrunk from the notice of the human eye, is beneath the condescension of His regard. Every addition to the powers of the one instrument extends the limit of His visible dominions. But by every addition to the powers of the other instrument, we see each part of them more crowded than before with the wonders of His unwearying hand. The one is constantly widening the circle of His territory. The other is as con-

stantly filling up its separate portions with all that is rich and
various and exquisite. In a word, by the one I am told that
the Almighty is now at work in regions more distant than
geometry has ever measured, and among worlds more manifold
than numbers have ever reached. But by the other I am also
told, that with a mind to comprehend the whole, in the vast
compass of its generality, He has also a mind to concentrate a
close and a separate attention on each and on all of its particulars, and that the same God who sends forth an upholding
influence among the orbs and the movements of astronomy, can
fill the recesses of every single atom with the intimacy of His
presence, and travail in all the greatness of His unimpaired
attributes, upon every one spot and corner of the universe He
has formed. They, therefore, who think that God will not put
forth such a power, and such a goodness, and such a condescension in behalf of this world, as are ascribed to Him in the
New Testament, because He has so many other worlds to
attend to, think of Him as a man. They confine their view to
the informations of the telescope, and forget altogether the informations of the other instrument. They only find room in
their minds for His one attribute of a large and general super-
intendence, and keep out of their remembrance the equally
impressive proofs we have of His other attribute, of a minute
and multiplied attention to all that diversity of operations
where it is He that worketh all in all. And when I think that
as one of the instruments of philosophy has heightened our
every impression of the first of these attributes, so another
instrument has no less heightened our impression of the second
of them—then I can no longer resist the conclusion, that it
would be a transgression of sound argument, as well as a
daring of impiety, to draw a limit around the doings of this
unsearchable God—and should a professed revelation from
Heaven tell me of an act of condescension in behalf of some
separate world, so wonderful that angels desired to look into
it, and the Eternal Son had to move from His seat of glory to
carry it into accomplishment, all I ask is the evidence of such
a revelation; for let it tell me as much as it may of God letting himself down for the benefit of one single province of His
dominions, this is no more than what I see lying scattered in
numberless examples before me, and running through the whole
line of my recollections, and meeting me in every walk of obser-

vation to which I can betake myself; and now that the microscope has unveiled the wonders of another region, I see strewed around me, with a profusion which baffles my every attempt to comprehend it, the evidence that there is no one portion of the universe of God too minute for His notice, or too humble for the visitations of His care.

The Devastation of Oude.

Had a stranger, at this time, gone into the province of Oude, ignorant of what had happened since the death of Sujah Dowla, that man, who, with a savage heart, had still great lines of character, and who, with all his ferocity in war, had still, with a cultivating hand, preserved to his country the riches which it derived from benignant skies and a prolific soil—if this stranger, ignorant of all that had happened in the short interval, and observing the wide and general devastation, and all the horrors of the scene—of plains unclothed and brown—of vegetation burnt up and extinguished—of villages depopulated and in ruin —of temples unroofed and perishing—of reservoirs broken down and dry, he would naturally inquire what war had thus laid waste the fertile fields of this once beautiful and opulent country—what civil dissensions have happened, thus to tear asunder and separate the happy societies that once possessed those villages—what disputed succession—what religious rage has, with unholy violence, demolished those temples, and disturbed fervent but unobtruding piety in the exercise of its duties ? What merciless enemy has thus spread the horrors of fire and sword—what severe visitation of providence has dried up the fountain, and taken from the face of the earth every vestige of verdure ? Or rather, what monsters have stalked over the country, tainting and poisoning, with pestiferous breath, what the voracious appetite could not devour ? To such questions, what must be the answer ? No wars have ravaged these lands and depopulated these villages—no civil discord has been felt—no disputed succession—no religious rage—no cruel enemy—no affliction of providence, which, while it scourged for the moment, cut off the sources of resuscitation—no voracious and poisoning monsters—no, all this has been accomplished by the *friendship, generosity*, and *kindness* of the English nation.

They have embraced us with their protecting arms, and lo ! those are the fruits of their alliance. What, then, shall we be told that, under such circumstances, the exasperated feelings of a whole people thus goaded and spurred on to clamour and resistance were excited by the poor and feeble influence of the Begums? When we hear the description of the paroxysm, fever, and delirium, into which despair had thrown the natives, when on the banks of the polluted Ganges, panting for death, they tore more widely open the lips of their gaping wounds. to accelerate their dissolution, and while their blood was issuing, presented their ghastly eyes to heaven, breathing their last and fervent prayer that the dry earth might not be suffered to drink their blood, but that it might rise up to the throne of God, and rouse the eternal Providence to avenge the wrongs of their country, will it be said that this was brought about by the incantations of these Begums in their secluded Zenana? or that they could inspire this enthusiasm and this despair into the breasts of a people who felt no grievance, and had suffered no torture? What motive, then, could have such influence in their bosoms? What motive? That which nature, the common parent, plants in the bosom of man, and which, though it may be less active in the Indian than in the Englishman, is still congenial with and makes a part of his being—that feeling which tells him that man was never made to be the property of man; but that, when, through pride and insolence of power, one human creature dares to tyrannize over another, it is a power usurped, and resistance is a duty—that feeling which tells him that all power is delegated for the good, not for the injury of the people; and that, when it is converted from the original purpose, the compact is broken, and the right is to be resumed —that principle which tells him that resistance to power usurped is not merely a duty which he owes to himself and to his neighbour, but a duty which he owes to his God, in asserting and maintaining the rank which He gave him in the creation!—to that common God, who, where he gives the *form of man*, whatever may be the complexion, gives also the *feelings* and the *rights of man*—that principle, which neither the rudeness of ignorance can stifle, nor the enervation of refinement extinguish!—*that* principle which makes it base for a man to *suffer* when he ought to *act:* which, tending to preserve to the species the original designations of Providence, spurns at the arrogant distinctions of man, and vindicates the independent quality of his race.

Philips' School Atlases.

PHILIPS' SYSTEMATIC ATLAS
For Higher Schools and general use. A Series of Physical and Political Maps of all the Countries of the World, with Diagrams and Illustrations of Astronomical and Physical Geography. 52 Plates, specially drawn by E. G. Ravenstein, F.R.G.S. With Index. Cloth, price 15s.
SCHOOL EDITION, 41 Maps, with Index, price 10s. 6d.

PHILIPS' "IMPERIAL" SERIES OF SCHOOL ATLASES.
Entirely New and greatly Enlarged Editions of these favourite Atlases.

PHILIPS' COMPREHENSIVE ATLAS of Physical, Political, and Ancient Geography, comprising 74 Maps (56 Modern and 18 Ancient), with a complete Index. Imperial 8vo, strongly half-bound, 10s. 6d.

PHILIPS' STUDENT'S ATLAS, comprising 56 Physical and Political and 4 Ancient Maps. With a complete Index. Imperial 8vo, bound in cloth, 7s. 6d.

PHILIPS' SELECT ATLAS, comprising 43 Physical and Political Maps. With a complete Index. Imperial 8vo, bound in cloth, 5s.

PHILIPS' INTRODUCTORY ATLAS, comprising 31 Maps of the Principal Countries of the World, with a complete Index. Imperial 8vo, bound in cloth, 3s. 6d.

PHILIPS' NEW POPULAR ATLAS of Astronomical, Physical, Political and Ancient Geography, comprising 76 Maps and Diagrams, with a complete Index. Imperial 4to, bound in cloth, 3s. 6d.

PHILIPS' ATLAS FOR BEGINNERS. Entirely new and improved Edition, comprising 60 Physical and Political Maps and Geographical and Astronomical Diagrams, printed in colours, and a new consulting Index. Crown 4to, strongly bound in cloth, 2s. 6d.

PHILIPS' NEW FIRST SCHOOL ATLAS, containing 50 coloured Maps and Diagrams, with a Classified Index on a new plan. Crown 4to, cloth, 1s.

PHILIPS "EXCELSIOR" ATLAS OF THE WORLD. New Edition, containing 100 Maps, Plans, and Diagrams, &c. Crown 4to, in stiff illustrated cover, 1s.

PHILIPS' FAVOURITE SIXPENNY ATLAS, containing 50 Maps, Plans, Illustrations, &c. Crown 4to, paper cover, 6d.

PHILIPS' GRAPHIC SCHOOL ATLAS, containing over 110 readable Maps and Diagrams, printed in colours. Size—7 in. by 4¾ in. Pictorial cover, stiff boards, 1s. ; cloth lettered, 1s. 6d.

GEORGE PHILIP & SON, LONDON AND LIVERPOOL.

Philips' School Atlases.

PHILIPS' ATLAS FOR JUNIOR CLASSES, containing 68 unusually clear and readable Maps. Medium 8vo (9¼ inches by 6½ inches), limp cloth, lettered, 1s. 6d.

PHILIPS' "UNIQUE" SIXPENNY ATLAS, containing 70 Maps and 10 Diagrams. Small crown 4to (8 inches by 6½ inches), stiff cover, illustrated.

PHILIPS' "UNIQUE" SHILLING ATLAS, containing 70 Physical and Political Maps and 10 Diagrams. Demy 4to (11 inches by 9 inches), stiff cover, illustrated.

PHILIPS' STANDARD ATLASES, a Series of 4 Atlases for Elementary Schools. No. 1, for Standard III., 2d.; No. 2, for Standard IV., 3d.; No. 3, for Standard V., 3d.; and No. 4, for Standards VI. and VII., 4d.

PHILIPS' SIXPENNY ATLAS OF THE BRITISH COLONIES, specially adapted for Standard VI., New Code. Crown 4to, illustrated cover.

PHILIPS' SCHOOL ATLAS OF PHYSICAL GEOGRAPHY, containing 20 Maps. Imperial 8vo (11 inches by 7 inches), strongly bound in cloth, 5s.

PHILIPS' PHYSICAL ATLAS FOR BEGINNERS, containing 12 Maps. Crown 4to (9 inches by 7 inches), stiff cover, 1s.; cloth lettered, 1s. 6d.

PHILIPS' SCHOOL ATLAS OF CLASSICAL GEOGRAPHY, a Series of 18 Maps, with complete Index. Medium 4to (11 inches by 8 inches), cloth, 3s. 6d.

PHILIPS' HANDY CLASSICAL ATLAS, containing 18 Maps. Medium 8vo (8½ inches by 6 inches), cloth lettered, 2s. 6d.

PHILIPS' SCHOOL ATLAS OF SCRIPTURE GEOGRAPHY, containing 16 Coloured Maps. Crown 4to (9½ inches by 7 inches), illustrated cover, 1s.; or bound in cloth, with Index, 1s. 6d.

PHILIPS' SMALLER SCRIPTURE ATLAS, containing 16 Maps. Foolscap 8vo (5½ inches by 3¾ inches), paper cover, 6d.; or bound in cloth, 1s.

GEORGE PHILIP & SON, LONDON AND LIVERPOOL.

Geographical Class-Books.

THE ADVANCED CLASS-BOOK OF MODERN GEOGRAPHY— Physical, Political, and Commercial. A Complete Manual of Geography for Students in Training Colleges, Senior Pupils in Middle and Higher Class Schools, Pupil Teachers, &c. By William Hughes, F.R.G.S. With Notes and Index. 883 pages. New Edition, revised to date. Crown 8vo, cloth, price 6s.

THE CLASS-BOOK OF MODERN GEOGRAPHY, illustrated by numerous Maps and Diagrams, with Examination Questions, Notes and Index. By William Hughes, F.R.G.S. New Edition, revised and largely rewritten by Albert Hill. 470 pp. Crown 8vo, cloth, 3s. 6d.

THE ELEMENTARY CLASS-BOOK OF MODERN GEOGRAPHY. With Examination Questions, and a comprehensive series of Maps and Diagrams. New Edition, revised and largely rewritten by Albert Hill. 272 pp. Crown 8vo, cloth, 1s. 6d.

AN INTRODUCTION TO THE STUDY OF GEOGRAPHY—Mathematical, Physical, Political, and Commercial. By William Hughes, F.R.G.S. With Index and Coloured Diagrams. 100 pp. Crown 8vo, cloth, 1s.

THE GEOGRAPHY OF THE BRITISH EMPIRE—Physical, Political, and Commercial. By William Hughes, F.R.G.S. With Coloured Map. 231 pp. Crown 8vo, cloth, 3s.

THE GEOGRAPHY OF THE BRITISH ISLES—Physical, Political, and Commercial. By William Hughes, F.R.G.S. With 3 Coloured Maps. 106 pp. Crown 8vo, cloth, 1s. 6d.

THE GEOGRAPHY OF THE BRITISH COLONIES AND FOREIGN POSSESSIONS. By William Hughes, F.R.G.S. With Coloured Maps. 240 pp. Crown 8vo, cloth, 2s. 6d.

THE GEOGRAPHY OF EUROPE—Physical, Political, and Commercial. By William Hughes, F.R.G.S. With Coloured Map. 240 pp. Crown 8vo, cloth, 2s.

THE GEOGRAPHY OF ASIA—Physical, Political, and Commercial. By William Hughes, F.R.G.S. With 2 Coloured Maps. 128 pp. Crown 8vo, cloth, 1s. 6d.

GEORGE PHILIP & SON, LONDON AND LIVERPOOL.

Geographical Class-Books.

THE GEOGRAPHY OF AFRICA—Physical, Political, and Commercial. By William Hughes, F.R.G.S. With Map, coloured to show the present political partition of the continent. 98 pp. Crown 8vo, cloth, 1s.

THE GEOGRAPHY OF AMERICA—Physical, Political, and Commercial. By William Hughes, F.R.G.S. With 3 Coloured Maps. 120 pp. Crown 8vo, cloth, 1s. 6d.

THE GEOGRAPHY OF AUSTRALASIA AND POLYNESIA—Physical, Political, Commercial. With Coloured Maps. 122 pp. Crown 8vo, cloth, 1s. 6d.

THE CLASS-BOOK OF PHYSICAL AND ASTRONOMICAL GEOGRAPHY, with a comprehensive series of Maps and Illustrations, Examination Questions, Notes and Index. By William Hughes, F.R.G.S. New edition, entirely rewritten and considerably enlarged by R. A. Gregory, F.R.A.S. Crown 8vo, cloth, 3s. 6d.

THE ELEMENTARY CLASS-BOOK OF PHYSICAL GEOGRAPHY, abridged from the larger Class-Book. New edition, revised and enlarged. 134 pp. Foolscap 8vo, cloth, 1s. 6d.

THE GEOGRAPHY OF THE OCEANS—Physical, Historical, and Descriptive, with Maps and Diagrams. By J. Francon Williams, F.R.G.S. 254 pp. Foolscap 8vo, cloth, 2s. 6d.

APPLIED GEOGRAPHY. By J. Scott Keltie, Assistant Secretary to the Royal Geographical Society. 170 pp. With Maps and Diagrams. Crown 8vo, cloth, 3s. 6d.

THE GOLDEN GATES OF TRADE, a Text-book of Commercial Geography. With Examination Questions. By John Yeats, LL.D. 354 pp. Crown 8vo, cloth, 4s. 6d.

MAP STUDIES OF THE MERCANTILE WORLD, a Text-book for the use of Students of Commerce. By John Yeats, LL.D. Supplementary to the "Golden Gates of Trade." 336 pp. Crown 8vo, cloth, 4s. 6d.

MANUALS OF COMMERCE. By John Yeats, LL.D., F.G.S., F.S.S. In Four Volumes, crown 8vo, strongly bound in cloth, price 24s., or in separate volumes, price 6s. each. Vol. I.—The Natural History of the Raw Materials of Commerce; Vol. II.—The Technical History of Commerce; Vol. III.—The Growth and Vicissitudes of Commerce in all Ages; and Vol. IV.—Recent and Existing Commerce.

GEORGE PHILIP & SON, LONDON AND LIVERPOOL.

www.ingramcontent.com/pod-product-compliance
Lightning Source LLC
Chambersburg PA
CBHW020243240426
43672CB00006B/622